$30

29957

DATE DUE

FE 07 '0			
MAR 2 1 2001			
APR - 4 2001			
APR 1 1 2001			
APR 2 5 2001			
MAY 2 2001			

DEMCO

GERMANY DIVIDED

PRINCETON STUDIES IN

INTERNATIONAL HISTORY AND POLITICS

Series Editors
John Lewis Gaddis
Jack L. Snyder
Richard H. Ullman

History and Strategy by Marc Trachtenberg (1991)

George F. Kennan and the Making of American Foreign Policy,
1947–1950 by Wilson D. Miscamble, C.S.C. (1992)

Economic Discrimination and Political Exchange: World
Political Economy in the 1930s and 1980s by Kenneth A. Oye
(1992)

Germany Divided: From the Wall to Reunification by A. James
McAdams (1993)

GERMANY DIVIDED

FROM THE WALL TO REUNIFICATION

A. James McAdams

PRINCETON UNIVERSITY PRESS   PRINCETON, NEW JERSEY

Library of Congress Cataloging-in-Publication Data

McAdams, A. James.
    Germany divided : from the wall to reunification / A. James McAdams.
        p.   cm. — (Princeton studies in international history and politics)
    Includes bibliographical references and index.
    ISBN 0-691-07892-0 (cl)
        1. Germany—Politics and government—1945–1990.   2. Germany—Politics and
    government—1990–   3. Germany (East)—Foreign relations—Germany
    (West)   4. Germany (West)—Foreign relations—Germany (East)   I. Title.   II. Series.
    DD257.M26   1992
    943.087—dc20   92-15654

To My Parents _____

Comrade L. I. Brezhnev: "When are you flying back? I've heard as early as tomorrow."

Comrade E. Honecker: "Yes, tomorrow afternoon. As you know, August 13, 1981, is the twentieth anniversary of the erection of the anti-fascist protective wall."

Comrade A. A. Gromyko to Comrade L. I. Brezhnev: "Yes, that is 'the Wall.' "

Comrade E. Honecker: "Yes, 'the Wall.' It has now existed for twenty years. That was a great event then."

Comrade A. A. Gromyko, jokingly: "Perhaps one should erect a monument to this event someday."

(A meeting in the Crimea, August 3, 1981. Courtesy of Central Party Archives, Berlin)

Contents

Preface   xi

Acknowledgments   xv

Abbreviations   xix

I. A Wall between the Germanys   3
  Accepting Germany's Division   5
  A German-German Consensus   13

II. One Germany, Two Alliances   16
  The Soviet Ultimatum   17
  East German Uncertainties   23
  The Persistence of West German Policy   30
  The Evolution of East German Policy   36
  Divergent Priorities   44
  The Construction of the Wall   49

III. Two Germanys: Confrontation or Accommodation?   56
  Changing Surroundings   57
  West Germany's Awkward Adaptation   64
  The Rigidity of East German Policy   71
  Bonn's Breakthrough: The Ostpolitik   79
  The End of the Ulbricht Era   87
  Two States in Germany?   93

IV. Two German States: New Relations, Bad Relations   96
  The Inter-German Dilemma   97
  The Benefits of Cooperation   102
  Handling Questions of Principle   106
  Whither Inter-German Ties: The View from Bonn   113
  Whither Inter-German Ties: Retrenchment in the GDR   121
  Toward a German-German Deadlock?   126
  Inter-German Ties in Question   133

V. Accepting a Divided Germany   134
  A Threat from the West   135
  An East German Opportunity?   141
  The Meeting at Werbellin   147

The "Wende"   152
A German "Coalition of Reason"   158
A New Era between the Germanys   164
A Working Visit to Bonn   173

VI. The Fall of East Germany   175

The Illusion of Success   177
A Path of Least Resistance   185
A New Political Force   193
The West German Response   199
Unity Despite the Germanys   204

VII. Germany without a Wall   207

Inter-German Tensions of a New Type   209
A Liberal Democratic Germany   216
The New Germany and the New Europe   222

Appendixes

A. Interview Locations, 1985–1990   229

B. GDR Oral History Project Interviews   231

Select Bibliography   233

Index   245

Preface

"THE WORLD will never again be as it was." These words, echoed with remarkable consistency by German politicians throughout the fall of 1989, seemed to encapsulate the tumultuous events that were brought about by the opening of the Berlin Wall, the fall of the East German government, and ultimately the reunification of the German nation. All that one could say with confidence at the time was that the face of Central Europe would be changed in ways scarcely conceivable during an era which for forty years had been based upon the existence of two German states, the German Democratic Republic (GDR) and the Federal Republic of Germany (FRG).

As much as any observer, I was taken by surprise by these developments and no more capable of foreseeing their twists and turns in the heady weeks of November and December 1989. However, in part because I had previously been so convinced that there would be two separate German states for my lifetime (as many a German policymaker had assured me in the past), I found myself focusing on something more than the German future to come. More deliberately than ever before, I also began to ask myself how one should understand the makeup of the *old* world that had been lost with these events. How had it come into being? In particular, how was one to explain the fact that the Germans themselves, in the East and West alike, had largely given up any realistic hopes of reunifying their nation?

It was part of the accepted wisdom of international relations that a good portion of the architecture of this old world was based upon the marvelous simplicity of the balance of power between the superpowers. This circumstance dictated that one part of Germany would be inalterably bound to the Soviet camp and the other to the Atlantic alliance. In fact, the Berlin Wall was built according to precisely the dictates of this bipolar logic. Furthermore, it was also part of the accepted lore of international studies that the challenge of adaptation to the Wall's existence was a crucial factor in subsequently forcing each of the German governments to come to terms with the division of the nation. Each in its own way and for its own reasons learned that its interests were best served by cooperating with its counterpart and putting remaining differences over the national question aside.

Still, as the old German reality disappeared from view, I found myself asking whether the fact that two very different kinds of states were separated by the Berlin Wall had not also played a role in this inter-German consensus. Beginning in 1981, I had had the good fortune of being able to develop a great number of professional contacts with politicians and political advisors in both German capitals. I had learned from countless discussions with these individuals that the rhythm of policymaking and the rationales according to which decisions were reached in East Berlin and Bonn were often so much at variance that the GDR and the FRG were not likely to agree on anything, much less on a manageable means for living with their nation's divided condition. What then, I wondered, had changed to make the German-German house appear so stable in the 1980s?

This study provides an answer to this question which suggests that the different political processes existing in East and West Germany were actually key factors in the behavior of both states up to the GDR's fall in 1989. This is by no means a reductionist account, since I would hardly want to deny that geopolitical considerations and the functional imperatives of inter-German bargaining were also important influences on the two governments. How could it have been otherwise? Nonetheless, I hope to provoke the reader into thinking about four decades of German history in a new way by contending that the concrete political setting in which the leaders of the GDR and the FRG made decisions about their priorities—state socialism in the former and multiparty democracy in the latter—was oftentimes more consequential for their actions than any other factors, even more than the well-known issues at stake between them. In this sense, this book is very much in line with the work of other political scientists who, in a number of fields, ranging from the study of trade unions to the administration of social policy, are now turning away from purely deductive models of political behavior to embrace the more traditional, historical study of political institutions and processes.[1]

By the same token, my argument about the "old world" that was Central Europe and the East-West divide is also something more than just an argument about the development of relations between two quite fascinating countries. It is really about the way we seek to account for an era. While many scholars prefer to emphasize the importance of "thinking big" about the roots of European stability in the postwar period—above all, in terms of the nuclear balance of terror between the superpowers and the Germanys' enmeshment in rival security alliances—I hope this book will show that one can also profit by "thinking mundane," in terms of the everyday world of politics and policymaking in different types of states. I first began to appreciate this issue myself when, in the earliest stages of my research, I pressed East and West German policymakers to reveal to me their "grand strategies" and visions—German intellectuals might say, *Konzepte*—of the national future. Invariably, they would respond by shaking their heads and then point instead to much more down-to-earth issues, many of which had little to do with popular definitions of the German question at all. Yet it

[1] For example, see Sven Steinmo, Kathleen Thelen, and Frank Longstreth, eds., *Structuring Politics: Historical Institutionalism in Comparative Analysis* (New York: Cambridge University Press, 1992).

seems that these factors too were a constituent part of the old European order. Even as I write, and Christian Democrats and Social Democrats debate whose strategy was better suited to insuring the reunification of their nation—an unresolvable debate if ever there was one—it is striking how few of these politicians now seem to remember that they were motivated by considerably less ambitious concerns in the 1980s.

Two notes of caution about my approach may be in order. The reader may feel that I display an unabashedly "elitist" bias in this study, in that almost all of my arguments are based upon the behavior of identifiable politicians and decision-makers on both sides of the German divide. This is not because I have no interest in or sympathy for the feelings and motivations of the German people, either West or East; to the extent that I have been able, I have addressed the issue throughout the study. It is only that it is so difficult to comment with any confidence about mass beliefs in both of the Germanys. Those familiar with the debates over the reliability of public opinion surveys on the national question in the FRG will readily acknowledge that, at least before the enlightening events of 1989, West German pollsters frequently came to contradictory conclusions about their population's commitment to and even interest in the goal of German reunification. Given the paucity of information that we have or will ever have about mass beliefs in the GDR, it is even harder to imagine how one would begin to assess the convictions of that state's population.

Fortunately for this study's purposes, it is not necessary to answer weighty questions such as: What did the East and West German people truly believe about their national destiny? Were there ever two fundamentally different types of national consciousness in the GDR and the FRG? Because I am primarily concerned with the more modest task of explaining changes in East and West German policy over a forty-year period, I have been able to confine myself to the perceptions of those individuals who were in the position to decide how their state's interests were best met. Whether their perceptions proved to be accurate over the long haul is really beside the point in view of the larger consideration that such decisions determined their government's policies. In this case, it is possible to write with confidence about these persons' calculations. Their publications and speeches have long been available to us; archives in the West, and more recently the Revolution of 1989 in the East, provide us with additional information about their less public stands;[2] and, conveniently, we can also ask many of the individuals themselves what they thought they were doing

---

[2]In this case, I have scrupulously adhered to the German "30-year" limitation in citing information from the Central Party Archives (Institut für die Geschichte der Arbeiterbewegung) in Berlin. I am grateful to the archives for lifting this regulation in the specific case of the Central Committee files, which has allowed me to refer to many more modern documents from the SED's history, including the curious Soviet–East German conversation about the Wall that opens this study.

when they made the decisions that shaped the world as it was before the Wall's fall.

My second note of caution concerns the manner in which I treat the former GDR and its policymakers. It has now become fashionable for students of German affairs to write about the German Democratic Republic as though the state were fated to collapse as a result of its "legitimacy deficit." This observation is probably true, although such retrospective crystal-ball gazing is not very relevant to this book's objectives. Whatever one thinks (or thought) of the East German regime, the more important and also more interesting fact, in my opinion, is that for four decades the GDR was controlled by a coterie of leaders who, for better or worse, lived up to the criteria that we normally associate with a state's existence: with the assistance of their Soviet allies and a vast police network, these individuals monopolized the means of coercion over their society and prevented the formation of alternative governments. Most telling of all, the GDR's Communist regime not only demanded that it be taken seriously but, by the 1980s, was in fact treated as a viable state by all of the countries surrounding it, including its principal rival, the Federal Republic of Germany. Just why this situation came to pass is the subject of this book.

January 1992

Acknowledgments _____

THE RESEARCH for this study has taken almost a decade to complete, and my debts are extensive. First, I owe much to the hundreds of German policymakers who were willing to speak with me over the years, particularly those with whom I conducted formal interviews during the 1985–1991 period. Given the spirit of the times, many of my discussions with politicians in 1987 and 1988 were conducted on an off-the-record basis. As a result, I have handled them in a differentiated manner. Some subjects later gave me permission to cite their remarks, and hence their names appear along with the dates and locations of the interviews. In instances when I could not obtain permission—often because I could no longer locate the interviewee—I have preserved anonymity. In all cases, however, as the reader will quickly see in the footnotes, I have sought to buttress my arguments with supplementary evidence from other primary and secondary sources as well. A complete list of the institutions represented by the subjects of my interviews is in Appendix A.

Following the opening of the Wall, I sought to make the findings of my interviews publicly accessible by creating a formal oral history archive with tape recordings of discussions with East German policymakers. This archive, still in formation as I write, will be housed in the Archives of the Hoover Institution for War, Revolution, and Peace at Stanford University. It is referred to in the footnotes of this book as OHP (Oral History Project), and the interviews thus far in the collection are listed in Appendix B.

Second, I owe a considerable debt to all of the institutes and government agencies that facilitated my many visits to both Germanys. Many of my earliest contacts with German decision-makers began not in the West but in the East, and I am particularly grateful to the scholars at the former Institute of International Relations in East Berlin and Babelsberg for arranging contacts from the early 1980s onward. Beginning in 1985, the Aspen Institute–Berlin brought me to West Berlin, East Berlin, Bonn, Dresden, and numerous other locations more times than I can now remember. The Deutsche Gesellschaft für Auswärtige Politik (DGAP) and its directors, Karl Kaiser and Eberhard Schulz, and the Seminar für Politische Wissenschaft and its director, Hans-Adolf Jacobsen, at the Friedrich Wilhelm University made possible a lengthy stay in Bonn in 1987 and 1988. I particularly profited from the use of the DGAP's famous archives. The Institute for State and Law of the GDR Academy of Sciences and its late deputy director, Karl-Heinz Röder, facilitated another long visit to East

Berlin in 1988. Finally, the Akademie für Gesellschaftswissenschaften and its director, Otto Reinhold, invited me for what was to be a final research visit to the GDR in 1989.

Third, I am also very grateful to all of those granting agencies that were willing to support my many trips to Germany: the International Research and Exchanges Board (IREX), which gave me two fellowships and which made the nearly impossible possible in East Berlin; the Alexander von Humboldt Foundation, which not only helped with many professional contacts in Bonn but also cared for me and my family during a long and fruitful stay in the FRG; the Fulbright-Hays Commission; the National Council for Soviet and East European Research; the GDR Studies Association; the American Council of Learned Societies; and finally, the Center for International Studies, the John Foster Dulles Fund, and the Committee on Faculty Research at Princeton University. I owe a particularly great debt to the Hoover Institution for War, Revolution, and Peace, which generously awarded me both a National Fellowship and the time I needed to write this book in a very congenial setting at Stanford University.

Finally, my greatest debt is to those individuals, friends and colleagues, who in various ways inspired me to undertake this project and then believed in me when it counted most. Many of them also read this book, in part or in its entirety. It is a pleasure not to have to identify them with any particular country: Donald Abenheim, Frank Anechiarico, Thomas Banchoff, J. D. Bindenagel, the late Cyril Black, Allen Blasucci, Heinrich Bortfeldt, George Breslauer, John Brown, Mark Cioc, Stephen F. Cohen, Forrest Colburn, Elena Danielson, Wolfgang Danspeckgruber, Peter Duignan, George Downs, William Griffith, Manfred Halpern, Iris and Richard Hunter, Ines and Gerd Kaiser, Stanley Katz, Ralf and Ines Kintzel, John Leslie, George Liber, Carlo Llenado, the late Richard Löwenthal, Willem Melching, Bowman Miller, Norman Naimark, Erich and Christiane Nickel, Fred Oldenburg, Kenneth Oye, David Paris, Agnes Peterson, Ingrid Reed, Hans and Evelyn Sachs, Olga Sandler, Jürgen Schnappertz, Peter Schneider, Matthew Siena, Mitchell Smith, Uwe and Inge Stehr, Manfred Stinnes, Robert C. Tucker, and Dale Vree. Many individuals also played crucial roles in helping me make contacts and providing useful advice along the way: Burkhard Dobiey, Gisela Gottwald, Rainer Hagen, Hans-Jürgen Kaack, Carl Christian Kaiser, Gerd Langguth, Claus Montag, Wolfgang Pfeiler, Karl-Ernst Plagemann, Wolfgang Schollwer, Thomas Simon, and Wolfgang Wiemer.

I owe an incalculable debt to William Stanton, who read this manuscript at a difficult stage and helped me to revise it with the same diplomatic candor that has made him famous at trouble spots at home and abroad. Gail and Richard Ullman played a major role in convincing me to write the book and then supported me the whole way through. Malcolm DeBevoise was an excellent editor, possessing a particularly healthy aversion to clichés of all types, and Alice Calaprice was an exacting copy editor. Finally, Anna Grzymala-Busse helped me with countless editorial tasks.

Without the support of those closest to me, however, it is clear that there would be no book. My wife, Nancy, and my daughters, Jackie and Erin, were as much a part of this project as I was, and I am indebted to them for their unceasing patience, love, and confidence. There are few authors that are as lucky to have a family so prepared to live and work abroad, especially in exotic cities and countries that no longer exist. Finally, I thank my parents, Helen and Jim McAdams, to whom this book is dedicated, for teaching me both to love learning and to assume that nothing is "obvious." The word does not appear in the following pages.

Abbreviations

CDSP	*Current Digest of the Soviet Press*
CDU	Christian Democratic Union (West German)
COMECON	Council of Mutual Economic Assistance
CPA	Central Party Archives (Berlin)
CPSU	Communist Party of the Soviet Union
CSU	Christian Social Union (West German)
DdZ	*Dokumentation der Zeit*
DzD	*Dokumente zur Deutschlandpolitik*
FDP	Free Democratic Party (West German)
FRG	Federal Republic of Germany (West Germany)
GDR	German Democratic Republic (East Germany)
JUSOS	Young Socialists (West German)
KPD	Communist Party of Germany
LDPD	Liberal Democratic Party of Germany (East German)
ND	*Neues Deutschland*
OHP	Oral History Project
RA	*Reden und Aufsätze*
SED	Socialist Unity Party of Germany (East German)
SPD	Social Democratic Party of Germany (West German)
TzD	*Texte zur Deutschlandpolitik*

GERMANY DIVIDED

I

A Wall between the Germanys

The Wall will remain as long as the reasons for
its presence have not been eliminated. It will still
be there in 50 and even 100 years.
  (Erich Honecker, January 20, 1989)

Today, the decision was taken which makes it
possible for all citizens to leave the country
through GDR crossing points.
  (Günter Schabowski, November 9, 1989)

FEW DECISIONS of greater historical consequence have been announced
with such nonchalance. On November 9, 1989, Günter Schabowski, a
member of the East German politburo, suggested in a passing remark
before a government press conference that exit visas from the German
Democratic Republic (GDR) would be made accessible to all who wanted
them. Within hours, the edifice that the world had known as the Berlin Wall
had opened. Schabowski apparently had something far less dramatic in
mind than proclaiming the barrier's demise. In an effort to stem the rising
tide of East German citizens who were fleeing his country to the West
through the open borders of Hungary and Czechoslovakia, his government
hoped that by liberalizing its travel laws, it could convince the GDR's
population to stay at home. Nevertheless, his unexpected statement un-
leashed instant confusion at official crossing points throughout East Berlin.
East German border guards struggled to make sense of the new policy and
in many cases just gave in to the crowds of people clamoring for access to
the West. Within an hour, thousands of GDR citizens were streaming freely
into West Berlin, where they were jubilantly received by their western
compatriots.

As scores of East and West Berliners celebrated the occasion by hoisting
themselves onto the top of the stretch of the Wall extending before the
Brandenburg Gate, one could see that the concrete barrier that had divided
the city since its erection on August 13, 1961, had for all practical purposes
ceased to exist. Nonetheless, the events that transpired in the wake of the
Wall's demise proved to be the most significant of all. On the first occasion
when the people of East Germany as a whole were able to express their

feelings freely, in the GDR's first truly democratic parliamentary elections on March 18, 1990, the majority voted for something unprecedented, to abandon their country altogether and support the fastest possible route to national reunification with the West German state, the Federal Republic of Germany (FRG).

As the previously unthinkable prospect of German reunification became apparent to all, one could not help but wonder how the Berlin Wall, having crumbled so quickly, should ever have appeared to be a lasting part of modern German history. Few monuments to man's inhumanity to man were more vivid than this edifice. Similarly, few acts could have represented a more blatant sign of weakness than the East German government's original decision to confine its population to a life behind such an artificial construct. Yet the Wall was a great deal more than the simple sum of the 102.4 miles of concrete blocks and steel fencing that encircled the island city of West Berlin. To all who beheld it, the barrier had become in the nearly thirty years following its erection the most visible symbol of the immutability of the East-West divide.[1] Certainly, the leaders of the major powers surrounding the Germanys—the Soviet Union, France, England, and the United States—could not conceive of a world in which their World War II foe was reunited.[2] But most important of all, the GDR and the FRG themselves, the two countries that had the greatest reasons for being opposed to accepting the division of their nation, had each managed to reconcile themselves to the situation by the 1980s. In their own distinctive ways, both German governments adopted accommodating stands on relations with each other that presupposed that the Wall would still be around, to quote Erich Honecker, the General Secretary of the East German Socialist Unity Party (SED), in "fifty and even one hundred years."

[1] On the relationship between German division and European stability, see, for example, the contributions to Edwina Moreton, ed., *Germany between East and West* (Cambridge, U.K.: Cambridge University Press, 1987), and Eberhard Schulz and Peter Danylow, "Bewegung in der deutschen Frage?" in *Arbeitspapiere zur Internationalen Politik*, no. 33 (Bonn: Deutsche Gesellschaft für Auswärtige Politik, April 1985). For a stimulating American account, see A. W. dePorte, *Europe between the Superpowers: The Enduring Balance* (New Haven, Conn.: Yale University Press, 1979), esp. chaps. 8 and 9.

[2] After the Germanys' reunification in 1990, however, it became fashionable for politicians and intellectuals to suggest that they had somehow had an inkling of these precipitous developments well before the event. For example, in his book, *The Future Belongs to Freedom* (New York: The Free Press, 1991), p. 131, former Soviet foreign minister Eduard Shevardnadze observes that he first began to have thoughts about the artificiality of the GDR and the "inevitability" of German reunification as early as 1986. Nonetheless, when Shevardnadze's former colleague and fellow politburo member, Yegor Ligachev, was asked about this observeration at a luncheon at Princeton University on November 6, 1991, he responded: "This was as much a secret to me as to you. If the foreign minister had broached such a plan, we would have gotten a new minister. We began to discuss German reunification only when one Germany began to swallow the other."

How striking it was, then, that on October 3, 1990, East and West Germany ceased to exist as separate states and the German nation was reunified. Nevertheless, the story of how the two polities moved from unremitting refusal to admit the fact of national division to gradual—complete in the case of the GDR, grudging in the case of the FRG—recognition of this condition, provides an illuminating opportunity to examine the sometimes fitful and frequently paradoxical ways in which states change their policies over time.[3] At some points in the history of both countries' relations, it was possible to anticipate the kinds of decisions that East Berlin and Bonn would make about their priorities. Yet, at others, the leaders of each state acted in ways that proved to be beyond prediction according to the most rational assessment of their interests. Precisely why the German governments made the choices they did in the period leading up to the fall of the Wall and finally came to very similar conclusions about their limited national options is the subject of this book.

Accepting Germany's Division

However ironic the Germanys' acceptance of a divided nation may have been only a few short months before reunification, the fact that they held such positions was not in itself surprising. As more and more time had elapsed since the Wall's erection to halt the first crippling exodus of refugees from the GDR—between 1949 and 1961, over two-and-one-half million people had fled the Communist state—it was to be expected that the leaders of the two regimes would *eventually* come to share the widespread perception among their populations that very little could realistically be done to bring the German nation back together again.[4] The intriguing

---

[3]This point is equally true of other types of historical change, as suggested by Stephen Jay Gould, *Wonderful Life: The Burgess Shale and the Nature of History* (New York: W. W. Norton, 1989).

[4]For example, in a 1984 poll by the Forschungsgruppe Wahlen, 52 percent of West German respondents considered reunification unlikely and 29 percent impossible; a mere 17 percent felt that reunification was possible. Cited in Gebhard Schweigler, "German Questions or the Shrinking of Germany," in F. Stephen Larrabee, ed., *The Two German States and European Security* (New York: St. Martin's Press, 1989), p. 94. So strong was this perception that even *after* the fall of the Wall, in late November 1989, when the polling agency, Emnid, asked West German citizens about relations with the GDR in a year's time, only 27 percent thought reunification "appear[ed] possible," whereas 44 percent thought relations would only be qualitatively better (like Bonn's ties with Austria); 25 percent thought that while relations would improve, the FRG would still be oriented toward the West and the GDR toward the East. See *Der Spiegel*, November 20, 1989, pp. 16–17. They might have found some support for their position among the East German populace. In an Academy of Sciences (East Berlin) poll in early December 1989, only 27 percent of GDR respondents favored forming "a common state with the FRG," while 71 percent wanted the GDR to remain "a sovereign state." See *Der Spiegel*, December 18, 1989, p. 89.

mystery, though, is why both states took as long as they did to act upon this seemingly self-evident conclusion.

One of the principal reasons that historians have long considered the Wall's construction to be a turning point (a "decisive watershed," in one analyst's estimation)[5] in East and West Germany's handling of the national problem is that the event took place against the backdrop of a fundamental shift in relations between the states' superpower allies. In the early years after the founding of both countries in 1949, the GDR's sponsor, the USSR, had been only a rising international presence. It was still uncertain about its claims in Eastern Europe and largely inexperienced in world affairs. But by the late 1950s and early 1960s, Moscow had begun to make its influence felt as a global power. One consequence of this development was the emergence of the rudiments of a relatively stable balance of power between the Soviet Union and the United States. The other result, the foundation for what would later be known as East-West détente, was the greater credence attached to the principle that world peace could be assured only if both superpower blocs respected the prevailing status quo.[6]

In view of the marked extent to which East and West Germany's interests and those of their allies were already intermeshed in a complex array of political, economic, and military commitments, it was reasonable to expect that the two states' sense of their priorities would immediately reflect this emerging bipolar balance in Europe. Nevertheless, the interesting fact about the behavior of both German governments well into the 1960s and 1970s is that each, while professing absolute loyalty to its superpower partner, still acted in ways that defied the international consensus that was taking shape around them.

The problem was that, for fear of precluding all chances of eventual reunification or inadvertently granting their opponents any advantages in the contest over the nation's future, neither state was prepared to recognize the legitimacy of the other. More than is commonly supposed, in fact, the GDR's founding father and First Secretary of the SED, Walter Ulbricht, seems to have believed that by refusing to give ground on his state's claims to a leading role in any settlement of the national question, he could at least hold open the possibility that Germany might someday be reunified under socialism. As a result, for years after the Wall's erection East Berlin was a persistent obstacle to its Soviet allies' hopes of resolving continental tensions on the basis of existing territorial realities. For their part, in contrast,

---

[5]See William Griffith, *The Ostpolitik of the Federal Republic of Germany* (Cambridge, Mass.: MIT Press, 1978), p. 102. Also see Wolfram Hanrieder, *Germany, America, Europe* (New Haven, Conn.: Yale University Press, 1989), p. 169; Peter C. Ludz, *Die DDR zwischen Ost und West* (Munich: C. H. Beck, 1977), p. 47; and Jean Edward Smith, "The Berlin Wall in Retrospect," *Dalhousie Review* 47, no. 2 (Summer 1967), pp. 173–184.

[6]An illuminating account of the culmination of these developments in the late 1960s is John Lewis Gaddis, *Strategies of Containment* (Oxford: Oxford University Press, 1982).

the FRG's leaders always regarded themselves as bound by the prescription of their constitution, the Basic Law, to work for the "completion of the unity" of the German nation. But throughout the first two decades of their state's history, they were so insistent that this provision gave them a "sole right" (*Alleinvertretungsanspruch*) to speak for the interests of all Germans, including those living in the GDR, that they refused to accede to any steps that might have led to even the slightest hint of normalcy for East Germany.

Given that international considerations alone cannot have been behind the Germanys' later adaptation to their divided condition, historians have also sought to account for the changes in East Berlin's and Bonn's actions by focusing on the many respects in which the physical presence of the Wall itself gave them no other choice but to attend to their bilateral relationship and, in the process, to recognize their adversaries.[7] Under other circumstances, one might assume, inter-German hostilities were so deeply felt that the two German governments might well have preferred a world in which they had few, if any, dealings with each other. Nonetheless, the severing of almost all ties between their populations in 1961 meant that both regimes were presented with compelling reasons for reassessing the way they went about pursuing their national objectives.

This shift became particularly apparent in the FRG as the 1960s progressed. Growing numbers of politicians and intellectuals concluded that Bonn did not have to approve of the policies of the SED regime to recognize that relations of some kind with East Berlin were unavoidable if the human costs of division were to be ameliorated. With the Wall in place, the East German government literally had the capacity to cut off its population completely from the West. Hence, as Egon Bahr, a close advisor to the mayor of West Berlin at the time, Willy Brandt, stressed in a famous address at the Lutheran Academy in Tutzing in July 1963, the Federal Republic really had no other option but to accept the GDR as a functioning state. Once one acknowledged that the country could no longer be "torn out of the Soviet sphere of influence" and that "every policy which was geared toward toppling the regime over there [was] hopeless," the best way to keep the dream of national unity alive was to convince East Berlin that greater inter-German contacts were in its best interest.[8]

Nor were Bahr's assumptions entirely fanciful in view of the situation

[7]Roughly speaking, this approach can be found in such works as Joachim Nawrocki, *Relations between the Two States in Germany* (Bonn: Verlag Bonn Aktuell, 1985); Wilhelm Bruns, *Deutsch-deutsche Beziehungen* (Opladen: Leske Verlag, 1982); and David Keithly, *Breakthrough in the Ostpolitik* (Boulder, Colo.: Westview, 1986). As a rule, however, scholars working on the subject, whether German or foreign, have not perceived themselves to be making the case for one scholarly approach over another.

[8]See Boris Meissner, ed., *Die deutsche Ostpolitik: 1961–1970* (Cologne: Verlag Wissenschaft und Politik, 1970), p. 46.

within the GDR following the Wall's erection. Although the East German government was apparently able to make great strides in stabilizing its relationship with its citizenry during the first decade after it had forcibly halted the refugee drain to the West, the difficulty with the solution, the Wall, was its almost sphinxlike character. Even if the country were to be transformed into a model of socialist well-being and abundance—and this was a driving theme behind all of the policies of the country's two most prominent postwar leaders, Ulbricht and Honecker—the East German Communist regime could never be certain that its population would remain in the GDR if the border in Berlin were ever to be reopened. Short of razing the barrier, one way of determining the depth of the East German people's fidelity to the country would have been to let it speak for itself; but the SED was never prepared to test its shaky legitimacy in a democratic vote. Thus the only other recourse open to the government was to go to the source of its troubles, the FRG, in the hope of convincing Bonn itself to abandon its campaigns to win over the hearts and minds of the East German population.

For these reasons alone, it might have seemed that the Germanys were finally able to agree upon a manageable means of accommodating themselves to their nation's division when, in the summer and fall of 1972, they successfully negotiated a treaty, known as the *Grundvertrag*, or Basic Treaty, to govern their relations. This accord not only brought the two regimes more closely back into harmony with the geopolitical imperatives of their superpower patrons, but, more telling still, it also seemed to represent a workable and lasting compromise on the basis of the status quo. All along, the GDR had sought some affirmation from Bonn of its sovereignty as a separate German state. It was therefore much to East Berlin's liking that the West German signatories of the treaty agreed to a de facto (but not a de jure) recognition of the GDR, pledging to respect its government's "independence and autonomy . . . in its internal and external affairs," to honor the "inviolability" of its borders, and to develop "good-neighborly relations . . . on the basis of equal rights."

In return, the FRG clearly profited from the arrangement with East Berlin as well. While stipulating that the national question was by no means settled with the agreement, Bonn obtained the East German government's assurances that a host of "practical and humanitarian questions"—problems of inter-German transit, cooperation in scientific and technical research, environmental dangers, legal matters, and popular exposure to Western media and communications—would be resolved, as the treaty put it, in the course of the normalization of the two states' relations.[9] In this

---

[9]For the text of the Basic Treaty, see *Verträge, Abkommen und Vereinbarungen* (Bonn: Presse und Informationsamt der Bundesregierung, 1973), pp. 17–26. The definitive work on the subject is Benno Zündorf, *Die Ostverträge* (Munich: Beck, 1979), pp. 211–319.

sense the FRG, too, seemed to have been provided with a means for living with the adversity of the Wall.

Nevertheless, the still ambiguous nature of the inter-German relationship was confirmed by the fact that the accord failed to lead to a satisfactory meeting of minds between the German regimes, and progress between East Berlin and Bonn over the first decade after the signing of the Basic Treaty was often desultory and disappointing. For all of the optimism that attended the agreement, the two states' few steps forward were just as frequently accompanied by equal numbers of backward steps. Sometimes, the disputes that arose between the GDR and the FRG were about fundamental issues. Many West German politicians worried, with some justification, that too close a bond with East Berlin might eventually undermine any meaningful semblance of German-German commonality by making it easier for the East German regime to propagate its cause as totally distinct from that represented by the FRG. Similarly, many East German politicians became concerned—quite rightly, as historical events would later testify— that exactly this degree of closeness could weaken their citizens' attachment to the GDR by providing an opposing model of German identity.

Yet, even without these differences to impede their relations, the Germanys' leaders just did not seem to want to get along. All too often in the 1970s, the two governments were able to reach agreements on matters of specific interest to each of them—for example, the construction of a freeway, the marking of common borders—but the general quality of relations between the GDR and the FRG scarcely improved. The East German regime was in the position to profit instantly from the considerable financial gains to be made from such projects, but in other areas, such as the treatment of West German journalists working in the GDR or the handling of its dissident population, its practices remained as oppressive as they had ever been in the past. In like manner, Bonn could benefit from East Berlin's readiness to allow for limited undertakings that enhanced the ability of West German citizens to travel to the GDR. But these gains rarely prevented prominent politicians in the FRG from belittling the SED's claims to legitimacy or making "Sunday speeches" that championed the goal of national reunification.

What was it, then, that still kept the German states from settling on a more amicable means of managing their differences? And what changed by the 1980s to allow each of them finally to come to terms with their nation's division? As we shall see in this study, above and beyond the influence exercised by the Germanys' superpower partners and quite separate from their leaders' appreciation for the benefits of greater cooperation, a deciding factor for both regimes' behavior was represented by the very different policymaking processes that set them apart as states. It is commonly recognized that the way governments make decisions about their priorities can often be just as important, if not even more so, as the substantive merits of the policies they adopt.[10] In the German case in particular, the fact that two opposing political systems were divided by the Wall—Marxism-Leninism in the GDR and pluralist democracy in the FRG—meant that East Berlin and Bonn were practically destined to be at odds. In large part because of this fundamental difference, from the time of both states' founding to the day the Wall was opened, their governments adapted to their shifting international surroundings and their sense for the ebb and flow of domestic opinion at conflicting and often contradictory tempos.[11]

To appreciate this issue, one has only to consider the significance of the high degree of centralization that typified policymaking in the GDR. In a system where all of the formal foreign-policymaking organs, such as the foreign ministry and the relevant central committee departments, were almost completely subordinated to the dictates of the ruling politburo and especially its First Secretary, there was never any doubt about the East German regime's monopoly on power. For all of its well-known weaknesses, the SED-led government had the capability to make the kinds of hard choices about its national options that were ultimately required to regularize relations with the Federal Republic.[12] In fact, this characteristic would prove to be one of East Berlin's greatest bargaining advantages over the four decades of its interactions with the West. The GDR's leaders repeatedly showed that they could act quickly and deliberately to defend their conception of their state's interests against any seeming threat presented by the FRG. Nonetheless, for two distinct reasons, both of which were related to the dictatorial structure of its government, the East German elite was still conspicuously slow to modify its policies when a greater propensity to innovate might have aided the cause of German-German understanding.

The first reason may be self-evident. As long as the GDR's Communist regime was incapable of assessing the extent of its citizens' commitment to socialism with any reliability, it was understandable that the country's leaders would be, almost without fail, reluctant to modify any of their government's policies. The risk of upsetting the delicate balance of East German stability was just too great. No one could doubt the dangers the

---

[10]For example, Peter J. Katzenstein, *Policy and Politics in West Germany* (Philadelphia: Temple University Press, 1987), pp. 6–7. More generally, see James March and Johan Olsen, "The New Institutionalism: Organizational Factors in Political Life," *American Political Science Review* 78, no. 3 (September 1984), pp. 734–779.

[11]My thinking about the impact of the Germanys' different political systems on their interactions has been influenced by three classic studies: Zbigniew Brzezinski and Samuel Huntington, *Political Power: USA/USSR* (New York: Viking, 1966); Raymond Aron, *Democracy and Totalitarianism* (New York: Praeger, 1968); and George Kennan, *Russia and the West under Lenin and Stalin* (Boston: Little, Brown, 1961).

[12]An excellent introduction to policymaking in the GDR is Gert-Joachim Glaeßner, *Die andere deutsche Republik* (Opladen: Westdeutscher Verlag, 1989).

country faced as the weaker and less prosperous of the two German polities. Even if the GDR's citizens were not directly exposed to their Western
counterparts through ties of family and friendship, the influence of the
affluent FRG was literally broadcast into their households and workplaces
on a daily basis through the media of radio and television. As a consequence, the SED was constantly in the position of battling for loyalties that
it could never truly confirm.

The second reason for the East German government's hesitancy was of
even greater moment. Because it was anyone's guess how to determine
which policies would serve East German interests and which not, the
authority to make the difficult decisions about the ordering of the country's
priorities invariably fell to those individuals who were considered best
positioned to speak for the collective will of the SED. This factor almost
always led the party faithful to turn to their First Secretary ("General
Secretary," from the mid-1970s onward), whose grip on political power
was strengthened all the more.[13]

Under these circumstances, on the questions that really counted, the
only reasonable hope that the East German government might be convinced to alter its policies lay with the inclinations of the SED's leader or
with those among his closest circle of confidantes. It was not that there was
always a "complete unanimity of views" (to use the party's own rhetoric)
within the leadership; major differences of opinion existed within the SED
just like in any other complex organization. In a highly politicized culture,
however, which placed a primacy on "revolutionary discipline" and the
maintenance of party unity at all costs, it was simply inconceivable that
anyone who disagreed with the First Secretary would have gone so far as to
voice dissenting perspectives publicly. This would have been to risk the
unpardonable sin of "factionalism." Thus, barring a major catastrophe,
such as a severe downturn in the economy or an international crisis, an
Ulbricht or a Honecker could practically dictate East German priorities
with impunity.

---

[13]Over time, the logic of this thinking tended to promote a virtual monopoly of decision-
making power in the hands of the SED's leader. For example, Erich Honecker's personal
involvement in foreign-policy questions grew with every year he was in office, so that by the
end of his tenure, he was not only making most of the crucial decisions about GDR priorities
himself—something not terribly unusual in Western polities—but also taking an interest in
the finest details of some policy issues. During the period when Honecker's involvement was
greatest in the late 1980s, one department director at the Ministry of Foreign Affairs grew so
concerned about offending his chief by choosing the wrong course of action that he decided to
pass the responsibility upstairs, inquiring in a written note whether a certain "course A" or
"course B" should be followed. Much to his dismay, Honecker returned the note the next day,
having scrawled only the single word *einverstanden* ("agreed") across the bottom. Author's
interviews, East Berlin. On Honecker's preeminent role in foreign-policymaking, see OHP
(Herbert Häber, March 19, 1990).

Naturally, this situation also meant that the FRG's leaders often found the challenge of dealing with the GDR maddeningly frustrating. Lacking either formal or informal groups within the East German elite to whom they could appeal for contrasting views, they were almost entirely dependent upon the SED chief's goodwill to have a chance of getting what they wanted. When it was lacking, simply put, relations with East Berlin went nowhere. Nonetheless, it would be far from correct to suggest that all of the problems that set the Germanys apart were due to East German intransigence. For practically the opposite reasons, the FRG's political system presented obstacles of its own to inter-German cooperation that were equally difficult to overcome.

As a liberal state, the Federal Republic had one strength that was forever denied the GDR. Thanks to the popular confidence enjoyed by the country's electoral system, its political parties, its courts, and its parliament, the FRG's leaders could always draw upon their ability, theoretically speaking, to lay the foundation for the broadest possible public consensus on even the most divisive issues. For, unlike the leadership of the SED, which was as a rule uncertain about its successes and therefore desperate for any signs of affirmation, West German politicians had no choice but to assess their population's wishes by testing their policies regularly at the ballot box. Yet, here as well, the FRG's advantage came with a price. As long as the country's reigning governments rose and fell on the basis of their leaders' skill in cultivating stable majorities—and this was a growing concern following the sharp political decline of Konrad Adenauer in the early 1960s—few politicians were likely to have the confidence that was required to question well-established policies. As a result, the Federal Republic, too, displayed its own distinctive aversion to major changes.

Had East Germany's leaders had their way with Bonn—and they were not at all reluctant to project their own strengths onto the West German system[14]—their adversaries would have acted without hesitation to implement changes in the Federal government's handling of the national question for which there was already broad public support in the 1960s and 1970s. Even in the official corridors of power, such as the Foreign Office, the Federal bureaucracies, and government-supported "think tanks," one did not have to look far to find considerable support for the proposition that the FRG's traditional approaches to the problem of national division were

---

[14]For example, one West German parliamentarian relates that in discussions with SED politburo member Hermann Axen in the late 1970s, he was almost incapable of convincing the latter that the Federal government was powerless to guarantee that the GDR would receive more favorable press coverage in the FRG. Evidently, Axen found it hard to believe that the West German government could not muzzle its newspapers in the way the official media were controlled in East Berlin. Author's interview, Hans-Jürgen Wischnewski, Bonn, January 11, 1988.

no longer effective. Nevertheless, the process of policy innovation was never so rational.

Quite frequently, the most mundane political considerations—the need to form manageable coalitions, the demands of intraparty bargaining—simply got in the way of these hopes for change and acted as brakes upon the inclinations of those who were in a position to challenge accepted ways of thinking. Of course, the influence of reform-minded politicians would eventually be felt in the parliamentary debates of the Bundestag and in the offices of the Federal chancellery. In large part, this was because of the way the competition of West Germany's political parties promoted the melding of new perspectives over time into old ones. But in the interim, many German officials, in East Berlin and Bonn alike, were likely to find the pace of adaptation in the FRG both indecisive and exasperatingly slow.[15]

Against this background, one can readily appreciate why any meeting of minds between West German decision makers and their GDR counterparts could only have occurred under unusual circumstances. Not only did the two German governments have manifestly different objectives, but they were also driven by very different policymaking imperatives. The East German government could act without interference to pursue its interests, but its leaders were constrained by their limited insight into the consequences of their actions. Conversely, the FRG's leaders may have known what their population expected of them. Yet the fact that they also had to build a consensus around their policies limited their ability to act as quickly as they might have liked. In these respects, because both states' shortcomings necessarily reinforced their governments' already risk-averse dispositions, one cannot help but wonder how East and West Germany ever reached the point where they could put enough of their differences behind them to cooperate successfully.

A German-German Consensus

One thing is certain. The 1980s presented a picture of German-German accommodation that was impossible to deny and difficult to ignore. As West German politicians traveled to East Berlin in record numbers—*Länder* presidents running for reelection, mayors of West Berlin seeking an independent profile for their city, Social Democratic parliamentarians exploring arms-control opportunities, and conservative notables establishing credibility in the new politics with the East—many of the explosive disputes of the German past seemed to be relegated to insignificance. Furthermore, the East German regime, too, began to open itself to a great

---

[15]Consider Raymond Aron's observation: "Regimes built on words and on debates will always find difficulty in making radical choices and will always be inclined to prefer compromise," in *Democracy and Totalitarianism*, p. 107.

variety of contacts that had only been dimly foreseen by the authors of the Basic Treaty. A long-sought agreement on cultural exchange was finally reached, regular discussions began on common environmental problems, and above all, years after the Wall had cut off most East Germans from the West, the GDR undertook a radical liberalization of its travel laws.

Had the Germanys been any other countries, their behavior might have been easily attributed to the broader phenomenon known as East-West détente. The fact that they were two opposing parts of the former German nation, however, made their accomplishments seem all the more distinctive, and important. Was there not a greater degree of "normality" to the GDR's and the FRG's relations, many outside observers wondered, as the two states' interactions seemed to become more and more akin to the everyday relations between other European powers?[16] And would not even closer ties between East Berlin and Bonn in the years to come, others speculated, finally lead the remaining skeptics in the GDR and the FRG about the benefits of inter-German reconciliation to the conclusion that there was no turning back from the fate that historical events had bestowed upon them?[17] It was as if the hoary German question were finally on the verge of being resolved on the basis of national division.

Against this setting, it is not hard to see why many Germans would have been completely taken unaware by the implications of the fall of the Berlin Wall in November 1989. To say that they had learned to live with the barrier throughout the nearly three decades of its existence is to say that they had come to terms with its reality and the larger issues it symbolized in every sense in which acceptance was possible. They had accepted the geopolitical implications of its construction; they had accepted the rationality of bargaining with each other under its shadow; and most important, they had finally come to accept the barrier's existence in a manner that was consistent with the constraints and opportunities presented to them by their own political systems.

In light of these factors, it might seem surprising that so little was required—the withdrawal of Soviet guarantees of East Germany's sovereignty and the opening of the Hungarian border—to bring the GDR crashing down in the late summer and fall of 1989, or that even less was

[16]For a German view, cf. Gebhard Schweigler, "Normalität in Deutschland," *Europa Archiv* 6 (1989), pp. 173–182. For a British view, cf. Edwina Moreton, "The German question in the 1980s," in Moreton, *Germany*, p. 4.

[17]"Contrary to widely held views abroad," an Austrian-American analyst, Eric Frey, noted in 1987, "a German-German rapprochement does not represent a movement toward reunification, but a movement away from it, toward the recognition of the division of Germany and the establishment of normal relations between two separate states." See *Division and Detente: The Germanies and Their Alliances* (New York: Praeger, 1987), p. xv. For a similar view by an English observer, cf. John Ardagh, *Germany and the Germans* (New York: Harper and Row, 1987), p. 384.

involved in the series of rapid-fire events that led to the merger of both German states into a single national entity less than a year thereafter. But in point of fact, these events serve to remind us that the division of Germany was never merely a geographical or physical reality. It was also a state of mind and an accepted political condition that had been decades in the making. Given the stubbornness with which individuals everywhere cling to their beliefs in the face of contradictory evidence, it is understandable that many German policymakers should have taken as long as they did before reaching the conclusion that they had no other choice but to live with the division of their nation. By the same logic, therefore, it was also predictable that once they had settled upon this conviction, they would each defend their new perspective with the same degree of confidence and certitude they had earlier displayed in holding onto the dream of national reunification.

As we shall see much later in this study, the consensus between East Berlin and Bonn about the meager prospects for German unity may provide one of the most useful means for conceptualizing the internal dilemmas that are likely to beset the reunified nation's future. For, just as the German policymakers of the past forty-plus years slowly came to believe that their destiny was to live apart from each other, so too will their western *and* eastern German successors have to convince themselves in the coming decades of the necessity and the desirability of living together again. Here as well, the single type of political system that governs reunified Germany—liberal democracy having emerged triumphant over Marxism-Leninism—will assume a central role in determining how and with what success future policymakers are able to overcome their population's differences and provide all of their citizens with a coherent sense of national purpose.

Nevertheless, even to speak about the German future at this point is to get ahead of ourselves. Worse still, it is to risk reading history backwards with a deterministic certainty that has nothing to do with the real German past.[18] First, it is necessary to recognize that as early as the 1950s there were already very good reasons for thinking that East and West Germany would somehow have to make their peace with their nation's division. Not the least of these was that, even before the Berlin Wall's construction, the GDR's and the FRG's superpower allies had begun to move toward an understanding about the balance of power in Europe that presupposed the lasting presence on the continent of two, diametrically opposed German states.

[18]On the dangers of thinking deterministically about the past, cf. Baruch Fischoff, "For Those Condemned to Study the Past: Heuristics and Biases in Hindsight," in D. Kahneman, P. Slovic, and A. Tversky, eds., *Judgment under Uncertainty* (Cambridge, U.K.: Cambridge University Press, 1982), pp. 335–354.

II

One Germany, Two Alliances

The governments of the Warsaw Treaty states
turn to the People's Parliament (*Volkskammer*)
and the government of the GDR, and to all
workers of the German Democratic Republic,
with the proposal that they introduce such an
order on the border of West Berlin which puts a
stop to the subversive activity against the
countries of the socialist camp and which
guarantees reliable surveillance and effective
control around the whole territory of West
Berlin, including its border with democratic
Berlin.
   (Warsaw Treaty Organization declaration,
   August 12, 1961)

Much less transpired during the implementation
of our measures than at an average Rock-'n'-Roll
concert at the West Berlin Sports Palace.
   (Walter Ulbricht, August 18, 1961)

IT IS NO WONDER that historians have been transfixed by the literal significance of the Berlin Wall. The barrier's construction on August 13, 1961,
marked the closing of the last gap between East and West Germany and, for
all appearances, the solidification of the physical division of the German
nation into separate states. Just as important, the event was also accompanied by a hardening of superpower policy on the GDR and the FRG, as
both the Soviet Union and the United States confirmed a trend that had
been visible for several years by defining their commitments to their respective German partners almost exclusively in terms of the status quo. If the
German nation were ever to be reunited, their actions showed, it would
only be on the improbable occasion that the division of Europe itself were
overcome and there were no longer any reasons to fight for the existence of
two distinct German states.

   Nevertheless, what makes the story behind the Wall's erection most
interesting is that the leaders of the GDR and the FRG did not respond to this

new circumstance as their allies might have hoped. Even with the Wall between them, many German policymakers, in the East and West, still acted as though the best way of preserving their interests was to resist the pressures around them to accord any legitimacy to the national divide. Well into the 1960s and 1970s, in fact, East Berlin's and Bonn's continuing adherence to such "policies of strength" (to use Konrad Adenauer's well-known terminology) accounted for a major imperfection in the way the priorities of each state meshed with the European balance of power.

Still, the situation might have been different. Understandably, neither of the two German governments wanted to show any signs of weakness or uncertainty that could have thrown to the opposing side the advantage in the contest over the nation's future. Yet there were politicians in both East and West Germany in the 1950s who had other ideas than their more famous leaders about how most reliably to pursue their national goals. Had their approaches been adopted, East Berlin and Bonn might have taken subtly and perhaps even significantly different courses of action on the national question. Then, quite possibly, the two states could have been better positioned to adapt to the shifting agendas of their superpower patrons. But somehow, these voices were never heard.

As we shall see in this chapter, the twin German policies that later proved to be such obstacles to inter-German contacts for over a decade after the Wall's construction were the products of unusual internal conditions within the GDR and the FRG in both states' first decade. Well beyond the influence of their turbulent international surroundings, Adenauer and his opponent, Walter Ulbricht, were able to benefit from unique policymaking circumstances that allowed each of them to approach the task of national reunification with almost no apprehension that their policies could be overturned. Yet, to appreciate why either of the German regimes might even have been called to rethink its priorities, one has to begin with the changes in superpower policy that predated the Wall itself.

The Soviet Ultimatum

For good reason, most accounts of the events leading to the Wall's construction start out with an incident that demonstrated, arguably better than any other before it, that Bonn's Western allies were no longer capable of fighting for German interests with the enthusiasm and commitment that had led them to make the state a member of the NATO alliance in the first place. On November 10, 1958, Nikita Khrushchev, First Secretary of the Soviet Communist Party (CPSU), used an address before a visiting Polish delegation at the Moscow Sports Palace to lash out at the United States, Great Britain, and France for ostensibly abusing their occupation rights in the island city of Berlin by conducting what he claimed were "subversive activities" against the GDR and the entire socialist bloc. If the Western powers really wanted to reduce tensions on the European continent, Khrushchev stressed, it was high time that they treated East Germany as a sovereign state, by respecting its capital, East Berlin, and accepting its authority over all matters that transpired on its territory. Otherwise, the Warsaw Pact would take steps to resolve the anomalous status of Berlin in the interests of socialism.[1] Rather than letting the matter rest with this verbal attack, Khrushchev's government formally advised all three Western occupation authorities on November 27, in a document that the First Secretary himself may well have drafted, that the USSR was committed to achieving a quick settlement of the Berlin problem, with or without their help. If they failed to end their occupation of West Berlin and to allow for the city's transformation into a "free," totally demilitarized entity within six months, the Soviet Union would sign a separate peace agreement with the GDR, which would then be entitled to resolve its differences with the city's western sectors as it saw fit.[2]

Of course, the Western powers did not need to be told that a "free city" of West Berlin would immediately fall under the shadow of Soviet and East German influence. The GDR's leaders would steadily tighten their grip over the access routes leading to the city, and soon they and their Soviet sponsors would determine the norms of all legitimate political activity. On these grounds alone, therefore, it is hardly surprising that Khrushchev failed to convince the allied powers to accede to his demands. Nonetheless, his ultimatum did succeed in one crucial respect. By forcing the allies to confine their interests more narrowly to Berlin's western sectors in the years after 1958—and not to the entire city, which lay within their legal provenance as occupying powers—he exposed a latent debate within the Atlantic community about how far one could go in defense of this and a host of other unresolved issues related to the destiny of postwar Germany. Ultimately at stake was a remarkable bargain that all three of the Western powers had struck with West Germany's first chancellor, Konrad Adenauer, in return for his cooperation in aligning the FRG militarily with the West.

As early as the London Declaration and Paris Agreements of October 1954, which originally set the stage for West Germany's incorporation into NATO, the allies had committed themselves to nothing less than a revisionist posture on the future of Europe, going far beyond their presence in Berlin to embrace all of the Federal Republic's reservations about the continental status quo. They had officially recognized Bonn's claim as "the only

[1]*Current Digest of the Soviet Press* (hereafter *CDSP*) 10, no. 45, pp. 7–9.
[2]*Pravda*, November 28, 1958. Also, see Khrushchev's press conference on November 27, in *CDSP* 10, no. 48, pp. 17–19.

German government freely and legitimately constituted" to speak for the entire German nation.[3] They had assured Adenauer that they would consult with the FRG whenever its interests in Berlin and in Germany as a whole were in question. And most important, in vowing "to achieve, by peaceful means, their common aim of a reunified Germany enjoying a liberal democratic constitution like that of the Federal Republic," they had bound themselves to a program for reshaping the face of central Europe that was potentially at odds with their public professions of interest in an orderly resolution of tensions in the region.[4]

Considering that the FRG had only recently been deprived of many of the attributes of state sovereignty, the chancellor's ability to extract these assurances was impressive. But this was not only because his country's occupiers had agreed to refrain from any initiatives that might have reinforced Germany's division. Since just about any Western attempt to negotiate with the East could have fallen into this restrictive category, Adenauer's bargain also meant, at least in his own selective reading of his country's position, that the FRG acquired something akin to a veto power over the West's relations with Communist Europe. Even on matters not directly tied to the German question, the Americans, the British, and the French were supposedly all kept from making overtures toward the Soviet Union and the other socialist states unless they could first secure the requisite West German support.[5]

Adenauer's bargain was also extraordinary for a more subtle reason, that is, the seeming ease with which he convinced the majority of his countrymen that a step which had the appearance of being contrary to the FRG's national goals—rearmament within the confines of the Atlantic alliance—was actually the best hope of one day restoring German unity. Scholars continue to be divided about whether the chancellor himself, a Catholic Rhinelander and longtime critic of his country's Bismarckian past, was as sincerely committed to German national objectives as he professed.[6] But there can be no doubt about the domestic forces that compelled him to address this issue and to keep it among his central priorities. Well into the

[3]"London and Paris Agreements," U.S. Department of State (September–October 1954), pub. 5659 (Washington, D.C.: GPO, 1954), p. 17.

[4]Rolf Steininger, ed., *Deutsche Geschichte: 1945–1961*, vol. 2 (Frankfurt: Fischer, 1987), pp. 403–404.

[5]Cf. Joseph Joffe, "The View from Bonn," in Lincoln Gordon, ed., *Eroding Empire: Western Relations with Eastern Europe* (Washington, D.C.: Brookings Institution, 1987), pp. 138–141.

[6]For contrasting views on this question by two of Adenauer's best-known interpreters, see Arnulf Baring, *Aussenpolitik in Adenauers Kanzlerdemokratie* (Munich: R. Oldenbourg, 1969), pp. 54–59, and Hans-Peter Schwarz, "Das aussenpolitische Konzept Konrad Adenauers," in R. Morsey and K. Repgen, eds., *Adenauer Studien*, vol. 1 (Mainz: Matthias Grünewald Verlag, 1971), pp. 71–108.

1950s, a majority of the FRG's population still regarded reunification as an uncompromisable national obligation.[7] Furthermore, Adenauer also had to contend on a daily basis with the demands of organized lobbies (for example, the so-called Federation of Expellees, claiming to represent the interests of over ten million Germans who in 1945 had been driven out of former German territories east of the Oder-Neisse boundary), which made it virtually impossible to ignore the national theme.

What made Adenauer's approach to this challenge distinctive, however, was that instead of merely contending that his government had made an unavoidable trade-off in joining the Western alliance, the West German leader went right to the heart of possible objections to his alliance policy by arguing that the West's assurances on reunification were in fact the only reliable guarantee that the two parts of Germany would ever be rejoined. As long as totalitarian regimes ruled in the East, he insisted, in what would become the rationale for the West German "policy of strength," compromises or concessions of any kind would only worsen the lot of those Germans trapped under communism. The FRG's sole chance of convincing the Soviet Union to relinquish control over East Germany, therefore, lay in demonstrating through its resolve and its democratic achievements (the "power of facts," Adenauer called these virtues) that there was no longer any point in resisting the demands of a united West.[8]

Such claims may seem fanciful, yet they possessed an irresistible appeal in the early 1950s. During the first half of the decade, events both within and outside central Europe, including the Stalinist purges in Eastern Europe and the outbreak of the Korean War, had created a political climate on the continent in which few Western leaders would have undertaken conciliatory steps toward the East in any case. Moreover, the American emphasis at the time on securing West German rearmament guaranteed that the United States would oppose serious talks with the Soviet Union until the FRG's integration in the Western alliance was concluded.[9] In this cause, Adenauer had the good fortune of sharing worldviews with the outspoken American secretary of state, John Foster Dulles, who, as much as he, be-

[7]Cf. Karl Deutsch and Lewis Edinger, *Germany Rejoins the Powers* (Stanford, Calif.: Stanford University Press, 1959), pp. 25–26.

[8]Cf. Hans-Peter Schwarz, ed., *Konrad Adenauer, Reden: 1917–1967* (Stuttgart: Deutsche Verlags-Anstalt, 1975), pp. 276–277. For a nice encapsulation of the "policy of strength," consider Adenauer's comments before the CDU congress on October 18, 1952: "My friends, a totalitarian state—we know this from history—does not even consider it worthwhile to talk to a weak country, but it will speak responsibly with a strong country, and for this reason, the West must be strong." Ibid., p. 285.

[9]Charles R. Planck, *The Changing Status of German Reunification in Western Diplomacy* (Baltimore: Johns Hopkins University Press, 1967), p. 10.

lieved that a "policy of Western unity and firmness" was a prerequisite for compelling Moscow to foreswear its aggressive aims in Europe.[10]

All along, the manifest weakness in such a stand was that an environment that supported a "policy of strength" could also change, and this was exactly what happened, although slowly and almost imperceptibly at first, to the Federal Republic. Yet, paradoxically, even as the Western powers were signing the agreements that would obligate them to defend the FRG's national goals, Adenauer's successes themselves contributed in an unexpected way to transforming the premises upon which the policy of nonrelations with the East was based. Almost by definition, a sovereign West German state was a different entity from the one that had previously been unable to act on its own.

Consider, simply, the impact of the FRG's rearmament on Moscow's overall strategy in Europe. While the Soviet Union had concentrated its energies in the early 1950s on preventing West German militarization, regularly expressing concern about the implications of any West German role in NATO, Bonn's accession to the North Atlantic alliance on May 7, 1955, meant that the Kremlin no longer had any choice but to coexist with a rearmed German state. Accordingly, Soviet leaders gradually began to search for ways of keeping the East-West standoff from becoming any more detrimental to their interests. They publicly combined offers to reduce the danger of war between the blocs, promises of troop cuts, and plans for the creation of zones of limited armaments with equally direct signals—no better represented than by the formation of the Warsaw Treaty Organization on May 14, 1955—showing how much the West stood to lose by maintaining the current level of tension in Europe.

Under these circumstances alone, it is impressive that the FRG's allies were willing to stick to their assurances to Adenauer *as long as they did* about pinning the question of European security to Bonn's conception of a satisfactory resolution of the German problem. At the Geneva arms-control summit of July 1955, for example, the Western powers peremptorily rebuffed Soviet pressures for a comprehensive disarmament agreement on the grounds that Moscow was still unprepared to allow for Germany's reunification along liberal-democratic lines. Even British prime minister Anthony Eden's cautious proposal to establish military inspection zones on both sides of the European divide foundered on Adenauer's objection that such measures would have accentuated the differences between the Germanys.

---

[10]Hans-Jürgen Grabbe, "Konrad Adenauer, John Foster Dulles, and West German–American Relations," in R. H. Immerman, ed., *John Foster Dulles and the Diplomacy of the Cold War* (Princeton, N.J.: Princeton University Press, 1990), pp. 121–122.

As public anxiety about the dangers of the East-West standoff rose on the continent, however, it was understandable that Western elites increasingly wondered whether they had not already done enough to meet West German interests.[11] At a London meeting of the United Nations' Disarmament Subcommittee in the spring of 1956, both the French and British representatives for the first time openly questioned whether the FRG's reading of European priorities alone could be used to judge the merits of arms-control initiatives. Throughout the following year, Western audiences were treated to an onslaught of proposals by noted personalities—George Kennan, Raymond Aron, and others—who sought to sever the link between German demands and the broader issue of European security through means as varied as German reunification under neutral auspices and even the recognition of the nation's division. Behind the scenes, the U.S. government cautiously sought to circumvent its obligations to Bonn by conducting informal talks with Moscow about ways of improving communications between the blocs and pursuing new avenues for arms reductions.

No issue, however, can have been more revealing of the potential fissures within the alliance than Berlin, for in no other case was the issue of war or peace so manifestly exposed. Even before Khrushchev's November 1958 ultimatum, there were indications that the Western occupation powers' readiness to go along with Bonn's objections to premature negotiations on the German question might be tested over the city's disputed status. In early 1958, for example, Soviet authorities consciously linked widespread hopes for the convening of a summit conference on disarmament with renewed pressure on the West to acknowledge East German interests in Berlin, including, most importantly, the GDR's claims to control the transit routes that passed over its territory between West Berlin and the FRG.

It may be that, in focusing on the city, the Kremlin had much broader objectives in mind, such as using Berlin to force the Western allies to reassess their views on discussions then underway about upgrading the FRG's role in NATO by equipping the Bundeswehr with nuclear weapons.[12] There could be no doubt, however, that the Soviets had touched a sensitive nerve for the West. Traffic to and from the city, including American military transit, was repeatedly interrupted and new border controls were implemented along the sectoral boundary separating East from West Berlin. By a strict interpretation of their rights of occupation, the three Western powers could have demanded that Moscow and its East German allies immediately lift all restrictions on movement within Berlin. However, John Foster Dulles signaled his country's desire to avoid any new conflicts with the Soviet Union by emphasizing in a press conference in early November that

---

[11] Mark Cioc, *Pax Atomica* (New York: Columbia University Press, 1988), pp. 6–11.

[12] On these themes, see the provocative argument by Marc Trachtenberg, *History and Strategy* (Princeton, N.J.: Princeton University Press, 1991), chap. 5.

the United States was "solemnly committed" to its obligations in *West* Berlin, but he omitted any mention of U.S. prerogatives to speak for the whole city.[13]

American officials were later to become even more deliberate about defining the extent of their interests in Berlin. Yet against this background alone, it is clear why Khrushchev's November ultimatum should have brought to the surface all of the hidden uncertainties about Adenauer's special bargain with the West. As authorities in Bonn readily sensed, the Soviet leader's demands called on everyone to make hard choices about their commitments. Once the Western allies had begun to draw the line between greater and lesser commitments to Berlin, one could reasonably wonder how long it would be before they would also rethink even the ultimate goal of German reunification.

In fact, only two weeks after Khrushchev's November 10 speech but still before the formalization of Moscow's threat to sign a separate peace with the GDR, West German anxieties were confirmed when Dulles himself casually broached the idea of using East German personnel to monitor the transit routes between West Berlin and the FRG, provided that such officials would be treated as "agents" of the Soviet Union and not signify a formal recognition of the GDR government.[14] No doubt the American secretary was only trying to devise a means for resolving the conflict that would be in everyone's interest. Yet, from the West German perspective, the U.S. role as a guarantor of the "policy of strength" was clearly unraveling. "We are standing before [a time of] difficult decisions," one of Adenauer's closest advisors, Heinrich Krone, noted in his diary on January 24, 1959: "The West wants to have quiet. With Berlin, the Kremlin has gotten the German question rolling. We will not come out of this struggle without some losses."[15]

East German Uncertainties

While the West German government had reason to be concerned about the support that it was receiving from its allies, it is less commonly recognized that the GDR's leaders themselves were discomfited by the Soviet Union's

[13]For Dulles's remarks, see Jean E. Smith, *The Defense of Berlin* (Baltimore: Johns Hopkins University Press, 1963), p. 163.

[14]On this and other aspects of the changing relationship between the FRG and its allies, see the illuminating accounts by Richard Löwenthal, "Vom kalten Krieg zur Ostpolitik," in R. Löwenthal and H. P. Schwarz, eds., *Die zweite Republik* (Stuttgart: Seewald, 1974), pp. 626–644, and Waldemar Besson, *Die Außenpolitik der Bundesrepublik* (Munich: R. Piper, 1970), pp. 166–70, 191–209.

[15]"Aufzeichnungen zur Deutschland- und Ostpolitik, 1954–1969," in R. Morsey and Konrad Repgen, eds., *Adenauer Studien III* (Mainz: Matthias-Grünewald, 1971), p. 149.

actions in the late 1950s, although in a less evident way. Undeniably, by taking on the West over Berlin, Khrushchev had assured his allies of getting exactly what they wanted. Were the ultimatum to have succeeded, the SED regime would have finally been able to control the Western presence in its midst and, by implication, would also have acquired the means drastically to curtail the use of the city's western sectors as a haven for the steady flight of refugees from socialism. Nevertheless, although the Soviet ultimatum represented a net gain for the GDR, this was only true relative to the two states' complex relations in the past. For unlike Bonn, East Berlin had rarely been able to get more than equivocal support from Moscow on the issues that mattered most to its leaders.

It may be that the United States and the West Europeans had often made their obeissances to German unity less out of real conviction than simple deference to the wishes of a vital ally. But in contrast, the restoration of a unitary German state was central to the broader objectives of Soviet foreign policy in the late 1940s and early 1950s. Both before and after the GDR's founding, the CPSU leadership and Josef Stalin in particular seem to have regarded the issue as the only available means for preventing the formation of a hostile Western alliance against the USSR. So long as the German people could be convinced that any kind of rearmament scheme would doom the chances for national unity, the reasoning went, the Soviet Union could at least hope to influence the role that such a state would play in a reconstructed Europe. Yet adherence to this objective also signified that Moscow had very mixed feelings about the fate of the socialist GDR. If the division of the German nation ever congealed to yield entirely separate states, the USSR's ability to exercise any impact on the evolution of political events in the West was bound to diminish accordingly.[16]

This stand meant that for all of the Soviet Union's outward efforts to play up the existence of an independent East German state after 1949, the GDR was always relegated to something of a second-class status among its East European allies.[17] It was never accorded more than associate membership in the Communist Information Bureau, and only in 1950, one full year after the founding of the Council of Mutual Economic Assistance (COMECON), was the GDR even invited to join the Eastern bloc's premier agency for economic integration. Only in 1952 did Moscow, apparently reluctantly, support the East German government's announcement that it, too, was ready to lay the foundations for a socialist economy, and even then

---

[16]On the Soviet position, see Wolfgang Pfeiler, *Deutschlandpolitische Optionen der Sowjetunion* (Melle: Verlag Ernst Knoth, 1987), pp. 36–47. Also see the excellent discussion of post-1989 archival findings by Dietrich Staritz, "Die SED, Stalin und der 'Aufbau des Sozialismus' in der DDR," *Deutschland Archiv*, July 1991, pp. 686–700.

[17]For example, N. Edwina Moreton, *East Germany and the Warsaw Alliance* (Boulder, Colo.: Westview, 1978), p. 19.

the Soviets seemed to have mixed feelings about the wisdom of the action. Finally, although the East German regime took part in the founding of the Warsaw Treaty Organization in May 1955, the GDR was not allowed to form its own army until January 1956.

Nevertheless, while the slow pace of East Berlin's incorporation into the Eastern bloc led to occasional friction between the Soviet and East German governments, Moscow's emphasis on German unity per se was not the primary source of these differences. To the contrary, despite the reputation the GDR acquired in the West as a "separatist state" (*Spalterstaat*), whose leaders were bent upon freezing the inter-German divide forever, the national ideal was probably as dear to the East German elite as it was to that of the FRG. In fact, the early leaders of the Socialist Unity Party—like the country's first (and last) president, Wilhelm Pieck, the old Social Democratic cochairman of the SED, Otto Grotewohl, and even Ulbricht—were at least as eager to portray themselves as German patriots as any of their rivals in the Federal Republic.

In part, this was a matter of straightforward political expediency. As representatives of the weaker of the two German polities, the GDR's leaders were driven by the sheer necessity of having to prove that "the natural place of the German people," as Pieck characterized it, "[was] in the camp of peace, democracy, and socialism."[18] With thousands of their citizens leaving the country permanently for the FRG, even in times when economic conditions in both Germanys were severe, and with many others (including many former Social Democrats, now members of the SED) clamoring for proof that their identities as Germans would not be lost under socialism, East German officials simply had no other option than to champion the national cause.

Yet it would be misleading to assume that the SED's leaders regarded these pretensions in merely instrumental terms.[19] From their perspective as Marxists, the division of the German nation also presented a priceless opportunity to make up for those times in the late 1920s and early 1930s

---

[18]*Protokoll der Verhandlungen des III. Parteitages der* SED (Berlin: Dietz, 1951), p. 28.

[19]Judging from my conversations with individuals who were actively involved in the making of the GDR's national policy, there seems to be much less dispute among former East German officials about their government's commitment to national reunification in the 1950s than among comparable West German authorities about Adenauer's objectives. Without exception, my East German discussion partners insist that politicians such as Ulbricht and Grotewohl really believed the conditions would one day be right for Germany's reunification under socialism. As one party official stressed in mid-1989, "We believed that the transformation to socialism was inevitable in the whole world. Why shouldn't this have been possible in all of Germany?" Author's interview with Heinz Hümmler, vice-rector of the SED Academy of Social Sciences, East Berlin, May 31, 1989. For another participant's description of his and others' anguish at having to move away from an emphasis on reunification to embrace the idea of two separate German states, see OHP (Böhm, December 5, 1990).

when many German Communists had underestimated the national question and failed to reach out to the diverse elements in the German working class who could have fought with them against the Nazi dictatorship. Decades later in the 1980s, in fact, East German ideologists still appealed to this rationale to justify their efforts to search for mutual points of interest with the FRG.[20] In the first half of the 1950s, however, the SED had some reason to think that its appeals to common German interests would not go unheard, not only among its own population but also in the Federal Republic. At a time when the strictures of the West German "policy of strength" kept the Adenauer regime from assuming almost any kind of ties with East Berlin—with the single exception of economic ties, which were tolerated on the grounds that the East German population should not be punished for the sins of its Communist rulers[21]—and when many West Germans had misgivings about the consequences of their government's decision to rearm, the GDR at least had the small advantage of appearing to do something to end the division of the nation. Thus Grotewohl and Pieck took the lead in advancing proposals—in late 1950, for example, for an all-German constituent council, later to be known by the popular slogan, "Germans at one table"[22]—which were meant to convince both German populations that the initiative on the national question lay with the GDR.

Where East German interests did collide with those of the Soviet Union, however, was on the issue of what was to become of the GDR if such appeals for German unity fell on fertile ground in the West. Would the reunified German state be a socialist entity, capable of leading the German working class down the road that Karl Marx and Friedrich Engels had prophesied a century earlier? Or would socialist values instead be sacrificed in the name of great power expediency? On several occasions in the GDR's early years, beginning with Josef Stalin's famous note to the Western powers of March 10, 1952, on the subject of a German peace treaty, the Soviets showed that they were prepared to exploit the attraction of an all-German government as a means of mobilizing popular sentiment in the FRG against rearmament. Yet, while it will never be known with certainty whether Stalin or any of his successors was sincerely interested in striking a deal with the West at the expense of the GDR—after all, Soviet reunification proposals

[20]Author's interviews, Ekkehard Lieberam and Jürgen Hofmann, Leipzig and East Berlin, May 9, 1988, and June 8, 1988. Also see Carola Stern, *Ulbricht* (Cologne: Kiepenheuer und Witsch, 1964), p. 191.

[21]Robert W. Dean, *West German Trade with the East: The Political Dimension* (New York: Praeger, 1974), p. 46.

[22]In 1951 Grotewohl also seemed to endorse the idea of some form of unitary German elections. However, because the East German regime later balked at the FRG's demands that any all-German vote be subject to international supervision, one must wonder whether the GDR's leaders would have been willing to accept truly democratic norms. On Grotewohl's and other proposals, see Gottfried Zieger, *Die Haltung von SED und DDR zur Einheit Deutschlands, 1949–1987* (Cologne: Verlag Wissenschaft und Politik, 1988), pp. 21–42.

were never put to a test[23]—there can be no doubt that the SED took every such overture seriously.[24]

As Moscow showed itself to be more and more willing to discuss the *terms* of unification with the West, even under conditions (such as free elections) that would have called into question the future of German socialism, doubts unavoidably arose in East Berlin about the USSR's long-term objectives. As one former member of the party apparatus later recounted, when the Soviets renewed their peace offering to the allied powers in August 1953, only two months after the GDR had been racked by the outbreak of massive antigovernment worker demonstrations on June 16 and 17, "[e]ven functionaries who had never deviated from the party line or doubted the infallibility of the Soviet Union or the party now began to ask uneasily what would happen if the Western powers accepted the Russian proposal."[25]

In this single respect, the FRG's entry into NATO may have been the best thing that could have happened to the East German government. Well before the Paris agreements were initialed in late 1954, the Kremlin signaled its recognition of its inability to slow the pace of West German rearmament by declaring its readiness to assume the same relations with the GDR that it already enjoyed with "other sovereign states."[26] On January 25, 1955, the Soviet Union unilaterally ended its state of war with Germany. Then it completed the reconciliation with the GDR on September 20 by signing a formal treaty of relations, which affirmed its ally's right to determine its own domestic and foreign policy, including "its relations with the German Federal Republic." In an attendant exchange of notes, the Soviets even acknowledged East Berlin's authority over civilian traffic between West Berlin and the FRG.[27]

[23]A well-known critique of Adenauer's role is Rolf Steininger, *Eine vertane Chance: Die Stalin Note vom 10. März 1952* (Bonn: Dietz, 1985).

[24]As one SED expert on national policy told me, "We had no doubt that [Stalin] would negotiate it all away with Washington if the U.S. gave him the smallest opportunity." Author's interviews, Jürgen Hofmann, May 29, 1989, East Berlin. For reflections on changing Soviet attitudes about the GDR by one of the country's leading theorists on the question, see OHP (Harald Neubert, December 4, 1990).

[25]Heinz Lippmann, *Honecker and the New Politics of Europe* (New York: Macmillan, 1972), pp. 160–161. According to Lippmann, the entire SED took the Soviet note with the utmost seriousness. Within the party, there were even discussions among some members about going underground in the event of the GDR's absorption into the West. When the young Erich Honecker was asked what would happen if the Western powers accepted the Soviet proposal, he replied: "Then we'll just have to fight and, if it comes to the worst, die like heroes."

[26]*New York Times*, March 26, 1954.

[27]Cf. see Hermann Weber, ed., *DDR: Dokumente zur Geschichte* (Munich: dtv, 1986), pp. 218–219. On the treaty and the exchange of notes between Moscow and East Berlin, see Melvin Croan, "Entwicklung der politischen Beziehungen zur Sowjetunion seit 1955," in Hans-Adolf Jacobsen et al., eds., *Drei Jahrzehnte Aussenpolitik der DDR* (Munich: R. Oldenbourg, 1980), p. 354.

Although several years were to pass before the full implications of this last point were spelled out, one would have erred in assuming that these steps alone would have satisfied the SED regime. For those in the party leadership who had feared that their allies might sell them out completely, there was some solace to be found in the fact that Moscow's geopolitical interests now made a special deal with the West unlikely. Khrushchev's predecessor as premier, Nikolai Bulganin, intimated as much at the Geneva summit in July 1955 when he let it be known—in what amounted to a major policy shift—that his government believed that two fundamentally different German states had emerged in central Europe. Because it was extremely unlikely, he contended, that the Germanys' opposing social and economic orders could ever be reconciled, the most for which the GDR and the FRG could hope would be a gradual rapprochement based upon reciprocal efforts to reduce tensions in the region.[28] Khrushchev himself had the pleasure of conveying the meaning of these observations directly, when, during a stopover in East Berlin after the Geneva meeting, he not only confirmed that his government regarded a "mechanistic unification" of the German states as no longer realistic, but expressly stated that the USSR had no intention of resolving the German question "at the cost of the German Democratic Republic."[29]

The remaining ambiguity, however, was whether East Berlin wanted to go quite this far. For unlike their partners in Moscow who were almost completely motivated by the international balance of power, the GDR's leaders could not be said to have made their peace with the status quo. By this time, Walter Ulbricht had emerged as very much in control of his country's national policy. Yet, while he may on occasion have echoed Soviet rhetoric about the existence of opposing states on German soil, neither he nor any of his colleagues gave any indication that they were willing to live with this situation permanently. In fact, a good part of the SED leader's attention was focused on exactly the issue the Soviets were at pains to overcome: the fluidity of conditions in central Europe.

In December 1956, for example, Ulbricht introduced the first of what would be numerous proposals, repeated well into the 1960s, for the formation of an all-German "confederation" between the GDR and the FRG. The idea might have seemed improbable at the time, and very few West Germans were prepared to take the East German party secretary at his word.[30]

[28]Zieger, *Die Haltung*, p. 75. Also see Bulganin's report on the conference to the USSR Council of Ministers, in *CDSP* 7, no. 29, pp. 15–16.

[29]Cited in Ernst Deuerlein, *DDR 1945–1970: Geschichte und Bestandsaufnahme* (Munich: dtv, 1972), pp. 167–168.

[30]Quite ironically, Ulbricht may have received the inspiration for his confederation proposal from two still mysterious visits to East Berlin by the West German finance minister and Christian Democrat, Fritz Schäffer, in the fall of 1956. Schäffer evidently broached such ideas in unofficial discussions with Vincenz Müller, an ex-Wehrmacht officer and collaborator with

But the logic behind the confederation plan was really not that different from the motives behind the FRG's successful *Ostpolitik* a full decade later: if the Germanys did not soon attempt to establish more active ties, Ulbricht argued, as if his government would never conceive of doing anything to impede inter-German contacts, there was a very real danger that there would be nothing left to unite in the event that "truly democratic elections" were ever held in both states.[31]

Still, Ulbricht chose to concentrate his energies on the unresolved situation in Berlin. Because of the attention Khrushchev's ultimatum received in late 1958, one may easily fail to notice that over an extended period between 1955 and 1957 Soviet officials barely mentioned the issue in their contacts with the West. Yet, over the same years, in contrast, the East German leader was actually pressing his allies on a routine basis to turn over the city to the GDR, including its western sectors, on the grounds that it was perfectly natural that Berlin in its entirety be steered down the path to socialism.[32] Most West Berliners, in Ulbricht's view, were opposed to seeing their city used as a "front-city" for Western aggression and "subversion" (*Wühltätigkeit*) against the German Democratic Republic; they would have much preferred to see relations between its sectors normalized so that Berlin could finally take its rightful place as "the capital of Germany" and become "a city of peace and progress."[33]

Undoubtedly, the ongoing East German refugee crisis was at the heart of the First Secretary's concerns. If the unity of Berlin were finally restored, then the last open border between the two Germanys would be eliminated. Nonetheless, it was just as important that control over the city and, with it, an end to the West's anomalous presence in West Berlin, would also have finally put the GDR on a more equal footing with the FRG. Thus, on October 27, 1958, Ulbricht became the first to signal the coming crisis over Berlin, when he announced publicly that his government was no longer disposed to tolerate the existing state of affairs. All of Berlin, he stressed, lay "on the territory of the GDR" and was within its "sovereign domain." The only logical solution to the conflict lay in the immediate termination of the Western military presence in the city which, in his mind, no longer enjoyed any legitimate justification anyway.[34]

We still know very little about Ulbricht's consultations with Khrushchev

---

the Soviet army. For what may be one of these exchanges, see the untitled and undated transcript of a discussion between one "Herr K" and one "Herr M" in the Ulbricht file (NL 182/897), Central Party Archives, Berlin (hereafter CPA).

[31] *Neues Deutschland* (hereafter *ND*), December 30, 1956, and *ND*, February 3, 1957. Of course, in Ulbricht's view, *truly* democratic elections were not possible under capitalism.

[32] Stern, *Ulbricht*, p. 203.

[33] See Ulbricht's speech at the SED's Fifth Congress on July 10, 1958, *Dokumente zur Deutschlandpolitik* (hereafter *DzD*), 3d ser., vol. 4, pp. 1398–1399.

[34] *ND*, September 28, 1958.

on this subject, either preceding the East German leader's statement or leading up to the latter's ultimatum two weeks later in November. How much did Ulbricht know about Khrushchev's intention to challenge the West on Berlin? To what extent was Khrushchev, in turn, responding to Ulbricht's entreaties to settle the city's contested status once and for all? Nevertheless, there was one very suggestive difference in the two leaders' emphases. Ulbricht was still pressing for radical change, and was therefore much more inclined to underscore the way in which the demilitarization of West Berlin fit into the larger picture of a reunified and presumably socialist Germany.[35] In comparison, the Soviet First Secretary's demands, even at this hour of great risk-taking, reflected the superpower's appreciation of the limited extent to which it could successfully press its adversaries to change their policies without simultaneously imperiling Soviet security.

For all of the dangers Khrushchev's threats of November 1958 seemed to conjure up, it is noteworthy that he only demanded that West Berlin be transformed into a "free city," and not be turned over to the GDR. Indeed, Khrushchev seemed to admit to the onlooking world that he and Ulbricht had not seen eye to eye on the matter. Pointedly referring to the "free city" proposal, he noted that East Germany's agreement "to set up such an independent political organism on its territory" had been "a concession, a definite sacrifice on the part of the GDR."[36] In this sense, while the East Germans had every reason to be pleased with their ally's decision to re-suscitate the Berlin controversy, they may have privately felt that their options were constrained much as they had been in the past. Like their West German adversaries, their ability to act upon their priorities appeared to remain subject in the final analysis to the dictates of the big powers around them. Were not the Soviet Union and the United States already softening their views on the negotiability of Berlin? And would not the Germanys' respective approaches to the problem of national division ultimately be the first interests to be sacrificed in the name of Soviet-American concord?

The Persistence of West German Policy

It is always the seductive temptation of the small power facing adversity to see its fate as determined exclusively by forces beyond its control. Nevertheless, while each of the German governments may have been irritated by the actions of its superpower partner, it is equally significant for understanding both states' national policies a decade later how tenaciously the GDR and the FRG remained committed to maintaining the East-West con-

[35]Ibid.
[36]CDSP 10, no. 45, pp. 7–10.

flict as the 1950s drew to a close. In both instances, one might be inclined to say that this was because the German problem was a special case which demanded unique solutions. Certainly, Ulbricht and Adenauer claimed as much. That there were quite prominent German politicians, however, who preferred less confrontational approaches to their governments' national goals is enough to make one wonder what accounted for the prevalence of one perspective over the other.

In the FRG's case, there was nothing startling about the antipathy most West German politicians felt about the prospect of having any contacts at all with the East German Communists. Not only did Adenauer's dominant Christian Democratic Union (CDU) hold no monopoly in its distaste for the GDR, but hatred for the SED regime ran, if anything, even deeper in the ranks of the opposition Social Democratic Party (SPD), since the party's eastern membership in the Soviet zone had been forcibly combined with the German Communist Party (KPD) to form the SED in 1946. Still, there were a number of prominent individuals across the West German political spectrum who felt that Adenauer's formula for linking the FRG's national ideals to an all-or-nothing policy of Western alignment was a mistake.

Some politicians, like the SPD's outspoken postwar leader Kurt Schumacher, simply felt that the best approach to the national question was one in which Bonn avoided making hard-and-fast alliance commitments, so that the theme of reunification would remain at the forefront of Federal objectives. Thus, although Schumacher was himself not opposed to rearmament in principle and shared many of the chancellor's pro-Western and anti-Communist sympathies, he and his party repeatedly voted against the FRG's participation in such institutions as the Council of Europe and the European Defense Community.[37] Other prominent personalities, however, such as Adenauer's chief antagonist in the CDU, Jakob Kaiser, who had once headed the Eastern branch of the party, advocated even more aggressive stands on their country's national priorities. They not only argued against taking any step that could compromise the long-term chances of reunification but also openly called upon their government to play the role of an intermediary (a "bridge," in Kaiser's terminology) in the conflict between the superpowers.

In fact, after both the Western allies and Adenauer failed to do anything to explore the Soviet "reunification notes" of 1952 and 1953, there was a noticeable upswing in the attention the national theme received in the FRG, as many politicians of diverse leanings contended that Bonn had missed a valuable opportunity to test the Soviets' readiness to negotiate. At least in

---

[37]See Lewis J. Edinger, *Kurt Schumacher* (Stanford, Calif.: Stanford University Press, 1965), pp. 170–171, 233, and Anselm Doering-Manteuffel, *Die Bundesrepublik in der Ära Adenauer* (Darmstadt: Wissenschaftliche Buchgesellschaft, 1983), pp. 40–43.

part for this reason, following Schumacher's death in late 1952, the leadership of the SPD became increasingly inclined to support neutralist and pacifist options for dealing with the national cause that questioned the FRG's burgeoning obligations to the Western alliance. Even the Free Democratic Party (FDP), Adenauer's small, liberal coalition partner in the Bundestag from 1949 to 1956, gave vent to nationalist feelings when party notables such as Karl Georg Pfleiderer and Thomas Dehler openly appealed to their government to adopt a more constructive *Ostpolitik*. For the first and only time in the 1950s, in October 1956, the FDP even went so far as to sponsor an official meeting in the GDR with its counterparts in the East German Liberal Democratic Party of Germany (LDPD) to discuss mutual national interests.[38]

Despite the existence of such contrasting perspectives, however, Adenauer never seemed to have any problem brushing off his critics' objections and acting, as he did throughout the 1950s, as though he alone were capable of adjudicating his country's priorities. German scholars even have a term for the haughty, autocratic style of leadership he brought to the FRG, *Kanzlerdemokratie* ("chancellor democracy"), which captures the extraordinary extent to which West Germany's first leader was able to centralize almost all decisions of consequence within the Federal chancellery.[39] Yet, while Adenauer's extraordinary past—his ties with German democracy extended back to the Weimar Republic, where on two separate occasions he was nearly elected chancellor—combined with a great deal of political acumen and not a little ruthlessness all had something to do with his strength at the time, it is most revealing that the 1950s was also a unique period in the political history of the FRG. In particular, Adenauer benefited from two institutional advantages over his competitors in shaping his administration's policy toward the East that would never again be available to any West German government.

Of greatest consequence was that he was the undisputed head of a party, the CDU, which could put him into a position from which he could build the broadest possible consensus for his policies. Whereas the historical antecedents to the CDU, such as the Center party of Weimar times, had been narrowly confessional associations and incapable of appealing to broad segments of the electorate, the postwar CDU had been founded upon a calculated decision by its leadership to adopt the posture of a modern catch-all party, or *Volkspartei* ("people's party"). On this basis alone, the early Christian Democrats were able to gain the support of a diverse array

---

[38]See Karlheinz Niclauß, *Kontroverse Deutschlandpolitik* (Frankfurt: Alfred Metzner, 1977), p. 46, and Doering-Manteufel, *Bundesrepublik*, pp. 58–61, 65–68.

[39]On these issues, see Arnold Heidenheimer, *Adenauer and the CDU* (The Hague: Martinus Nijhoff, 1960), pp. 207–218, and Gordon Craig, *From Bismarck to Adenauer: Aspects of German Statecraft* (New York: Harper and Row, 1958), chap. 5.

of groups across West German society by presenting themselves as the only sensible alternative to the class-based, religious, and regional antagonisms that had pitted Germans against each other in the past.[40]

Indeed, one may regard the "policy of strength" itself as a kind of catchall policy in the number of different interests to which it appealed. For CDU stalwarts in the Catholic West and South, the policy's attractiveness lay in the priority the chancellor assigned to the FRG's role in the Atlantic alliance. For the Protestant and expellee elements in the CDU's ranks, as well as for other members of the early coalition governments, such as the FDP and the short-lived German Party, it was Adenauer's refusal to abandon the goal of national unity which made his policies most attractive. Finally, still other groups, such as the Bavarian Christian Social Union (CSU), were willing to go along with Adenauer because they regarded German rearmament as the most effective way to combat the threat of communism.

Whatever the sources of the CDU's overall appeal, however, there can be no dispute about its successes. From the FRG's first elections in 1949, when the Christian Democrats barely defeated the SPD with only 30 percent of the national vote, the party climbed to a dominating 45 percent of the popular vote by 1953. And by 1957 Adenauer was even able to rid himself of his critics within his governing coalition (the FDP had already left the government under the weight of its own internal dissension) when the Union forces won a still unrepeated absolute majority of the national vote.

Had the other dominant West German party, the SPD, been able to present an effective political challenge to the CDU, Adenauer's fortunes and the ensuing history of the Federal Republic might well have been different. But it was here, quite aside from the CDU's efforts to maintain electoral respectability, that the chancellor's second advantage lay. The postwar SPD was a much more traditional party organization than the CDU. It brought to modern West German democracy all of the lessons its leaders claimed to have learned from their long struggle against the Communists and the National Socialists—above all, the need for constant vigilance and discipline. Yet, particularly after Schumacher's death, the party's leaders became practically obsessed with the idea that they had to present a hard-and-fast alternative to Christian Democratic rule. As a result, the SPD quickly became known in the public mind as the party of the nay-sayers, which opposed West German recovery along capitalist lines and which campaigned against the FRG's rearmament and membership in NATO.

In point of fact, such perceptions were only partly accurate. There were individuals within the Social Democratic movement—Carlo Schmid, Fritz Erler, and the young Willy Brandt—who quietly pressed behind the scenes

---

[40]See the classic study by Geoffrey Pridham, *Christian Democracy in West Germany* (London: Croom Helm, 1977), pp. 14–15.

to reform the party's stand on a number of issues, including Bonn's role in the Western alliance.[41] Still, as long as the majority of the SPD leadership persisted in defining the party's purposes in principled rather than pragmatic terms, Adenauer was easily able to portray his rivals as dogmatists and extremists who, as he argued frequently, would sell out their country to its adversaries the moment they found themselves in power. As a consequence, without an effective opposition to force him to be more flexible, the chancellor could practically operate from a position of political impunity. The Social Democrats could criticize him for his failure to make the most of opportunities to take action on the division of the German nation. But the burden of proof in the eyes of many West Germans still lay with the SPD, whose leaders were as yet unable to offer a program of their own that would reconcile the pursuit of the FRG's national goals with the policy choices already reached in Bonn.

If such domestic considerations accounted for Adenauer's unusual ability to present himself as the exclusive arbiter of his country's national options by the mid-1950s, there was one ironic respect in which they constrained West Germany's leader as well. For on those few occasions when the chancellor himself sought to introduce a note of flexibility into the FRG's foreign relations, even he found that his room for maneuver was limited. In these instances the reason seems to have been that the "policy of strength" itself, in part because of the diverse constituencies to which it appealed, tended to bind the FRG to a confining logic of its own once its initial premises were accepted.

For example, in September 1955 Adenauer surprised even members of his own cabinet with the decision to make his first official trip to the Soviet Union. In return for agreeing to establish full diplomatic ties with Moscow, a step the Soviets had pursued as part of their efforts to improve their credentials as advocates of better East-West relations, he was able to negotiate the release of nearly ten thousand German prisoners of war and at the same time, no doubt, help to overcome his image in the West as an unthinking opponent of serious contacts between the blocs. It was what the trip could not accomplish, however, that left many onlookers with the impres-

---

[41]Some high CDU officials, such as Kaiser, were not only aware of the SPD's diversity but were also apparently open, unlike Adenauer, to developing better ties with the party. For an early exchange between Kaiser and the chancellor on this theme on December 15, 1952, see Günter Buchstab, ed., *Adenauer: Es mußte alles neu gemacht werden* (Stuttgart: Klett-Cotta, 1986), pp. 229–231. On the different currents within the SPD, see Hans-Peter Schwarz, *Die Ära Adenauer: 1949–1957* (Stuttgart: Deutsche Verlags-Anstalt, 1981), pp. 239–246, and the nicely contrasting accounts by Stephen J. Artner, *A Change of Course: The West German Social Democrats and NATO* (Westport, Conn.: Greenwood, 1985), and Gordon D. Drummond, *The German Social Democrats in Opposition* (Norman: University of Oklahoma Press, 1982).

sion, well before the two states had exchanged ambassadors, that the FRG's relations with the East remained thoroughly stalemated.

First, there was very little left for the Soviets and the West Germans to discuss beyond their initial overtures. Adenauer made a forceful, if predictable, speech to his hosts, in which he demanded that they begin immediate negotiations with the Western occupying powers on German reunification, while the Soviets, in return, simply insisted that they no longer recognized the West's authority to make decisions affecting the GDR.[42] Thus, by the time Adenauer returned to Bonn, the national question itself remained largely untouched. Yet this was by no means the end to the story of the chancellor's breakthrough to the East. After relations had been established between West Germany and the USSR, it became painfully evident to Adenauer's advisors—especially to those who had counseled him against the journey—that the FRG's claim to be the only legitimate representative of German national interests had been put at risk, since Moscow already had such ties with the GDR. Was it not possible, many worried, that other countries might follow the Soviet lead and decide that they too were entitled to diplomatic missions with East Berlin?

Accordingly, in what became known as the Hallstein Doctrine, the Foreign Office announced that the West German government would regard any such steps as "unfriendly acts" against the FRG. The stand itself was intended only to convey Bonn's displeasure at the prospect that its allies might unwittingly help to give the GDR legitimacy. But it soon became an inflexible threat to break ties with any offending country, including even those states which by virtue of their membership in the socialist bloc already had relations with East Germany. In January 1957 the FRG was forced by the logic of its own position to decline an offer of diplomatic ties with the government of Poland, despite having actively sought such a reconciliation for years. In October 1957 Bonn even found itself compelled to sever relations with Yugoslavia after Belgrade dared to exchange ambassadors with the GDR.[43]

Adenauer's defenders contend that, in the latter part of the decade, even he became aware of these shortcomings in his national policy and cautiously began to search for ways out of the predicament. For example, we know from the chancellor's memoirs that he conducted confidential discussions with the Soviet ambassador to West Germany, Andrei Smirnov, in March 1958, in which he hinted that his government would be prepared to go along with an "Austrian solution" for the GDR, under which Bonn

---

[42]*DzD*, 3d ser., vol. 1, pp. 324–325, 327–328.

[43]On Adenauer's visit to Moscow and the origins of the Hallstein Doctrine, cf. Besson, *Außenpolitik*, pp. 192–203. Although the name of the former state secretary, Walter Hallstein, is associated with the doctrine, the policy's author was Wilhelm Grewe, director of the Foreign Office's Political Department.

would forego discussions about German reunification for an unspecified period in return for East Germany's transformation into a neutral but democratic state. Unquestionably, the concession in the offer lay in the chancellor's willingness even to broach a resolution of the German question on something less than his customary maximal terms. Nonetheless, the proposal also illustrated the bind in which the West German regime found itself only half a year before the enunciation of Khrushchev's Berlin ultimatum. Can Adenauer have failed to recognize that his new terms would still be unacceptable to Moscow? Even if Bonn agreed to alter its rhetorical stance on German unification, it was never clear what compensation the Soviets would have won for losing the GDR, particularly after West Germany had been fully incorporated into NATO. In any case, it was just as revealing of the constraints under which Adenauer operated that he also appealed to his Soviet interlocutor to treat the proposal with the utmost confidentiality. If it were made public, he conceded only half jokingly, he would risk being "stoned by my own people."[44] In itself, this was a stunning admission. The one figure in the FRG who was in the position to redefine his country's foreign policy in light of its changing surroundings was held captive by his own success.

The Evolution of East German Policy

In comparison to Adenauer, Ulbricht was virtually unbendable on the handling of the national question in 1958. Yet what makes the story behind the evolution of his equivalent stand to the "policy of strength" particularly compelling, and atypical by later East German standards, is how long it took for his government to agree on its priorities. This delay was not for want of effort on Ulbricht's part. Rather, quite unlike the liberal-democratic FRG, where foreign policy was, equally atypically, dominated by a single individual throughout the decade, the uncertain internal conditions in the GDR in the early 1950s made it much harder than is commonly assumed for the SED chief to consolidate his power.

Surely, no one will contest the fact that Ulbricht had more advantages at the time of the GDR's founding in October 1949 than any of his contemporaries. Like Adenauer in the West, he too had been present at the creation. In April 1945 he had led the first group of German emigrés who returned to their homeland from the Soviet Union with the expressed aim of setting up a new type of German state. He had personally presided over the formation of the Socialist Unity Party in 1946, engineering the German Communist

---

[44]Cf. Löwenthal, "Vom kalten Krieg," p. 641. Also Konrad Adenauer, *Erinnerungen*, vol. 3 (Stuttgart: Deutsche Verlags-Anstalt, 1967), p. 378.

Party's merger with the Social Democratic Party in the Eastern zone. Perhaps most important, Ulbricht also had the indisputable advantage of years of close association with Moscow, and he could draw on his direct line of communication with the Soviet occupation forces in Karlshorst ("the friends," as they were known within the party) to present himself as the authoritative interpreter of Soviet interests in the GDR.[45]

Still, it would be a mistake to assume that the East German leader enjoyed the degree of control over the SED in the GDR's early years that he would at the end of the 1950s. Although he was able to follow Stalin's example by successfully stocking the party Central Committee and its bureaucracy with faithful disciples, Ulbricht still had regularly to contend with colleagues in the party politburo and in the leading state institutions who were much less beholden to him than the rank and file. Some had established independent reputations during the war by remaining in Germany to fight the Nazis or participating in the Spanish Civil War, while others, such as Otto Grotewohl, had come to the SED by way of the SPD. Among the former Moscow exiles, there were also ill feelings about Ulbricht's dictatorial style and dogmatic personality.[46] Furthermore, the First Secretary's close relationship with the Soviet Union was never the undiluted blessing it may have appeared to be. During those periods when Ulbricht's conception of the GDR's main interests coincided with theirs, those policymakers in the Kremlin who counted most were always willing to lend the East German party chief every conceivable form of assistance. But on other occasions, when Moscow's needs shifted, the Soviets were never averse to looking among his colleagues for alternative means of serving their purposes.[47]

These internal uncertainties were bound to be especially salient in the handling of the national question, because on this issue in particular there were significant differences among the SED elite. All of the representatives of the party's upper echelons, Ulbricht included, could agree that reunification was their long-term goal. Plus, all were united in the belief that a

[45] Arnulf Baring, *Außenpolitik*, p. 15. Because it was up to Ulbricht to decide what information passed from Soviet authorities to the SED politburo, his colleagues were often rightly suspicious that he was not presenting them with the full story. As the head of the party's Control Commission, Hermann Matern, is said to have remarked on one occasion in the early 1950s: "Let's hope Walter lets us know if we are at war." See Stern, *Ulbricht*, p. 133.

[46] Author's interview with Erich Nickel and Michael Lemke, Humboldt University and Academy of Sciences, East Berlin, June 11, 1988. Also see Stern, *Ulbricht*, pp. 124–135, and, for the roots of these differences, Wolfgang Leonhard, *Child of the Revolution* (Chicago: Henry Regnery, 1967), chap. 8. For a perspective on why a German communist might have taken a different route and even sympathized with the Social Democratic cause, see my interview with Karl Schirdewan, OHP (July 9, 1991).

[47] There was nothing very subtle about the assistance the Soviets chose to offer. Until 1954, the Soviet ambassador routinely sat in on meetings of the SED politburo.

narrowly defined version of state socialism was the only appropriate model for the distant German future. Yet, despite this outwardly disciplined image, the one area in which the SED's leaders were sorely divided was on which steps to take first in addressing their national future.

For most members of the SED, the problem could be framed in classic Marxist terms: whether the "class question" was to be resolved before the "national question."[48] If the party pressed too quickly to finish the transition to socialism, some argued, it ran the twofold risk of antagonizing both its own population and those elements of the West German working class that might be sympathetic to the GDR's cause but not yet ready to accept the sacrifices involved in the creation of a postcapitalist society. From this perspective, it was better for the SED to wait before committing itself completely to the harsher aspects of social and economic transformation. In contrast, those members of the ruling elite who were associated with Ulbricht called for decisive action, contending that the elimination of the "class question" on East German soil took precedence over all other goals. If the party concentrated only on appeasing its domestic critics and its possible Western supporters, these individuals warned, it faced the even greater risk of compromising its principles and irretrievably weakening itself in the contest with capitalism.

As a consequence, when Ulbricht announced the long-postponed decision in July 1952 to begin the "planned construction of socialism in the GDR,"[49] he was immediately opposed by those in the East German government who felt that the country was not yet strong enough to undertake the challenge and who also feared that an emphasis on socialism alone might freeze relations forever between the two German populations. Had the adoption of socialist production principles (already a reality in every other state in the Soviet bloc) led to a visible economic upswing in the GDR, the possibility of an open conflict between these two currents in the SED might have been precluded. But quite unlike the successes the FRG's social-market economy was slowly registering in the West, the East German measures proved to be devastating. The regime's efforts to collectivize large sections

---

[48]As Rudolf Herrnstadt maintained in his critique of Ulbricht's policies: "The class question can only be solved after the national question." Cited in Walter Osten, *Die Außenpolitik der DDR* (Opladen: Leske, 1969), p. 15. On the tensions within the party, see Henry Krisch, *The German Democratic Republic: The Search for Identity* (Boulder, Colo.: Westview, 1985), p. 11.

[49]I say "his decision" because Ulbricht was clearly one of the architects of the accelerated transition to socialism at this time, although at least one of my sources (Otto Reinhold, former rector of the SED Academy of Social Sciences) contends that the final decision was Stalin's. Author's taped interview, East Berlin, March 23, 1990. There can be no doubt, however, that Ulbricht announced the move without sufficiently discussing the issue with his politburo colleagues. On this, see the memoir by Ernst Wollweber, "Aus Erinnerungen. Ein Porträt Walter Ulbrichts," *Beiträge zur Geschichte der Arbeiterbewegung* 32, no. 3 (1990), p. 357.

of the agrarian economy fueled the refugee flight from the countryside—
ironically, in view of what was to come, the right to "freedom of movement" was still guaranteed by the GDR constitution—and as a result, by
early 1953 East Germany was facing a food crisis. In factories throughout
the country, workers staged protests and work stoppages in response to
higher production quotas imposed by the government. Even within the
SED, unrest grew at the prospect that Ulbricht was on the verge of purging
the party apparatus of all who did not support his policies.[50]

By themselves, these disturbances were a revealing demonstration of
how far the East German regime still fell short of the image of disciplined
dictatorship of Marxist-Leninist lore. Indeed, when Stalin died in March
1953, touching off a power struggle within the Soviet Communist Party,
those of his successors who were bent upon promoting more lenient domestic policies in the USSR and a more forthcoming relationship with the
West did not have to look any farther than the GDR for support for their
plans. By this juncture, opposition to Ulbricht was so great that a number
of the SED's most powerful members, grouped around Rudolf Herrnstadt,
the editor of the party daily, *Neues Deutschland*, and Wilhelm Zaisser, the
minister of state security, favored removing their leader from office in order
to slacken the pace of the transition to socialism.

Who is to say how the future of the GDR as well as its government's stand
on relations with the West would have changed had the Soviets and these
reformists in the SED leadership been able to replace Ulbricht. In early June
1953 the party politburo moved, with direct Soviet backing,[51] to rescind
many of the coercive measures that had been associated with the drive to
transform the GDR, and in a provocative step even banned the word "socialism" from its official vocabulary. New directives were issued, emphasizing consumer goods over heavy industrial production. The private trade in
retail goods was restored. And farmers who had left East Germany for the
West were encouraged to return to their old holdings with assurances that
the collectivization decrees would be repealed.[52]

Most suggestive, however, the SED also sought to use these steps to add
credibility to its appeals for a relaxation of East-West tensions and some
form of inter-German dialogue. Not only were travel restrictions between
the GDR and the FRG reduced, but the party leadership immediately returned to themes that affirmed a sense of commonality between the Ger-

[50]For a participant's view on the period, see Heinz Brandt, *The Search for a Third Way*
(Garden City, N.Y.: Doubleday, 1970), pp. 186–187.

[51]For evidence on the Soviet role, see Yuri Shpakov, "Komanda brat'iam po lageryu,"
Moskovskie Novosti, July 15, 1990, p. 13.

[52]On these developments, see Arnulf Baring, *Uprising in East Germany, June 17, 1953*
(Ithaca, N.Y.: Cornell University Press, 1972), pp. 22–28, and Martin Jänicke, *Der Dritte
Weg* (Cologne: Neuer Deutscher Verlag, 1964), pp. 23–39.

manys. In a June 11 communiqué, the politburo explicitly declared that the more relaxed internal course had been introduced with "an eye toward the great goal of restoring the unity of Germany," and pointedly stated that "both parts" of the nation had a responsibility to their populations to do what they could to bring about a rapprochement. The reference to the two "parts" of Germany, and not to two states, was in itself a revealing indication of the remaining fluidity in the SED's conceptions of the national question.[53]

Yet just a few days after this decree, the outbreak of mass demonstrations and industrial strikes in East Berlin and more than two hundred other locations on June 16 and 17 put an end to the hopes of those who had hoped to steer the GDR in a more moderate direction. It made no difference that the upheavals were largely brought about by Ulbricht's refusal to renounce one of the most hated aspects of the drive toward socialism, the industrial production quotas. As first the Soviets and then a majority of the East German leader's original critics in the party politburo came to appreciate in the weeks after the debacle, the workers' uprising placed them all in the position where any further indecision and vacillation could have jeopardized the existence of the GDR.[54]

As a result, Ulbricht was not only able to remain in office but, thanks to Moscow's apprehensions that similar disturbances might break out elsewhere in Eastern Europe, actually found his position at the head of the party strengthened as never before. In a number of ways, this turn of events meant that the SED chief could return to his conceptions about what was, and was not, appropriate for the GDR. Once he had seen to the removal of

---

[53]*ND*, June 11, 1953. On the communiqué, see Heinz Brandt, *Search*, p. 193. Of course, no one in the SED leadership wanted to compromise Germany's eventual reunification under socialist auspices. The main concern of Ulbricht's critics was that the GDR first put its own house in order, so it could compete with the Federal Republic. As Herrnstadt later reflected: "We believed that the point of departure for a practical and successful struggle to create a democratic and socialist Germany [*Gesamtdeutschland*] had to reside in bringing the relationship between party, class, and people [back] into order." See Nadja Stulz-Herrnstadt, ed., *Das Herrnstadt Dokument* (Reinbek bei Hamburg: Rowohlt, 1990), p. 108. Also see the document, "Der neue Kurs und die Erneuerung der Partei," produced by the hopeful reformers in June and early July 1953 as an outline for the post-Ulbricht order: "Life has shown that the right political and economic conditions do not exist for the accelerated construction of socialism in the GDR. It has shown that such an orientation does not promote the solution of all-German questions, but hinders it." See *Beiträge zur Geschichte der Arbeiterbewegung* 32, no. 5 (1990), p. 659.

[54]Still, it took several weeks before this revelation led the majority of the SED politburo to abandon Herrnstadt and Zaisser and return to Ulbricht. Indeed, on July 7, 1953, at least nine of the body's thirteen members voted to remove Ulbricht from office, with only two (Erich Honecker and Hermann Matern) voting to support him. Ulbricht was apparently saved only when the Soviets themselves abruptly changed course on July 8. On these events, see Herrnstadt's moving account in Nadja Stulz-Herrnstadt, *Herrnstadt-Dokument*, pp. 126–131.

his most prominent critics from the party leadership, Herrnstadt and Zaisser included,[55] Ulbricht gradually reasserted his government's grip over East German society, reintroducing collectivization, although on a less extensive scale than before, and setting the tone for years to come by explicitly rejecting supposedly "false theories" about the primacy of consumer goods production over heavy industry. Then, in a particularly telling display of his enhanced powers, Ulbricht adopted a posture on the national question that practically mirrored Adenauer's approach in the West.

As in the past, reunification remained, for the SED chief, the GDR's official goal, the "main question of the German people," as Ulbricht still described it.[56] In two respects, however, there was a noticeable hardening in his stand on the negotiability of its national interests. First, we have already seen that from mid-1955 onward, Ulbricht sought to reintroduce the issue of West Berlin's uncertain future into public debate, demanding in contrast to the Soviets' lack of attention to the subject, that the situation in and around the city be normalized ("by closing its secret-agent and spy centers," it would seem).[57] Even more revealing, however, was a second development in the way he characterized the GDR's historical task. Whereas in earlier years the party had at least been willing to entertain the notion that there were two distinct representatives of German interests in Europe, one in East Berlin and the other in Bonn, now Ulbricht emphasized that the GDR was the *only* "legitimate German state."[58]

In this sense, it might seem as though the SED leader's later calls for an inter-German confederation were an exception to the tougher line on the national cause. Nonetheless, while Ulbricht undoubtedly counted on using such appeals to embellish his image as a spokesman for German interests, his appeals for dialogue were really not that different from Adenauer's professed willingness to accept a liberal-democratic GDR. Both of the seemingly more forthcoming policies were a contradiction in terms. One did not have to read very closely between the lines of Ulbricht's speeches to see that West Germany would have made all of the sacrifices to enter such a union. The FRG would have been required to leave NATO and to purge its offices of everyone (supposedly "revanchist forces" and "Nazi functionaries") who did not live up to East Berlin's definition of democratic purity. Rendering the prospects of such a confederation even more unlikely, Ul-

---

[55]Ulbricht's efforts to cleanse the party of dissenting elements went far beyond the top leadership. By 1954, 62.2 percent of the members of the SED's *Bezirk* (regional) committees had been removed from office and 71 percent of the First and Second Secretaries of the *Kreis* (county) committees. See Martin McCauley, *The German Democratic Republic* (New York: St. Martin's, 1983), p. 70.

[56]Zieger, *Haltung*, p. 66.

[57]Ibid., p. 74.

[58]Ibid., pp. 78–79.

bricht also made it clear that before his government became involved in talks with Bonn, the West German working class, "in alliance with the middle classes and elements of the national bourgeoisie," would have had to move in East Germany's direction first, by setting in motion the social and economic transformation of the FRG.[59]

Such fundamentally uncompromising positions are worth keeping in mind because Ulbricht's claims to undisputed authority over the SED still had to withstand one final assault before the end of the 1950s, as a result of Khrushchev's famous denunciation of the errors of the Stalinist past at the CPSU's Twentieth Congress in February 1956. Once again, but this time for a period lasting almost two years, the SED was thrown into turmoil as a disparate group of party officials, including Ulbricht's principal deputy, Karl Schirdewan; the minister of state security, Ernst Wollweber; and the Central Committee secretary for economics, Gerhart Ziller,[60] seemed to come from out of nowhere to challenge their leader on a range of issues. These included his dictatorial style; the harsh economic measures that were promoting the flight of, in Schirdewan's later testimony, so many "workers and farmers from the workers-and-farmers state"; and, finally, his inflexible handling of the national question.[61]

In a remarkable paper prepared for the upper party leadership in mid-1956, Schirdewan made what was to be the final stand for those in the SED who still favored a more differentiated approach to the FRG by outlining a "Program for a Special German Road to Socialism" that went beyond any previous critique of Ulbricht's policies. According to this plan, the party was immediately to abandon the most draconian aspects of Ulbricht's march to socialism and open direct contacts with potentially sympathetic elements in the West, like the SPD, in order to explore ways of preserving the best traditions of both German states. Negotiations were to be pursued on a host of subjects, ranging from the preservation of such East

[59]ND, February 3, 1957. This is an important but difficult speech, because Ulbricht seems to have confused those changes that were necessary for reunification with those that were sufficient for the formation of a common German council and an inter-German confederation.

[60]For Wollweber's views, see "Aus Erinnerungen," p. 377. As an indication of just how disparate this group of Ulbricht's critics was, another key figure, the SED secretary for science and culture, Kurt Hager, apparently limited his challenge to supporting the Polish model of economic development then espoused by Wladyslaw Gomulka. Hager's and others' uncertainty at the time was reflected in the debates at the Central Committee's Twenty-sixth Plenum of March 22, 1956 (IV 2/1/79), CPA, Berlin. For Hager's later reflections, see OHP (December 3, 1990).

[61]See Schirdewan's interview with the Berliner Zeitung, February 10/11, 1990, and his even more detailed testimony before the SED Central Committee preceding his removal from the party leadership in February 1958, "Karl Schirdewan: Fraktionsmacherei oder gegen Ulbrichts Diktat?" in Beiträge zur Geschichte der Arbeiterbewegung 32, no. 4 (1990), pp. 498–512.

German achievements as land reform to the implementation of Social Democratic reforms in the FRG, until it was finally possible to call all-German elections. Then, all foreign troops would be withdrawn from the two states' territories and reunification would become feasible under a reformed version of socialism suiting Germany's specific needs.[62]

Even at this difficult juncture, it is hard to imagine that Schirdewan's program would have met with a favorable response had it seen the light of day in the West. What his plan did indicate, nonetheless, if only in the lengths to which its author was willing to go, was the high degree of uncertainty about the GDR's options, national and otherwise, which still prevailed in the uppermost circles of the SED. By implication, it confirmed that Ulbricht had not yet consolidated his authority. Astonishingly, despite the appearance of these signs of discontent in 1956, it took Ulbricht until late 1957 to marshall the forces to oust his critics from the party leadership. Even then, the East German leader was only sure of his victory when Khrushchev finally chose to support him.[63]

Against this background, the reader can easily appreciate the stubborn determination with which Ulbricht subsequently went about implementing his particular vision of the GDR's priorities. He continued to assign places of prominence to his party's national goals and such themes as the inter-German confederation in all of his speeches. Yet, what now made Ulbricht's orientation so much like that of his adversaries in the FRG was his insistence that the only sensible approach to the national cause lay in first finishing the task he had begun in 1952: the domestic transformation of the GDR. Only when his country had completed the passage into socialism would it be able to negotiate from strength with its enemies and ensure that its vision of the German future would be realized.[64]

In this sense, there was a certain logic to the defiant air Ulbricht assumed

---

[62]I first came upon Schirdewan's program (complete with the marginalia of the First Secretary of the SED!) in the Ulbricht *Nachlaß* (NL 182/893, also IV 2/1/228) in CPA, Berlin. Although it is unclear that Schirdewan ever presented his plan before the full Central Committee—the Soviet invasion of Hungary in November 1956 seems to have changed his plans—one is still astounded by the boldness of his challenge to SED orthodoxy. Among his other demands, one finds the following: the right to strike, the closing of unprofitable collective farms, the abolition of the Ministry of State Security, an end to the GDR's "one-sided" relationship with the Soviet Union, a plea for "the unrestrained self-criticism" of past SED policy, and the replacement of the current politburo.

[63]As in 1953, Ulbricht's efforts to eliminate challenges to his authority extended far beyond the ranks of the politburo. By the party's 1958 congress, twenty-one of the formerly eighty-nine full members and sixteen of forty-four candidate-members of the central committee had been replaced. Cf. Jänicke, *Der dritte Weg*, p. 91.

[64]Thus in a May 1958 critique of the so-called Schirdewan group, an internal SED report emphasized that "the strengthening of the GDR is a basic precondition for securing the peace and *later* bringing about reunification." In Hermann Weber, *Kleine Geschichte*, pp. 235–236 (italics added).

at the SED's Fifth Congress in July 1958. In one of his first official acts after surmounting his internal critics, he simply brushed aside the few remaining voices of caution within his government to unveil a radical new program of accelerated economic development, the so-called Main Economic Task, which was supposed to enable the GDR to catch up with and then surpass the FRG in the production of most food stuffs and essential consumer items.[65] Naturally, it was also this same reasoning which emboldened the East German leader, now both unchallenged and unchallengeable in setting his country's priorities, to push for some sort of victory over the West in the battle to control Berlin. This brings us back to Khrushchev and the Soviet ultimatum of November 1958.

Divergent Priorities

It is easy to see why, when Berlin once more became an object of international controversy at the end of the 1950s, the GDR's and the FRG's interests were bound to be at least slightly, if not significantly, out of harmony with those of their superpower patrons. Still, if anything can have surprised the leaders of both German states after the enunciation of Khrushchev's ultimatum, it must have been the sheer alacrity with which both the Soviet Union and the United States moved to distance themselves from their involvement in the inter-German imbroglio.

Almost immediately, from the moment they received Khrushchev's demands, the Western powers sought to defuse the conflict. Naturally, they all observed their formal obligations to the FRG by reaffirming their rights and responsibilities for Berlin and repeatedly underscoring their refusal to abandon West Berlin to Soviet pressure. But in the same motion, the allies showed that they were just as concerned to emphasize, to friend and foe alike, that the new crisis could be resolved through reasoned negotiation. In early February 1959, the ailing John Foster Dulles used his last visit to Bonn to urge Adenauer to consider the idea of expanding contacts with the East, even if this meant recognizing the East German regime on a de facto basis.[66] More generally, the United States, Great Britain, and France together proposed to Moscow that their foreign ministers meet once again to discuss ways of resolving the various aspects of the German stalemate. This time the three allies even agreed to allow representatives of both German states, the FRG *and* the GDR, to participate as observers at the meeting, the farthest that they had ever gone toward acknowledging the existence of a separate East German state.

---

[65]*ND*, July 11, 1958, and *ND*, July 12, 1958.
[66]Peter Bender, *Neue Ostpolitik* (Munich: dtv, 1986), p. 59.

Yet it was when the conference of foreign ministers finally convened in May and June 1959 in Geneva that the Western allies proved to be most forthcoming of all, offering the Soviets a package of recommendations on German reunification (known as the Herter Plan, after Christian Herter, Dulles's replacement as secretary of state) which envisioned, among other things, the creation of a special German-German committee to regulate the two states' relations *before* the calling of national elections. At later stages in the talks, the allies even bandied about proposals—to the evident horror of some West German observers—that were geared to meeting the Soviet Union's demands halfway. These included major cuts in the Western troop presence in West Berlin, limits on intelligence activities, and following Dulles's earlier suggestion, provisions to allow East German authorities to monitor the transit routes to and from Berlin, provided that the Soviet Union was willing to guarantee "continued free access to the city."[67]

None of these signals would have made sense had the Soviets been unwilling to take note of the Western overtures. Hence, it was equally significant that for someone who had nearly seemed ready to go to war with his adversaries, Khrushchev proved to be suddenly, even astonishingly conciliatory after he had succeeded in getting their attention. As early as January 10, 1959, he had already indicated a readiness to talk when he essentially lowered the ante in the contest with the West by broadening his demands, dispatching an outline for a comprehensive German peace treaty to all of the states that had fought in the Second World War. Admittedly, there was little that was novel in his proposal, which called for the demilitarization of West Berlin and the removal of all foreign troops from German soil. Nevertheless, Khrushchev and his representatives were at least allowed to make the important point that the Soviet Union was not looking for a fight. During a visit to the United States not long thereafter, the Soviet deputy premier, Anastas Mikoyan, suggested that the six-month deadline on West Berlin applied only to the convening of negotiations, not to a settlement of the city's status. It was Khrushchev himself, however, even before the Geneva foreign ministers' meeting, who broke the sad news about the ultimatum to his East German allies. While passing through the GDR in March, he let the SED's leaders know, and the onlooking world through them, that they would have to wait a great while longer before they got what they wanted and what the Soviet Union surely wanted for them. "Do not hurry," Khrushchev advised. "The wind does not blow in your face. . . . The conditions are not ripe as yet for a new scheme of things."[68]

---

[67]Smith, *Defense of Berlin*, pp. 204–205, and Planck, *Changing Status*, pp. 27–28. At the time, the Soviets summarily rejected these proposals for not going far enough. In view of the more modest gains they later made with the Quadripartite Accord on Berlin of 1971, one wonders whether they regretted their haste in rejecting the Western proposals.

[68]Cited in Smith, *Defense of Berlin*, p. 199.

The big problem was that both of the Germanys' leaders had anything but patience. In the FRG, Adenauer maintained a familiar pose throughout the crisis, apparently worried as much that his allies might soften their demands of the USSR as a result of Khrushchev's more agreeable stance as that the Soviet leader might follow through on his threats. Thus he routinely cautioned the Western powers against falling into the Soviet trap of thinking that tensions in Europe could be reduced merely by giving in on Berlin's status and urged them to recognize instead that their presence in the city was the free world's best trump in containing Soviet expansionism. "It was necessary to have strong nerves," the chancellor ruminated years later in his memoirs, "and to do everything to keep the West united and firm."[69]

For those, however, who could tell the difference between action on the German question and a lively romanticization of the Federal government's options during the period, it was also abundantly clear that Adenauer was quite short of options. Historians may remind us that in 1959 as well, there were again hushed discussions behind the scenes in Bonn about the need for a new approach to the German problem. For example, Adenauer's state secretary, Hans Globke, outlined the first of several variants of a plan to settle the German question definitively, which would have allowed the FRG and the GDR to establish full diplomatic ties one full year before they each conducted democratic elections to determine the fate of the nation. Not long thereafter, a leak in the Foreign Office revealed that ministry officials were also contemplating ways of working around the strictures of the Hallstein Doctrine to enable Bonn finally to establish relations with the socialist states of Eastern Europe.[70]

Still, what stands out about these later years in Adenauer's tenure is not that the West German regime was filled with a renewed sense of national purpose and determination in the face of Khrushchev's demands but rather that it was acting from weakness. It was refusing to rethink its traditional stands for want of any other means of contending with the new order emerging between the superpower blocs. But this situation was in no small measure due to the government's inability to break away from the person of Adenauer himself.

By the end of the decade, many members of the CDU and its parliamentary partner, the CSU, had actually become disillusioned with their chancellor's inclination to dominate every matter of consequence within his purview.[71] Consequently, a loose alliance of diverse elements within the

[69]For Adenauer's reading of the situation, see *Erinnerungen*, vol. 3, pp. 463–468, 478–482; also see Besson, *Außenpolitik*, pp. 215–218.

[70]Besson, *Außenpolitik*, p. 222.

[71]For example, Eugen Gerstenmaier argued that Bonn should try to break the deadlock with the East by pursuing a general peace treaty with the Soviet Union. See Schwarz, *Die*

ruling parties, ranging from the Bavarian conservative, Franz Josef Strauß, to the more liberal, Protestant president of the Bundestag, Eugen Gerstenmaier, made an abortive effort in March and April 1959 to deprive Adenauer of his office by seeking to arrange his "promotion" to the largely ceremonial post of Federal president. That even such dominant figures within the Union leadership were unable to make the chancellor budge testified to the extent to which his personal charisma, if not his policies, still held the CDU/CSU together. But far from being a sign of strength, it was an indication of how inflexible and how bereft of alternatives the Union forces had become since they had first sought to reach out to all elements in the West German political spectrum.

How different the situation might have been, then, if the opposition Social Democrats had been able to muster a competing conception by this time of how best to meet the FRG's national goals. The prospect is worth considering because, in the wake of a disastrous showing in the parliamentary elections of 1957—where the party received only 31.8 percent of the national vote, in contrast to the CDU/CSU's 50.2 percent—the SPD had displayed definite signs of wanting to shed the dogmatic and sectarian cast that had hampered its efforts to gain broader public credibility in earlier years. In mid-November 1959, in a now famous meeting in Bad Godesberg, the party adopted a domestic reform program that was unabashedly crafted to win the approval of middle-of-the-road voters by putting its revolutionary heritage formally behind it and actively embracing the social-market economy already championed by the CDU. Had the Social Democrats only been willing at this point to make an equally unequivocal stand in favor of Bonn's participation in the Atlantic alliance, they could have found themselves perfectly positioned to carve out a more moderate foreign-policy course and to benefit from the discontent within the CDU/CSU. Nevertheless, this was not yet to be the case, as the majority of the party's leaders still clung to their idealistic hopes of somehow managing to surmount the conflict between the blocs. It was in this vein, also in 1959, that the SPD advanced a new "Germany plan," which endorsed the not very new idea of reunifying the nation by first withdrawing all foreign troops from German soil.[72]

In comparison to Adenauer's policy, which continued therefore to rule as much by default as by design, Ulbricht's equally confrontational stance toward the West was driven by the First Secretary's determination to prove

---

Ära Adenauer, p. 60. On these trends within the CDU, see especially Heidenheimer, *Adenauer*, pp. 221–224.

[72]Löwenthal, "Kalten Krieg," pp. 648–649. Historians tend to discount the seriousness of this SPD plan, although one of the plan's architects with whom I have spoken, Eugen Selbmann, insists that the proposal was a realistic way of diverting Moscow's attention from Berlin. Author's interview, Bonn, November 30, 1987.

that, after all of the years in which his authority had been in question, now he alone was capable of setting his country's priorities. In particular, with the death of Wilhelm Pieck in 1960, the last symbol of collective rule in the GDR, Ulbricht took the pointed step of abolishing the East German presidency and replacing it with another organ, the State Council, to which he not surprisingly had himself appointed chairman. This meant that by 1960 his aims and GDR's were literally identical.[73]

Formally, the SED First Secretary again assumed the pose of the great German peacemaker, pleading with the West for universal disarmament, a general peace treaty to end the Second World War, and a final solution to the West Berlin problem ("a part of our capital") that would guarantee the city's independence and allow for its demilitarization along the lines of Khrushchev's ultimatum.[74] However, if there was any doubt about his intentions, Ulbricht also let his listeners know that the realistic chances of reaching a short-term solution to the national problem were slim. The Bonn government, it seemed, had already "manifestly written off any peaceful form of reunification," and it was unlikely to support a peace treaty because it did not "want peace for either the German people or for Europe."[75] Hence, in his estimation, as long as the forces of militarism and monopoly capitalism still reigned in the FRG, the best that the SED could do was to fulfill the promise of East Germany's socialist system by proving its superiority over its rival in the West. One would have to wait for the day on which the West German working class too might rise to the challenge of waging its own successful revolution.[76]

While such a formulation may have seemed a mirror image of the West German chancellor's policy of benign neglect toward the East, there was at least one major respect in which the force of circumstances may have made Ulbricht more inclined than his counterpart to make hard choices about the contours of his national policy. By the end of the decade, it was clear that his attempts to speed up the GDR's socialist transformation were endangering the country's future by making life intolerable for many of its citizens. From 1959 to 1960, the number of refugees fleeing the GDR rose dramatically, from 144,000 to nearly 200,000, in direct response to shortcomings that were already evident in the Main Economic Task, including

[73]Ulbricht also became the head of a new National Defense Council, making him the chief military officer in the GDR. Lest there be any doubt about which East German institution had the greatest authority, however, he also presided in 1960 over a secret Central Committee decision which, in contravention of the GDR constitution, formally subordinated the country's state organs to the SED. Author's interview, Gerhard Keiderling, East Berlin, March 21, 1990.
[74]See Ulbricht's speech of October 4, 1960, in Walter Ulbricht, *Zur Geschichte der deutschen Arbeiterbewegung*, vol. 9 (Berlin: Dietz, 1966), pp. 212–244.
[75]Ibid., pp. 222, 236.
[76]See Ulbricht's speech of September 10, 1960, in *DzD*, 4th ser., vol. 5, pp. 252–253.

bottlenecks in the supply of basic goods and tougher work conditions. Furthermore, Ulbricht's stubborn insistence on completing the long-delayed collectivization of the East German countryside did not help matters either.[77]

In this respect, it cannot have been coincidental that while the GDR's leader continued to harangue his Soviet colleagues in the late summer and fall of 1960 about how much his country deserved to control Berlin in its entirety, the SED regime began to concentrate its attention on the much less ambitious implementation of border controls between the eastern and western sectors of the city.[78]

The Construction of the Wall

In view of the time that has passed since the Warsaw Pact first issued its declaration of August 12, 1961, about the forthcoming measures to establish a new "order" on the border of East and West Berlin, it is noteworthy how little we still know about the erection of the Berlin Wall.[79] How was the final decision reached to construct the barrier? To what extent was there disagreement within the Soviet and East German leaderships?[80] Would the Warsaw Treaty states have backed down if the Western allies had resolved to use force to preserve their rights in the entire city of Berlin? We can say on the basis of the preceding analysis, however, that by the summer of 1961, the Germanys and the superpowers subscribed to very different perspectives about what was at stake in Berlin and what, therefore, the barrier might signify for Germany as a whole.

It would be excessive to accuse the Americans and the other Western powers, as some West German leaders, such as Adenauer, later did, of welcoming the Eastern bloc's answer to the GDR's refugee crisis or regard-

[77]Ernst Richert, *Die Sowjetzone in der Phase der Koexistenz* (Hannover: Niedersächsischen Landeszentrale, 1961), p. 47.

[78]Smith, *Defense of Berlin*, pp. 225–227. These controls were largely confined to West Germans wishing to enter East Berlin, but in retrospect it seems likely that the regime was using them to test its leeway in supervising traffic over the sectoral boundary.

[79]There is a good reason why this is the case—very few individuals were actually involved in the decision. For example, Kurt Hager, then a candidate-member of the politburo, insists that he was not informed of the decision until August 12, when Ulbricht instructed him to persuade the leaders of the GDR's so-called bloc parties that the barrier's construction was justified. See my interview with Hager, OHP (December 3, 1990). Also, see Peter Möbius and Helmut Trotnow, "Das Mauer-Komplott," *Die Zeit*, August 16, 1991, pp. 13–14.

[80]For example, an unpublished letter in the Ulbricht *Nachlaß* from the SED First Secretary to Khrushchev on October 30, 1961, suggests that M. G. Pervukhin, Moscow's ambassador to the GDR and a former member of the CPSU praesidium (politburo), opposed the elimination of many of the border control points between East and West Berlin on the grounds that the steps violated the city's four-power status. CPA, Berlin.

ing it as a "good thing."[81] It is indisputable, however, that particularly after the arrival of the Kennedy administration in Washington in early 1961, the United States and its allies were actively searching for ways of putting the Berlin problem behind them. Hence, they were frankly disposed to accept both a more exacting definition of Western responsibilities in the city and to negotiate an end to the conflict with Moscow. It was indicative of Kennedy's own youthful idealism that when the president met with Khrushchev for the first time on June 3–4, 1961, in Vienna, he evidently expected to persuade his Soviet counterpart to explore new ways of dealing with both Berlin and Germany. He sorely underestimated, however, the pressures under which the Soviet leader was then operating— from a flagging economy at home to a vitriolic dispute with the People's Republic of China—and hence was unprepared when Khrushchev presented him with a detailed aide-mémoire formally renewing the 1958 ultimatum on West Berlin. If the three Western occupying powers did not take steps to transform the city into a neutral entity by the end of the year, Khrushchev threatened again, his government would have no alternative but to sign the long-promised peace treaty with the GDR.[82]

Against this backdrop, one might conclude that Khrushchev's motivations must have been fundamentally different from those of the Western allies. Yet in retrospect, we can see that he too was seeking the easiest means of eliminating Berlin once and for all as an object of contention between the blocs. As early as March 28–29, 1961, the Soviet leader had been presented with another way out of the controversy when Ulbricht appealed at a meeting of the Warsaw Pact to allow his government to seal the intersectoral boundary in Berlin with barbed wire. At *that* time, however, Khrushchev and the majority of Pact members rejected the proposal as being too provocative, apparently because no one could be sure how the Western powers would react to such an assault upon their rights in East Berlin.[83] In this sense, the renewed ultimatum in June may have been little

[81]As Adenauer argued years after the Wall was built, quietly ignoring his own passivity at the time: "Although the Russians broke the treaties and built the Wall, the Americans made their peace with it. The Americans even tried to tell us that it was a good thing because it stopped the refugee exodus. The German people were shocked. It was a terrible success for Moscow. The Americans were too fearful." Cited in Bruno Bandulet, *Adenauer zwischen Ost und West* (Munich: Weltforum, 1970), p. 282, n. 136.

[82]Arthur Schlesinger, Jr., *A Thousand Days* (Greenwich, Conn.: Fawcett, 1965), pp. 347–348.

[83]Hermann Zolling and Uwe Bahnsen, *Kalter Winter im August* (Oldenburg: Gerhard Stalling, 1967), pp. 102–103. For a suggestion that Ulbricht may have called for such measures earlier, see the unpublished letter from Khrushchev to the SED First Secretary on October 24, 1960, in Monika Kaiser, "Ulbricht schrieb das Drehbuch für die Mauer," *Die Welt*, August 12, 1991.

more than a less risky method of prodding the United States and its allies into accepting a speedy Berlin settlement before the GDR collapsed.

Apart from all of Khrushchev's bluster and bravado, however, there was a subtext to his discussions with Kennedy at Vienna which, although barely detectable, bordered on compromise. In the aide-mémoire, Khrushchev conceded for the first time that a contingent of Western (and Soviet) troops might remain in West Berlin to guarantee the city's independent status. And, distinguishing the offer slightly from past threats, he also suggested that the Western powers could sign a German peace treaty with his government *without* having to recognize the GDR explicitly.[84] Just as important, while Kennedy let the Soviet leader know in unequivocal terms that he was willing to go to war to safeguard American interests in West Berlin, he also allowed—and this was crucial—that he would not interfere with any steps the Soviet Union chose to take in its own sphere of influence.[85]

No one could have recognized it at this juncture, as the specter of an imminent conflict hung over the United States and the Soviet Union for some time thereafter, but Kennedy's rejoinder, later formalized in a July 25 address to the nation, provided exactly the kind of information that Moscow needed to erect the Wall.[86] For the president's emphasis on West Berlin alone was, as Egon Bahr, then a young associate of Willy Brandt, put it, "almost like an invitation to the Soviets to do what they want[ed] with the eastern sector."[87] Certainly, this was how both the Soviet and East German leaderships interpreted the signal.[88] Ever since the articulation of

---

[84]Smith, *Defense of Berlin*, pp. 232–233. For a less charitable interpretation, however, see Michael R. Beschloss, *The Crisis Years: Kennedy and Khrushchev, 1960–1963* (New York: HarperCollins, 1991), pp. 215–224.

[85]Honoré M. Catudal, *Kennedy and the Berlin Wall Crisis* (Berlin: Berlin Verlag, 1980), p. 118, and Smith, *Defense of Berlin*, p. 234.

[86]For Kennedy's address, in which he emphasized the United States' readiness to go to war to defend "three essential" commitments to West Berlin, its military presence in the city, unimpeded access rights, and the preservation of West Berlin's democratic institutions, see *Public Papers of the Presidents: John F. Kennedy, 1961* (Washington, D.C.: GPO, 1962), pp. 533–540.

[87]Cited in Wilhelm Grewe, *Rückblenden: 1976–1951* (Frankfurt: Propyläen, 1979), p. 480. Grewe, Adenauer's argumentative ambassador to the United States during the crisis, undoubtedly spoke for his silent chancellor when he observed in early 1961 that Kennedy's emphasis on only West Berlin was "the minimum of what could be expected" (pp. 463–464). Unfortunately, although perhaps revealingly, Adenauer never completed the part of his memoirs dealing with the crucial weeks surrounding the construction of the Wall, even though he did manage to address events in later years in detail. For a general account of the period, see Hans-Peter Schwarz's classic biography, *Adenauer. Der Staatsmann: 1952–1967* (Stuttgart: Deutsche Verlags-Anstalt, 1991), pp. 640–671.

[88]According to one East German historian, GDR authorities took Kennedy's stand into account when they erected the Wall, recognizing that the United States would not use force to

Khrushchev's ultimatum, the East German population's fears that *something* was about to happen in Berlin, *Torschlußpanik*, or "gate-closing panic," had driven the refugee flight to unprecedented heights. Twenty thousand people fled the GDR in June alone, and more than thirty thousand in July. Despite the government's efforts to slow the exodus by implementing more extensive controls on movement between the two parts of Berlin—restrictive measures were taken in July against the so-called *Grenzgänger* ("border-crossers") who lived in East Berlin and worked in West Berlin—even these steps merely added to the number of those fleeing to the West. As a consequence, when the member states of the Warsaw Pact met again on August 3–4 in Moscow, they finally voted to support the construction of the Wall.

Since that time, much has been made by historians about the extent to which the leaders of the Western alliance were taken by surprise by the barrier's erection. On August 13, President Kennedy, French president de Gaulle, and British prime minister Macmillan were all, almost too conveniently, on vacation. Hence, it took days before a formal Western protest was even lodged with Soviet authorities. Surprised or not, there can be no doubt that the allied leaders were prepared to treat the Wall as the end to the Berlin crisis and not the beginning of a new one. Little was made of formal demands that the Soviets reopen the border, and there was even a certain amount of self-congratulation in Western decision-making circles that the allies' major goal of protecting West Berlin had been achieved.[89] Similarly, it was not much longer before the Soviets themselves showed, as Khrushchev steadily moved away from his "free city" demands, that they too were content to live with having secured their minimal objectives, assurance of the GDR's existence and the West's tacit acknowledgment of a socialist sphere in Eastern Europe.

It is no wonder, then, that had the choice been up to the superpowers alone, the Wall should have marked (to use one analyst's piquant expression) "the last step in the consolidation of the status quo" in Europe.[90] The only problem with such an assessment is that it would have left out the very parties, the Germanys, which still stood in the way of a final settlement to the political shape of the continent. In each case, Ulbricht and Adenauer seemed practically driven to prove that their respective stands on the national question remained unaffected by the Wall.

This can have been no mean challenge for Adenauer, since well before the barrier's appearance, the West German leader had been presented with

---

defend its rights in East Berlin. Author's interview, Gerhard Keiderling, East Berlin, March 21, 1990.

[89]Walter Stützle, *Kennedy und Adenauer in der Berlin Krise, 1961–1962* (Bonn–Bad Godesberg: Verlag Neue Gesellschaft, 1973), pp. 138–9.

[90]Besson, *Außenpolitik*, p. 263.

daily reminders about the flaws in his approach to the German problem. If a fundamental premise of the "policy of strength" was that the FRG's ties to the Western alliance would bring Germany closer to reunification, one of the troubling ironies with which the chancellor had to live was that his allies were intent upon moving in quite the opposite direction. Thus, in the spring of 1961, even before the enunciation of Khrushchev's second ultimatum, Adenauer found himself in the unenviable position of having to counsel a new American president to defend U.S. interests in Berlin in its entirety and to persevere in the face of Soviet pressure, even while recognizing that Washington no longer shared his definition of alliance priorities.[91]

In any other year, the challenge would have been serious enough. But 1961 was also an election year in the FRG, with a new Bundestag to be selected in the fall. On top of his own weaknesses within the CDU, Adenauer also had to contend with the new circumstance that his rivals in the SPD, led by the charismatic mayor of West Berlin, Brandt, and the party's deputy chairman, Herbert Wehner, had finally begun to make their break with the overtly anti-NATO stands of the past and to embrace the Atlantic cause unequivocally.[92] As a result, for the first time in the FRG's history, it was no longer self-evident which of the West German parties could be counted upon to be most supportive of the alliance.

Faced therefore with the failure of his policy and rising uncertainty about the internal makeup of his country's domestic politics, Adenauer was almost immobilized when the Wall was put up in August. There was no quick trip to West Berlin to show solidarity with the city at a time of crisis; instead, the chancellor confined himself to receiving assurances from the Soviet ambassador that the conflict would not escalate further. Nor did Adenauer even hurry to convene the Bundestag to consider possible responses to the loss of East Berlin. Indeed, if the West German leader expressed his frustration at all with the GDR's action, it was not against the country's Communist leadership but instead, improbably, against the SPD in the context of the fall election campaign. Perhaps this was because Brandt distinguished himself by being among the few West German leaders to call for swift Western countermeasures against the Wall, drafting an angry letter to the American president in which he demanded more determined action from the United States.[93] In one particularly venomous

---

[91]On the U.S.–West German relationship, see Stützle, *Kennedy und Adenauer*, pp. 89–103.

[92]The benchmark for this shift is usually taken to be Herbert Wehner's Bundestag speech of June 30, 1960, recognizing NATO as the "foundation and framework" of any steps toward national reunification, in *DzD*, 4th ser., vol. 4, pp. 1278–1292. Throughout the 1961 election campaign, Adenauer reviled the SPD for its about-face on past policy, although one suspects he was most aggrieved that it was becoming so much more competitive with the CDU.

[93]*DzD*, 4th ser., vol. 7, pp. 48–49.

speech, Adenauer indirectly impugned the mayor's character and his pa-
triotism. Later in the month, he even suggested that the GDR had erected
the Wall to aid the electoral fortunes of the Social Democrats.[94]

On no account, however, did the West German chancellor give any
indication that the crisis had altered his thinking. He did make occasional
references to the need for the two superpowers to begin discussions about
controlled disarmament measures; this at a time when, as one of his interpreters has observed, there was no chance the United States and the Soviet
Union would engage in serious negotiations.[95] Still, he proved to be as
inflexible as ever about the German contribution to any reconciliation
between the blocs. His government was interested in sincere talks with the
East, Adenauer proclaimed on August 18, to discuss a final settlement of
the German problem and the Berlin question, but only on the same terms
that had seemed so sensible to him over a decade earlier: "To the German
people must be returned the right, which is refused to no other people in
the world, freely to establish a government of its own enjoying the legitimate task of speaking, acting, and making decisions for all of Germany."[96]

For Ulbricht, in contrast, the task of responding to the Wall's erection
was considerably easier. Supposedly, in what would become his regime's
favored mythology for justifying the barrier over the next three decades,
the East German government had discovered that the NATO powers had
been preparing to launch "open military provocations" against the GDR
just after the upcoming West German elections, and thus the SED had no
choice but to act quickly to save the peace in Europe. Yet even before this
date, Ulbricht emphasized, it was clear "for anyone who [had] eyes to see
and ears to hear" that the Berlin situation had grown intolerable. Something had to be done if the continent were to be spared another Sarajevo.
Hence, the Wall was really only a sensible way of demonstrating that the
GDR's existence was not negotiable.[97]

There remained, however, a telling ambiguity in much that Ulbricht had
to say about the events of August 13. Whereas his allies in Moscow were
content to rest comfortably with the thought that they had survived their
risky challenge to Western rights in Berlin, the East German First Secretary
clearly regarded the Wall as the springboard to other objectives. The
"Bonn ultras" may have been defeated at the foot of the Brandenburg Gate,
but in his estimation Europe could still not live without a general German
peace treaty. Furthermore, the situation in West Berlin itself could hardly

[94]See Adenauer's controversial references to "Herr Brandt alias Frahm," in *Union in
Deutschland*, 15, no. 33 (1961); and Schwarz, *Die Ära Adenauer*, p. 150.

[95]Stützle, *Kennedy und Adenauer*, p. 152.

[96]*DzD*, 4th ser., vol. 7, p. 79.

[97]See Ulbricht's television address of August 18, 1961, in Walter Ulbricht, *Zur Geschichte
der deutschen Arbeiterbewegung*, vol. 10 (Berlin: Dietz, 1966), pp. 15–21.

be considered settled until the city had been transformed into a "free city" along the lines of Khrushchev's earlier proposal.[98]

Most revealing, Ulbricht still regarded the future of the German nation as unresolved. Naturally, there was no point in deluding oneself into thinking that relations between the now-separated populations of the Germanys would be any easier as a result of his regime's action. It was not the fault of the GDR, Ulbricht insisted, that the nation was divided. That condition could only be overcome when those who had caused it, the West German militarists and their NATO allies, were themselves overcome. In the meantime, however, one could at least be thankful that one decisive step had been made in the true interests of the German nation: "Thanks to the political clarity, and to the capabilities and energies of the citizens of the GDR," he advised, "we will all be able to create the preconditions for a time when Berlin, our Berlin, will become the capital of Germany in its entirety, a Germany in which there is no militarism, no imperialism, and no black-brown-yellow dictatorship, but only the working class, which in alliance with the farmers and all other peace-loving forces is able to shape the destiny of the new Germany."[99] Far from being an abstract philosophical observation, this perspective, like Adenauer's very different conception of the ideal German future, would present a significant challenge to anyone who assumed that the German question had been neatly redefined with the erection of the Wall.

[98]Ibid., pp. 16, 34–35.
[99]See Ulbricht's speech of August 25, 1961, in ibid., p. 61.

III

Two Germanys: Confrontation or Accommodation?

> In August 1961 a curtain was drawn aside to
> reveal an empty stage. To put it more bluntly, we
> lost certain illusions that had outlived the hopes
> underlying them—illusions that clung to
> something which no longer existed in fact.
>   (Willy Brandt, *People and Politics*)

> Herr Adenauer has determined with sadness that
> his revanchist German policy has collapsed at the
> Brandenburg Gate. The great wheel of history
> cannot be turned back. Herr Adenauer has had
> to accept the fact that the GDR is here to stay.
>   (Walter Ulbricht, August 25, 1961)

THE GREATEST impediment to a better understanding of the relationship between the Berlin Wall and the dynamics of the German question may be that we know how the story eventually ended. We know that some twenty-five years after the barrier's erection, the leaders of both the GDR and the FRG had set aside many of the confrontational policies that had been at the heart of their difficulties during their first decade and basically accommodated themselves to their nation's division. Furthermore, we also know that there were key developments in the interim that helped to set the stage for this shift. In 1970 Bonn went a long way toward reconciling itself with its World War II enemies by signing renunciation-of-force pacts with Moscow and Warsaw, and it concluded a similar agreement with Prague in 1973; in 1971 Berlin's four occupying powers finally reached an accord managing their differences over the city's status; and in 1972 the Germanys completed negotiations on their own Basic Treaty. Nonetheless, the passage from the policies of strength of the 1950s to even the formal agreements of the 1970s was by no means the straightforward undertaking it might appear to be in retrospect.

Decades after the event, the Wall's erection may seem to be the sole reason behind the change in both states' policies. Certainly, this was what Willy Brandt had in mind when he suggested, writing in his memoirs in the late 1970s, that the events of August 1961 had exposed an "empty stage" in the GDR's and the FRG's handling of the national dilemma.[1] The simultaneous shift in superpower priorities in Europe showed that the Germanys could no longer hope to look to their allies for support in their efforts to remake the status quo. Additionally, with the closing of the last open border between them, it also seemed to be self-evident that any realistic hope of preserving the national ideal would have to begin with the realization that two completely separate states had sprung up on German soil.

Nevertheless, while the time would come when both East Berlin and Bonn acted as though their interests were in fact best served by emphasizing prevailing conditions on the continent rather than seeking to deny them, Ulbricht's and Adenauer's contrary perspectives on the German future still exercised an undeniable, if baffling, hold on their governments' behavior throughout the 1960s.[2] In both cases, the persistence of old ways of thinking was particularly striking, because the policies seemed literally to be larger than the personalities themselves. In no small measure, this was because they reflected the considerable difficulty of recasting East and West German national policy when the internal conditions that were required for such a shift were still unavailable.

Changing Surroundings

It is a truism that the Berlin crisis did not simply expire with the building of the Wall but lingered on uneasily for several years as each of the superpowers struggled to sort out the implications of the events of August 1961. Nevertheless, the depth of the discontinuity between Soviet and American perspectives, on the one hand, and those of their respective German allies, on the other, could not have been more blatant. Even as the great powers were seeking to put many of their differences about the European balance of power behind them, East Berlin and Bonn seemed to be almost defiantly set upon resisting the idea that the world was any different than at the height of the Cold War in the 1950s.

This problem was apparent in the degree to which West German and American policymakers found themselves at loggerheads in only the first few months after the construction of the Wall. Already in September 1961, only a month after the barrier's construction, President Kennedy had begun a confidential exchange of letters with Nikita Khrushchev in which he

---

[1] Willy Brandt, *People and Politics* (London: William Collins, 1978), p. 20.

[2] As one East German participant relates: "The conflict between capitalism and socialism was ideologized *and* personalized in Adenauer and Ulbricht. So long as they remained, nothing could be changed." Author's interviews, Klaus Zechmeister Institute for International Politics and Economics, East Berlin, June 8, 1988.

sought to convince the latter that there was nothing to be gained by further attempts to settle the Berlin problem unilaterally. So long as the Soviet Union was prepared to respect Western rights in West Berlin, Kennedy suggested, his administration was willing to consider a number of ways of putting the conflict to rest, including the adjudication of the issue by the World Court, the creation of a Central European security zone, and the establishment of an international access authority to link West Berlin with the FRG.[3] At several points over the ensuing months, Kennedy's secretary of state, Dean Rusk, met privately with his Soviet counterpart, Andrei Gromyko, in New York to flesh out possible compromises on these issues.

At the very least, perhaps one should have expected the Adenauer government to be irritated by such initiatives. Still, given the lessons that Bonn might also have gleaned from earlier Berlin crises and the centrality of its relationship with Washington, the extent of West German displeasure with the United States was telling. For example, the FRG's ambassador to the United States, Wilhelm Grewe, publicly expressed his indignation at, what he termed, the American government's habitual inclination "to answer the maximal demands of the Eastern side with maximal concessions on the Western side." Going right to the heart of the U.S.–West German relationship in an address in early October, Grewe even suggested that Washington had violated a sacred trust. Had the Americans forgotten, he inquired, that his government had only been able to sell its population on rearmament in the 1950s by obtaining the West's commitment not to make decisions about the European status quo that might one day impair a satisfactory German settlement? Now the United States seemed oblivious to this compact.[4] For his part, Adenauer managed to be only a little bit more diplomatic than his emissary when, during a November visit to Washington, he pressed Kennedy to refrain from giving in any further to Soviet blackmail on Berlin. For the first time, the chancellor intimated that his government would be willing to put up with limited exploratory talks with Moscow about the fate of the city—on the double condition that these contacts would not interfere with the White House's own commitments or the FRG's special claims to West Berlin—but he also begged the president to refrain from broaching any other issues that might inadvertently solidify the status quo.[5]

It was, however, testimony to the inherent fragility of U.S.–West German ties that by early 1962 Washington was again showing that it was not about to let the FRG's Central European priorities get in the way of the need to resolve more pressing differences with the Soviet Union. On April 12, the

[3]Theodore C. Sorensen, *Kennedy* (New York: Harper and Row, 1965), pp. 598–599.
[4]On Grewe's remarks of September 22 and October 8, 1961, see Walther Stützle, *Kennedy und Adenauer in der Berlin Krise, 1961–1962* (Bonn–Bad Godesberg: Verlag Neue Gesellschaft, 1973), pp. 163–164.
[5]Ibid., pp. 170–177.

Kennedy administration presented the FRG government with a confidential package of proposals on Berlin that envisioned going beyond even the formation of an international control authority for the city to embrace a broad range of tension-reducing measures in the region: a Soviet-U.S. agreement limiting the proliferation of nuclear arms, which would effectively have deprived the FRG of such weapons; an exchange of "nonaggression declarations" between NATO and the Warsaw Pact; and on a particularly sensitive note, even the formation of special German-German commissions to foster technical and economic contacts between the GDR and the FRG.[6] In large part because of the way the message was handled— the West Germans were given but twenty-four hours to respond—the U.S. initiative exploded upon its arrival in Bonn, as the FRG's leaders perceived with some justice that they were not being given due consideration of the matter.[7] Although efforts were subsequently made on both sides to paper over the dispute—Grewe was replaced as the FRG's ambassador and the U.S., in turn, withdrew its proposals—the episode showed many Germans, if not Adenauer himself, just how much the FRG had become out of step with its ally's priorities.

True, Adenauer tried to act as though he was unaffected by the further consolidation of the shift in American thinking. He did not have the "slightest conviction," he noted at one point, that the Soviet-U.S. talks would amount to anything anyway, and in any event, his government was not about to engage in an enterprise that helped to legitimate the "Pankow people."[8] Over the following months, however, the chancellor's behavior suggested that he was nevertheless very much at a loss for ways of restoring the leverage his country had once enjoyed over matters affecting the German future. In an apparent effort to forestall any other U.S. actions that would further harden the inter-German divide, Adenauer made an unusual yet, as in the past, secret proposal to the Soviet ambassador on June 6 that Moscow accept a ten-year moratorium—"a kind of cease-fire," as he described it—on any future deliberations over the German question. In return, he asked only that the Soviets help stop the killing of innocent citizens on the inter-German border.[9] For his part, however, the Soviet emissary acted as though it was already clear that Adenauer's room for maneuver

<hr>

[6]Jean Edward Smith, *The Defense of Berlin* (Baltimore: Johns Hopkins University Press, 1963), p. 333.

[7]Consider Heinrich Krone's diary entry of April 14, 1962: "The Americans aren't the Americans they were in the past. They are looking for an understanding [*Man will sich verständigen*], and this will come only on the backs of the Germans. Over the long haul, however, it will also cost the West and the United States," in "Aufzeichnungen zur Deutschland- und Ostpolitik," in R. Morsey and K. Repgan, eds., *Adenauer Studien III* (Mainz: Matthias-Grünewald, 1971), p. 169.

[8]*Dokumente zur Deutschlandpolitik* (hereafter *DzD*), 4th ser., vol. 8, p. 487.

[9]*DzD*, 4th ser., vol. 8, p. 624. For Adenauer's rationale, cf. *Erinnerungen*, vol. 4 (Stuttgart: Deutsche Verlags-Anstalt, 1967), p. 225.

was limited, remarking only that his government was prepared, as ever, to sign a peace treaty with both Germanys.

It may have been for want of other options to deal with the national question that throughout 1962 the chancellor began aggressively to court political ties with France's president, Charles de Gaulle, in whom he seems to have found a willing soulmate in his suspicions about U.S. motives and his concern over Washington's proclivity to negotiate with Moscow "for the sake of negotiations alone."[10] Here too, however, the West German leader's alternatives were limited. When he subsequently tried to put the Franco-German relationship at the center of his government's foreign policy by pushing for a comprehensive treaty on military, economic, and cultural cooperation with Paris, he found himself immediately under pressure by the increasingly pro-American SPD, as well as members of his own party and the FDP, to water down the agreements by affirming the FRG's special bond with the United States.[11]

In the end, oddly enough, Adenauer's only comfort may have been provided by Moscow's role in bringing about the Cuban missile crisis in the fall of 1962, which introduced a temporary pall over U.S. and Soviet efforts to reduce tensions. When the chancellor visited Washington in November, he found what appeared to be a new Kennedy, hardened in his response to the Soviet action and agreeably opposed to making further concessions to the East.[12] But this was not to last. After the crisis was resolved, the president was, as one of his biographers has noted, still "rather more impressed by the risks of war than by the risks of *détente*."[13] Kennedy made the point explicit in a famous address at American University in Washington on June 10, when he called upon the American people to "reexamine [their] attitude toward the cold war" and to support negotiations with the Soviet Union on all matters—he specifically proposed a ban on nuclear-weapons testing—that would reduce the risk of nuclear war.[14] As if to insure that there was no room for misunderstanding, the U.S. leader practically lectured Adenauer about Bonn's limited options two weeks later, when he emphasized in a speech at the Free University in West Berlin that there was no alternative to détente. The whole world could see, Kennedy declared, that a police state had been imposed on Berlin's eastern sector, but no one was helped by indulging in "self-deception" or thinking

[10]Adenauer, *Erinnerungen*, p. 173.

[11]F. Roy Willis, *France, Germany, and the New Europe* (London: Oxford University Press, 1968), pp. 314–316.

[12]See, for example, Krone, "Aufzeichnungen," p. 172.

[13]Arthur M. Schlesinger, Jr., *A Thousand Days* (Greenwich, Conn.: Fawcett, 1965), p. 811 (italics in original).

[14]*Public Papers of the Presidents: John F. Kennedy, 1963* (Washington, D.C.: GPO, 1964), p. 459–464.

"merely in slogans." Instead, he insisted, in language that would eventually provide the intellectual rationale for Bonn's own *Ostpolitik*, the West was best served by doing "what [it] could do . . . to improve the lot and maintain the hopes of those on the other side."[15]

If the GDR's leaders, in contrast, found life somewhat easier with their ally, the Soviet Union, it was only because the realization came somewhat more slowly to Moscow that relations between the superpowers needed to be put on a more stable footing. Even after the Wall's erection, Khrushchev seems to have been torn between competing alternatives. On the one hand, he could seek to soften those frictions with the West that had been generated by the Berlin ultimatum and the sealing of the East Berlin border. But on the other hand, he could hardly fail to see that neither his state nor the GDR had yet obtained any of its principal demands on the issue of Berlin's status.

Certainly, the kinds of behind-the-scenes talks about the city that went on between the superpowers throughout the fall of 1961 would have been unimaginable had Khrushchev not taken to heart the desirability of easing tensions in the region. The Soviet leader himself had been behind the September exchange of letters with Kennedy in the first place by letting the American president know through an intermediary that, as far as he was concerned, "the storm in Berlin [was] over."[16] At the CPSU's Twenty-second Congress in October 1961, Khrushchev even took a public stand on the issue with the curious observation that Western politicians were suffering from an "erroneous" impression when they contended that his country had issued an ultimatum on Berlin. The Soviet Union, he asserted, had only *proposed* that a German peace treaty be concluded by December 31, 1961, whereas Moscow would be satisfied if the Western powers only showed "a readiness to settle the German problem."[17]

Nevertheless, the SED leadership was not the least bit inclined to help Khrushchev forget his previous assurances to sign a peace accord of some kind with the GDR. When Ulbricht was called to speak at the same CPSU congress, he could scarcely conceal his displeasure with the Soviet about-face on the ultimatum, emphasizing pointedly that the conclusion of a peace treaty was the "most urgent task" facing the socialist world. It was "good," Ulbricht granted, that Moscow and Washington were considering further talks on the German problem, but his Soviet colleague could not afford to blind himself to the fact that some powers—he specifically men-

[15]Ibid., pp. 527–528. Egon Bahr, for one, later claimed to be directly influenced by Kennedy's reasoning. Author's interview, Bonn, January 21, 1988.

[16]Robert Slusser, *The Berlin Crisis of 1961* (Baltimore: Johns Hopkins University Press, 1963), p. 207.

[17]*Current Digest of the Soviet Press* (hereafter CDSP) 13, no. 41, p. 5.

tioned the flowering of relations between the FRG and France—were pursuing quite different, potentially more dangerous agendas on the continent.[18]

Given the conventions of the Soviet–East German relationship, this was strong language. Yet at this juncture in particular, the GDR's leader at least had the benefit of Khrushchev's ambivalence. In response to Ulbricht's pleas, Khrushchev insisted that his government was by no means oblivious to the intentions of its enemies. Still, the Soviet Union would not impose any new deadlines on the West as long as its adversaries were willing to negotiate in good faith: "We are not superstitious people," he lectured, in words that were just as appropriate for the GDR as for the United States, "and we believe that both the figures 31 and 13 can be lucky."[19]

By referring to the hypothetical date of the peace treaty, Khrushchev no doubt intended to remind the East German First Secretary that he had already gained a great deal from the "lucky" events of August 13, 1961. In fact, however, the Soviet leader had himself not quite gotten over his inability to extract a favorable Berlin settlement from the West. Nor could he evidently resist the temptation to employ the convenient lever of West Berlin to remind the West that the city's status had still not been settled. Thus, beginning in the early spring of 1962 and continuing through the following summer, Soviet authorities once again began to apply intermittent pressure on the city, initially harassing western air traffic and then conducting military maneuvers on the transit routes linking West Berlin with the FRG. At least at first, these measures may have reflected little more than Moscow's hopes of gaining the upper hand in the talks with the United States about access to the city.[20] Nevertheless, it is also true that by the summer of 1962 Khrushchev's personal situation had become complicated by the fact that hostile critics from as far away as Beijing and Tirana and as close as his own politburo were challenging him to reestablish the Soviet Union's international credibility. In this case, Berlin, along with one other issue—the fate of Fidel Castro's Cuba—seemed to offer just the opportunities he needed.

Although the exact connection between Berlin and the Cuban missile crisis of October 1962 may never be known, it does seem that the two questions were linked in the Soviet leader's thinking. The surprise TASS

[18]*Neues Deutschland* (hereafter *ND*), October 22, 1961.
[19]*CDSP* 13, no. 46, p. 23.
[20]Yet, even in this instance, the East German government was in no mood to see its allies strike a bargain on the Berlin question. In an April 29, 1962, interview with two Soviet editors, one of whom, A. I. Adzhubei, happened to be Khrushchev's son-in-law, Ulbricht coolly advised that his country was "neither a colony, a protectorate of any imperialist power, nor a leaderless territory, and it would not even come into question that an international organ would receive the right to violate the GDR's sovereignty by exercising administrative functions on the territory of the GDR," *Dokumentation der Zeit* (hereafter *DdZ*, no. 263, p. 35.

announcement of early September 1961 that first informed the world that Moscow had begun arms deliveries to Havana also raised the possibility that the Soviet Union might soon return to its demands for a speedy German settlement. As U.S. officials speculated one month later when the crisis broke out, Khrushchev may have gambled that his one bold stroke in the Caribbean, the deployment of intermediate-range nuclear missiles only 90 miles off the American coast, would give him all the leverage he needed to induce the West to compromise on a host of other issues, including Berlin.[21]

Nonetheless, there was also a striking similarity between Ulbricht's pose at the time of the Cuban crisis and that of Adenauer. Much like the latter in his relationship with Kennedy, Ulbricht suddenly found reason to be optimistic that his Soviet allies were ready to redress the balance of forces in central Europe to the GDR's advantage.[22] However, when the United States and the Soviet Union came within inches of war over Cuba, and Khrushchev, not Kennedy, was ultimately forced to back down by agreeing to withdraw his country's missiles, Ulbricht's hopes died as quickly as they had been reawakened, as the Berlin crisis, in the form that it had taken since the late 1940s, came to a definitive end. The East German leader seemed to acknowledge as much in a speech in early December, when he grudgingly conceded that just as the Soviet and American governments had been forced to "compromise" for the sake of avoiding a nuclear inferno, so too his country would have to look for ways of coexisting with the Adenauer government in the interest of peace.[23]

As if to insure that his allies really understood the meaning of the Cuban debacle, Khrushchev used the occasion of the SED's Sixth Congress in January 1963 to suggest that the GDR had been given just about everything that its leaders could expect from the Soviet Union with the erection of the Wall. "Our ally and friend, the German Democratic Republic," he emphasized, noticeably distancing himself from any further demands to refuel the dispute over Berlin, "has obtained what every sovereign state requires, the right to control its borders and to take measures against those who try to weaken [its] socialist system."[24] The fact, however, that Khrushchev felt

---

[21]Sorensen, *Kennedy,* pp. 676–678. Also see Adam Ulam, *Expansion and Coexistence* (New York: Praeger, 1968), p. 669.

[22]In early October 1962, for example, Ulbricht emphasized that the "peace treaty [could] not be endlessly postponed," almost as though he hoped the Soviets would again take the issue in hand. *ND,* October 6, 1962.

[23]From a speech on December 2, 1962, cited in *DzD,* 4th ser., vol. 10, p. 249.

[24]*CDSP* 15, no. 3, p. 6. The Soviet Union conveyed the finality of Khrushchev's words in signing a long-awaited Treaty of Friendship, Mutual Aid, and Cooperation with East Berlin a year later, in June 1964. Although the accord paid homage to such truisms as the need of all peoples for peace, it also fell noticeably short of addressing the demands (e.g., the "free city" solution for West Berlin) the GDR's leaders had once considered among the minimal requisites for a Central European settlement.

moved to make such a statement was itself enough to suggest that even he was unsure where East Germany's leaders stood, much as U.S. leaders too might have wondered how far their own allies had progressed on the national question.

West Germany's Awkward Adaptation

Admittedly, it would have been a strange development had either of the German states accommodated itself with no hesitation to the emerging Soviet-U.S. consensus about the continental status quo. After all, so much more was at stake for the Germans—the future of their nation and the right to define the social and economic order of a reunified Germany—in the shifting superpower balance than for other Europeans, that both East Berlin and Bonn were understandably reluctant to part with their earlier policies. At least in the case of the FRG, however, it says something about the impact of the Wall's construction that even before Adenauer's retirement in October 1963, the first signs of a new *Ostpolitik* and of a more conciliatory Germany policy were already beginning to challenge the chancellor's past priorities. Nevertheless, it is also clear that one of the chief factors that delayed the process of adapting national policy to the new reality represented by the Wall was the absence of anyone with Adenauer's clout and prestige capable of forcing through such a shift. This was no accident. Ironically, with the chancellor's passing from the scene, foreign policymaking in the FRG not only became more democratic, in that more and more voices were included in the shaping of official policy, but also more complex. These conditions made the regime much less amenable to the kinds of adaption the situation demanded.

The casual observer of West Germany's domestic debates in the early 1960s would not have had much trouble finding evidence of dissatisfaction with Adenauer's inability to accept the fact that a new international order was emerging, which in turn called Bonn to reevaluate the way it pursued its national objectives. In the wake of the Wall's erection, a number of major liberal publications such as *Der Spiegel* and *Die Zeit*, leading intellectuals such as Werner Heisenberg, Golo Mann, Rudolf Augstein, Karl Jaspers, and Carl Friedrich von Weizsäcker, and vocal representatives of the country's Lutheran churches, had all begun to advance the sorts of ideas that would one day provide the philosophical rationale for the breakthrough treaties of the early 1970s. These included, for example, the need finally to recognize the Oder-Neisse border in the name of Polish–West German reconciliation—although millions of Germans had lost their homes as a result of the Soviet definition of Poland's postwar boundaries, there was a growing recognition that nothing could be done to regain these lost territories; the desirability of moving beyond the Hallstein Doctrine to promote greater international maneuverability; and perhaps most pressing, the necessity of taking up routinized contacts with the other German state to ease the human burdens of national division.[25]

Many of these convictions were also taking hold, slowly and tentatively, within the ranks of the political parties that were already in the position to change West German policy. Although Willy Brandt's Social-Liberal coalition of 1969 is often exclusively credited with authorship of the West German *Ostpolitik*, the policy's origins can actually be found in the early, if still cautious, efforts of Christian Democratic standard-bearers such as Kurt-Georg Kiesinger and Gerhard Schröder, the West German foreign minister between 1962 and 1966, to carve out a workable alternative to the "policy of strength." For these politicians, Adenauer's obstinate refusal to keep pace with the changes in U.S. foreign policy had brought the FRG dangerously close to a rupture in relations. What was worse, the chancellor's stand had also played right into the hands of the CDU/CSU's rivals in the SPD, who were eager to say that their party was best equipped to lead Bonn into an era of realistic détente with the East. As Schröder emphasized, so long as the Soviet Union was determined to retain its grip on its satellites, the GDR included, Bonn simply had to accept that its hopes of keeping alive the dream of German unity were contingent upon having some kind of relationship with the communist regimes it had previously shunned.[26]

For this reason alone, the West German foreign minister is rightly best remembered for his efforts in the final years of the Adenauer chancellorship and in the government of Adenauer's more accommodating successor, Ludwig Erhard, to free the FRG of many of its self-imposed restraints by opening negotiations with a host of East European governments, just below the level of full diplomatic recognition. These contacts, known under the rubric of "the policy of movement" (*Politik der Bewegung*), led in 1963 and 1964 to a series of noteworthy breakthroughs in the region, when Bonn successfully concluded trade treaties with Poland, Romania, Hungary, and Bulgaria. In a similar vein, Schröder arranged to have Nikita Khrushchev invited to make an unprecedented state visit to the FRG in 1964, only to find his efforts wasted by the latter's ouster at the end of the year.

Yet, following Adenauer's retirement, it was just as significant that Schröder was shown to be a captive of the distinct institutional circum-

---

[25]Hans-Peter Schwarz, *Geschichte der Bundesrepublik Deutschland: Die Ära Adenauer, 1957–1963* (Stuttgart: Deutsche Verlags-Anstalt, 1981), pp. 299–300; Peter Bender, *Neue Ostpolitik* (Munich: dtv, 1986), p. 118.

[26]On the early signs of flexibility among the various West German parties, see the seminal study by Karl Kaiser, *German Foreign Policy in Transition* (London: Oxford University Press, 1968), pp. 90–95.

stances that facilitated his initiatives. On the positive side, Erhard had brought to Bonn a manifestly more democratic style of policymaking than had existed under the "chancellor democracy" of the Federal Republic's first decade. While this change should have provided an ideal setting for domestic and foreign-policy innovation, however, the new chancellor's insistence upon portraying himself as a man of the people (a *Volkskanzler*) proved to be his and his government's undoing. Because Erhard refused to involve himself in the internal politics of his party and failed to develop an independent base of support, his administration was swiftly caught up in the multifarious political struggles—among regional interests in the *Länder*, parliamentary factions, and both within and between the coalition parties—which had long been held at bay by Adenauer's charisma and authoritarian proclivities. Under these conditions, Schröder soon ran out of room to move. For his efforts, he was routinely, if unfairly, assailed by CDU fundamentalists such as his predecessor, Heinrich von Brentano, for selling out the German future, reviled by Silesian and Sudetan expellees for ostensibly accepting the status quo, and even taken to task by the so-called Gaullist forces among the Union parties, Franz Josef Strauß and Adenauer included, for too readily acceding to American pressures for détente with the East.[27]

It was revealing, however, of the Bonn government's fixation on past policy that even a more compliant constellation of political forces within the CDU/CSU would probably not have led the West German government to entertain initiatives toward the GDR comparable to even those limited overtures already undertaken toward the rest of the socialist bloc. For much like their conservative critics, Schröder and Erhard were still set on preserving Bonn's claim to sole responsibility for the German nation and accordingly looked askance at any steps that might have had even the slightest chance of legitimating the East German regime.[28] As late as March 1966, in fact, when the chancellor sought to express his administration's sense of its international priorities in a famous "peace note" to the East, he did not even mention the GDR at all in his remarks.[29]

In contrast, it is well known that other Germans would have had the Bonn government go much farther at the time. These included an influential group of Social Democratic advisors to Brandt in West Berlin—Bahr, Klaus Schütz, and Heinrich Albertz—and a smaller but equally vocal contingent in the FDP, represented by an iconoclastic foreign policy intel-

---

[27]See, for example, Strauß's October 14, 1964, address to the Bundestag, in Franz Josef Strauß, *Bundestagsreden* (Bonn: Verlag AZ Studio, 1968), pp. 217–224.

[28]For example, see Schröder's speech of March 30, 1965, before the CDU's Düsseldorf congress, in *DzD*, 4th ser., vol. 11, p. 1, 1965, pp. 339–48.

[29]Boris Meissner, ed., *Die deutsche Ostpolitik, 1961–1970* (Cologne: Verlag Wissenschaft und Politik, 1970), pp. 120–124.

lectual, Wolfgang Schollwer, who argued (in language that would one day be used to justify the Basic Treaty) that the only way the FRG could hope to hold onto its national ideals was by recognizing the GDR's existence as a separate state and enlisting the aid of potentially reformist forces within its government to promote change from within.

Nevertheless, in this case as well, both the SPD and the FDP were suffused with an abiding conservatism of their own making. Whatever one called the approach, whether a "policy of enmeshment (*Verklammerung*)" (Schollwer) or "change through rapprochement" (Bahr), the national leaderships of both parties were initially inclined to regard such proposals as political dynamite.[30] True, the two organizations did occasionally join forces (the Free Democrats more often behind the scenes than directly) in promoting policies that amounted to de facto recognition of the East German state. For example, in 1963 there were negotiations with the GDR that allowed for a staggering 1.2 million visits by West Berliners to East Berlin over the 1963/64 Christmas holidays, the first substantial contacts between the two halves of the city since the erection of the Wall. Yet, aside from these talks and a few other contacts with the GDR—the Free Democratic Minister for All-German Affairs, Erich Mende, was instrumental in arranging the first of tens of thousands of deals under which Bonn quietly paid for the release of political prisoners from East Germany—the SPD and the FDP still seemed to go out of their way to avoid unnecessary controversy by restraining the calls for a more aggressive courtship of the East.

In part, this degree of caution was exercised because the leaderships of both parties had to be concerned about retaining their memberships. As a small party that hovered uncomfortably close to the 5 percent barrier of the national vote necessary for entering the Bundestag, the FDP could scarcely afford to lose even a portion of its national wing, as it might if its leaders were to have broken too quickly with the prevailing orthodoxy.[31] The SPD, too, had its share of members who approvingly remembered the days when Social Democratic policy had put the cause of national reunification above all other concerns.[32] Still, the appeal of holding office may have exercised

[30]For Schollwer's "policy of enmeshment," which was first broached in June 1962, see *DzD*, 4th ser., vol. 8, pp. 376–389. For Bahr's famous address in Tutzing, in which he first articulated the notion of "change through rapprochement," see *DzD*, 4th ser., vol. 9, pp. 572–575. It also seems likely that Bahr was influenced by Schollwer's thinking as well. Author's interviews with Bahr and Schollwer, Bonn, January 21, 1988.

[31]On the party's calculations, and particularly on the complex personality of Erich Mende, the FDP chairman at the time, see Heino Kaack, *Zur Geschichte und Programmatik der FDP* (Meisenheim am Glan: Verlag Anton Hein, 1976), pp. 22–23, and Karl Moersch, *Kurs-Revision: Deutsche Politik nach Adenauer* (Hof: Societäts-Verlag, 1978), p. 43.

[32]On the different currents within the SPD, see the useful Diplomarbeit by Wolfgang Behrendt, "Die innerparteilichen Auseinandersetzungen um die Ostpolitik in der SPD, 1960 bis 1969," Freie Universität Berlin, 1972.

the greatest moderating influence of all on both parties. As a member of the governing coalition, and a vulnerable one at that, the FDP probably had no other choice but to abide by the dictates of its partners in the CDU/CSU. However, the SPD was also limited by its political ambitions, and party spokesmen, such as Herbert Wehner and Fritz Erler were not shy about admitting that the Social Democrats did not want to make themselves easy targets for the Union's right wing. In particular, as the SPD's post-Godesberg strategy of deliberate moderation showed signs of paying off at the polls, the prospect of finally gaining political office—even in the once unthinkable form of a coalition with the CDU—was enough to harness the impulses of even the most radical reformers.[33] Although the SPD had first broken the 30 percent barrier in 1961 by winning 36.2 percent of the national vote, by 1965 it had bettered even that mark by exceeding the 39 percent level, and party regulars could practically taste the acquisition of power.

The SPD's calculated appeal to the political mainstream paid off in December 1966 with the party's entry into a coalition government, the Grand Coalition, with the CDU/CSU. Furthermore, given the record of strained relations between the Social Democrats and the Union parties, it was equally significant that this unlikely marriage gave rise to a remarkably stable consensus about the pursuit of needed reforms in Federal policy—in every area from the handling of the country's economy, then beginning to feel the weight of its first recession to its social policy, and finally to its foreign relations as well. Nevertheless, while the new coalition may have had all of the advantages of a wider degree of political support, in large part thanks to the conciliatory political style of Kurt-Georg Kiesinger,[34] who became its chancellor, the Grand Coalition's efforts to devise a more flexible approach to the communist bloc were also beset with all of the political limitations of a policy reached on the basis of mutual self-restraint and compromise.

As we have already indicated, it would be a mistake not to give moderate Christian Democrats like Kiesinger credit for moving their party out of the doldrums to which it had descended in Adenauer's final years. In his inaugural address on December 13, 1966, the new chancellor not only made the cause of improved relations with the Soviet bloc one of his administra-

---

[33]Consider Brandt's remarks at the SPD's national congress of June 1966. He went out on a limb somewhat by calling for a "qualified, orderly, and temporally limited modus vivendi [*Nebeneinander*]" with the GDR. But he also protected himself by summoning the traditional demand that his government still "prepare [itself] for a solution to the German question." Cited in Meissner, *Deutsche Ostpolitik*, pp. 131–132.

[34]On Kiesinger's skill as a "management specialist," see Gerard Braunthal, "The Policy Function of the German Social Democratic Party," *Comparative Politics* 9, no. 2 (January 1977), p. 153.

tion's chief goals, but he also came noticeably close to violating an old taboo about the GDR. Although he balked at giving up the FRG's claim to represent the whole German people, Kiesinger did break new ground by indicating his willingness to assume formal contacts with East Berlin (in the interest of "our countrymen in the other part of Germany"), provided that this step did not lead to the recognition of a second German state.[35] Five months later, in April 1967, he followed up on these statements with a number of concrete proposals on practical measures to facilitate trade and transit between the Germanys, which led to an unprecedented exchange of exploratory notes with the East German premier, Willi Stoph.

It is indisputable that the SPD's presence in the governing coalition had much to do with the new chancellor's confidence in seeking to enliven his government's foreign policy. From the first, the party's leaders had made the pursuit of a more progressive *Ostpolitik* a precondition for joining the coalition.[36] Then, too, Brandt's appointment as foreign minister in the new government unquestionably gave the Bonn coalition exactly the leverage it needed to take on such relics of the past as the Hallstein Doctrine, which even many conservative leaders agreed had outlived its usefulness. Thus, in a flurry of diplomatic activity and with Kiesinger's blessing, formal relations were opened with Romania in January 1967; a trade mission was set up in Czechoslovakia the following summer; and finally, in January 1968, eleven years after Bonn had been forced by its own illogic to sever ties with Belgrade, the FRG reestablished diplomatic ties with Yugoslavia.

Nevertheless, even if the structure of the Grand Coalition was conducive to some significant adjustments in Bonn's foreign policy, it is instructive of the limits of democratic decision-making that Kiesinger and his cabinet could still not get far away from their predecessor's policies. Just as the composition of the new coalition forced his government to be attentive to the interests of the SPD, the FRG leader also had to be sensitive to opposing pressures from fundamentalist and expellee elements within his own party and from the CSU.[37] This may be one of the main reasons why the chancellor himself displayed a remarkable lack of consistency in his own Eastern initiatives. For example, when he was pressed to justify his exchange of letters with Stoph—clearly the closest step the FRG had yet taken toward recognizing the factual existence of the GDR—Kiesinger insisted that nothing had actually changed in his government's policy toward the GDR; he had not been corresponding with representatives of a real state at all, but

[35]Meissner, *Deutsche Ostpolitik*, pp. 161–163.

[36]Christian Hacke, "Von Adenauer zu Kohl: Zur Ost- und Deutschlandpolitik der Bundesrepublik, 1949–1985," *Aus Politik und Zeitgeschichte*, December 31, 1985, p. 11.

[37]Peter G. J. Pulzer, "The German Party System in the Sixties," *Political Studies* 19, no. 1 (1971), p. 9.

only of a "phenomenon" (*Phänomen*).[38] And when, in early 1968, Brandt sought to prod the coalition into finally seeking a compromise settlement with Poland of the Oder-Neisse controversy, Kiesinger appealed to political expediency—the expellees were "breathing down his back," he confided to the Social Democratic leader—in dissuading his foreign minister from acting with undue haste.[39]

An even greater indication of the limitations upon the Grand Coalition's foreign policy, however, was the conspicuous reluctance of the SPD leaders themselves to push the chancellor too far, for fear of upsetting the delicate balance of forces upon which his government was built. The influence of this constraint can be seen by juxtaposing the SPD's comparatively cautious approach to foreign affairs questions against the turmoil over these issues that engulfed the Free Democrats after they were excluded from the government in 1966. With the possibility of being totally shut out of office by a permanent CDU-SPD coalition—a threat reinforced by efforts in the CDU to change the FRG's electoral system to a pure winner-take-all system of direct elections—pressures grew within the FDP to adopt positions that would help the party stand out against its rivals. Accordingly, as reformers such as Schollwer, Hans-Wolfgang Rubin, and Walter Scheel, who was to become the FDP chairman in 1968, gradually gained the upper hand in their party, the Free Democrats became more outspoken than ever about the need for a new relationship with the East.

Privately, many Social Democrats supported the direction in which their FDP colleagues were progressing. However, their immediate obligations to the governing coalition limited their ability to act on their convictions. In a notable controversy in September 1968, when the CDU tacked a reference emphasizing Bonn's right to represent the German nation onto a Bundestag resolution condemning the Soviet invasion of Czechoslovakia, the Social Democrats, unlike the FDP, chose to support the measure.[40] Similarly, in January 1969, when the FDP proposed breaking the logjam in

---

[38]See his October 13, 1967, statement, in *DzD*, 5th ser., vol. 1, p. 1820. Even some of Kiesinger's more liberal allies within the CDU opposed limited contacts with the GDR, arguing that such steps would inevitably solidify the national division. Eugen Gerstenmaier, for example, condemned the exchange of letters as the "opening of a fatal path." See his *Streit und Friede hat seine Zeit* (Frankfurt: Propyläen, 1981), p. 456. Those closer to Adenauer's tradition were quite unforgiving. As Heinrich Krone lamented on September 21, 1967, "Our Ostpolitik is progressing further down the path of the status quo. We're not allowing ourselves to be bothered by this. Undisturbed, we press on"; see "Aufzeichnungen," p. 196.

[39]Brandt, *People and Politics*, p. 183.

[40]Karlheinz Niclauß, *Kontroverse Deutschlandpolitik* (Frankfurt: Alfred Metzner, 1977), p. 48. Notably, the SPD explicitly accepted the CDU's wording: "Recognition of the other part of Germany as a foreign country or as a second, sovereign state of the German nation is not conceivable [*kommt nicht in Betracht*]." For the Bundestag resolution, see Meissner, *Deutsche Ostpolitik*, pp. 290–292.

relations with the GDR by offering East Berlin a general treaty and the exchange of "permanent representatives" between the German capitals, the SPD again, if grudgingly, voted along with the CDU/CSU in rejecting the proposal. Herbert Wehner may have expressed his party's position best, however, when he informed the Free Democrats in the parliamentary debate over the accord that it was only a matter of time before such a treaty would be possible.[41] Evidently, the political conditions for such a breakthrough were still not quite right.

The Rigidity of East German Policy

While the 1960s were therefore understandably frustrating for those in the FRG who hoped that their government would adopt a more flexible stand on the national question, the decade would have been doubly trying for anyone who secretly hoped to see changes of an even lesser magnitude in the GDR. Within the confines of the West German party system, at least some sort of incremental adjustment was conceivable in the FRG's policy. In the GDR, however, Ulbricht's hold on the party leadership was sufficient to make any revision of SED policy virtually impossible without his express approval.

It is worth making this relatively self-evident point because if it had not been for Ulbricht's personal involvement, the determined manner in which the East German regime continued to highlight the national issue in the early and mid-1960s could have appeared less than inevitable. In the murky world of what might have been, SED historians have hinted that for some leading party officials, such as Kurt Hager and Hermann Axen,[42] both of whom were to play a key role in redefining the government's German policy a decade later, the Wall had already marked the definitive caesura in the history of the German people. They felt that the GDR's interests would better be served by deemphasizing any commonalities, much less national ties, which their citizens might have with their counterparts in the Federal Republic. What sense did it make, after all, to remind the East German population of everything that it shared with the West, when the party's primary focus was on creating a new and different socialist order?[43]

---

[41]"*Kommt Zeit*," he noted optimistically, "*kommt Vertrag*" ("With time, the treaty will come"). See Klaus Hildebrand, *Von Erhard zur Grossen Koalition, 1963–1969* (Stuttgart: Deutsche Verlags-Anstalt, 1984), p. 350.

[42]This relative lack of interest in the national question is suggested between the lines in the interview with Kurt Hager, OHP (Hager, December 3, 1990).

[43]Author's interviews, Ministry of Foreign Affairs and Academy of Social Sciences, East Berlin, May 31, 1988, and June 8, 1988. For example, in the arcane language of internal party

Yet Ulbricht was apparently of two minds on this perspective. On the one hand, in the immediate period following the closing of the border in Berlin, he and his colleagues agreed about the importance of demonstrating, both to East Germany's skeptical citizenry and to those beyond the country's borders, that the GDR really was building a viable and humane alternative to Western capitalist society. Thus, in the wake of the Twenty-second Congress of the CPSU, Ulbricht practically leaped onto Khrushchev's bandwagon in denouncing the crimes of the Stalinist past. He presided over numerous reforms in his government's criminal code, and for a few years at least even tolerated a significant loosening of restraints on the East German artistic and intellectual community. He also put his own prestige behind the first extensive economic reforms to be implemented in East Europe, the so-called New Economic System, which returned the GDR to a balanced program of economic growth, compared to the excesses of the late 1950s and addressed the need for greater efficiency in state planning by encouraging the use of "capitalist-sounding" tools such as profitability and enterprise autonomy.[44]

Yet, on the other hand, Ulbricht evidently refused to be deterred in his quest to portray the GDR's existence as a "stroke of luck" for all Germans, arguing that only his country could offer the positive example according to which the peaceful reunification of the nation might be achieved.[45] In part, the steady decline in Adenauer's political fortunes emboldened the First Secretary to think that this was the time for the GDR to make its move on the national question.[46] Those who were associated with Ulbricht during the period insist that the SED chief was also quite earnest in asserting that a

---

debates at the time, Hermann Axen suggested that national issues were playing a lesser role thanks to the victories of the world socialist system, while "general socialist characteristics" were expressing themselves more. See ND, December 2, 1961. Furthermore, in a June 7, 1962, address, Kurt Hager tried to steer attention away from the question of reunification by suggesting that the GDR was already developing its own "socialist nation." Cited in Jürgen Hofmann, *Ein neues Deutschland soll es sein* (Berlin: Dietz, 1989), pp. 194–195. For other hints of differences with Ulbricht, see Dietmar Säuberlich, "Das Problem der Nation in der Strategie und Taktik der SED," *Forschungen zur Geschichte der deutschen Arbeiterbewegung*, ser. A, no. 48 (Berlin: Akademie für Gesellschaftswissenschaften, 1985), pp. 61–80.

[44]For more detailed accounts, see Martin McCauley, *The German Democratic Republic since 1945* (New York: St. Martin's, 1983), pp. 105–121; Peter Ludz, *Die DDR zwischen Ost und West* (Munich: C. H. Beck, 1977), pp. 38–79; and my *East Germany and Detente* (Cambridge, U.K.: Cambridge University Press, 1985), pp. 41–47.

[45]ND, March 27, 1962. Also see "Die geschichtliche Aufgabe der DDR und die Zukunft Deutschlands," in *DdZ*, no. 260, pp. 30–40.

[46]Author's interview, Gerhard Keiderling, East Berlin, March 21, 1990. Also, see Ulbricht's assessment of "the end of the Adenauer era" in his speech before the national congress on, notably enough, June 17, 1962, reprinted in Walter Ulbricht, *Zur Geschichte der deutschen Arbeiterbewegung*, vol. 10 (Berlin: Dietz, 1966), pp. 514–518.

way could still be found to reconcile the two parts of Germany under socialism.[47]

Be that as it may, one must admit that Ulbricht did have one important advantage in the contest with Bonn over which German state was best suited to articulate the nation's interests. In the absence of an effective West German policy on relations with the GDR, it was no problem at all for the East German leader to play the role of the eager suitor, ready and willing to take up all manner of contacts with the FRG if only Bonn would abandon its reserve. Hence, throughout 1963 and 1964, he was the source of constant initiatives to the FRG, ranging from the most mundane (for example, the exchange of newspapers) to the most ambitious (for example, the formation of a German council of parliamentarians), which he must have known would in many cases never be acceptable to the West. He routinely appealed to the rank and file of the SPD for talks ("Our common opponent is the CDU/CSU");[48] he persisted in presenting the GDR as the most interested party in the resolution of tensions over Berlin (astonishingly, still along "free city" lines);[49] and in late 1965 he even presided over the formation of a State Secretariat for All-German Affairs that was supposed to function as a clearinghouse for a new era of inter-German contacts.

When these overtures met with a rare response, as was the case with the negotiations over the 1963 Christmas visits by West Berliners to East Berlin, Ulbricht basked in the luxury of being able to say that his negotiating partners (in this case, the West Berlin Senate) had acted sensibly by choosing to recognize the GDR as a legitimate discussion partner. But when the West rebuffed his offers, which was more often the case given the Erhard government's disinclination to deal with the GDR formally, Ulbricht could simply reply that it was not his regime's fault that the Germanys were making such slow progress in overcoming their division.[50] All virtue, therefore, supposedly lay on the side of socialism.

We can appreciate the inherent complexity of the First Secretary's position, however, by asking what would have happened if the West German government had chosen instead to call his bluff and attempted to engage

[47]Author's taped interviews with Otto Reinhold and Herbert Häber, East Berlin, March 19, 1990, and March 23, 1990.

[48]ND, April 14, 1963. Also see his address in Leipzig a month earlier on March 9, 1963, in DzD, 4th ser., vol. 9, pp. 159–186.

[49]In "view of the fact that all of Berlin legally belongs to the territory of the GDR," Ulbricht informed an audience in Budapest on May 11, 1964, almost three years after the Berlin crisis should have ended, "[it is] our proposal to neutralize this special territory of West Berlin, to turn it into a peace-loving free city without an occupation regime, a considerable concession for the GDR to make and a further proof of its detente and peace policy." Cited in DzD, 4th ser., vol. 10, p. 558.

[50]See, for example, Ulbricht's interview with Der Stern, reprinted in ND, November 28, 1963.

the SED in serious talks about the nation's future. Although Erhard would never have gone so far, the leadership of the West German SPD actually made this question something more than an academic issue in April 1966 when, at Herbert Wehner's instigation, the party chose to respond to a proposal by the SED central committee to engage in an experimental exchange of high-level speakers. In all likelihood, the GDR's leaders had never anticipated that the Social Democratic leadership would even acknowledge the overture; hence, the proposal was originally addressed only to the rank-and-file delegates of the party's upcoming annual congress in Dortmund. Nonetheless, the fact that the SPD agreed to consider the exchange seems to have provided the SED with its first clear indication of the dilemma it would face only a few years later during conditions of sustained exposure to the FRG. How could the GDR's leaders convincingly claim, as Ulbricht desired, that they were equipped to speak for the national ideal if they were not prepared to act on every opportunity to reaffirm German commonalities? By the same token, how could they risk opening the delicate East German social order to the West without simultaneously awakening false hopes about the prospects for a meaningful rapprochement with their adversaries?

For the few short months in which the idea of the speaker exchange was alive, this uncertainty reached directly to the heart of the SED itself. Initially, some of the party's leaders, including Ulbricht, seem to have considered the mere possibility of meeting with prominent SPD representatives as a tantalizing opportunity to prove their abilities as legitimate spokesmen for German interests.[51] But for others the risks of any interaction with the Social Democrats, who were still none too restrained about expressing their distaste for SED policies, were just too great. For a short while, those who focused on the merits of dialogue with the SPD seem to have gained the upper hand, as the two parties moved ahead with preparations to meet in Karl-Marx-Stadt and Hannover. However, as the date of the exchange neared, those who argued for caution, evidently including the man who would one day govern the GDR, Erich Honecker, were able to convince Ulbricht that the circumstances were not yet right for such a test of their population's commitment to socialism. In late June 1966, the SED used the pretext that its opponents could not guarantee its members' safety to call off the exchange.[52]

[51]Author's interviews, Herbert Häber, East Berlin, June 1, 1989, and Otto Reinhold, East Berlin, March 23, 1990. Certainly, this attitude was reflected in Ulbricht's enthusiastic endorsement of the exchange at the Twelfth Central Committee Plenum on April 28, 1966. File number IV 2/1/192, pp. 1–4, Central Party Archives, Berlin (hereafter CPA).

[52]According to some of my discussion partners, others who were skeptical of the talks, aside from Honecker, included politburo members Kurt Hager, Paul Verner, Horst Sindermann, and Albert Norden. Author's interviews, Gerhard Keiderling and Otto Reinhold, East

   This is not to say, however, that Ulbricht or any of the GDR's other leaders were oblivious to the potential significance of a more active Social Democratic *Ostpolitik*.[53] When a marked downturn in the West German economy in the late summer and early fall of 1966 raised the possibility that the Erhard government might fall, the SED could barely conceal its enthusiasm at the prospect that the SPD might form a progressive coalition with the Free Democrats against the CDU. Accordingly, Ulbricht lost no time in announcing that he was ready to assume contacts with all of the "democratic forces" in the SPD.[54] When, however, the Social Democrats showed that they were more impressed with the long-term gains they could make by collaborating with the CDU/CSU, the SED First Secretary treated the decision as an outright betrayal of the national cause. The SPD had been presented with a historic opportunity, Ulbricht lamented openly, to pursue a policy of moderation in the question of relations with the GDR and, in so doing, to contribute to an easing of tensions in Europe. Yet, while his government was prepared to do everything in its power to reciprocate any signs of fruitful dialogue that might emerge from the new Grand Coalition, he had no doubt that the party's unholy alliance with the forces of reaction was the harbinger of a new right-wing course that would inevitably lead to "intensified attacks on the GDR."[55]

   However propagandistic such assessments may have seemed, Ulbricht was not entirely off the track. In its comparative flexibility and its readiness to reassess its relations with the Eastern bloc as a whole, the CDU-SPD alliance was in fact more threatening to East Berlin than any previous West German government. For example, when Kiesinger and Brandt finally took the first unequivocal steps in early 1967 toward putting to rest the Hallstein Doctrine by exchanging diplomatic missions with Romania, the GDR's leaders readily saw that they were in danger of losing the support of all of their other allies on the national question. Behind the scenes, the Czechoslovaks, Bulgarians, and Hungarians all hoped to share in the economic and technological benefits promised by better relations with the

---

Berlin, March 21 and March 23, 1990. Hints of differences about the speaker exchange were already evident at the Twelfth Central Committee Plenum. See, for example, the addresses by Hermann Matern and Heinz Hoffmann. File number IV 2/1/193, pp. 122, 138–140, CPA, Berlin.

   [53]Even after the collapse of the speakers' exchange, Herbert Häber, then deputy head of the State Secretariat for All-German Affairs, defended the idea that there were responsible elements in the SPD to whom it was worth talking. "Das Wesen der Demokratie und Freiheit: Der Kampf um demokratische Verhältnisse in Deutschland," unpublished lecture, Central Committee of the SED, July 8, 1966, pp. 5–30, Archives of the Academy for Social Sciences, East Berlin.

   [54]*ND*, November 14, 1966.

   [55]*ND*, November 30, 1966.

FRG. Furthermore, Khrushchev's successors in Moscow, Leonid Brezhnev and Alexei Kosygin, were sorely tempted by the Grand Coalition's more forthcoming gestures in the area of foreign affairs and actively sought Bonn's aid in their own efforts, first enunciated in the summer of 1966, to convene a continentwide security conference to affirm Soviet hegemony over Eastern Europe.[56] As a result, Ulbricht found himself by the spring of 1967 in a position that was not that different from Adenauer in the late 1950s, trying desperately to convince his allies that they should refrain from negotiating with the West until Bonn had first shown its willingness to take East Berlin's demands seriously.

An even greater, if more subtle, danger for the East German regime was to be found in the Grand Coalition's additional intimations of interest in a formal relationship with the GDR below the level of full diplomatic relations. As the probability grew that East Berlin might be compelled by the logic of its own position to take up active talks with the FRG, many of those members of the party leadership who earlier had had reservations about Ulbricht's emphasis on the national issue began, ever so tentatively, to express their doubts about their leader's constant appeals to all-German themes. For them, it simply made more sense to emphasize those issues that *separated* the GDR's citizens from their West German cousins. Werner Lamberz, a full member of the politburo, introduced a new accent to his government's national vocabulary when he told a meeting of Central Committee secretaries in January 1967 that the main task before them was to develop a distinct "GDR consciousness." "We are speaking about a socialist GDR," he emphasized, "a sovereign GDR. West Germany no longer has any influence on the development of the GDR, economically, politically, [or] culturally."[57] At the same forum, his colleague, Axen, went even further by explicitly denouncing speculation about German unity as "nonsense" (*Unsinn*). "There is no partner in West Germany," he stressed, in an unmistakable jab at Ulbricht's past policies, "either for a confederation or for reunification."[58]

In this light, even well-informed members of the party elite were led to expect that the final break would be made with Ulbricht's national policy when the SED's Seventh Congress convened in April 1967. In the first part of the year, the regime already appeared to be seeking to refashion its institutions and the language of political discourse in a way that would set the GDR apart from everything that could remind its citizens of a national

[56]Gerhard Wettig, *Die Sowjetunion, die DDR und die Deutschland-Frage* (Stuttgart: Verlag Bonn Aktuell, 1977), pp. 52–53.

[57]Cited in Klaus-Uwe Koch, "Das Problem der Nation in der Strategie und Taktik der SED in der zweiten Hälfte der sechziger Jahre," unpublished dissertation (A), Academy of Social Sciences, East Berlin, July 1985, p. 69.

[58]Ibid., p. 65.

bond with the FRG. The State Secretariat for All-German Affairs was re-designated to deal with West Germany alone. A new citizenship law was promulgated that eliminated past references to a single German citizenship. Some party leaders even went so far as to remove the "D" (for "Deutschland") in their public references to the SPD!

However, quite unlike the situation in the FRG, where interparty competition at least opened the way for compromises on select aspects of the country's national policy, it was a proof of the decisive influence Ulbricht retained over his government that, despite the pressures around him, the SED stuck to its old course. To be sure, there were subtle indications at the party congress that the shift in the West German approach to the GDR embodied by Kiesinger's call for formal contacts had forced the SED to alter its tactics somewhat. Instead of speaking of "reunification," party leaders began to refer to the historically less problematic concept of German "unification." Also, there was almost no mention in the congress proceedings of the First Secretary's decade-long proposals for a German confederation. Still, Ulbricht showed that he was not yet ready to abandon the GDR's claims to a special role in the resolution of the national question when he emphasized, to the surprise of many of his colleagues, that the "unification of the German states" remained his government's chief goal. "We German Marxists and Leninists," he stressed, "have never written off the unitary, peaceful and progressive German state . . . and we will never do so."[59]

Despite the seeming irrationality of his stand, Ulbricht's determination not to change course may have been based on perfectly sound reasoning about the sorts of reversals that his population was likely to welcome in the government's national policy.[60] At the time, SED internal opinion polls revealed that popular attachment to the German nation continued to be strong among East Germans; apparently some citizens even felt that their party had gone too far in distancing itself from its national heritage.[61] Nevertheless, it is also important to recognize that Ulbricht was driven by higher ideals than his population's wishes alone. As in the past, he seems to have remained convinced that the best way of combatting the challenge

---

[59]*ND*, April 18, 1967.

[60]Ulbricht did the right thing if the behavior of the participants at the party congress may be used as a measure. One participant relates: "Everyone expected that this [congress] would be the last word on the national question, that we would finally delimit [*abgrenzen*] ourselves from the FRG. But Ulbricht said something quite different—he still insisted that the working class would establish unity. There was tremendous applause! A proof that this idea of German unity was very hard to get rid of. I think Ulbricht probably thought that the masses wouldn't accept a change. We had been telling them, and members of the SED, for years that unity would come; many had come from other parts of Germany. We still wanted to experience a whole Germany." Author's interview, Heinz Hümmler, East Berlin, May 31, 1989.

[61]Koch, "Das Problem," pp. 72–73, 110–112.

from the West was to stay out front on the national issue, openly competing with the FRG for the stewardship of the nation.

It is noteworthy, therefore, that during those years when the Grand Coalition was stumbling toward a coherent German policy, the SED kept up its barrage of seemingly conciliatory, if ultimately unworkable, overtures to the FRG. It was not the GDR's fault, the First Secretary insisted in an address in March 1968, that Bonn still refused to recognize Europe's prevailing borders, that it maintained its revanchist claims to speak for all of the German people, or that it continued to pursue the "totally unrealistic" goal of annexing the "special political entity" of West Berlin. All the West German government had to do if it sincerely wished to break the deadlock between the Germanys was to recognize reality, which meant accepting the GDR as a separate and equal state and establishing normal diplomatic relations. Then, he argued, one could begin to overcome the national divide.[62]

Once again, the trouble with these offers, as Ulbricht had to have realized, was that they provided almost no room for compromise. Yet this was precisely the point. If, by compromise, one meant that the GDR would have sacrificed its pretensions to play the role of the rump state for a reunified Germany—Ulbricht still left no doubt that he expected such an entity to be socialist eventually[63]—then the East German leader was not interested in talking. In fact, his public posture at the time seems most striking because of the extent to which it mirrored the stands that he had taken almost a decade earlier about the GDR's model character. Not only was the East German economy sure to hold its own in the race to keep up with the West in offering its citizens modern living standards, but it now seemed that it was perfectly positioned to lay the foundations for what the First Secretary called a "human community" (Menschengemeinschaft), in which the citizens of East Germany would share in their common achievements and relate to each other in new ways.[64]

Had such boasting been limited to words alone, one might have written off Ulbricht's proclamations as little more than empty bravado. However, his words also had direct implications for a wide range of the GDR's priorities, since almost no aspect of East German policymaking seemed to be immune to the First Secretary's drive to compete on a par with the Federal Republic. In 1968, Ulbricht proved to be so eager to establish his country's claims to distinction that he took the radical step of abandoning the relatively well-balanced Five Year Plan that his government had introduced in

[62]ND, March 14, 1968.
[63]Ibid.
[64]Author's interviews with Heinz Hümmler and Günter Tschacher, Academy of Social Sciences, East Berlin, May 31, 1989, and June 2, 1989.

1. Chancellor Konrad Adenauer, middle, presents the Allied High Commission with his cabinet, September 21, 1949. Third from left, Minister of All-German Affairs Jakob Kaiser. (Courtesy German Information Center [GIC])

2. Konrad Adenauer (chancellor, FRG, September 15, 1949–October 16, 1963). (Courtesy GIC)

3. Walter Ulbricht (General Secretary, later First Secretary, of the Socialist Unity Party, July 25, 1950–May 3, 1971). (Courtesy GIC)

4. Konrad Adenauer, visiting for the first time the fortifications that would become the Berlin Wall, August 24, 1961. (Courtesy GIC)

5. Konrad Adenauer with his successor Ludwig Erhard (chancellor, FRG, October 16, 1963–December 1, 1966). (Courtesy GIC)

6. Kurt Georg Kiesinger (chancellor, FRG, December 1, 1966–October 21, 1969). (Courtesy GIC)

7. Walter Ulbricht, speaking at the twentieth anniversary celebrations of the GDR's founding, October 7, 1969. (Courtesy GIC)

8. Willy Brandt (chancellor, FRG, October 21, 1969–May 16, 1974) meeting for the first time with GDR prime minister, Willi Stoph, in Erfurt, March 19, 1970. (Courtesy GIC)

9. Egon Bahr, left, and Michael Kohl sign the Basic Treaty, December 21, 1972. (Courtesy GIC)

1966 and replaced it with a program of accelerated economic growth. By funneling investment capital into only the very strongest sectors of East German industry (for example, chemicals, machine tools), this scheme was supposed to enable the GDR quickly to attain world-class economic standards.[65]

Steps such as this one were important because they slowly but surely led to the alienation of many of those who had supported Ulbricht since the GDR's founding, both within his country and in the Soviet Union as well. Nevertheless, the existence of dissatisfaction alone can hardly have pushed the East German leader to embrace a new German policy. In a system where so much power was concentrated in the office of the First Secretary, only the removal of Ulbricht himself could allow for the kind of break- through that was finally achieved with the negotiation of the inter-German treaty in the summer and early fall of 1972. To appreciate this point, however, and especially its later relevance for the evolution of East Berlin's ties with Bonn, it is helpful to see why very different conditions led to a corresponding shift in the Eastern policy of the FRG. For the change in West German policy was at once a signal of how far the FRG's leaders might go to accommodate the East if the political circumstances were right and an indication of how uncertain their options could be if these same conditions were to turn against them.

Bonn's Breakthrough: The Ostpolitik

There are two facts that no one will dispute about the changes that were introduced to West German foreign policy in 1969. The first is that when Brandt made his inaugural address on October 28 as the leader of a newly formed coalition of the Social Democrats and Free Democrats, he an- nounced a definitive break with the confrontational vocabulary that had typified past West German approaches to the East. In one breath, the new chancellor made known both his government's hopes to seek a reconcilia- tion with its old adversaries on the continent (a "European peace order," he called it) by exchanging renunciation-of-force agreements with the So- viet Union, Poland, and Czechoslovakia and also its desires to include the GDR fully in the process. Brandt's only qualification was that his admin- istration would never be willing to treat East Germany as a separate nation. It was "not a foreign country" (*nicht Ausland*). Nevertheless, the fact that he failed even to mention the term "reunification" in his speech and openly

[65]Michael Sodaro, "Ulbricht's Grand Design: Economics, Ideology, and the GDR's Re- sponse to Detente," *World Affairs* 142, no. 3 (Winter 1980), pp. 147–168.

acknowledged the existence of two separate German *states* showed that he was ready to put the immediate benefits of cooperation with the GDR before his country's dreams of national reunion.[66]

Just as indisputably, Brandt could not have been presented with more propitious external circumstances for taking such a stand, since all of the major powers around him, the Soviet Union and the United States included, had reason to welcome Bonn's readiness to make its peace with the continental status quo. Moscow had stepped up its efforts to convene the conference on European security, which it had first proposed in 1966, and it was commonly understood that only the West Germans' acquiescence would have made such a meeting feasible. At the same time, a new American president, Richard Nixon, had also let it be known that the United States' interest in a more stable relationship with the USSR was contingent upon the resolution of the remaining conflicts of the Cold War period. To this end, Nixon informed the Soviets that he hoped finally to reach an amicable settlement of the old Berlin conflict.

Nonetheless, while the new chancellor may have felt heartened by the happy convergence of his regime's interests with those of the states surrounding the Federal Republic, it is hard to imagine how the shift in Bonn's priorities could have come about as quickly or as completely as it did if Brandt had not also had political fortune on his side. As it was, there was nothing inevitable about the formation of the new governing coalition, which enjoyed only a slim electoral advantage (just over 2 percent of the national vote) over the CDU/CSU. Both Wehner and the SPD's parliamentary leader, Helmut Schmidt, had actively flirted with the idea of maintaining the Grand Coalition with Kiesinger to retain the confidence of the West German voting public.[67] Plus, there were even hopeful signs (for example, in the CDU's Berlin program of November 1968)[68] that the Christian Democrats were open to being slightly more flexible in their handling of the national question.

Still, it is doubtful that the Union forces would ever have agreed to Brandt's pace of innovation, if only because the fundamentalist elements within the conservative parties would have ripped the coalition apart. Nor for that matter does it seem likely that the formation of a coalition between the CDU and the FDP would have produced any better results. Given the Liberals' small numbers and the resistance within the party to moving any faster to revise Bonn's national policy, an alliance with the CDU would

[66]Cited in Meissner, *Deutsche Ostpolitik*, pp. 380–383.

[67]Arnulf Baring, *Machtwechsel: The Ära Brandt-Scheel* (Stuttgart: Deutsche Verlags-Anstalt, 1983), pp. 171–173.

[68]See the excerpts in Meissner, *Deutsche Ostpolitik*, pp. 317–319.

probably have neutralized the efforts of other Free Democrats to promote more extensive contacts with the East.[69]

This is why the existence of the Social-Liberal coalition must be regarded as nothing less than an integral part of Brandt's later success. For one thing, the FDP was the perfect coalition partner for the SPD. The Liberal leadership had never really forgiven the CDU for dropping it from the governing coalition in 1966,[70] and those Free Democrats who had risen to the top of the party during its years of isolation (for example, Walter Scheel, who became foreign minister under Brandt) were determined to free the FDP of any association with the policies of the Christian Democratic past. Scheel's minimal exposure to foreign policy proved to be an added bonus for the SPD, since Brandt was able to draw upon his own experience and the advice of a close circle of confidantes to concentrate most foreign policy decision-making within the Federal chancellery.[71]

The new coalition's greatest advantage, however, was undoubtedly provided by the CDU/CSU's inability to mount an effective challenge to its policies. From the very first, both of the Union parties were divided over how best to respond to Brandt's opening to the East. A sizable minority within the CDU leadership, including the party's *Fraktion* leader, Rainer Barzel, believed that some form of accommodation with the Communist bloc was unavoidable, both because the West German public was increasingly showing signs of favoring such overtures and because the United States had already given its blessing to the cause of East-West dialogue.[72] Nonetheless, an equally powerful group of opposition critics, centered in the CSU and among the various expellee organizations, was much less charitable to the SPD-FDP government. Politicians like Strauß argued that,

---

[69]See Kaack, *Zur Geschichte*, p. 41. Kaack notes that because the FDP Bundestag representation was so small (thirty voting members), it was difficult for the party's somewhat stronger reformist wing to replace its critics with younger members more likely to favor innovation.

[70]Kiesinger did not help matters either. Upon learning that the Liberals were unwilling to form a coalition with his party in 1969, he declared that it would be the CDU's priority in the five upcoming *Länder* elections of 1970 to "catapult" the FDP out of office. See Baring, *Machtwechsel*, pp. 152–170. On the FDP's cooperation with the SPD, see Reinhold Roth, *Aussenpolitische Innovation und Politische Herrschaftssicherung* (Meisenheim am Glan: Verlag Anton Hain, 1976), p. 45.

[71]On the institutional strengths of Brandt's chancellorship, see Günther Schmid, *Entscheidung in Bonn: Die Entstehung der Ost- und Deutschlandpolitik, 1969/1970* (Cologne: Verlag Wissenschaft und Politik, 1979), pp. 181–193.

[72]Author's interview, Hansjürgen Schierbaum, Bonn, October 21, 1987. For background perspectives on U.S. interests, see Kurt Birrenbach, *Meine Sondermissionen* (Düsseldorf: Econ, 1984), pp. 300–308, and Paul Frank's unusual pseudonymous portrayal of the adventures of diplomatic advisor "Caspar Hilzinger," *Entschlüsselte Botschaft* (Stuttgart: Deutsche Verlags-Anstalt, 1981), pp. 214, 286–287, passim.

at best, the Brandt coalition was acting naively in opening itself so easily to negotiations with the East; at worst, however, it was running the risk of signing away the leverage the FRG still enjoyed on the national question.[73]

By themselves, the policy differences between these groups would have been enough to frustrate any efforts to generate a common position within the Union ranks. Yet, quite apart from their substantive disagreements, the debate about the *Ostpolitik* also reflected the CDU/CSU's deeper inability to come to terms with the reality that it was no longer in power. The Christian Democrats had led every West German administration since the FRG's founding in 1949. In view of the narrow margin with which Brandt's government had been formed, it was understandable that many Union members, moderates and conservatives alike, viewed the Social-Liberal coalition as nothing more than a "factory mishap" (*Betriebsunfall*) that would soon be remedied when they were returned to power. The absence, however, of an easy consensus about how this task was to be accomplished meant that the diverse constituencies that supported the CDU/CSU frequently spent more time arguing among themselves than fashioning a coherent challenge to the SPD-FDP regime.

In this sense, Brandt's situation was, by the standards of West German party competition in the 1960s *and* what was still to come in the 1970s, quite atypical and probably more akin to the period of Adenauer's dominance than any other. Yet this situation also meant that the administration's achievements were bound to be atypical as well. Far from having constantly to heed the complaints of his opposition critics, the chancellor was able to take steps toward the East already in his first year in office that would scarcely have been conceivable in the FRG's first decades. His first accomplishment, ultimately crucial for the opening of serious negotiations with the GDR, was the successful conclusion of the renunciation-of-force agreements with Moscow in August 1970, and with Warsaw only a few months later, in December 1970. In both instances, the treaties were masterpieces of the art of diplomatic compromise. The FRG's leaders assured their Soviet and Polish counterparts of their readiness to treat all existing state boundaries in Europe as "inviolable," and this promise included the touchy matter of Poland's western Oder-Neisse border. But Brandt and his coalition partners, not wanting to forsake their national options completely, nevertheless managed to hold open the possibility that the continental status quo might someday be changed by peaceful means.

[73]For a detailed analysis of the contending positions within the CDU/CSU, see Clay Clemens, *Reluctant Realists* (Durham, N.C.: Duke University Press, 1989), esp. chap. 2. Additionally, for some reflections on Franz Josef Strauß's approach to the national question, which say more about his lust for power than about any sincere interest in national unity, see Klaus Bloemer, "Außenpolitische Vorstellungen und Verhaltensweisen des F. J. Strauß," *Liberal*, July–August 1980, pp. 609–624.

In the rarefied political atmosphere of the time, however, Brandt's even greater accomplishment may have been the initiation of the contacts with East Berlin that led to the first face-to-face meeting between the heads of government of East and West Germany. In early 1970, Brandt and the GDR premier, Willy Stoph, began an exchange of letters on the requisites for an equivalent inter-German agreement in which they staked out many of the issues—diplomatic representation, citizen contacts, and legal recognition—that would define the substance of their regimes' negotiations throughout the 1970s. Yet nothing could match the significance of the highly publicized, face-to-face talks the two leaders held, first in the East German city of Erfurt, on March 19, and later in the West German city of Kassel, on May 21, 1970. Brandt's presence in the GDR alone was a telling demonstration that Bonn was truly coming to terms with East Germany's existence as a separate state.

To be sure, the West German chancellor and his East German interlocutor were unable to reach any agreements of substance during their meetings. Consistent with his government's policy, Stoph maintained that serious negotiations could begin only when the Federal government was prepared to accord the GDR full diplomatic recognition. Then, too, while Brandt must have pleased the East German premier with his explicit renunciation of the FRG's claims to speak for the entire German nation, there was enough in his catalog of demands to demonstrate that Bonn was intent upon preserving a special relationship with the other German state. This was practically the opposite of East Berlin's intentions. In a famous list of twenty points, for example, which Brandt introduced in Kassel, he called on the GDR to allow for more "freedom of movement" over its borders and to act in the interests of "the nation's cohesion."[74] Still, in view of the near absence of contacts between the Germanys over the preceding decades, the incalculable value of the two meetings was that they had taken place at all. Each suggested, as the Basic Treaty was to confirm two years later, that neither the GDR nor the FRG could any longer hope to conduct its national policy without some form of interaction with the other.

Of course, we know where these contacts eventually led. But to understand the manifold difficulties that the Social-Liberal coalition would encounter in the implementation of its national policy some five to ten years down the road, it is also important to underscore the painful awareness of Brandt's opponents in the CDU/CSU of how much the chancellor was able to exploit his good fortune—and their disorganization—to cultivate support for his policies among the West German electorate. Indeed, many of his

[74]*Kassel, 21. Mai 1970: Eine Dokumentation* (Bonn: Presse- und Informationsamt, 1970), pp. 86–88.

advantages at the turn of the 1970s would later come back to haunt the governing coalition and his successor, Helmut Schmidt.

The depth of the CDU/CSU's disarray was first made apparent in its leaders' inability even to agree upon an effective response to the Moscow and Warsaw treaties. For a while, Barzel, who became the CDU chairman in 1971, was able to cover up the Union's ambivalence by emphasizing that an American-inspired provision in both treaties made ratification of the two agreements contingent upon the conclusion of a four-power accord on Berlin.[75] Yet when on September 3, 1971, the United States, the USSR, Great Britain, and France finally reached a Berlin settlement, effectively circumventing their old disputes about the city's status by agreeing on a number of practical measures to guarantee the integrity and accessibility of West Berlin, Barzel and other moderates in the opposition ranks were once again at the mercy of Brandt's accelerated pace of foreign policy change.

Had he had his druthers, the CDU leader himself would evidently have been happy to portray the opposition parties as simply honest critics of the Eastern treaties who, if given the chance, would merely seek to improve the agreements by assigning greater weight to the FRG's long-term national goals.[76] But Barzel's problem was that he could never be sure of his ability to maintain this position. Despite an improving climate between the Soviet Union and the United States, which was itself causing growing numbers of Christian Democrats to reevaluate their opposition to East-West détente, there were still many other individuals within the CDU, not to mention the CSU, who remained unalterably opposed to any such agreements, including even the Berlin accord. The CDU chairman's only choice, therefore—or so Barzel interpreted his options as the ratification debates over the Moscow and Warsaw agreements began in early 1972—was to bring the Union forces first back to power and then to attempt, with the excuse of governmental responsibility to justify his actions, to hammer out an acceptable agreement on the treaties.

Decades later, leading members of the CDU/CSU would still ask themselves whether the means Barzel chose to resolve this dilemma were appropriate for the circumstances. On April 27, 1972, he took the unprecedented step of calling for a "constructive vote of no-confidence" in the Brandt government. Had he waited and, as some of his colleagues (like the young Helmut Kohl) urged at the time, sought instead to focus his party's criticisms on matters in which the Brandt coalition was more vulnerable (for example, economic policy), Barzel might ultimately have assured him-

---

[75] Clemens, *Reluctant Realists*, pp. 108–109, 112.

[76] See Barzel's famous "*So nicht!*" ("Not this way!") speech of February 23, 1972, in which he argued that the basic idea behind the treaties was correct but their formulation needed improvement. See *Texte zur Deutschlandpolitik*, vol. 10 (1972), p. 168.

self of the votes necessary for toppling the Social-Liberal coalition.[77] Nevertheless, while the CDU leader did come breathtakingly close to unseating the chancellor, thanks to the defection of key Social Democratic and Free Democratic parliamentarians to the Union ranks,[78] the decision of three members of Barzel's own party not to vote against Brandt kept the government from falling, and the passage of the Eastern treaties was assured.

Who can say how the history of the Federal Republic might have been altered if Barzel had succeeded in forming a new governing coalition. Certainly, the path of the *Ostpolitik* and all of Brandt's efforts to regularize relations with the GDR would have been slowed. Still, it is one of the abiding ironies of policymaking in the FRG that later governments might also have been spared the years of tense interparty antagonism that were to come in the 1970s. Had Barzel lived up to his hopes of encouraging all the West German parties to come to a mutually acceptable compromise on the accords, this explosive element in their relations might have been defused. After the vote's defeat, however, deeply felt political divisions remained to impair Brandt's opening to the East. This meant that just about every effort to locate an acceptable middle ground between the Bonn government and its critics was bound to come to naught.

Admittedly, during the last days of the debates over the Eastern treaties, there was a certain pathos to the CDU chairman's futile attempts to convince other conservatives to support the accords, providing that Brandt would accept subtle changes in the agreements' language about the way in which they addressed German national concerns. In the end, however, Barzel only managed to save the CDU/CSU the public opprobrium of wrecking the accords by convincing his colleagues to abstain on the final votes.[79] Nevertheless, although the Moscow and Warsaw treaties did pass through the Bundestag, this was a pyrrhic victory at best. For the vote of no-confidence had weakened the Brandt regime just enough to insure that the Social-Liberal coalition would have to call early elections to regain its governing majority at precisely that juncture when it was poised to begin the most important negotiations of all, over the inter-German Basic Treaty.

For quite some time, at least since the late fall of 1970, the two German states had been conducting talks behind the scenes on a host of technical matters relating to the establishment of ties between their gov-

---

[77]Author's interviews, Kurt Biedenkopf, Bonn, March 10, 1988. For Kohl's alternate position, see Geoffrey Pridham, "The CDU Opposition in West Germany, 1969–1972," *Parliamentary Affairs* 26, no. 2 (Spring 1973), pp. 201–217.

[78]Even prominent Social Democrats, Willy Brandt among them, seem to have become convinced that their government would fall. See Baring, *Machtwechsel*, p. 419.

[79]A number of CDU and CSU parliamentarians still refused to heed his advice and voted against the accords. For Barzel's reasoning, see *Auf dem Drahtseil* (Munich: Droemer Knauer, 1978), p. 167.

ernments. The Berlin accord a year later, however, gave the two states' representatives—Michael Kohl, on the Eastern side, and Egon Bahr, on the Western side—exactly the impetus they needed to begin work on the mechanics of the agreement that would become the Basic Treaty. The four-power agreement explicitly directed the GDR and the FRG to resolve the practical issues involving transit between West Berlin and the FRG that had been such a burden to the East-West relationship since the 1950s. But in addition, it also provided a ready excuse for conducting talks about facilitating inter-German travel on an even broader level, with the result that contacts between the two states were finally formalized. For the first time since the Wall's construction, the Transit Treaty of May 26, 1972, created conditions that enabled average West Germans to make private visits to their relatives and friends in the East on a regular basis. To a very limited extent, the same possibility was even offered to their East German counterparts to make short trips to the FRG in cases of "urgent family need."

Once again, however, the Brandt government's motives in conducting these negotiations were very much intertwined with its domestic political agendas. Because its rivals in the CDU/CSU had always insisted that "humanitarian improvements" (*menschliche Erleichterungen*) should be an integral part of any long-term understanding with the GDR, there was no way that the Union parties could have objected to the new transit agreement. Nonetheless, as Bahr and Kohl began negotiations in earnest over the following summer about the more comprehensive inter-German agreement to come, it became fully apparent just how politicized Bonn's dealings were with the GDR. With evidence to suggest that the majority of West Germans now supported the Eastern initiatives, the governing coalition would have been foolhardy not to have made the question of expanded contacts into a central theme in its campaign to regain a parliamentary majority.[80] Still, the government would later have reason to regret the calculating way in which it linked considerations of sheer political expediency with national policy.

---

[80]This was particularly true among young voters. As early as July 1969, 67 percent of young respondents in one poll favored coming to a "good relationship" with the GDR; perhaps more telling, 62 percent of young CDU/CSU voters (versus 65 percent for the SPD, and 82 percent for the FDP) were of this opinion. In successive polls among all voters between November 1967 and January 1971, support for recognizing the GDR as a separate state went from 27 percent to 42 percent. More generally, when eligible voters were asked in August 1972 what appealed to them about the party of their choice, 74 percent replied positively to the statement, "It wants to continue reconciliation and détente with the East." See E. Noelle-Neumann and E. P. Neumann, *Jahrbuch der öffentlichen Meinung, 1968 bis 1973* (Allensbach: Verlag für Demoskopie, 1974), pp. 322, 332, and 510. See Ludolf Eltermann, Helmut Jung, and Werner Kaltefleiter, "Drei Fragen zur Bundestagswahl 1972," *Aus Politik und Zeitgeschichte*, November 17, 1973, pp. 1–22, for evidence that many CDU voters supported the governing coalition because of the *Ostpolitik*.

It can have been no coincidence, for example, that the chancellor chose September 20, 1972, the very day the Bundestag was scheduled to vote on the transit accord, to arrange for his government to fall, since this event cleared the way for what was to become a national referendum on the *Ostpolitik*. Yet it was the unabashedly self-serving manner in which the SPD sought to exploit its dialogue with the GDR to its electoral advantage, by pressing for a quick conclusion to negotiations over the Basic Treaty, which made the subsequent election battle even more acrimonious than it might otherwise have been. In particular, when Brandt arranged to have the treaty initialled but *not* formally signed on November 8, just eleven days before the parliamentary elections, his message was just as clear to the parties in the West German opposition as to his potential supporters: a vote for him and for the Social-Liberal coalition was a vote for a new and hopeful relationship with the East, whereas a vote for the CDU/CSU was at best a matter of risking the unknown.[81] This coupling of power politics with the appeal of a substantively new policy clearly served the SPD's and FDP's short-term purposes, for on November 19 the coalition was returned to power with its largest majority ever.[82] Nevertheless, the victory also left a legacy of bitterness and a longing for revenge in the ranks of the coalition's opponents that would haunt the inter-German accord for almost a decade.

The End of the Ulbricht Era

If atypical political circumstances were required for the initial breakthrough in the West German *Ostpolitik*, it stands to reason that even more unusual conditions must have been required to bring the East German government to reevaluate its options. At least in the FRG, the conservative opposition parties were agreed about the need to modify an outdated policy. But in the GDR, in contrast, the absence of any institutional mechanisms to force a review of past approaches to the West meant that Ulbricht's reading of his country's national priorities was practically unassailable.

It was perhaps to be expected that the East German government would

[81]One of the members of the West German negotiating team for the Basic Treaty relates about the final talks with East Berlin that "our whole emphasis was on getting the initialing (*Paraphierung*) done in eight days, so that the regime could say 'if you elect us, we'll get this [document] ratified.'" Author's interview, Antonio Eitel, Bonn, January 19, 1988. On the bitterness with which both the ruling coalition and the opposition forces conducted the election contest, see Jaeger's account in *Republik im Wandel*, pp. 86–90.

[82]For evidence about the connection between the *Ostpolitik* and the Social-Liberal victory, see Max Kaase, "Die Bundestagswahl 1972, Probleme und Analysen," *Politische Vierteljahresschrift* 14 (1973), pp. 145–190.

evince a certain amount of tactical flexibility in the late fall of 1969 when its Soviet allies signaled their willingness to pursue the renunciation-of-force talks with Bonn that would lead to the Moscow Treaty of the following summer. Suddenly, everyone from Erich Honecker to Willi Stoph to Ulbricht himself seemed to be transformed into thoughtful, if qualified, supporters of the new Social-Liberal coalition. In particular, they credited Brandt with finally acknowledging the GDR's existence as a separate German state and for abandoning Bonn's "revanchist" claims to speak for all Germans. The remaining question, a fundamental one, was whether the new chancellor would go on to draw the relevant conclusions from his statement about the GDR's equal standing under international law.[83] Accordingly, in late December 1969 the SED regime sought to push the Brandt government in its direction by sending the West German president, Gustav Heinemann, a treaty outlining the establishment of full diplomatic relations.

In itself, East Berlin's readiness to talk with the Bonn regime was a significant event, although it quickly became clear that the country's leaders (Ulbricht above all) still expected the FRG to meet their main demands before they would consider even the most practical issues surrounding an inter-German agreement.[84] This was the unmistakable tone which Stoph adopted in the first of his meetings with Brandt in Erfurt. While the West German chancellor spoke of his hopes of improving the two states' ties in the spirit of "good-neighborly cooperation" and "respect for the territorial integrity and borders of the other side," Stoph not only insisted that Bonn completely abandon its policy of attributing a "special" character to the inter-German relationship but also imposed a new demand on the FRG—that it pay the GDR DM 100 million in reparations for the damage ostensibly done to the country's economy in the years of open borders. When the two leaders met again in Kassel in May, Stoph proved to be no more forthcoming. Rather than respond to Brandt's twenty-point plan on formal relations—in its essentials, the eventual basis for the Basic Treaty— he simply broke off all further talks, contending that his West German counterpart clearly needed more "time for thought" (a *Denkpause*, as he put it) to see that there was no alternative to recognizing the GDR completely.

[83]See *ND*, November 10, 1969; *ND*, November 12, 1969; and *ND*, December 14, 1969.
[84]See Ulbricht's statement in *ND*, January 15, 1970, making the exchange of full diplomatic ties a prerequisite for any improvement in relations. Behind the scenes, Ulbricht was even tougher, as one can see from the background report for a meeting he held with Soviet leaders on December 3, 1969, in Moscow: Brandt was practicing a policy of differentiation toward the Warsaw Pact, he warned; yet, "only" (*erst dann*) when the Bonn government was prepared to recognize the GDR would East Berlin's East European allies be justified in assuming formal ties with the FRG. See his report (IV 2/1/230), CPA, Berlin.

For at least two distinct reasons, however, this show of East German toughness masked some very real uncertainties that were on the rise in the SED politburo about the wisdom of continuing along the party's traditional course. First, the fact that these high-level talks were met with an unexpectedly volatile outpouring of popular feelings among the East German citizenry seems to have prompted many in the SED leadership—such as Ulbricht's heir apparent, Honecker—to wonder whether they could successfully balance their government's tributes to national reunification with their simultaneous efforts to create a separate socialist consciousness in the GDR. In the Erfurt meeting in particular, the dangers of the country's reexposure to the West after so many years of isolation were graphically illustrated by the spontaneous show of support Brandt received from the city's local population, as thousands of East German citizens crowded around the Hotel Erfurter Hof, jubilantly calling out his name.[85]

But in addition, for many in the party leadership, again including Honecker, there was also a growing sense of unease about Ulbricht's handling of relations with the Soviet Union. Already, by the end of the 1960s, tensions had arisen between Soviet officials and the GDR over the First Secretary's various claims to distinction for his country. On numerous occasions, Leninist ideologues, such as Boris Ponomarev and Mikhail Suslov had let their counterparts in East Berlin know that they disapproved of the East German leader's forays in the realm of ideological innovation and his use of such ambitious concepts as *Menschengemeinschaft*. More important, complaints about Ulbricht's arrogance and "air of superiority" (to quote Leonid Brezhnev himself) were to be found at the highest levels of the Kremlin leadership.[86] Even the GDR's role in arranging the Erfurt and Kassel meetings was considered suspect. Despite the fact that the encounters were grudgingly tolerated by Moscow, they too seem to have occurred largely as a result of Ulbricht's independent initiative.[87]

[85]However, for a nuanced and for the most part positive assessment of the Brandt-Stoph meeting in Erfurt, see the confidential report by the first secretary of the Leipzig *Bezirk*, Paul Fröhlich, to Ulbricht, in Gerhard Naumann and Eckhard Trümpler, *Der Flop mit der DDR-Nation 1971* (Berlin: Dietz, 1991), pp. 171–175.

[86]Author's interviews, Heinz Hümmler and Günter Tschacher, East Berlin, May 31, 1989, and June 2, 1989. Brezhnev addressed the issue in an impassioned letter to Erich Honecker on July 28, 1970: "People say that in the GDR the best model of socialism has been developed or will be. . . . I know how Walter handles this question, from personal experience. . . . He drives all of my [advisers] into a corner, he works me over [as if I were] in a hot room, I begin to sweat, but he won't give in. . . . One needs to get over this sense of superiority in the GDR. It hurts us all." Cited in Peter Przybylski, ed., *Tatort Politbüro: Die Akte Honecker* (Berlin: Rowohlt, 1991), pp. 284–285.

[87]One participant relates that as preparations began for the meetings, Soviet officials made nervous inquiries at the SED Central Committee in their efforts to keep abreast of the East German initiative. Author's discussion with Herbert Häber, East Berlin, March 21, 1990.

Against this background alone, it is easy to see why Moscow's efforts to reach its own understanding with the FRG at the end of the decade were bound to have led to a test of wills with the SED First Secretary, if only because they illuminated the divergence of Soviet and East German priorities. During the negotiations over the Moscow Treaty in the summer of 1970, the Kremlin had simply abandoned its long-standing efforts to press Bonn into granting the GDR full diplomatic recognition when it saw that the treaty was on the line. Furthermore, as part of a quid pro quo to guarantee that the accord would be ratified, the Soviets even gave their tacit blessing to a West German proviso that linked the agreement to the conclusion of a Berlin accord safeguarding the FRG's ties with the city. Yet, while Ulbricht tried to get his way by insisting that peace in Europe could only be insured if Bonn finally consented to the de jure recognition of his country, it was symptomatic of Moscow's disinclination to accede to his complaints any longer that Soviet spokesmen merely emphasized that compromise was required on all sides. Some states still needed "to reconcile themselves to the fact," as the CPSU daily *Pravda* lectured on August 18, "that West Germany has its own interests, like any other state, and seeks to pursue a policy which takes the real situation and real possibilities into account."[88]

Moscow's subsequent role in the four-power negotiations on Berlin, however, caused the most pronounced differences of all with the GDR's leader. As we have seen in the First Secretary's behavior in the 1950s, if any issue symbolized Ulbricht's commitment to a distinctly East German perspective on the national question, it was his conviction that his regime was entitled to a direct role in any settlement on the city's status. Despite this concern, when the Berlin talks first began to show signs of progress in September and October 1970, the Soviets demonstrated that they were no longer willing to let their ally's interests get in the way of an agreement. Even more openly than before, the two countries came close to a public conflict. No doubt spurred on by the fact that the West Germans were allowed to play an active part behind the scenes, Ulbricht let it be known that his government would not accept being left out of the negotiations. And, as if to prove that one could not ignore his regime's wishes with impunity, he again returned to the favored tactic in the 1950s of disrupting the Autobahn traffic to and from Berlin. If Leonid Brezhnev was impressed by his colleague's protests, however, he did not show it, and merely responded to Ulbricht with the chilly observation that the Soviet Union intended to take into account the needs of *all* of the parties to the conflict, including the "wishes of West Berlin's population."[89]

[88] *Pravda*, August 18, 1970. For Brezhnev's concern that Ulbricht might still come up with some "surprises" and even a veiled threat to use force to secure Soviet interests, see his letter to Honecker of July 28, 1970, in Przybylski, *Tatort*, pp. 280–282.

[89] Compare Ulbricht's remarks in *ND*, November 9, and *ND*, November 15, 1970, with Brezhnev's in *Pravda*, November 30, 1970.

How then could the GDR get back into step with the shifting priorities of its principal ally and at the same time adapt its own policies in such a way that the country would be sufficiently prepared to withstand the onslaught of a new era in East-West contacts? That quite a few of Ulbricht's colleagues were asking themselves these questions by the early fall of 1970 was demonstrated by a marked shift in the political idiom, epitomized above all by the arcane term, "delimitation" (*Abgrenzung*), which personalities such as Honecker, Stoph, Axen, and Hager used to characterize their state's emerging national agenda. While Ulbricht remained intent upon continuing his competition with the FRG for the leadership of the German nation, these individuals began to speak in ways that suggested that the specter of a fundamentally new relationship with the West called for a correspondingly new approach. In their view, the GDR had no other alternative than to concentrate on the immediate task of defining ("delimiting") for the East German population exactly where its interests lay in the contest with capitalism. Yet, for those who could see through the new terminology, "delimitation" meant nothing less than putting the whole theme of national reunification, not to mention the existence of any inter-German commonalities, on hold.[90]

Had these differences merely been confined to the realm of semantic controversy, it is conceivable that the East German leader could have remained in office for much longer than he did, since, failing Moscow's direct intervention, the domestic configuration of forces necessary to unseat a reigning First Secretary could not have been easily obtained within the secret sessions of the politburo. Even at this juncture, the sense of deference many still felt toward Ulbricht personally, as well as the abiding fear of dividing the party, were just too great. In this respect, it was not only important but also a crucial consideration that Ulbricht's ability to demonstrate the concrete benefits of his policies was also fading rapidly at the time. Even before his national policy came under scrutiny, the SED leader's grandiose efforts to compete on a par with the West German economy were clearly running aground. Severe bottlenecks had arisen in East German industrial production along with shortages in the supply of consumer goods, which no number of idealistic proclamations about the socialist future could overcome. It may have said something for the risk-averse political culture of the SED that many members of the party leadership were

---

[90]A close Soviet observer, Marina Pavlova-Silvanskaya, has suggested to me that the concept of "delimitation" was originally meant to be a direct assault on Ulbricht's policy of seeking to hold open the national issue. For evidence that the idea was, in fact, borrowed from Soviet sources, see Naumann and Trümpler, *Der Flop* p. 59. For the first Soviet use of the term in the context of GDR-FRG relations, see *ND*, January 29, 1967. For the earliest East German uses of the term, see Stoph in *ND*, October 7, 1970; Hager in *ND*, November 28, 1970; and Honecker in *ND*, January 31, 1971. Notably, because the concept cast doubt upon his national aspirations, Ulbricht rarely mentioned the term.

still agonizingly slow to acknowledge these problems and to appreciate the necessity of pursuing a more balanced economic course.[91] Yet, as evidence mounted of serious discontent among the country's work force, the almost religious devotion to the principle of party loyalty apparently could not survive the threat of economic collapse. With the outbreak in mid-December 1970 of work stoppages and antigovernment riots in neighboring Poland, the SED leadership was finally compelled to confront the possibility, really for the first time since the Wall's construction, of serious instability in the GDR. If it did not quickly alter its ways, the East German population might rise up against it, too.[92]

The SED's decision instead to rise against Ulbricht in the spring of 1971 said two things about the party's position. First, the politburo's role in ousting its longtime leader meant that any potential conflict that might have emerged with the Soviet Union over who should govern the GDR was automatically defused; both the SED and the CPSU had reasons, even if they were only indirectly related, for wanting Ulbricht replaced. Second, it would soon become apparent that the whole question of the country's opening to the West was also greatly simplified by the considerably more black-and-white perspective that the SED's new chief, Honecker, brought to East German policymaking in light of the failure of his predecessor's maximalist positions.

The difference in the Honecker government's style was immediately evident in the comparative ease with which East and West German negotiators were able to conduct their part of the follow-up agreements—on transit and tourism—to the four-power Berlin accord of September 1971. Whereas in the past, Soviet leaders might have genuinely feared that Ulbricht would seek to block any agreement that did not resolve the thorny

[91]Incredibly, as signs grew that the East German economy was in difficulty, some functionaries like Günter Mittag proved to be so set upon following Ulbricht's course that they recommended economic steps (e.g., major price increases) that would have made the situation worse. See Gerhard Naumann and Eckhard Trümpler, *Von Ulbricht zu Honecker* (Berlin: Dietz, 1990), pp. 26–30.

[92]The Polish events played a key role in the opposition to Ulbricht, although the first unequivocal sign that he was in trouble came a few days earlier at the Fourteenth Central Committee Plenum on December 9–11, 1970. See Paul Verner's slightly critical remarks in *ND*, December 10, 1970, as well as the then-unpublished criticisms by Hanna Wolf and Alfred Neumann, in Naumann and Trümpler, *Von Ulbricht zu Honecker*, pp. 114–126. One East German observer notes that although Ulbricht was formally deposed on May 3, 1971, the first concrete sign that he would be deprived of his powers came during a conference of *Kreis* (county) leaders on April 16–17, when a minor member of the Berlin delegation was charged with the task, in the First Secretary's presence, of openly attacking Ulbricht's views on the national question and the *Menschengemeinschaft*. "Then for the first time in the history of the GDR there was a great silence, the entire delegation stood up and left the room, and Ulbricht and Honecker sat alone. They all saw that Ulbricht had lost." Author's interview, Erich Nickel, East Berlin, June 11, 1988.

question of West Berlin's status in the GDR's favor, Honecker preferred (albeit, at times, to the point of misrepresenting the understanding that had been struck among the occupation powers)[93] to emphasize only those aspects of the accord which enhanced his government's claims to independence. Indeed, to the extent that the Soviets even became involved in the inter-German transit negotiations—as Brezhnev apparently did in a hastily arranged meeting with the new SED leader in early November 1971—it was only to bring the talks to a faster conclusion, since both parties, Moscow and East Berlin, could already take the favorable outcome of the negotiations for granted.

The best indication, however, of the Honecker government's readiness to accommodate itself to a revised definition of East German priorities was shown in the discussions that finally began in the summer of 1972 over the Basic Treaty. In stark contrast to Ulbricht's utopian visions about the GDR's contributions to the German future and his hopes of sustaining the dream of reunification under socialism, Honecker's strictly dichotomous image of the national dilemma was a breath of fresh air to those who were involved in the two states' talks. Under the new First Secretary's direction, it now seemed that history had already decided the German question, with the outcome that two fundamentally irreconcilable states were squared off against each other on either side of the national divide. If one were sincerely committed to the welfare of the East and West German people, Honecker advised, the only sensible approach was for both parties to accept each other for what they were, completely independent, self-sustaining entities that would best learn to live "with each other" (*miteinander*) in the interest of peace in Europe.[94]

Two States in Germany?

The appealing simplicity of this line of reasoning and the Brandt government's readiness to accept the factual existence of another German state were by no means easy guarantees that the inter-German negotiations that began on June 15, 1972, would proceed without complications. For months, the GDR and the FRG were at loggerheads over their maximal objectives. The one side continued to demand a status approximating de jure recognition with all of the accoutrements of national sovereignty (the exchange of ambassadors, United Nations membership, etc.), while the

---

[93]In an address on September 24, 1971, for example, he claimed (incorrectly) that the four occupation powers had for the first time "confirmed" the GDR's existence according to international law. See *Reden und Aufsätze* (hereafter *RA*), vol. 1 (Berlin: Dietz, 1975), p. 304.

[94]For example, Honecker's speech of June 6, 1972, in *RA*, vol. 1, p. 548.

other insisted that the Germanys' ties would still retain a "special" character, regardless of the normalization of relations. Given these stands, the two
states' representatives were frequently on the verge of an impasse throughout their talks during the summer of 1972.[95] Yet this was before one event
intervened that cast the German-German negotiations in an entirely new
light—Willy Brandt's decision to dissolve his government and prepare the
way for national elections by mid-November 1972.

We have already seen how, from the FRG's perspective, the prospect that
the Social-Liberal coalition might fall added an undeniable note of urgency
to Bonn's negotiations with the GDR, which can only have sped up the inter-
German talks. Those who were involved on the West German side admit
that the event induced them to be more forthcoming on key sticking points
with East Berlin, such as the way in which they addressed the Germanys'
differences on the national question.[96] However, although somewhat less
apparent at the time, the West German election may also have weakened
East Berlin's bargaining position as well. Up to this juncture, the GDR's
leaders had been able to comfort themselves with the knowledge that they
had one great advantage over Bonn. This was the luxury of being able to act
quickly and decisively in defense of their country's interests, since they did
not share the FRG's burden of having to appease a diverse domestic constituency.[97] Nonetheless, the ability to define the country's priorities and then
to realize them in practice were by no means the same thing once the GDR
had begun to interact with the FRG. After the SED recognized that some
form of inter-German agreement would be reached, the loss of support for
Brandt's government brought all of the vagaries of West German liberal
politics directly home to the East German elite. Provocatively, Honecker
and his colleagues had to ask themselves with whom they would rather do
business, the SPD and the FDP or a new West German administration
dominated by the Christian Democrats.

Evidently, the SED's new leader drew the predictable conclusion to this
question. "It cannot be a matter of indifference to us," he informed Egon

[95] Author's interview, Antonio Eitel, Bonn, January 19, 1988.

[96] Ibid. In later correspondence on January 2, 1992, Antonio Eitel qualified this point as
follows: "The possibility of a collapse of the Social-Liberal coalition certainly did have
consequences. On the one hand, the fact that some [Bundestag] deputies went over to the
opposition relieved the government of the necessity of having to make concessions to these
deputies. To this extent, [policymaking] was perhaps made easier. On the other hand, the need
to preserve the ever-decreasing majority also meant there had to be even greater consideration
of the views of the remaining members of the coalition. In this respect, one certainly became
less flexible."

[97] On this theme, see the illuminating dissertation (in part based on internal sources from
the GDR Ministry of Foreign Affairs) by Barbara Vogel, "Die Politik zur Herstellung verträglicher Beziehungen zwischen der DDR und der BRD in der ersten Hälfte der siebziger
Jahre," Akademie für Gesellschaftswissenschaften, Berlin, July 1987, pp. 44–46.

Bahr confidentially in mid-October, "who forms the new government in the FRG."[98] As a result, first tacitly and then openly, East German negotiators began to make concessions of their own to Bonn that were deliberately designed to return the Social-Liberal coalition to power. In a curious bargain in October, for example, the SED explicitly followed through on one of Bahr's suggestions when it announced a general amnesty for all East German citizens who had fled to the West before 1972. This decree allowed such individuals to return for short visits to their former home and at the same time may also have helped the governing coalition in Bonn to profit from the appearance that the inter-German talks were already bearing fruit.[99]

There is no way of determining how much such efforts to keep Brandt in office (jokingly referred to as "Brandt-protective weeks" [*Brandtschutz-wochen*] in internal party circles)[100] influenced the outcome of the negotiations over the Basic Treaty. It does seem that East Berlin was forced to accept an array of qualifications in the agreement (for example, on the exchange of "permanent representatives," and not full ambassadors) which cast doubt on its government's claims that this was an internationally binding treaty like any other. Nonetheless, Honecker seemed to speak for a majority in the SED when on November 16—just eight days after the initialing of the inter-German agreement—he openly criticized those in his party who still felt they could have gotten a better deal from Bonn: "Comrades, such transparent talk about a 'better' treaty is no help at all. There is no such thing as a better *Grundvertrag*."[101]

Just the same, the nagging question that had to have been on the minds of both the GDR's and the FRG's leaders in late 1972 was whether, after having come so far, they could count on a treaty alone to foster a self-sustaining relationship between the Germanys.

[98]Ibid., p. 72.

[99]Ibid., p. 73.

[100]The term is a pun on the German term for "fire-prevention week."

[101]*RA*, vol. 2 (Berlin: Dietz, 1977), p. 94. For example, in September 1972, East Berlin made a major concession by consenting to Bonn's demands to have a special "Letter on German Unity" accompany its signing of the Basic Treaty. This was evidently an acceptable compromise for Honecker. As he told Bahr in a meeting on September 9, "Whatever the FRG might declare unilaterally at the treaty's conclusion is its affair. The GDR will not contradict such assertions as long as they don't come too close to the positions of Barzel and Strauß." Cited in Vogel, "Die Politik," p. 50.

IV

Two German States: New Relations, Bad Relations

The process of the normalization of relations
between the GDR and the FRG has already begun.
  (Erich Honecker, June 6, 1972)

Previously, we have had no relations. [Now] we
will have bad ones, and this is progress. It will be
a long time before we have better ones.
  (Egon Bahr (1973)[1]

AFTER YEARS of almost no relations of any kind between the two German states, no one in East Berlin or Bonn could have expected their leaders to turn their attention to the Basic Treaty with the unqualified enthusiasm of individuals who had been apart only for a short time. It was widely accepted that hostilities ran deep between the GDR and the FRG, and only the most favorable circumstances were likely to encourage either of the countries' governments to put aside the unpleasant experiences of the recent past in the interest of cooperation. Thus, it was no accident that when East and West German authorities sought years later to account for the varied difficulties that they encountered in attempting to sort out their differences in the 1970s, they often reached for Egon Bahr's pithy formulation about the inter-German agreement: an era of no relations between East Berlin and Bonn would almost certainly be followed by one of bad relations.[2]

Yet Bahr's famous assessment of the treaty's prospects should not be taken as a sign of outright pessimism. In the immediate aftermath of the negotiation of the Basic Treaty, there was also reason for both German governments to be cautiously hopeful about the prospects before them. While the conditions for a healthy relationship were far from ideal—few could have expected them to be—there was no question that they were much more propitious than ever before. Additionally, with the FRG's agree-

---

[1] This is only one of many examples of Bahr's use of this phrase, from an interview in Günther Schmid, *Politik des Ausverkaufs* (Munich: tuduv, 1975), p. 257.

[2] When I conducted interviews on the Basic Treaty a decade and a half after its negotiation, Bahr's formulation was by far the most frequent characterization of the challenges facing the treaty that I encountered. This was true in the West German Foreign Office and Ministry of Intra-German Relations *and* the East German Ministry of Foreign Affairs alike.

ment to its renunciation-of-force accords with the Soviet Union and Poland in 1970, and then finally with Czechoslovakia in 1973, plus the flowering of superpower détente between the USSR and the United States, the two states were also in something of a novel position. For the first time in their short histories, German-German concerns were almost completely separable from the world around them. Although no one would have said that the Basic Treaty was a perfect document—no treaty ever is—it at least presented a framework according to which those who hoped for a more "pragmatic" national policy could act. Conveniently removed from the rhetoric about distant national goals (to use one participant's characterization of their objectives), East and West Germany could finally begin to clarify the many obstacles before them and calmly seek to build upon areas of mutual interest.[3]

In this respect, the negotiators of the inter-German agreement had good reason to be pleased with the evolution of the ties between the GDR and the FRG in the early 1970s. Contrary to the expectations of some skeptics, both governments showed that they could learn from their errors and make the kinds of concessions and compromises that were needed to foster a satisfactory working relationship between the two German capitals. What no one could foretell, however, was whether even the "bad relations" that had seemed so out of reach in Ulbricht's and Adenauer's days could be kept from frustrating those individuals who had higher expectations for the GDR and the FRG.

The Inter-German Dilemma

Even the most respectful student of the Basic Treaty would have a hard time denying an elementary fact about the agreement: in order for the accord to have been reached in the first place, East and West Germany's representatives had had no choice but to gloss over many of the major differences that had separated their governments throughout the 1950s and 1960s. In itself, this circumstance made the treaty no more unusual than countless other international understandings in which the parties in a dispute successfully bring their negotiations to a close by "agreeing to disagree" about fundamentals. Nonetheless, this condition also meant that the inter-German accord was replete with ambiguities and potential conflicts, which the leaders of the GDR and the FRG were sure to exploit to their respective advantage in later years.

[3]In the view of one West German participant, a staff member of the Ministry of Intra-German Relations, about the spirit of the times: "We all needed to accept only one thing conceptually, that reunification would not happen and that the old policy had led to tensions. Hence, we needed a more pragmatic policy." Author's interview, Bonn, February 24, 1988.

For example, it was almost predictable that the Germanys would have been unable to agree about their opposing interpretations of the national question; even the accord's preamble acknowledged that they had "different views" on the subject. This dispute meant, though, that from the very first, East Berlin and Bonn were at odds about the whole point of the Basic Treaty. From the GDR's perspective, the fact that the treaty emphasized its signatories' "independence and autonomy in their internal and external affairs" was not only evidence enough that the hoary German question was no longer open to discussion, but also established a guiding principle for all future relations with the Federal Republic: if Bonn wanted to have productive ties with the GDR, it was up to its leaders to demonstrate their respect for East German sovereignty. Yet nothing could have been further from the FRG's objectives. For the West German government, in contrast, the exchange of subambassadorial "permanent representatives" and its success in attaching a letter to the agreement (the so-called Letter on German Unity) that affirmed its commitment to the goal of national reunification served to underscore quite the opposite message: inter-German relations would always be relations of a "special" type, fundamentally different in character from those between any other states.

As a consequence of these differences, even an issue as fundamental as the criteria for judging German citizenship was left unresolved in the inter-German accord. Bonn carefully safeguarded its claims to treat Germans living in the GDR as no different than Germans residing in the FRG by emphasizing in a protocol note to the treaty that all matters having to do with German citizenship were unaffected by the treaty. In this fashion, years of subsequent bad feeling between the two states were guaranteed, since the Federal government accordingly reserved for itself such rights as the ability to hand out West German passports to any East German requesting its citizenship. In response, all that the GDR's leaders could do, in their hopes of forcing the FRG to change this policy, was to append their own note to the treaty, which stipulated that the resolution of citizenship disputes would be "made easier" by the accord. Finally, even issues that seemed beyond the Germanys' direct control—the most prominent being those involving four-power authority over Berlin—were brought into the agreement, notably with all of the controversies associated with them, thanks to a provision that specified that the Basic Treaty could not interfere with agreements with other powers "involving" the two German states.[4]

Given these ambiguities, it was to be expected that even before the inter-German agreement was in force, East Berlin and Bonn were poised to

---

[4] "Vertrag über die Grundlagen der Beziehungen zwischen der Bundesrepublik Deutschland und der Deutschen Demokratischen Republik," in *Zehn Jahre Deutschlandpolitik* (Bonn: Bundesministerium für innerdeutsche Beziehungen, 1980), pp. 205–211.

insure that those interpretations of the accord that were best attuned to their immediate understanding of their interests would be accepted. Yet what made such disputes even more difficult than they might have been otherwise was that neither the GDR nor the FRG was ever very far removed from the domestic circumstances that shaped its particular approach to the national question. As a result, neither of the German governments ever had to look very far for good reasons to play up their differences, nor could they easily afford to ignore such considerations when making policy.

In the Federal Republic, the partisan bitterness and acrimony that preceded the negotiation of the Basic Treaty could not have helped but filter into every aspect of the Brandt government's handling of the inter-German accord. Although the ruling coalition's victory in the elections to the Bundestag in 1972 had already provided the Social-Liberal regime with the majority that it technically required to assure the accord's ratification, the West German parliament debated the inter-German treaty for over three months before finally accepting it in May 1973. Even then, although the Union parties were unable to block the agreement when they voted almost unanimously against its implementation—only four CDU/CSU deputies chose to break ranks and support the Basic Treaty, among them the future president of the FRG, Richard von Weizsäcker—Brandt and his colleagues could hardly have been indifferent to the implications of this challenge. For all of the controversy that had already attended their opening to the East, they could see that they were still far from achieving a national consensus about the improvement of relations with the GDR. Indeed, if there was any doubt about the matter, the state of Bavaria demonstrated that there were no grounds for self-satisfaction when it brought a debilitating, if ultimately unsuccessful, legal challenge to the inter-German accord before the Constitutional Court in the summer of 1973.

At least in part for these reasons, Brandt was practically at pains to emphasize to his country's citizens that the governing coalition's national goals remained unchanged from those of the FRG's founding. The whole purpose of the inter-German agreement, he insisted in mid-February 1973, had been to serve German national objectives, to "aid in hindering a further drifting apart, a further living apart [of the two German populations]" by insuring that the "will and consciousness of togetherness as preconditions for the continuing existence of the nation" would not be lost with the passage of time.[5] The practical consequence of such emphases, though, was that the chancellor could not have helped touching upon themes that were bound to be a constant irritant for the East German government. He regularly championed positions (for example, the claim to

[5]See his speech of February 15, 1973, in *Texte zur Deutschlandpolitik* (hereafter *TzD*), vol. 12 (Bonn: Bundesministerium für innerdeutsche Beziehungen, 1973), p. 143.

a unique West German relationship with West Berlin) that gave evidence to the unresolved character of the national question. Moreover, he routinely pressed the GDR to live up to its obligations to allow for the maximum amount of contacts between the German populations, even to the point of going out of his way to keep public attention focused on the continuing inhumanitarian practices (such as the shooting of would-be refugees) of the SED regime.[6]

Yet, not unlike Bonn, the East German government, too, had its own distinctive reasons for emphasizing a very different reading of the Basic Treaty, and these were equally likely to raise obstacles to the cause of inter-German cooperation. After all, with many of the barriers to contacts between the GDR and the FRG being lifted for the first time since 1961 and with the two states' long-separated populations being reexposed to each other through a diverse array of new contacts, it is not surprising that the SED's leaders should have begun to wonder whether the monopoly on truth they had sought to cultivate during ten years of isolation was in danger of vanishing. Would average East German citizens now be even more prone than before to question their destiny under socialism? Would the allure of the West prove irresistible? As in the past, the party's problem was that it still lacked an effective means of assessing the success or failure of its efforts to generate a separate GDR consciousness. Therefore, many of its members quite naturally tended to assume the worst.

In this respect, it made sense that for every speech that Brandt gave about the undecided character of the German question, Honecker seemed to be intent upon getting his population to focus on the differences between the GDR and the FRG and their lack of any commonality. Relations between East Berlin and Bonn would only prosper, he would typically emphasize, if the two states' ties were premised on the same international standards that governed relations between other countries as well: "With the Basic Treaty . . . we are talking about a normal treaty under international law, which was concluded by two independent and sovereign states." This meant, in Honecker's mind, that Bonn had no legitimate claim to a special relationship with the GDR: "The GDR is not a part [*kein Inland*] of the FRG, and the FRG is not a part of the GDR."[7]

At times, the logic of this desire to set the East German state physically and psychologically apart from the West seemed to achieve almost absurd proportions, as some SED leaders were tempted even to make a complete

---

[6]See Brandt's speeches in ibid. of January 18, 1973, pp. 17, 21, and of April 15, 1973, p. 269.

[7]See Honecker's speech of March 28, 1973, in *Reden und Aufsätze* (hereafter *RA*), vol. 2 (Berlin: Dietz, 1977), p. 234.

break with the theme of the GDR's Germanness.[8] As early as July 1972, for example, while negotiations over the inter-German treaty were still underway, one ranking member of the politburo, Albert Norden, the former secretary of the Volkskammer's Committee for German Unity, flatly declared the entire issue of the unitary German nation to be a "fiction." There were no longer "two states in one nation," he asserted, as if all one had to do to resolve the problem of national identity was to wish it away. Instead, there were "two nations in states of different social orders."[9]

Nor were such sentiments absent from other segments of the party. In a striking contrast with the era not so many years before this period when Ulbricht had sought to deny the FRG's credentials as a legitimate German state—because it had supposedly abandoned any sensible path for pursuing the goal of reunification—much of the SED leadership suddenly seemed prepared to accept denuding the GDR's best-known institutions and political shibboleths of any association with its national past. In 1973, for example, the National Front of Democratic Germany, the forum in which a variety of non-Communist parties nominally participated to give the GDR the appearance of democratic legitimacy, was renamed the National Front of the GDR. The country's principal radio station, the *Deutschlandsender*, became the *Stimme der DDR* ("Voice of the GDR"). Finally, in late 1974, the East German government again moved to revise its constitution, only just rewritten in 1967, to exclude all of its earlier references to the German nation and the goal of reunification.[10]

Although there were members of the SED leadership, apparently including Honecker himself, who may have balked at the idea of attempting such a total divorce from their country's German heritage—the General Secretary preferred instead a formula that conceded his population's German nationality while emphasizing its separate "GDR citizenship"[11]—the desideratum remained essentially the same throughout the party. In times of enhanced exposure to capitalism and the West, there was no such thing as being too cautious about insulating the East German social order from the unwanted consequences of its opening to the FRG. Most prominently, steps were taken to increase ideological education about the dangers of the "bourgeois enemy" in the country's schools and among its work force; the party's leading role and its "fighting spirit" were reaffirmed in the press;

[8]I say "absurd" (in the words of Karl-Heinz Röder, the late deputy director of the Institute of State and Law, GDR Academy of Sciences) because this was the perception of many SED members who were involved in implementing the policy.

[9]See his speech of July 3, 1972, reprinted in *Deutschland Archiv*, November 1972, pp. 1223–1225.

[10]*Neues Deutschland*, however, was not renamed.

[11]*RA*, vol. 3 (Berlin: Dietz, 1978), p. 262.

and an entirely new class of citizens was created of so-called *Geheim-nisträger* (or "secret-carriers")—prominent SED members, state officials, scientists, and soldiers—who by virtue of their supposedly sensitive positions were forbidden to have any interactions with Westerners. In short, it was remarkable that average East Germans were allowed any contact at all with the FRG or with its alien culture.

The Benefits of Cooperation

In view of such overtly contradictory objectives, it does not require a great deal of imagination to see why the two German governments were practically programmed for conflict in the early 1970s. While the FRG's leaders were seeking nothing less than to tear down the many barriers to inter-German contacts that had first been put in place with the Wall, their counterparts in the GDR seemed to be striving to accomplish exactly the opposite goal of constructing new impediments—new walls, in effect—to any serious rapprochement with their rivals. To the extent, however, that East Berlin and Bonn were able to confound the skeptics and recognize that there were some benefits to be gained through cooperation, it cannot have hurt that the decades of virtually no ties at all had left a number of issues to be resolved, many of which were quite mundane, that represented little or no threat to their divergent national policies.

First, as policymaking intellectuals such as Bahr and Schollwer had recognized years earlier, there was the undeniable fact that the Federal Republic really had no other alternative but to seek East Berlin's cooperation in reopening many of the old channels of communication that had once united the divided German population. This was the East German regime's greatest advantage. In this single regard, the early 1970s were to show that Bonn had everything to gain by retaining the GDR's goodwill with respect to those passages of the Basic Treaty that specified that the Germanys would work together to resolve the "practical and human-itarian" burdens of national division. In 1973 alone, thanks to the treaty and its attendant accords, over 2.27 million West Germans were able to make extended visits to the GDR, marking an increase of more than a million persons over the preceding year. Additionally, beginning in July 1973, West Germans living in "border areas" (*grenznahen Gebieten*) on the boundary between the FRG and the GDR were provided with their first opportunity to travel to neighboring regions in East Germany; nearly 200,000 persons took advantage of this privilege in 1973 alone, and over 330,000 in 1974. Even more impressive, the number of West Berliners who were able to make any visits at all to East Berlin or the GDR as a whole went from a mere handful of exceptional cases before the conclusion of the inter-

German transit agreement in the spring of 1972 to over 3.3 million by the end of the year, and then rose to 3.8 million by the end of 1973.[12]

Then, too, the Basic Treaty's promise from Bonn's perspective was also spelled out in scores of follow-up negotiations with the GDR. For example, a variety of improvements were registered in 1972 and 1973 in postal and telephone communications. Thus, over the first three quarters of 1973, West Berliners were able to make over 2.2 million calls to East Berlin, whereas less than three years before, there had been no official telephone links at all between the two halves of the city. The Germanys signed their first agreement on cooperation in the fields of health care and medicine in April 1974, and then reached an equivalent accord on sports contacts the following May. And, in 1973 and 1974, the two states were also able to make substantial progress in laying the groundwork for the settlement of a number of territorial and environmental disputes along the inter-German border.[13]

By the same token, it stands to reason that the Basic Treaty must have served East Berlin's purposes equally well, since the majority of these gains would have been inconceivable had the accord not in some way contributed to East Germany's campaign to be recognized as a separate state. Here, too, the benefit of decades of no contacts was immediately tangible. Following the years of isolation during the era of the Hallstein Doctrine, it is understandable that many SED members and government officials were simply exhilarated at the prospect that their state—and hence, they themselves as individual policymakers—might finally receive serious international attention.[14]

East Berlin had first broken Bonn's embargo on relations with the non-Communist world in a small way in the spring of 1969 by taking advantage of anti-Western hostility in the Middle East growing out of the 1967 Arab-Israeli war. Nonetheless, the countries that were willing to exchange diplomatic missions with the GDR at the time—Iraq, Syria, Egypt, and the Sudan—were for the most part developing states and hence little more

---

[12]Bundesministerium für innerdeutsche Beziehungen, *Zahlenspiegel*, February 1979, p. 97.

[13]See Dettmar Cramer, "Zwischen Kollision und Kooperation," *Deutschland Archiv*, February 1974, pp. 113–118, and Dieter Mahncke, "Abschluss der Neuordnung der Beziehungen zwischen der Bundesrepublik Deutschland und Osteuropa," in *Die Internationale Politik 1973/1974* (Munich: R. Oldenbourg, 1980), pp. 193–215. As an example of what the two states could accomplish, a close West German participant, Hansjürgen Schierbaum, emphasizes the novel agreement they reached on September 20, 1973—more than a decade before the famous nuclear catastrophe at Chernobyl in the USSR—on cooperative measures to clean up radioactive waste in the event of a nuclear accident on the inter-German border. Author's interview, October 21, 1987. Cf. *Zehn Jahre Deutschlandpolitik*, p. 245.

[14]"We were then a sovereign baby," one East German observer notes, "that had to learn to walk." Author's interview, East Berlin, May 25, 1988.

than symbolic gains for the East German leadership. But in this light the Basic Treaty was unquestionably liberating. Once Bonn had signaled its approval on recognizing the GDR, the floodgates opened for a wave of international ties.[15] By the end of 1974, 110 countries had chosen to establish formal relations with East Berlin, in contrast to a mere 13 five years earlier. Most important from the SED's perspective, these states included all of the world's major industrial powers—Great Britain, France, the United States, and Japan. Adding to these gains, and again with Bonn's approval, the GDR was also admitted to membership in numerous international organizations, including UNESCO, the World Health Organization, and the World Postal Union, and in September 1973, it was finally able, along with the FRG, to achieve a long-standing objective by becoming a full member of the United Nations.

Yet East Germany's vastly improved international standing was not only significant from a psychological perspective. This new-found status also had the advantage of helping to improve the country's international economic position by enabling its leaders to begin finally to diversify their trade relations. For most of the GDR's history, its trade relations had been very rigidly structured around the narrow needs of the Soviet economy and the blocwide Council for Mutual Economic Assistance (COMECON), and hence were unfavorable to many of the state's immediate economic interests. As East Berlin's exposure grew with the signing of the inter-German agreement, however, and West European and American lending institutions became more willing than in the past to provide the credits to finance the purchase of Western technology and consumer goods, East German planners were able, albeit ever so carefully at first, to take the initial steps to reduce the extent of their state's overall dependence on the Eastern bloc. Notably, between the years 1970 and 1974, the proportion of the GDR's total trade with the Soviet Union declined from 39.1 percent to 31.4 percent, while the proportion of its total trade with the West rose at a corresponding rate, from 24.4 percent to 30.9 percent.[16] At the same time, even Honecker himself began to look to the capitalist world as a welcome

[15]In some cases, West German authorities may have gotten more than they bargained for. True to the principle from Adenauer's times that German policy should take precedence over other priorities, one of their greatest fears while working on the Basic Treaty was that their allies would recognize East Berlin before they had spelled out how their agreement with the GDR was to be understood. Author's interview, Günther Meichsner, Bonn, February 11, 1988.

[16]See Thomas A. Baylis, "Explaining the GDR's Economic Strategy," *International Organization* 40, no. 2 (Spring 1986), p. 391. As Baylis emphasizes, part of the increase in trade with the West must be attributed to inflation; still, the general trend favoring trade diversification continued well into the 1980s. Also see Hanns-Dieter Jacobsen, "Strategie und Schwerpunkte der Aussenwirtschaftsbeziehungen," in H.-A. Jacobsen et al., *Drei Jahrzehnte Aussenpolitik der DDR* (Munich: R. Oldenbourg, 1980), pp. 298–308.

source of financial assistance in his efforts to reward East German consumers for their devotion to socialism.[17]

In view of the SED leadership's concern simultaneously to "delimit" its state from the Federal Republic, it may seem paradoxical that this upgrading of economic relations with the West should have included economic ties with the FRG as well. Yet in a revealing indication of his flexibility in comparison with Ulbricht, Honecker was not averse to admitting his government's willingness to take advantage of every opportunity it could find to strengthen the East German economy.[18] If Bonn were disposed to devote its resources to the stabilization of the GDR, he seems to have reasoned, there was every reason to use such ties to achieve the SED's purposes. Thanks to West Germany's insistence on preserving a "special" German-German relationship, GDR exports to the FRG (although not, as is commonly supposed, to the rest of West Europe) were already treated as "internal" German trade and therefore exempt from Common Market tariffs. Furthermore, East Berlin had also benefited for years from Bonn's willingness to finance a special overdraft credit (or "swing"), which saved the GDR millions of Marks in interest payments annually, and which the FRG generously raised to DM 600 million in 1974.

With the Basic Treaty, however, Honecker apparently recognized that the country stood to gain all the more from the practical aspects of the regularization of inter-German ties. After decades of neglect, many of the GDR's highways had to be rebuilt, its train tracks modernized, and a complex variety of services coordinated (everything from the provision of electricity for West Berlin to the disposal of its waste in the East) in order to make the new relationship between the two states function effectively. In these respects, as the everyday benefits of East Berlin's contacts with the Federal Republic became fully apparent—between 1972 and 1975, for example, the East German government received payments of over 235 million Marks annually from the FRG for transit fees alone[19]—it would have been strange if the GDR's leaders had not been inclined to pursue what, from the perspective of the time, appeared to be other relatively low-risk arrangements with their adversaries.

[17]Günter Schabowski, *Der Absturz* (Berlin: Rowohlt, 1991), pp. 121–122. Schabowski also notes that Honecker was criticized at the time by his planning chief, Gerhard Schürer, for too quickly assuming such foreign debts. For Schürer's reflections on the period, see OHP (Schürer, July 10, 1991).

[18]See his interview with *New York Times* columnist C. L. Sulzburger in *RA*, vol. 2, p. 110. For a relevant East German dissertation, based on sources within the Ministry of Foreign Trade, see Detlef Nakath, "Zur Geschichte der Handelsbeziehungen zwischen der DDR und der BRD in den Jahren 1961 bis 1975," Humboldt University, East Berlin, May 1988.

[19]See Jochen Bethkenhagen, Siegfried Kupper, and Horst Lambrecht, "Die Aussenwirtschaftsbeziehungen der DDR vor dem Hintergrund vom kalten Krieg und Entspannung," *Beiträge zur Konfliktforschung* 4 (1980), pp. 59–60.

Handling Questions of Principle

Of course, amicable arrangements between the Germanys were much harder to obtain in some areas than in others, particularly when matters of principle were involved. Yet, provided that there were concrete benefits to be gained by both sides over the long term, there were also encouraging signs in 1973 and 1974 that East Berlin and Bonn might be able to move beyond many of their earlier differences. Quite frequently, all that was required to overcome the most prominent obstacles to cooperation was the time and experience necessary to convince both governments that they might eventually stand to lose more by failing to get along.

One instructive case involved the seemingly straightforward matter of German-German representation. It was a given that the GDR and the FRG had to exchange representatives if they were ever effectively to attend to the routine business of the Basic Treaty. Nevertheless, while one might have expected the two governments to make the establishment of their permanent missions one of their first priorities, it was illuminating of the difficulties still remaining between them that when negotiations on the subject began in the spring of 1973, these offices became their first field of battle.

From the standpoint of the GDR's leaders, their country had already lost an important contest with Bonn in the inter-German accord's emphasis on permanent missions as such, below the level of full embassies. Still, this defeat did not keep East German officials from persistently seeking to insure that when their representatives were finally in place, their presence would come as close as possible to symbolizing their state's recognition under international law. The negotiator of the Basic Treaty, Michael Kohl, probably put it best when he said about the new mission in Bonn that it would have the "same character" as its embassy in Brussels.[20] Hence, East Berlin insisted that both of the permanent missions be subject to the 1961 Vienna Convention on Diplomatic Relations and accredited directly to the foreign ministries of the two German states.

In stark contrast, however, West German authorities would have nothing to do with any effort to water down one of the principal respects in which, in their reading of the document, the Basic Treaty affirmed the unusual quality of relations between the Germanys. Thus, Bahr and his colleagues responded to the East German demands by contending that if the new diplomatic offices were to be accredited at all, it could only be as special entities before the GDR Council of Ministers and the Federal chancellery. In fact, some West German officials, spurred on by the CDU/CSU's opposition to the Basic Treaty, went even further than the government position, de-

[20]*Der Spiegel*, August 25, 1975, p. 23.

manding that the East German mission be accredited only to the Ministry of Intra-German Relations.[21]

Despite these differences, the sheer volume of talks taking place between the states may have been the deciding factor that led East Berlin and Bonn to settle their differences in March 1974. In January 1974, negotiations were being conducted in thirteen different areas, and all of these required the kinds of administrative support that only the permanent missions could afford. Nonetheless, the dispute was illustrative of two principles that would accompany the inter-German relationship throughout the coming decade. Given the time that elapsed between the start and close of negotiations, almost a year, the first principle was that even the most trivial issues could serve to inhibit cooperation between the two governments. But the second and no less important issue was that if the Germanys were ever to resolve their differences, it was crucial that each state also sense that it had in some respect attained its objectives.

In the case of the permanent missions, West German authorities could say that they had achieved their goal regarding the character of the new offices after all, because the inter-German protocol that set up the agencies stipulated only that they would be treated in a manner "corresponding," and not according, to the Vienna Convention. At the same time, however, it was equally significant from East Berlin's standpoint that the West German parliament passed a law that allowed the GDR's representatives, for all intents and purposes, the same rights and prerogatives as other diplomats. Furthermore, the GDR also registered a small victory when Michael Kohl was able to present his credentials as the first East German representative to the FRG directly to the West German president, while his counterpart presented his letter to Honecker, acting in his capacity as a member of the State Council. Finally, East Berlin and Bonn were essentially able to split the difference over the question of where their new missions would be accredited. Pursuant to the wishes of most West German officials, the GDR's mission was tied to the Federal chancellery, reaffirming for Bonn the special character of the German-German relationship, while in a similar act of diplomatic legerdemain, East Berlin's demands were met by having the FRG's mission assigned to the East German Ministry of Foreign Affairs.[22]

On other occasions in the early 1970s, however, such understandings were much harder to achieve for the simple reason that both of the German

---

[21]Author's interviews, Ministry of Intra-German Relations, Bonn, January 28, 1988. Cf. *Deutsche Zeitung Christ und Welt*, November 2, 1973. For the views of the conservative opposition, also see the parliamentary debates in *Das Parlament*, March 23, 1974, pp. 1–2.

[22]Dettmar Cramer, "Zwischen Kollision und Kooperation," *Deutschland Archiv*, February 1974, pp. 113–118, and Ernest D. Plock, *The Basic Treaty and the Evolution of East-West German Relations* (Boulder, Colo.: Westview, 1986), pp. 138–140.

governments could not help but succumb to the temptation of taking advantage of their respective bargaining strengths in the hopes of generating conditions that their rivals would be powerless to overcome. In these instances, manageable relations could only be restored when the offending party had literally been compelled to see that short-term gains were not in its long-term interests.

One of the most frequent matters on which the Federal Republic continually sought to gain the advantage over the GDR, for example, was in its peculiar relationship with the city of West Berlin. Clearly, few issues were better suited to demonstrating the open and unresolved character of the national question than Bonn's claims to a piece of territory inside of the GDR. But in this case in particular, the West German government also had the benefit of all the ambiguities that were built into the Quadripartite Accord. Reflecting the four powers' 1971 agreement to disagree, the accord was conspicuously contradictory with respect to the FRG's rights in West Berlin, specifying *both* that the city's ties with the West were to be "maintained and developed" and also that West Berlin was not a "constituent part of the FRG."[23] Yet because Bonn had the advantage of already having a substantial presence in the city, West German leaders were almost predictably inclined to exploit every opportunity they could find to support their reading of the accord. Visits were scheduled by the Federal president to West Berlin on a regular basis, as were even more provocative meetings of Bundestag deputies and cabinet officials in the city. Likewise, it was just as predictable that East Germany and the Soviet Union would immediately protest that such acts were illegal.

This is not to say that all of the disputes over Berlin's status were of the same intensity or consequence during that decade. In the majority of instances, East Berlin and Moscow were apparently quite willing to let the FRG's routine demonstrations of the West German presence in the city go by with equally perfunctory notes of warning. Yet there was also a limit to the Honecker regime's tolerance. In the late fall of 1973, at the urging of Brandt's Free Democratic interior minister, Hans-Dietrich Genscher (popularly known as the *Bremse*, or the "brakesman," because of his tough-minded views on the national question), the Federal government announced its intention to set up an Environmental Protection Office in West Berlin as one way of showing that the city had not been abandoned by the FRG.[24] In this case in particular, however, the Social-Liberal government

---

[23]The English version of the Quadripartite Accord is reprinted in David Keithly, *Breakthrough in the Ostpolitik* (Boulder, Colo.: Westview, 1986); on these themes, see Annex II, p. 213. Also see Joachim Nawrocki, "Schwierigkeiten mit den 'drei Z,' " *Deutschland Archiv*, June 1974, pp. 582–595.

[24]Cf. Olga Sandler, "Shades of Center: Hans-Dietrich Genscher and West German Policy towards the Soviet Union," unpublished manuscript, April 14, 1989, pp. 13–14. However,

may have underestimated the East's likely reaction. For, in the GDR's estimation, the new agency appeared to be nothing less than a West German bid to raise the stakes in the long-standing contest over the city.

True to form, when the office was first proposed, East German and Soviet officials immediately condemned the plan as a violation of the letter of the four-power agreement; Honecker even insisted (incorrectly) that the Berlin accord had required that all such political ties with West Berlin be "dismantled."[25] Nonetheless, when Federal authorities made known their determination on January 25, 1974, to follow through on the proposal, the GDR showed its muscle.[26] For twenty-four hours on the day thereafter, the city seemed to have returned to the crisis atmosphere of the late 1950s. East German police brought traffic to and from West Berlin to a virtual standstill with time-consuming searches of vehicles passing over border checkpoints. To guarantee that Bonn had correctly interpreted its message, the SED regime then repeated these demonstrations throughout mid-February and early March, and disturbances of various kinds related to the Federal agency were recorded during the following summer.[27]

In large measure because of Genscher's involvement in the conflict, the West German government chose to ignore these measures and finally set up the environmental office on July 22, 1974.[28] Nevertheless, although one might think that the FRG emerged the victor in the clash with East Berlin, it was what did *not* happen after the dispute had quieted down that conveyed the limits upon the Federal Republic's leverage. In view of the trouble the GDR caused for the West by disrupting the Berlin transit routes, not to mention the attendant strains in Soviet–West German relations that were

---

the decision to erect the new agency, and particularly Genscher's role in it, was met with misgivings within the governing coalition. See, for example, the internal memorandum of October 23, 1973, from West Berlin's mayor, Klaus Schütz, to the members of the SPD parliamentary *Fraktion*, Archives of the Friedrich-Ebert-Stiftung, Bonn.

[25]For example, see his interview in *RA*, vol. 2, p. 451.

[26]Behind the scenes, however, the East Germans let the FRG know unequivocally that they considered the erection of the Environmental Protection Office a serious violation of the Quadripartite Accord. In private discussions, Deputy Foreign Minister Kurt Nier warned the FRG's soon-to-be permanent representative to the GDR, Günter Gaus, that the step was sure to damage the Germanys' relations. However, when Gaus (who was struck by Nier's "earnestness") informed Brandt and Genscher of the warning, both West German leaders resolved not to allow themselves to be intimidated. Author's interview with Gaus, Bonn, March 29, 1988.

[27]East German authorities were not shy about suggesting that they intended to convey a message with such actions. As Willy Stoph lamented on January 26, the first day of the traffic disturbances, "If only the gentlemen in Bonn would think through the lessons of history and finally jettison all of the hopeless illusions of their policy toward the GDR." Cited in *Frankfurter Allgemeine Zeitung*, January 28, 1974.

[28]On this conflict, see the documents in Hans Heinrich Mahnke, ed., *Dokumente zur Berlin-Frage, 1967–1986* (Munich: R. Oldenbourg, 1987), chap. 26.

brought about by the controversy, the most revealing fact of all was its impact on Bonn. Brandt's government and, even more so, that of his successor, Helmut Schmidt, apparently recognized the dangers of pressing their advantage on the Berlin question and concluded that they had already gone far enough. It can have been no coincidence that for the remainder of the decade and well into the 1980s, the FRG's leaders pointedly avoided taking any new measures (aside from minor symbolic demonstrations of the West German presence in West Berlin) that their adversaries could have regarded as unnecessarily raising the stakes in the battle over the city.[29]

In comparison, East Berlin had quite sensible reasons of its own, the most prominent being the SED regime's uncertainties about the East German population's loyalties in the face of heightened contacts with the West, for being inclined to act upon the few bargaining strengths that it enjoyed in its relations with Bonn. In the rapidly changing environment of the early 1970s, Ulbricht's successors could readily appreciate that their ability to control access to West Berlin and, more essential, to the GDR in its entirety, was the most effective means at their disposal to counter the adverse effects of Bonn's Eastern policy. As it was, SED internal opinion polls in 1972 and 1973 had already revealed what appeared to be an alarming weakening in the commitment average East Germans felt toward the GDR, which many party members regarded as a direct consequence of the proliferation of contacts. Moreover, there was a general sentiment within the party that the country's citizens showed too much sympathy for Willy Brandt and far too much enthusiasm for West German television. Even the number of those who were seeking to escape to the West seemed to have risen sharply over the preceding year, again in direct proportion to the successes of the Ostpolitik.[30]

On these grounds alone, it is not difficult to understand why in early November 1973 East Berlin should have taken the bold move of doubling the amount of currency (known as the Mindestumtausch) that Westerners were required to exchange for East German Marks when entering the GDR, to 10 Marks for day visits and to 20 Marks per diem for visits lasting more than one day.[31] As the costs of entering the country rose, the SED leadership knew, the number of those who could afford to visit the country was sure to decline correspondingly. True to expectation, this was exactly what happened. While West Germans had made nearly 2.8 million short-term or

[29]Wolfgang Jäger and Werner Link, Republik im Wandel (Stuttgart: Deutsche Verlags-Anstalt, 1987), pp. 293–294.
[30]On the polls, see Gerhard Wettig, "Dilemmas der SED-Abgrenzungspolitik," Berichte des Bundesinstituts für ost-wissenschaftliche und internationale Studien 22 (1975), p. 4. On the escape attempts, which rose in 1973 by 16 percent over 1972, see Neue Zürcher Zeitung, January 8, 1974.
[31]For this decision, see Mahnke, Dokumente, chap. 27.

extended visits to the GDR in 1973, this number dropped by more than 350,000 visits in 1974. Similarly, the number of West Berliners traveling to the GDR was cut by more than a third over the same period, from more than 3.8 million visits in 1973 to 2.56 million visits in 1974.[32]

Nevertheless, although it may be easy to explain why the GDR's leaders acted when they did to constrict access to their territory, it is somewhat more challenging to account for the calculations they made about the likelihood of carrying off such a manifest challenge to the spirit, if not the letter, of the Basic Treaty. Perhaps Honecker and his colleagues reasoned that Bonn would be taken off guard by the doubling of the currency exchange requirement and, given its vested interests in the maintenance of stable ties, prove to be unwilling to make the kinds of serious countermoves against the GDR that could have put at risk the two states' entire relationship.[33] Here too, however, as in the FRG's efforts to increase its advantage on the Berlin question, the East German regime soon discovered that it had miscalculated.

West German officials reacted with a mixture of shock and anger to the new exchange requirements—to quote one participant, like "disappointed suitors"[34]—and immediately announced their determination not to allow their adversaries to get the better of them. Publicly, Brandt delivered a somewhat milder rebuke of the SED action than one might have expected under the circumstances, observing merely that the East Germans had not helped the cause of understanding between the blocs in taking such steps: "The leadership of the GDR must know," he advised, in his State of the Nation address on January 24, 1974, "that it cannot raise the level of tensions without at the same time provoking consequences which extend beyond the relationship of the two [German] states."[35] Yet, behind the scenes, the chancellor's representatives to the GDR proved to be much more unforgiving bargainers, drawing a direct link between the return of the exchange requirements to their previous levels and the outcome of another area of discussions only then beginning with East Berlin over the extension of the inter-German overdraft ("swing") credit.

Policymakers in the Federal chancellery were aware that the success of these negotiations was a preeminent concern for the East German regime.

---

[32]These figures are cited in *Zehn Jahre Deutschlandpolitik*, p. 44.

[33]At least at first, such a judgment may have been well founded. Only a few days after the new East German rates were introduced, Egon Bahr told the SPD parliamentary *Fraktion* that while the Federal government was considering "whether and what kind of countermeasures might come into question," the FRG had to be careful not to cultivate "too high expectations: the minimum exchange rates for other states in the Warsaw Pact were equally high." SPD *Fraktion* protocol of November 6, 1973, p. 3, Archives of the Friedrich-Ebert-Stiftung, Bonn.

[34]Author's interview, Hans Heinrich Mahnke, Bonn, January 28, 1988.

[35]Cited in *Zehn Jahre Deutschlandpolitik*, p. 14.

In 1972 alone, the GDR had availed itself of over 585 million Marks in interest-free credits to balance its trade with the FRG. If the talks over the renewal of the "swing" had collapsed, however, East Berlin would have seen the ceiling of the credit fall from 600 million Marks annually to its 1968 level of only 200 million Marks. In this sense, the West Germans could not have spelled out the trade-off in a more straightforward fashion.

In private communications, the FRG's representatives were careful to assure their East German counterparts that they had no intention of embarrassing the Honecker government by promoting a public impression that it was vulnerable to economic blackmail.[36] Nevertheless, they also quite deliberately emphasized that the failure to return the *Mindestumtausch* to its earlier levels would hurt the GDR most in the long run by making the inter-German relationship all the more susceptible to the attacks of the West German Right.[37] So it was that, almost a full year after the conflict between the two states had erupted, the East German government was finally induced to lower the mandatory exchange requirements, with the almost immediate consequence that Western visits to the GDR picked up once again.

Later, Honecker and his associates may have been able to congratulate themselves at their ability to reach a relatively comfortable settlement of their differences with the FRG, despite the tensions between the two states. East Berlin was able to get away with reducing the minimum exchange rates only by about one-third, which left them still substantially above their 1973 levels (although pensioners were eventually excluded from the requirements entirely). Furthermore, in fulfillment of its part of the implicit bargain, the FRG not only agreed to a new "swing" settlement but even increased the credit's upper limit to a high of 750 million Marks annually for the period from 1975 to 1981. Finally, there was even a suggestion at the conclusion of the negotiations that Bonn was prepared to begin a new round of talks about a host of lucrative joint undertakings—such as the construction of an Autobahn between Hamburg and Berlin—that were meant to restore some stability to the inter-German relationship.

Nonetheless, even if one took these gains into account, the FRG had established a powerful precedent for turning the GDR's weaknesses against

[36] Yet this was precisely what happened. As one of the negotiators recounts: "We blackmailed the GDR with the 'swing'!" Author's interview, Federal chancellery, Bonn, February 12, 1988.

[37] Author's interview, Hansjürgen Schierbaum, Bonn, February 24, 1988. It is possible that the Soviet Union as well had a hand in encouraging the GDR to back down on the *Mindestumtausch* question; at least the new West German chancellor, Helmut Schmidt, pleaded for as much in his communications with Leonid Brezhnev. However, participants in the "swing" negotiations contend that the GDR's own financial considerations played the greatest role in East Berlin's decision.

it. Just as the West German government had apparently learned that it could not afford to burden the Germanys' ties with excessive claims on West Berlin's status, the leaders of the GDR too were evidently forced to conclude that their own interest in further contacts with the FRG was dependent on the ability to show restraint. Thus, as long as this rudimentary principle was acknowledged on both sides of the national divide—"a tacit agreement in thinking," as one East German participant later described the realization[38]—it was reasonable to expect that some form of inter-German progress was assured. Still, the unavoidable question to be raised for both states after they had mastered such lessons in the first half of the 1970s was whether either would be psychologically disposed to make the extra effort that was required to transform the cause of inter-German cooperation and compromise from a necessary evil into a positive good in itself.

Whither Inter-German Ties: The View from Bonn

In a world in which all other things were equal, East Berlin and Bonn might well have continued to make steady, incremental progress in the second half of the 1970s in much the same way they had exhibited in the first half of the decade, routinely encountering difficulties along the way and then equally routinely seeking to surmount these obstacles by appealing to no less authoritative a norm than their own self-interest. Nonetheless, what makes this part of the decade such a provocative period from the comparative standpoint of East and West German foreign-policymaking is that the inter-German relationship seemed to lose even the passing sense of importance that it had previously held for both governments, and the most noticeable characteristic of their interactions became what was *not* taking place between them.[39] The intriguing question is why this transpired.

On balance, it is no wonder that almost all observers of the Germanys' relations have looked for personalistic explanations for this shift, since the West German government's interest in the GDR seems to have declined at just about the time that a new chancellor, Helmut Schmidt, rose to replace Willy Brandt in May 1974. Certainly, no one familiar with Schmidt's career or disposition can have been surprised that the new leader of the FRG—more the strong-willed board chairman than a visionary like

[38]Author's interview, Institute for International Politics and Economics, East Berlin, June 14, 1988.

[39]See Kenneth Oye, "Explaining Cooperation under Anarchy," *World Politics* 38, no. 1 (October 1985), p. 7. As Oye stresses, states are sometimes unable to cooperate for reasons no more complicated than the absence of mutual interests. In this circumstance, no amount of "learning" will lead to cooperation.

Brandt—was eager to leave a distinctive mark on West German foreign policy. As the chancellor made clear in his inaugural address on May 17, his administration would concentrate its attention, "with realism and sobriety," as he put it, on only "the most essential matters, on [those issues] which are now necessary, and leave everything else aside."[40] Yet, for those who hoped that any aspect of the *Deutschlandpolitik* would be included on Schmidt's list of priorities, his further remarks were definitely disappointing.

In his inaugural address, Schmidt made no more than a few obligatory comments about the subject, emphasizing instead the quite different themes that would later epitomize his chancellorship—Western security and close ties with the United States, an expanded role for the FRG in the European Community, and the importance of a stable world economy. Nor were his subsequent assessments of the subject of Bonn's relations with East Berlin any more forthcoming. Even within the SPD's internal planning sessions, the chancellor's few references to the inter-German cause seem to have been designed merely to defuse the issue of its potentially explosive content. He assured his colleagues that there would be no change in the basic contours of Federal policy. But, by the same token, he apparently had no plans to pay any renewed attention to the question of his country's national policy either.[41]

It is here, however, that interpretations of the chancellor's motives diverge. In seeking to account for his approach, many of Schmidt's former associates contend that his reticence on the subject of GDR-FRG ties had less to do with his own desires than with the nature of the inter-German challenge in the aftermath of the negotiations over the Basic Treaty. Whereas Brandt had the good fortune, they emphasize, of dealing with issues that called for dynamism and leadership and allowed him to impose his personal imprint on the grand questions relating to the German future, Schmidt had suffered the comparative misfortune of arriving at a time when implementation, and not innovation, was the order of the day in the specific case of German-German affairs. In this sense, it was no mystery why his enthusiasm was bound to be dampened when mundane concerns, such as fishing rights, water quality control, and waste disposal (all matters

---

[40]*Bulletin*, May 18, 1974, p. 593, Bonn, Presse und Informationsamt.

[41]Thus, Schmidt seemed to straddle the fence when he spoke about the GDR in his first meeting with the SPD Bundestag *Fraktion* on May 13, 1974. Although he emphasized that it would occasionally be necessary to raise "a carefully balanced word about the fulfillment of treaties" with East Berlin, he also stressed that one should "avoid fanning already existing emotions." Cf. the *Fraktion* protocol of May 13, 1974, Archives of the Friedrich-Ebert-Stiftung, Bonn. Notably, by the next meeting of July 10, 1974, Schmidt was not even mentioning his country's relations with the GDR. Cf. Anlage 1 to the *Fraktion* protocol, Archives of the Friedrich-Ebert-Stiftung, Bonn.

that were the subject of extended negotiations between East Berlin and Bonn in 1974), rose to a superordinate level of importance on the scale of inter-German priorities.[42]

Such an explanation of the chancellor's behavior may appear completely satisfactory on the surface. But one must still grapple with the fact that quite a few members of Schmidt's own party and, for that matter, of the Union parties as well, were of a different mind on these questions at the time and felt that the Germanys' relations were deserving of greater attention. By the late 1970s, in fact, as we shall see shortly, some of these individuals were even beginning to speak tentatively about the advent of a "second phase" of the *Ostpolitik*, in which Bonn would have to look beyond the initial purposes of the Basic Treaty.

In this vein, others who were close to the chancellor at the time underscore the extent to which Schmidt was also affected by the demands presented by the FRG's quickly changing international surroundings, which, they argue, kept him from attending to other objectives.[43] According to this view, while Brandt had been able to focus his attention on themes that were at the center of the early Soviet and American détente initiatives—the grand initiatives toward Moscow and Warsaw and the vision of a "European peace order"—Schmidt could not have avoided being preoccupied with other, more immediate challenges. His government was just beginning to feel the consequences of the collapse in 1971 of the Bretton Woods monetary system and the first Arab oil embargo in 1973 and, in tandem with the onset of Soviet-U.S. arms-control negotiations (SALT I, MBFR), the FRG was being called to assume a new role in the Atlantic alliance. Who, then, could have expected the West German leader to do otherwise than turn his attention from central European concerns to matters that were increasingly global in scope?

Still, as accurate as these observations may appear, the international climate does not seem to have interfered with the travels Schmidt made elsewhere in the socialist world in the 1970s. By the end of the decade, the chancellor had conducted formal talks with just about every leading politician in the Soviet bloc. He had several high-profile meetings with Leonid

[42]Author's impression from numerous interviews in Bonn, 1987–88. Also see Jonathan Carr, *Helmut Schmidt: Helmsman of Germany* (London: Weidenfeld and Nicolson, 1985), p. 104.

[43]Author's interviews, Hans-Jürgen Wischnewski, January 11, 1988, and German Bundestag, March 30, 1988. In correspondance on February 10, 1992, Wischnewski later explained: "Helmut Schmidt was always active in the making of German policy, but naturally other concerns channeled his energies to a great extent elsewhere." Also see Jäger and Link, *Republik im Wandel*, p. 353; Christian Hacke, "Nur Reformidylle und Entspannung? Die siebziger Jahre," in Werner Weidenfeld, ed., *Politische Kultur und deutsche Frage* (Cologne: Verlag Wissenschaft und Politik, 1989), pp. 101–103; and Wolfram Hanrieder, *Germany, America, Europe* (New Haven, Conn.: Yale University Press, 1989), pp. 209–210.

Brezhnev in the middle of the decade, signing major economic accords with the USSR in 1974 and 1975. He developed a close working relationship and a personal friendship with the Polish party chief, Edward Gierek, leading in August 1975 to an agreement allowing over 120,000 ethnic Germans to emigrate to the FRG from former German territories, in particular Silesia and Pomerania. Finally, he also found the time for relatively cordial exchanges with most of the other East European leaders as well—Nicolae Ceausescu of Romania, Janos Kadar of Hungary, and Todor Zhivkov of Bulgaria.

Yet, for all of the matters that might have been discussed in great detail between East Berlin and Bonn, it is noteworthy that Schmidt chose to have only two very brief encounters with Erich Honecker during the entire decade. Both of these meetings, which were scheduled only two days apart, took place on the occasion of the signing of the Final Acts of the European Conference on Security and Cooperation in late July and early August 1975, when the two German leaders happened to be seated next to each other in Helsinki. Moreover, both were, by all accounts of the chancellor's perspective at the time, stiff and uncomfortable. It is little surprise that they accomplished nothing of consequence.[44] If it were not for Schmidt's readiness to speak with the other East European leaders, one might attribute his lack of attention to the GDR simply to a personal aversion to Communist functionaries of the type Honecker so well embodied. Cool, seemingly colorless politically, and—so the prevailing interpretation of his personality held at the time—almost religiously devoted to the Soviet Union, Honecker was unlikely to support the sorts of inter-German undertakings that would have captured the chancellor's imagination. But even here, one must wonder whether a more flamboyant East German leader would have made a difference at this point. For the other clue that we have to Schmidt's behavior may lie in the fact that, domestically speaking, any chancellor would have found the task of promoting a closer relationship with East Berlin in the second half of the 1970s much harder than in the first.

It certainly cannot have helped Schmidt that one of the reasons for the fall of Willy Brandt's government in 1974 was the discovery that one of his closest personal advisors, Günter Guillaume, had long been a spy for East German intelligence, and hence East Berlin had been secretly privy to most aspects of the negotiations over the inter-German transit accord and the Basic Treaty. Still, in an even deeper sense, the German-German relationship was also burdened by its early successes. In large measure because of

[44]In the words of a former mayor of West Berlin, Dietrich Stobbe, the chancellor found Honecker "petty and insignificant." Author's interview, Bonn, December 11, 1987. Schmidt's assessment of Honecker's skill and intelligence apparently changed when he wrote his memoirs two decades later. Cf. *Die Deutschen und ihre Nachbarn* (Berlin: Siedler, 1990), pp. 32–39.

the readily identifiable gains that had been recorded just after the signing of the inter-German treaty, relations with the GDR probably could not have avoided becoming the subject of rising expectations in West Germany. This meant that public support for the relationship with East Berlin was bound to be high as long as Bonn's interactions with the East went well. Yet, with growing signs of difficulties, and especially with every suggestion that the GDR was unwilling to comply with the FRG's understanding of the inter-German agreements, it made sense that the weight of public opinion in the Federal Republic should slowly but inexorably have swung the Schmidt government in the direction of more uncompromising policies toward the East.[45]

There can be little doubt that only a few years earlier, a Social Democratic politician, like Schmidt, could have defended a conciliatory policy toward the GDR by arguing for patience and understanding about the pace at which meaningful changes in policy could be expected of a Leninist regime. Was this not, after all, the approach both Brandt and Bahr had employed at the turn of the decade, the essence of the latter's philosophy of "change through rapprochement"? "Bad relations" with East Berlin were presumably better than no relations at all. However, for reasons that were in part quite removed from the rationale behind the Social-Liberal coalition's original stand on the FRG's national priorities, the precise political circumstances that existed in West Germany in the mid-1970s imposed a variety of constraints upon the Schmidt government that it would have been foolish to ignore.

For one thing, Schmidt himself had come to power with the expressed intention of bringing his party back from what he and many other moderate Social Democrats perceived to be two potentially harmful developments in the last years of Brandt's tenure. The first was, in their estimation, an unnecessary drift to the political Left that was epitomized by many younger SPD members' criticisms of German middle-class values and the country's ties with the United States. The second factor was a marked increase in internal strife within the leading circles of the governing coalition. To offset these tendencies and maintain his party's majority with the

[45]A study by the polling institute, EMNID, in March 1974 revealed a dramatic swing in public opinion in favor of more resolute ("*energischere*") stands in the FRG's relations with East Europe and the GDR. Whereas in June 1972 (five months before the Bundestag election) only 29 percent of those surveyed favored a harder course, by December 1973 (after the raising of the *Mindestumtausch*), 47 percent supported such a policy, and 50 percent in February 1974. A similar poll conducted around the same time by the Konrad-Adenauer-Stiftung found that 50 percent of the respondents had had "previous experiences" with the GDR that were negative (as compared to only 16 percent that were positive), whereas those who were asked about the Soviet Union were only 23 percent negative (and 27 percent positive). Both polls are cited in Werner Kaltefleiter, *Vorspiel zum Wechsel: Eine Analyse der Bundestagswahl 1976* (Berlin: Duncker und Humblot, 1977), p. 30.

FDP, Schmidt seems to have concluded that the Social Democrats had no choice but to make a greater effort to portray themselves as a "party of the middle" (Brandt had spoken idealistically about a "new middle"). This meant that the SPD had to move away from all of the issues, relations with the GDR included, that fueled public uncertainty about its political identity.[46] Furthermore, the chancellor also seems to have reasoned that by encouraging policies of moderation, he had a good chance of overcoming the inevitable strains that were then engulfing his party and the FDP on a number of contentious issues ranging from the management of the West German economy to the handling of the national question itself.

By themselves, these calculations could probably have sufficed to make the case for moderation. Yet Schmidt was equally concerned at this juncture to insure that his policies not become the object of renewed attacks by the CDU/CSU opposition. With the passage of time, there had been some noteworthy change in the Union parties' stand on the Social-Liberal Ostpolitik, and particularly on the Basic Treaty. Following the ratification of the Eastern treaties, even many of the most strident critics of the opening to the East had recognized that there was no longer any alternative to going along with the legal obligations the Federal government had assumed in signing the accords. "*Pacta sunt servanda*!" Franz Josef Strauß proclaimed in 1973, in what would become the leitmotif for most conservatives' efforts to come to terms with the agreements, "Treaties are meant to be observed!"[47] Still, Schmidt and all of his advisors could easily appreciate that Strauß's maxim potentially cut two ways. While the administration was assured that the CDU/CSU would no longer contest the legality of the accords, it was also evident that Union fundamentalists had been provided with a powerful tool for taking the coalition to task every time the GDR, or any other communist regime, failed to live up to the expectations attending its agreements with Bonn.

The crucial question, therefore, was not what the Schmidt administration ideally wanted of its foreign relations but instead how interested the opposition parties were in again making criticism of the *Ostpolitik* a centerpiece of their attacks on the government. After the Christian Democrats' disastrous showing in the 1972 Bundestag elections, there were strong indications that the CDU was prepared to do just about everything it could to regain the favor of the West German electorate. Rainer Barzel had been replaced as CDU chairman by Helmut Kohl, the former minister-president

---

[46]On these issues, see ibid., pp. 21–41; Jäger and Link, *Republik*, p. 291 and passim; and Arnulf Baring, *Machtwechsel* (Stuttgart: Deutsche Verlags-Anstalt, 1982), pp. 702–708.

[47]For the first of Strauß's numerous references to the concept, see his January 24, 1973, speech before the Bundestag, in *TzD*, 2d ser., vol. 12, p. 32. Also see Clay Clemens, *Reluctant Realists: The Christian Democrats and West German Ostpolitik* (Durham, N.C.: Duke University Press, 1989), p. 129, passim.

of the Rhineland-Palatinate, in 1973, and, together with the party's General Secretary, a dynamic professor of law, Kurt Biedenkopf, the Union leadership had begun a major internal reorganization. By laying greater weight upon its national organization and attempting to deemphasize the policymaking role of the conservative parliamentary alliance with Strauß's CSU, the leaders of the CDU hoped to bring the party back to power as a voice of the entire German people, a modern *Volkspartei*.[48]

Precisely because such credibility could be won only if the Christian Democrats were willing to tone down some of their more extreme stands, one could be forgiven for wondering whether conditions were not propitious for the party finally to adopt a more conciliatory line on the Eastern policy.[49] At a later date, in fact, just such a shift would come to pass, as greater numbers of Christian Democrats were brought around to support the *Ostpolitik*—many already did privately[50]—and as it served their party's political purposes. Nonetheless, the paradoxical nature of liberal politics once again intervened to stay the opposition's hand. Because Kohl also had to be attentive to the challenge of maintaining the unity of the CDU as he sought to rebuild it and because the CSU chose to be especially intransigent on the issue of relations with the Soviet bloc, the Union leadership remained for the time being artificially bound to its past. Not only did the party turn out to be considerably less flexible on foreign affairs questions than one might have otherwise anticipated; but in much the same manner that it had previously acted in the debates over the Eastern treaties, the CDU even rejected initiatives to reduce tensions on the European continent that already enjoyed wide popularity with the West German electorate.

In the greatest blow of all to many of the party's rank-and-file members and not a few of its hopeful reformers, the CDU/CSU Bundestag *Fraktion* went so far as to vote against the FRG's participation in the Helsinki Final

[48]Author's interviews, CDU Bundesgeschäftsstelle and CDU/CSU *Fraktion*, Bonn, 1987–1988. Also see Geoffrey Pridham, *Christian Democracy in Western Germany* (New York: St. Martin's, 1977), esp. chap. 6; and Wulf Schönbohm, *Die CDU wird moderne Volkspartei* (Stuttgart: Ernst Klett, 1985).

[49]See the CDU's program of renewal, the "Mannheim Declaration" of November 12, 1975, in *Argumente, Dokumente, Materialien*, no. 5408. On Kohl's flexibility, cf. Heiner Geißler, *Zugluft* (Munich: Bertelsmann, 1990), p. 244.

[50]Early revisionist views within the CDU could be found in the journal *Sonde*, many of whose youthful editors and contributors, Wulf Schönbohm, Detlef Stronk, Friedbert Pflüger, and Gerd Langguth, were to play important roles in the intellectual leadership of the party in the 1980s. See, for example, the article by Walther Leisler Kiep, the CDU treasurer and a supporter of the Social-Liberal *Ostpolitik*, "Zur Entspannungspolitik—Bilanz und Ausblick," *Sonde* 1 (1975), pp. 72–78. For an early Christian Democratic defense of *Ostpolitik* by a young political scientist and eventual architect of Helmut Kohl's foreign policy, see Horst Teltschik, "Plädoyer für eine konstruktive Ost- und Deutschlandpolitik," in Gerd Langguth, ed., *Offensive Demokratie* (Stuttgart: Seewald, 1972), pp. 162–187.

Acts, on the specious grounds that the Conference on European Security and Cooperation was merely a cleverly designed Soviet scheme to seal the division of Germany. Thus it was that for more than a decade thereafter the Social Democrats were still able to call into question their opponents' sense of responsibility for continental peace by pointing to this misstep. Almost perversely, the democratic CDU/CSU was joined by only two other European parties in opposing the Helsinki accords—the Albanian Communists and the fascist Italian Social Movement (MSI).[51]

These circumstances also demonstrated, however, that Helmut Schmidt had quite rational reasons for exercising caution throughout the later 1970s. The chancellor's actions suggested that he saw no domestic advantage to be gained by engaging in renewed battles with the Union forces over the touchier aspects of the *Ostpolitik*. To the contrary, one indication of the West German leader's desire to stay abreast of the shifting public mood about the GDR in particular was shown in his annual State of the Nation address of 1975, when he even went to the unusual length, for his tastes, of emphasizing the "continuing existence" of the German nation and the "feeling of commonality" (*Zusammengehörigkeitsgefühl*) between the people of East and West Germany. In fact, neither of these issues had played any role at all in his inaugural address a year earlier.[52] Moreover, it was also unmistakable that Schmidt carefully avoided taking any step that could have been interpreted as a sign of conciliation toward East Berlin during his campaign for reelection in 1976.[53]

Were the Union parties, then, somehow on the right track in working to impede any future initiatives toward East Germany? If the West German population expected a more forthcoming policy on the GDR, it was at least notable that this sentiment was not reflected at the polls. While the SPD-FDP coalition was returned to office in October 1976, its victory was made possible only by the slimmest of margins, and apparently only thanks to the chancellor's personal reputation for efficiently keeping his government on its middle-of-the-road course. At the same time, corre-

---

[51]See, for example, CDU deputy Werner Marx's critique of the Helsinki accords in *TzD*, 2d ser., vol. 3, pp. 181–184. Years later, some Christian Democratic parliamentarians would admit that they had underestimated the potential value of the Helsinki Basket III provisions on human rights: "Ironically," one of them reflected in 1988, "we saw things exactly as the Soviet Union did. Neither of us believed this would lead anywhere." Author's interview, Kurt Biedenkopf, Bonn, March 10, 1988. On these decisions, see Christian Hacke, "Parlamentarische Opposition und Entspannungspolitik—Die Position der CDU/CSU zur KSZE," in H. Haftendorn, W.-D. Karl, J. Krause, and L. Wilker, eds., *Verwaltete Außenpolitik* (Cologne: Verlag Wissenschaft und Politik, 1978), pp. 263–278; Carl-Christian Kaiser, "Gespaltene Opposition," *Die Zeit*, July 11, 1975; and Clemens, *Reluctant Realists*, pp. 156–160.

[52]*TzD*, 2d ser., vol. 3, p. 21.

[53]Gerard Braunthal, *The West German Social Democrats, 1969–1982* (Boulder, Colo.: Westview, 1983), p. 274.

spondingly, in an apparent vindication of its tactics, the CDU/CSU once more became the largest party in the Bundestag, winning 48.6 percent of the national vote, its best showing since 1957.[54]

Whither Inter-German Ties: Retrenchment in the GDR

In comparison with the political dynamics of the FRG, it is clear that Honecker and his colleagues in the East German government could much more easily have chosen to keep the inter-German relationship at the center of their priorities had this been their desire. Although some aspects of policymaking had changed with the new East German leader's ascent to power—above all, Honecker's associates emphasize his less overbearing style in contrast to Ulbricht[55]—the GDR's principal political institutions, and particularly the power in the office of the First Secretary (or General Secretary after May 1976), remained the same as ever.[56] The greater uncertainty throughout much of the 1970s, however, was exactly where foreign policy lay on the list of the SED chief's concerns.

That Honecker was both ready and able, despite his reputation as a

---

[54]The CDU/CSU share of the national vote rose by 3.7 percent over 1972, while the SPD's share dropped by 3.2 percent (from 45.8 to 42.6 percent), despite Schmidt's high standing with the West German population. In part, this outcome may be explained by the unusual circumstances that led to the Social-Liberal coalition's victory in 1972. But one must also take into account the extraordinary showing of Strauß's CSU in Bavaria, which increased its share of the state vote by 4.9 percent. The *Ostpolitik*'s role in the election was confirmed by a postelection survey in November 1976 which found that the desire for a tougher policy toward the East ranked a high fourth among the reasons voters supported the CDU/CSU; 56 percent said they wanted "to elect a party that [was] not too compliant in dealing with the East, that [did] not make concessions without getting something in return." More specific to inter-German relations, 49 percent of voters interviewed in a February 1977 survey said they favored a "harder course" against the GDR; when broken down according to political orientation, 61 percent of CDU/CSU supporters held this view but also 43 percent of FDP supporters and 39 percent (a plurality!) of SPD supporters. For the two surveys, see Elisabeth Noelle-Neumann, ed., *Allensbacher Jahrbuch der Demoskopie: 1977* (Vienna: Molden, 1977), pp. 61, 128.

[55]Author's taped interview with Otto Reinhold, East Berlin, March 23, 1990.

[56]One indication of continuity was that even during the early 1970s, when Honecker's attention was not focused on foreign policy questions, no one emerged to rival his authority on such issues. When I asked numerous policymakers who were active during the period, "Who made GDR foreign policy at this time?" I invariably received the answer "Honecker" or merely the names of individuals (e.g., Hermann Axen, the politburo member directly responsible for relations with other Communist parties) who were both perceived to be *and* perceived themselves to be Honecker's subordinates. Axen, in particular, was famous for his deferential demeanor, both toward Ulbricht and toward Honecker. Cf. OHP (Neubert, December 4, and Böhm, December 5, 1990). Although, for a more favorable account of Axen's role, see OHP (Manfred Uschner, October 4, 1991).

colorless bureaucrat, to give a distinctive cast to his government's *domestic* policies became instantly apparent at the party's Eighth Congress in June 1971. Without even waiting for time to pass following his predecessor's departure, he made a decisive break with the era of economic experimentation that had prevailed under Ulbricht by associating his government with a radically different set of economic priorities which emphasized not the utopias of a distant future but instead the concrete benefits of socialism in the here-and-now. Assuming the pose of a beneficent despot, Honecker announced that the SED's "Main Task" (*Hauptaufgabe*) would henceforth be to concentrate on the kinds of down-to-earth concerns—the quality and quantity of consumer goods available to the mass public, the need for better housing and for improved health services and pensions—that would make the personal sacrifices involved in the creation of a socialist society worthwhile.[57] In many ways, in fact, he saw to it that these promises were fulfilled. Over one million new units of housing were constructed in the GDR between 1971 and 1980, and almost half as many were renovated; social expenditure per capita rose by 90 percent; and the quality of overall health care showed marked signs of improvement as well.[58]

Given the favorable reception the East German population was likely to give such a shift in its government's practices, there is little need to puzzle over Honecker's motivations in breaking with past policy. From his vantage point, the quick payoffs that could be gained in popularity and prestige were probably as attractive as the need to address the many problems which had gone unattended during the later years of Ulbricht's rule. True to design, by the 1980s, the Unity of Social and Economic Policy (as the Main Task became known after the SED's Ninth Congress in 1976) had achieved almost mythic proportions in party lore. It supposedly embodied—if one were to take the elite's self-assessments seriously—the advent of a more hopeful era in state-society relations in East Germany and Honecker's personal contribution to the improvement of everyday life in his country.[59]

In comparison with these domestic innovations, however, the making of

---

[57]*RA*, vol. 1, pp. 158–167. About the break with the accelerated pace of socialist construction during Ulbricht's time, one participant has observed: "We could feel what was necessary, just like a farmer when he milks a cow and knows how to get the milk out." Author's interview, Heinz Hümmler, East Berlin, May 31, 1989.

[58]Martin McCauley, *The German Democratic Republic since 1945* (New York: St. Martin's, 1983), pp. 180–183, and Hermann Weber, *Kleine Geschichte der DDR* (Cologne: Verlag Wissenschaft und Politik, 1980), pp. 153–155.

[59]In discussions with East German policymakers and SED members throughout the 1980s, I rarely encountered anyone who spoke about the "Main Task" and Honecker's role in implementing the policy in anything less than reverential terms. In the fall of 1989, however, when the shortcomings of the policy had become public knowledge, I routinely heard exactly the opposite remarks; for example, from politburo member Günter Schabowski on October 30, 1989, East Berlin.

foreign policy was a field in which it was less immediately self-evident how either the General Secretary could profit from a heavy investment of his energies or the GDR government was to benefit from greater flexibility. Although the years following the signing of the Basic Treaty were unquestionably encouraging times for all of those within the party leadership who felt that they had finally surmounted the "recognition embargo" (Honecker's term) that had made their efforts to achieve credibility so difficult in the past, it is useful to appreciate that the terms of this wave of international recognition for East Berlin may also have been spoiling for the SED. Precisely because the country's isolation from its non-Communist neighbors had been so artificial, there was really very little that Honecker and his politburo associates needed to do to lay the groundwork for the GDR's entry into diplomatic relations with other states. Exchanging embassies and receiving the credentials of scores of ambassadors were practically technicalities by the time they occurred. Nevertheless, while all of these accomplishments may have been quite positive from the standpoint of East Berlin's long-range goals, the ease with which they were made also seems to have fostered a sense of self-satisfaction within the SED elite which carried over to practically all of the party's interactions with the outside world. Many could inquire, had not their state's ostracism been unjust all along? And, was not its inclusion as an equal and completely sovereign member of the international community simply a matter of putting things aright in the interest of world peace?

For those in the West, however, who had hoped that the GDR would become a more accommodating participant in East-West affairs, the problem with such easy accomplishments was that Honecker and his colleagues then seemed to draw quite narrow lessons from their experiences. Their government was prepared to reciprocate the attention it received, provided that others were willing to serve the GDR's needs. But significantly, the logical corollary to this position was that the SED's leaders almost instinctively seemed to feel that it was not their place to make the concessions necessary to facilitate such contacts in the first place. Given the high domestic stakes involved in the maintenance of East German internal stability, it may be that the party elite also had very good reasons for being slow to revise its opinion on this issue.

Clearly, Honecker was disinclined initially to commit himself and the powers of his office on anything more than a very selective basis to foreign-policy concerns, and only then to those interactions with the West that directly served his state's interests. This is not to suggest, however, that relations with Bonn never captured his attention. Günter Gaus relates that shortly after his installation as permanent representative to the GDR in 1974, Honecker unexpectedly emerged from the unknown realm that was East German policymaking to involve himself personally in the first contacts with the West German mission, even though it was not until 1976 (when Honecker assumed Ulbricht's old post as chairman of the State Council) that such meetings were justified by East German protocol. The guiding principle behind each of these contacts, however, seems to have been how little the SED chief had to risk by making the overtures, and how much to gain. In Gaus's view, Honecker simply could not resist the opportunity "to show the world that there were finally inter-state relations [between the Germanys]," and conveniently for his purposes, contacts with the West German representative were an almost cost-free means of accomplishing this objective.[60]

However, it was in a more widely publicized inter-German encounter—Honecker's back-to-back meetings with Schmidt in Helsinki in late July and early August 1975—that the East German leader may have first acquired a taste for foreign affairs.[61] We have already suggested that the West German chancellor was not impressed by the discussions or by his interlocutor. But for the SED leader, in contrast, this first "exchange of views between me and Chancellor Helmut Schmidt" (as Honecker later described the encounter) appears to have been something of a personal breakthrough. For an individual who had been cut off from the non-Communist world for the better part of his political career, the opportunity of even seeming to conduct business with his nemesis was a tantalizing indication that the GDR could take even greater strides forward, in guaranteeing its acceptance as an equal by its main opponent.[62]

Thus, Honecker evidently tried to treat the exchange with Schmidt as a matter of clearing up old misunderstandings, as if all that still needed to be accomplished between his government and Bonn was to rid the Germanys' relations of any unrealistic or unhelpful attachment to the policies of the past. "You and I," he counseled Schmidt, "we are both practical people, and we know that we're dealing with two sovereign states. What use can talk of reunification be to anyone? This just awakens [false] hopes, which then later lead to disappointments."[63] Just as in the East German leader's

[60]Author's interview with Gaus, Bonn, March 29, 1988.

[61]OHP (Böhm, December 5, 1990). Joachim Böhm, a former deputy director of the Central Committee's International Department accounts for the shift in Honecker's interests as follows: "As the GDR's representative, *he* had signed the Helsinki document, for the first time *he* had developed contacts beyond the confines of the communist world, with Gerald Ford, Helmut Schmidt. . . . As a result, psychologically speaking, Honecker developed a taste for foreign policy."

[62]*RA*, vol. 3 (Berlin: Dietz, 1978), pp. 471–472. Honecker had tried to develop a personal tie with Schmidt a year earlier during the inter-German dispute over the Federal Environmental Office, by calling for a face-to-face meeting with the chancellor, but Bonn declined the offer.

[63]Cited in Helmut Schmidt, *Die Deutschen und ihre Nachbarn*, p. 33. Since Schmidt cites Honecker's words at length, I am assuming that he is drawing from transcripts of the talks.

previous contacts with Gaus, however, the advantage of giving such advice was that it did not require anything in return from the GDR.

Nonetheless, it is undeniable that from the mid-1970s onward, Honecker did show signs of seeking to add to his foreign-policy profile. For example, he quite deliberately moved to involve himself more directly in the affairs of his foreign ministry, which only then had begun to feel a sense of institutional competence thanks to the scores of new diplomatic representations it had established abroad. Moreover, by relying more and more on a small circle of close friends and confidantes to handle some of the trickiest aspects of the GDR's foreign relations—such as Wolfgang Vogel, the negotiator of hundreds of the most famous trades of political prisoners between the Germanys, and Alexander Schalck-Golodkowski, the shadowy intermediary in many of the GDR's secret trade and credit arrangements with the West—Honecker also seems to have increased his discretionary authority as well.[64]

The question that still had to be asked of the East German leader's behavior at the time, however, was: Authority to what end? No one would have disputed that the General Secretary was left ideally positioned to adjust his country's priorities as he saw fit, above all in its relations with the Federal Republic. Yet the one factor that was conspicuously lacking was the compelling motive for him to act. He and the rest of the SED leadership made no secret of the fact that they were looking for unequivocal signs that their West German adversaries were finally prepared to make the kinds of concessions that they considered essential to maintaining the momentum behind the inter-German relationship. Nevertheless, the different rhythm of policy innovation in the Federal Republic made it highly unlikely that the Schmidt government would even consider the kinds of compromises that would satisfy the GDR. Accordingly, one could just about predict that each of the Germanys' subsequent actions would convey to its counterpart that it was still lacking in the good intentions that were required to make the pursuit of better ties worthwhile. For those who were interested in a deeper relationship, these were the wrong messages at the wrong time.

[64]On Vogel's legal career, see Jens Schmidthammer, *Rechtsanwalt Wolfgang Vogel* (Hamburg: Hoffmann und Campe, 1987), and for a somewhat romantic characterization of the individual whom most people knew simply as "Schalck," see Klaus Bölling, *Die fernen Nachbarn* (Hamburg: Goldmann, 1985), pp. 218–226. Honecker's relationship with Vogel provides a telling example of the greater worth the General Secretary attached to personal versus institutional ties. Several years later, in 1981, Vogel played an important behind-the-scenes role in arranging Helmut Schmidt's first visit to the GDR. Evidently, when the two German leaders and a small group of their advisors met for dinner, it came to light that Vogel was not even a member of the SED, and Honecker had to admonish his friend to take care of the oversight.

Toward a German-German Deadlock?

If the West German government was kept from investing more of its energies in its ties with East Berlin, it was not for want of inspiration or insight into the vagaries of inter-German bargaining. In 1976 and 1977, Gaus gave a series of widely publicized interviews in which he used his position as the FRG's chief representative in East Germany to show that there were indeed ways in which the Federal government could act creatively to serve its interests in dealing with the GDR. His key contention was that one had first to recognize what was—and what was not—possible between the Germanys. Echoing views that were already privately shared by many less prominent policymakers within the Schmidt administration,[65] Gaus maintained that the relationship between East and West Germany had already entered a "second phase" in which, like it or not, one could no longer be confident of reaching agreements that possessed the "luster and spectacular quality" of the first stages of the two countries' negotiations. The second phase would "be very much more characterized by small steps" which, although positive in the long term, were likely to be appreciated "only by the experts or people affected by them."[66]

It was the upshot of these conclusions, however, that proved most controversial. To insure the success of any future negotiations with East Berlin, Gaus emphasized that the Federal Republic could no longer afford to deceive itself about its leverage over the GDR. While no one could deny that the East German leadership had definite weaknesses that could occasionally be exploited for the maintenance of stable ties—above all, its interest in favorable economic relations with Bonn—the FRG had to recognize the strengths of the Communist regime as well. It could quite easily cut itself and its population off from the West the moment it felt that its sovereignty was at stake.[67] Hence, in his view, the only possible way to assure continued progress between the Germanys lay in finally accepting the SED's leaders for what they were, an elite "with the capacity to act on its own." In practical terms, this standpoint meant not only that Bonn should learn to deal with the East German regime on a basis of genuine equality but also that it would see the wisdom of excluding all of those "unbridgeable differ-

---

[65]In late 1976, for example, an internal chancellery report that was leaked to the press revealed that the Schmidt government had already concluded that it had no choice but to recognize the East German system "as such," if it wanted to achieve its objectives from the GDR. There could be no doubt, the report's authors had concluded, that the GDR could live without Western contacts if its leaders felt their survival depended on such a policy. *Frankfurter Allgemeine Zeitung*, September 9, 1976.

[66]*TzD*, 2d ser., vol. 4, pp. 281–282.

[67]See Gaus's interview with the *Süddeutsche Zeitung*, March 18, 1976, as well as his interview in *Evangelische Kommentare* 9, no. 4 (1976), pp. 223–226.

ences of opinion" that had repeatedly served to exacerbate tensions in the past. In this case, Gaus specifically emphasized the question of a unitary German citizenship.[68]

Quite predictably, Gaus's readiness even to broach this sensitive issue was met with a wave of protests and cries of indignation from the ranks of the Social-Liberal coalition's parliamentary opponents. There were some questions that one just did not raise publicly. Still, after a few years of experience with the Basic Treaty, the logic of his arguments cannot have been lost on the majority of West German politicians. Behind the scenes, even the CDU/CSU had shown some signs of accepting the reality (if not the desirability) of the GDR's existence as an independent state. This was all on a very unofficial level, of course, but from the mid-1970s onward, contacts between Union representatives and the East German regime had grown appreciably. In part thanks to Helmut Kohl's encouragement but also for their own private purposes, at least half of the senior CDU leadership had made private visits to the other German state by the end of the decade. In addition, by this time as well, the Union parties had also quietly begun to establish a network of back-channel contacts with SED officials through meetings at the permanent missions in Bonn and East Berlin and at such forums as the biannual industrial fair in Leipzig. In some instances, news of these exchanges was soon leaked to the press, as was the case with the increasingly routine contacts between the CDU treasurer, Walther Leisler Kiep, and the director of the Central Committee's Department on Western Affairs, Herbert Häber.[69] In other instances, however, even supposed hard-liners within the Union ranks, such as Olaf von Wrangel, Manfred Abelein, Gerhard Reddemann, *and* Strauß, found the time for off-the-record exchanges of views with their adversaries, in which they reportedly assured their East German interlocutors that they were no less interested than the SPD and the FDP in working to achieve a state of "normality" between the Germanys.[70]

---

[68]*TzD*, 2d ser., vol. 4, pp. 406–408. The FRG was "trying to be a little bit pregnant," Gaus reflected years later about his country's ambivalent attitude on relations with East Berlin. "I was on the front, and I saw how negotiations with the GDR had gotten cooler and cooler . . . whereas I wanted to bring the GDR into the game, assuming that the more they played, the more they would be bound by the rules." Author's interview, Gaus, Bonn, March 29, 1988.

[69]The Kiep-Häber tie reached back to the early 1970s, when the latter was the director of the Institute of Politics and Economics. It was probably the strongest link between the CDU/CSU and East Berlin in the period leading up to 1984 and 1985, when Häber enjoyed a short appointment as a full member of the politburo.

[70]According to one of my sources, a former top official at the East German Permanent Mission in Bonn, Strauß had "roundabout" (*auf Umwegen*) meetings with the GDR negotiator, Michael Kohl, on several occasions during the 1970s, some of which were at his own instigation. Author's interviews, Bonn and East Berlin, November 3, 1987, June 8, 1988, and

The problem, as one could readily detect in the public record of both German governments' efforts to resolve the broad range of questions relating to the implementation of the Basic Treaty, was that politics itself all too frequently got in the way of the best of intentions. This predicament was perhaps nowhere more evident than in one particularly glaring example of the irrationality of the inter-German relationship during the period when the Germanys became mired in negotiations over a seemingly insignificant 94-kilometer stretch of the Elbe River between the cities of Schnackenburg and Lauenburg.[71]

The dispute itself grew out of a supplementary protocol to the Basic Accord which specified that East Berlin and Bonn should come to an understanding about marking the formal location of the inter-German border. As early as May 1953, with regard to this stretch of the Elbe, a British representative to the Allied High Commission had ruled that the boundary between the then-existing German zones of occupation ran squarely down the middle of the river. Yet, while this judgment seemed on the surface only to serve East Berlin's interests by demonstrating that the GDR's boundary with the West was defined according to the same principles of international law that governed relations between other sovereign states, the lawyers representing the Federal government were actually able to devise a means of their own for accepting the ruling. According to their rationale, the British statement had only been a temporary "determination" (*Feststellung*) of convenience, since it lacked the legitimacy of a long-term "definition" (*Festlegung*) of German borders which could only come from a four-power settlement of the national question. Therefore, it did not threaten Bonn's interests at all.

Here, the matter might have rested to the satisfaction of all of the participants. Nevertheless, when the issue arose again two decades later, the Schmidt administration, ever attentive to its domestic interests, was apparently unwilling to appear too eager to appease its adversaries. Hence, hoping to gain the upper hand in later negotiations, it temporarily insisted on retaining control over the whole extent of the Elbe. Had the SPD not had to deal with a parliamentary opposition, the impasse might have been resolved in a year or two. Yet, once again, politics intervened. Not long after Bonn had taken its stand, a CDU-dominated government was

June 14, 1988. Also see Clemens, *Reluctant Realists*, p. 174, and OHP (Hans Schindler, October 3, 1991).

[71]My account of the Elbe boundary dispute is largely drawn from Link's analysis in Jäger and Link, *Republik im Wandel*, pp. 361–363. In 1987 and 1988, I encountered considerable optimism in my discussions of the dispute with officials in the Federal chancellery in Bonn and the Ministry of Foreign Affairs in East Berlin, all of whom seemed to think that, politics aside, the Elbe controversy would soon be resolved. The problem remained, however, that the issue could not be separated from its political context.

installed in Lower Saxony, where the contested portion of the river lay, and its minister-president, Ernst Albrecht, decided that what had originally been a negotiating tactic was no longer negotiable. Soon, with Strauß's vocal backing, a conflict that had begun as a technical uncertainty had become a *cause célèbre* for the CDU/CSU, which for reasons of pure political expediency used the Elbe controversy to attack the Social-Liberal coalition every time it sought to modify its original stand. The real burden of the controversy, however, was borne by the inter-German relationship, since East Berlin could hardly resist the opportunity to accuse the Bonn government of a lack of good faith. In the end, despite the amount of time and energy invested on both sides, the Germanys never were able to settle their differences about the border, and the gap between them widened.

When viewed from the GDR's perspective, it is not hard to see why the FRG's behavior in such minor disputes would have fallen far short of the minimal expectations that individuals like Honecker had about the acceptable conditions for any sustained dialogue with Bonn. If better relations with the West had been palatable to the East German elite in the first place because it could assume that the Federal Republic would take the first step in most of the inter-German undertakings that were to ensue, the FRG's intransigence can only have made the SED doubly determined not to allow itself to be pushed around at what it perceived to be its adversaries' whim. In turn, however, it was exactly this sort of defiance on the GDR's part that convinced many West Germans that East Berlin had never seriously intended to live up to its part of the Basic Treaty.

The refusal to compromise East German interests was probably best spelled out in the period immediately following the Helsinki conference when much of the outside world (and the West German government above all) was waiting to see whether the GDR would live up to the so-called "Basket III" provisions of the conference's Final Acts. These specified that the documents' signatories would allow for the free flow of information and populations over their borders and guarantee basic human rights. In this case, the East German regime recognized that there were benefits to be had, both in international prestige and domestic credibility, by at least seeming to abide by such standards. Accordingly, Honecker was especially interested in fostering the impression that his government was at peace with the "world-open conditions" in which it now found itself. When East Berlin played host to a major conference of European Communist parties in June 1976, for example, and the Italian and Spanish delegates set themselves apart from the other fraternal parties by frankly criticizing the dictatorial methods of the CPSU and openly calling their colleagues' attention to the shortcomings of modern socialism, the General Secretary himself intervened—notably against the advice of other more cautious members of the SED politburo—to allow the publication of the complete texts of the conference speeches in the official East German press.[72]

By the same token, however, the SED leadership was also intent upon demonstrating that it would not allow itself to be cowed by outside pressures about how best to interpret the Helsinki agreements.[73] Domestic conditions alone in the GDR in the mid-1970s left the regime in no mood to bargain. At this juncture, the East German economy, and hence Honecker's "Main Course" policy of purchasing his citizens' loyalties with consumer goods and higher standards of living, was encountering an array of unanticipated difficulties. Sharp increases in the cost of Western imports (a delayed consequence of the OPEC oil embargo of 1973–1974) and an upward valuation of Soviet energy prices made it harder and harder for the regime to balance its needs for sound investment strategies with the rising demands of its population. Concurrently, East Berlin also had to contend with a staggering increase in the number of its citizens—most estimates put the figure over 100,000—who sought to take advantage of the Helsinki agreements by applying for official permission to emigrate to the West.

In response to these difficulties, the Honecker government proved to be, if anything, even less accommodating than before in the way it dealt with its critics. Whereas the General Secretary had begun his tenure with a variety of seemingly conciliatory gestures toward the East German cultural community and hinted that his country's artists and intellectuals would be allowed greater room for self-expression provided that they showed a modicum of respect for the essentials of socialism, these policies were abruptly exchanged for a much less forgiving line not long after Helsinki. The most prominent case of all was in mid-November 1976, when the outspoken songwriter and satirist, Wolf Biermann, was unexpectedly shorn of his citizenship while on a concert tour in the Federal Republic. When many of Biermann's fellow artists and compatriots responded by initiating a mass letter-writing campaign to protest the measure and attempted to take their grievances to the level of the politburo—marking really the first instance that any significant protest had been organized against government policies since the 1950s—the regime moved swiftly and mercilessly to restrain its critics. By the end of the decade, it said

[72]According to Joachim Böhm, Honecker could not resist the opportunity to play up the GDR's image as a supposedly "world-open country." In contrast, Hermann Axen opposed publication of the controversial texts from the conference: "We won't print that crap!" he is said to have declared; see OHP (Böhm, December 5, 1990). The official Soviet press went along with Axen's admonition.

[73]Indeed, Böhm relates (ibid.) that when he told his colleagues that Helsinki would put heavy demands on them, he was met with incredulity: "We've signed the thing," many noted, "and that's all that needs to be done." In Böhm's view, for individuals like Honecker, it was not a matter of misunderstanding the full meaning of the documents. "Honecker did not want to understand."

something for the limits of the SED's tolerance that scores of East Germany's most famous literary and cultural figures had been either intimidated into silence or forced into permanent exile.

Predictably, these incidents could not have contributed to fostering goodwill in the FRG. Yet, if one looked at the way in which the Honecker government treated the very few West German journalists who were stationed in the GDR, it should have been apparent anyway that there were still serious limits to its desire to cultivate Western public opinion. In December 1975, the correspondent for *Der Spiegel*, Jörg Mettke, became the first of many journalists to be expelled from East Germany for "defaming" his hosts, because of an article in which he examined the forced adoption of children in the GDR. In January 1978 the magazine's East Berlin office was closed down completely after it published a lengthy document purporting to be the manifesto of a hidden opposition group within the ruling circles of the SED.[74] Then, in April 1979, the East German government introduced a series of new provisions in its legal code which severely limited the rights of foreign journalists, requiring them to have formal permission for every interview they conducted.

Once again, the inter-German relationship suffered. Much as one might have anticipated, for every apparent East German violation of the Helsinki spirit, hard-liners in the CDU/CSU promptly took up the call for countermeasures against the GDR, including the resort to economic sanctions. Yet the reaction of Union moderates to these developments may have been most revealing of all. While personalities such as Kohl, Biedenkopf, and the latter's successor, Heiner Geißler, were still concerned to steer their party away from the unprofitable extreme stands of the not-so-distant past, even they could not resist the opportunity to chide the Schmidt government for having achieved so little leverage over its East German counterpart. Had not the Basic Treaty, many inquired, been meant to bring the Germanys closer together and to lighten the load of those Germans who were forced to spend their lives under socialism? Instead, the Honecker regime seemed to have gotten the better half of the bargain. In this case, the best for which the West German population could hope—so the Union argument went— was that real leaders, capable of regaining the FRG's advantage over the GDR and reaffirming Bonn's essential commitments on the national ideal, would control the chancellery after the parliamentary elections of 1980.[75]

[74]For provocative (if perhaps inaccurate) speculation about the identity of the document's authors, see Böhm, ibid. For a contrasting view, see OHP (Hager, July 11, 1991). For some hints about the real authors, see the letter from Humboldt University historian Heinz Niemann in *Deutschland Archiv*, May 1991, pp. 533–538.

[75]Clemens, *Reluctant Realists*, pp. 176–180; *Frankfurter Allgemeine Zeitung*, August 5, 1978, and October 6, 1978; and, from a Social Democratic perspective, Herbert Prauß, "CDU/CSU Außenpolitik—nichts dazugelernt," *Neue Gesellschaft* 25 (May 1978), pp. 402–

Under these circumstances, even if Schmidt had been personally disposed to do more to develop ties with East Berlin—and there was an isolated group of individuals within the SPD, primarily composed of former Brandt associates, such as Bahr, Gaus, Wehner, and even the former chancellor himself, who hoped to see him move in this direction[76]—there would have been little political justification for such an undertaking. Thus, it can hardly have been unexpected that the majority of the agreements Schmidt's government chose to pursue with the East German regime at the end of the 1970s—the decision in 1978, for example, to go ahead with the construction of the new Autobahn between Hamburg and Berlin—were noteworthy for their totally uncontroversial and highly technical character. It was almost as if they had been selected on the basis of their domestic feasibility alone.[77]

Outside of the official channels between the two countries' permanent missions, the few contacts that did exist between East Berlin and Bonn at decade's end were of notably limited scope and consequence. Schmidt's advisor and confidant, Hans-Jürgen Wischnewski, made two trips to East Germany in 1978 and 1979 on behalf of the chancellor. But these visits were largely confined to removing bottlenecks in specific negotiations between the two states. In 1978 Dieter Haack, the FRG's construction minister, became the first cabinet member from the Schmidt administration to visit the GDR when he accepted an invitation to meet with his East German counterpart. Yet, as Haack himself later admitted, the trip proved to be "a political nothing," which vanished from the public eye only days after it had taken place.[78] Otherwise, the only other interactions between the two countries—such as two largely unpublicized meetings, in June 1977 and July 1979, between representatives of the East and West German foreign ministries[79]—were limited to routine exchanges of information. What all of these efforts at inter-German dialogue lacked, noticeably, was the most

---

406. In contrast, when conservative leaders met with East German officials behind the scenes, they brushed away the latters' complaints about the Union forces' harder line by underscoring the necessity of retaining the support of their right-wing constituencies. Their East German interlocutors supposedly said they understood this. Author's interviews, East Berlin, June 8, 1988.

[76]Author's interviews, Dieter Haack and Dietrich Stobbe, December 11, 1987. For example, an outspoken advocate of greater attention to relations with the GDR was the new mayor of West Berlin, Dietrich Stobbe. See his report to the SPD Bundestag *Fraktion* in *Informationen*, no. 1159, December 13, 1977.

[77]Author's interview, Dietrich Stobbe, Bonn, December 11, 1987.

[78]When he returned to Bonn after the trip, Haack was struck by how little interest there was in his talks with East German officials. Author's interview, Dieter Haack, Bonn, December 11, 1987.

[79]Officials whom I interviewed in the Foreign Office in 1987 and 1988 insisted that there was nothing unusual about these contacts, in which a state secretary, Günter van Well, represented the FRG and Michael Kohl the GDR, since the two sides never went beyond

fundamental element of all—the conviction that such contacts should or even would ever amount to anything more substantial.

Inter-German Ties in Question

As the 1970s ended, in short, it was understandable that those individuals on both sides of the national divide who had been cautiously optimistic about the Germanys' prospects as the decade began should have had substantial grounds for disappointment. Would the two governments ever find any bases for taking their relations beyond their halting, and for the most part uninspired, efforts to achieve the greatest possible advantage from the least conceivable investment of their energies? In comparison with the nonrelations of the 1960s, it was undeniable that the GDR and the FRG had at least acquired a formal agreement to guide them and some hope of achieving their minimal objectives. The East German regime had been given the chance to whittle away at Bonn's insistence upon treating the national issue as a matter still open to debate. Also, for all that its leaders could determine about their population's attachment to the GDR, they may even have made some progress toward attaining this goal. Similarly, the West German government had been provided with means of its own for contending with the many walls, material and otherwise, that had arisen between the German populations over the years of separation. Its leaders, too, could point to concrete achievements in pursuing this objective.

Nevertheless, half a decade after the signing of the Basic Treaty, both German regimes seemed to have lost the original impetus to *have* relations at all and to work to overcome the many hurdles that were still associated with the Germanys' differences on the national question. Evidently, the leaders of each government were motivated by factors lying above and beyond their identity as Germans. Given this fact, it was reasonable to expect that the breakthrough in relations between East Berlin and Bonn that had begun, for some, so hopefully with Willy Brandt's ascendancy in the late 1960s would only be completed when both states had found their own distinctive reasons for concluding that a healthier relationship would serve these other ends.

---

exchanging information about official policy. Still, in two respects, the contacts did prove significant. First, they established a powerful precedent for the later efforts by the SPD to press for an expansion of inter-German dialogue on security questions (see chapter 5). Second, because they took place directly between the foreign ministries (although representatives of Bonn's Ministry of Intra-German Relations were present as observers), they also gave East German officials grounds for confidence that they were eroding Bonn's position on the "special" character of German-German contacts. Also, see Link's analysis in Jäger and Link, *Republik im Wandel*, p. 377.

V

Accepting a Divided Germany

All fruitless discussion about how open the
German question is should be ended. It doesn't
bring us anything. As the Basic Treaty specifies,
we should cultivate as good relations as we can
with the GDR, a state that is very much different
from our own, but which is just as sovereign and
independent as any other state in the Warsaw
Pact. We should look for commonalities in spite
of and within the division.
  (Willy Brandt, in *Reden über das eigene Land*,
  1984)

Both German states have a vital, common
interest in preserving peace. . . . Now that
"reunification" has proven to be a big illusion,
their differences over the German question have
the drama of a dream, which occasionally recurs,
but is gone once one wakes up.
  (Erich Honecker, November 22, 1984)

NO ONE in the 1970s could have imagined a proliferation of contacts
taking place between East and West Germany in the 1980s. Yet, this was
exactly what happened. During the decade, city partnerships suddenly
sprang up everywhere, major economic deals were struck, the GDR-FRG
border became more permeable, and most prominently, millions of Germans were temporarily reunited with relatives and friends with whom they
had had little or no contact for decades. If only because the two German
governments had been so far apart just a few years earlier, these developments were both striking and, simultaneously, perplexing. East Berlin and
Bonn may have had reason to cooperate on the technical matters to which
their ties had descended in the late 1970s, but there was nothing to account
for the two states' newly acquired enthusiasm for the relationship. Moreover, everything about the timing of this explosion in contacts was wrong,
as a triple set of international crises—the conflict over NATO's December
1979 decision to deploy a new generation of intermediate-range missiles

(INF) in Western Europe, the Soviet invasion of Afghanistan, and the outbreak in the summer of 1980 of worker unrest in the Polish Baltic shipyards—threatened to set the German governments permanently against each other.

Was it simply that the Germanys' leaders finally came to recognize, as almost all studies of the period have emphasized, how much they stood to lose from a dramatic deterioration in relations and, therefore, sought to do what they could to preserve a semblance of inter-German stability? The point is true enough, but it begs the question of what exactly transpired to make a better relationship suddenly compatible with both states' seemingly divergent interests. The shift seems to have begun with a sequence of events that precipitated the first inter-German summit between Erich Honecker and Helmut Schmidt.

A Threat from the West

By itself, it was surprising that the leaders of the GDR and the FRG should have been able to come together at all as the 1970s ended. The idea of a summit meeting between Honecker and Schmidt was not entirely new, since East Berlin had occasionally broached the possibility of bringing the two figures together during the decade, although there is every reason to suppose the SED regime doubted its counterparts would go along with the proposal. It was clear all along why Honecker would have looked hopefully to the symbolic gains that might be made from such an encounter. He had nothing to risk by meeting with Schmidt and, in view of the GDR's continual search for external sources of legitimation, could only gain from a situation that put Bonn's chief representative in the position of having to demonstrate his respect for and recognition of East German sovereignty. The more difficult question, therefore, given the pressures that impinged on the West German government, was why Schmidt should have suddenly concluded that such a meeting was in his own political interest.

The answer, not unexpected in view of the record of GDR-FRG ties which we have already examined, is that the chancellor's readiness to talk with Honecker was only very indirectly related to developments in the inter-German relationship itself. In October 1977 Schmidt had given a much-publicized lecture at the International Institute for Strategic Studies in London in which he called upon his NATO allies to redress a growing disparity in tactical nuclear and conventional forces in the East-West balance that had emerged from the Strategic Arms Limitation Talks (SALT) between the superpowers. At the time, the West German leader was vague about the specific response that he had in mind, since he was determined only to convince the United States to counter ongoing Soviet deployments of intermediate-range SS-20 missiles in the European USSR. There can, however, be no question that his initiative played a key role in the INF decision of December 1979. It prodded U.S. President Jimmy Carter's administration into taking seriously the theme of the Eurostrategic balance and, just as significantly, also set the stage for NATO's "two-track" response to the Soviet buildup. According to this approach, the stationing of Pershing II and cruise missiles in Western Europe was not to begin until the fall of 1983, and only then if the West were unable to persuade the Soviet Union to reduce its nuclear forces on the continent.[1]

Schmidt himself seems to have been convinced that if he could make the USSR's leaders believe that the West was prepared to go ahead with the modernization of its nuclear forces, Moscow would have no choice but to foresake its military advantage. In May 1978 he thought that he received Leonid Brezhnev's assurances to curtail the SS-20 buildup on the occasion of the General Secretary's long-awaited visit to Bonn. Yet, even when this assumption proved to be wrong—Schmidt rationalized that infighting in the Soviet politburo had somehow limited Brezhnev's ability to fulfill his promise—the chancellor could still tell his party that the Soviet leader appreciated the gravity of the problem and was prepared to discuss it with the West.[2] Less clear, however, is why Schmidt should also have wanted to speak with Erich Honecker. After all the years of basically snubbing his counterpart, there was nothing to suggest that, at least at this early date, he regarded contacts with the East German general secretary as a serious means of influencing Moscow.

A greater clue to Schmidt's behavior may lie in the fact that by 1979 he was by no means in firm control of his own party. To be sure, his continuing high opinion ratings with the West German public assured that the SPD could be counted on to retain him as its chancellor, particularly after the CDU/CSU announced Franz Josef Strauß as its candidate in the upcoming fall 1980 national elections. Nevertheless, it was also true that after a decade in power, there were unmistakable signs of internal dissension within the Social Democratic Party. A growing Left-wing contingent within the SPD, revolving around the Young Socialists (JUSOS), was becoming more and more vocal in its criticisms of Schmidt's mainstream social and environmental policies, and especially his support for nuclear energy.

[1]For Schmidt's 1977 speech, see "The 1977 Alastair Buchan Memorial Lecture," *Survival* 20 (January–February 1978), pp. 2–10. For analysis of his role in the INF decision, see Helga Haftendorn, *Sicherheit und Entspannung* (Baden-Baden: Nomos Verlagsgesellschaft, 1983), pp. 235, 239–248; and Wolfram Hanrieder, *Germany, America, Europe* (New Haven, Conn.: Yale University Press, 1989), pp. 109–113.

[2]See, for example, the SPD *Fraktion* protocol of February 6, 1979, p. 11, Archive of the Friedrich-Ebert-Stiftung, Bonn. Also Jonathan Carr, *Helmut Schmidt: Helmsman of Germany* (London: Weidenfeld and Nicolson, 1985), p. 128.

Misgivings had also arisen in the party, even among the chancellor's closest supporters, about Schmidt's emphasis on relations with the United States, thanks to the Carter administration's maladroit handling of such issues as human-rights policy in Eastern Europe, the neutron bomb, and American fiscal and monetary affairs.

But INF proved to be a catalyst to an explosive debate within the party. Although the nuclear-force modernization decision itself was still far from the intense public controversy that it would become in only a year's time, a number of former Brandt associates, including Wehner, Bahr, and Horst Ehmke, and parliamentarians such as the SPD spokesman for security questions, Alfons Pawelczyk, were already evincing mixed feelings about the implications of a Western military buildup in response to the SS-20s. Wehner in particular called attention to the need for more pacific solutions, such as new forms of cooperation with the East—he especially favored the term "security partnership"—to overcome the psychological impediments to arms control talks between the blocs. Urging his government to move beyond its obsession with the primacy of national reunification, he singled out the GDR in his list of worthwhile discussion partners.[3]

In light of these circumstances, one can more easily understand why, when Schmidt met with his party's assembled delegates at the SPD's Berlin Congress on December 3–7, just days before the INF decision was to be formalized, he took the occasion to announce his plans to meet with Honecker in the GDR in early 1980 to discuss ways of improving the inter-German relationship. Very little may have changed between the Germanys themselves, but so long as Schmidt had to sell the party on his determination to keep negotiations between the blocs on a par with the necessity of restoring the military balance with the Soviet Union, the possibility of even a limited dialogue with East Berlin represented one way of proving his commitment to the cause of détente. Even for a chancellor who was not particularly interested in the GDR, it was, as a former member of the Bonn government has put it, "a theme to rebind the party."[4]

Nonetheless, the invasion of Afghanistan by the Soviet Union on December 27, 1979, put the West Germans, arguably more than any other state involved in the Western response to the Soviet action, into the uncomfortable position of having to choose between two desiderata. On the one hand, there was their fidelity to the Atlantic alliance, and particularly the demands of the American superpower, and on the other, their countervailing desire to carry on business more or less as usual with the East. In the first months after the conflict erupted, Schmidt and his foreign minister,

[3]*Neue Zürcher Zeitung*, April 19, 1979, and Jäger and Link, *Republik im Wandel* (Stuttgart: Deutsche Verlags-Anstalt, 1987), p. 368.

[4]Author's interview with Günter Gaus, Bonn, March 29, 1988.

Hans-Dietrich Genscher, went out of their way to show that their priorities still lay with the alliance, a point the West German leader reluctantly confirmed by agreeing to go along with a U.S. boycott of the Moscow Olympics. At the same time, nevertheless, Schmidt also insisted on practicing what he called "quiet crisis management." He prodded Washington, sometimes to the consternation of American officials, not to write off every chance of convincing Moscow to rethink its actions, while simultaneously he also pressed his Soviet interlocutors to recognize their responsibility for the exacerbation of East-West tensions.

This context helps to explain why the GDR slowly began to occupy a more prominent place in the chancellor's thinking. The inter-German relationship, such as it was, was both a potential victim of the troubles surrounding the two states as well as a convenient symbol of the kinds of cooperative undertakings that Schmidt had in mind in a time of growing "speechlessness" (again, his terminology) between the superpowers. He experienced firsthand the consequences of external uncertainty when, as a result of Soviet pressure, East Berlin chose to postpone the upcoming summit with Honecker only a month after he had announced it. Schmidt, however, proved to be uncharacteristically curious about what might be gained from such a summit. Thus, in May 1980, at the funeral of the Yugoslav president, Josip Broz Tito, he actually met with Honecker for a short exchange of views on steps to minimize the damage already being done to East-West relations.[5]

Even this gesture was not without some risk for the West German leader. Especially because 1980 was an election year, Schmidt could not afford to be oblivious to the possible objections from the ranks of the conservative opposition to any of his contacts with the East. Politicians such as Strauß and Kohl were already criticizing him for supposedly neglecting the "life interests" of the German nation by not doing enough to keep the goal of German unity at the forefront of his government's dealings with the GDR. According to this line of argument, the chancellor needed to be tougher in the way that he broached human-rights issues with the East, and above all, he had to avoid the temptation, of which some of his Social Democratic colleagues were ostensibly guilty, of thinking that his country's relations with the communist bloc were a holy "island of détente" that could be insulated from its international environment.[6]

[5] Klaus Bölling, *Die fernen Nachbarn* (Hamburg: Goldmann, 1983), pp. 78–79. An unpublished transcript of the Schmidt-Honecker exchange in Yugoslavia (IV 2/1/360) provides evidence both of the chancellor's interest in reducing tensions between the superpowers—medium-sized states like the GDR and the FRG, he suggested, could see to it "that the big brothers didn't become nervous"—and of his eagerness to set up a more formal meeting with the East German leader, Central Party Archives, Berlin (hereafter CPA).

[6] For example, see Kohl's June 17, 1980, speech in *Texte zur Deutschlandpolitik* (hereafter, *TzD*), 2d ser., vol. 8, esp. pp. 120–122; also Clay Clemens, *Reluctant Realists* (Durham, N.C.: Duke University Press, 1989), pp. 196–197.

Accordingly, if there were to be a German-German summit in the post-Afghanistan climate, Schmidt recognized that he still had to approach the issue carefully. In fact, this was one of the main reasons why he decided to postpone a second meeting with Honecker, which was scheduled for late August 1980. Up to this point, Schmidt's representatives had insisted that one leg of his planned visit to the GDR include a side trip to the northern port of Rostock, where the chancellor would take the opportunity to stroll through the city and thereby demonstrate his interest in communing with the East German man-on-the-street. Yet the international situation once again intervened, as this time the outbreak of strikes and workers' protests in the northern cities of Gdansk and Gdynia, Poland, gave the GDR's leaders reason to worry about their own domestic stability. As the crisis worsened, the SED's representatives withdrew the invitation to visit Rostock, and Schmidt felt that he had no other choice but to put off the visit again.[7]

It was not long after these developments, however, in mid-October 1980, that the West German leader was presented with a more ominous set of challenges that had to have reminded him of the fragility of the Germanys' modest achievements over the preceding decade. Against the background of the Polish developments, Honecker's government took Bonn by surprise by announcing that as of October 13, 1980, all West Berliners and West Germans wishing to make extended visits to the GDR would have to exchange twice as much currency as they had in the past and four times as much to make day-long visits to East Berlin. Whereas some groups, such as children and retirees, had been previously exempted from these requirements, now they too were included in the currency exchange rules.

This incident alone showed that the SED regime was as capable as ever of exploiting the bargaining advantage provided by the Wall in Berlin. In the ensuing months, all categories of travel into the GDR declined.[8] Neverthe-

---

[7] Author's interview, Dietrich Stobbe, Bonn, December 11, 1987. As the GDR's negotiators informed Schmidt at the time who was clearly concerned about the international ramifications of a Soviet decision to intervene in Poland: "The Russian fleet is already in Rostock." In a letter of January 14, 1992, Stobbe reflected that the message may well have been conveyed by Honecker, but the General Secretary's motives were still unclear: "It is conceivable that the Soviet Union at that point in time sent a unit of the fleet to Rostock because of the disturbances in Poland and that this was actually interpreted as a threat by the SED leadership. It is just as conceivable, however, that the whole incident was made up as a way of warding off the Schmidt visit, since this visit would have to have led to inter-German concessions from the SED that were possibly not wanted at that time by the [party's] 'hardliners.' In this case, the SED leadership would have only used the disturbances in Poland to defend against the Federal Republic's pressures for détente."

[8] According to the end-of-year figures for 1981, the number of West Germans traveling to the GDR fell by 31.6 percent, the number of West Germans taking part in so-called border (*grenznahen*) visits by 40.1 percent, and the number of West Berliners visiting the GDR by 34 percent. See Ernst Martin, *Zwischenbilanz: Deutschlandpolitik der 80er Jahre* (Stuttgart: Bonn Aktuell, 1986), pp. 93–94.

less, as if to guarantee that Schmidt and his advisors really understood how much was at stake for the inter-German relationship, Honecker used the very day on which the new exchange requirements went into effect to deliver a stinging address in Gera, in which he basically called into question the compromise foundations of the Basic Treaty. He demanded that Bonn finally recognize the GDR's separate citizenship, that it agree to the immediate exchange of full ambassadors between the two German capitals, that it settle the Elbe boundary dispute, and that it abolish a monitoring station located in the city of Salzgitter which it used to record human-rights violations in the GDR.[9] Needless to say, because the two most important issues in Honecker's list—those involving citizenship and the exchange of ambassadors—ran directly against long-standing West German policy, there was no way that the Federal government could have acceded to the East German demands. But this fact alone had to have said something to Schmidt about the precariousness of the two states' ties.

We shall later consider Honecker's possible calculations in intensifying the inter-German conflict at this time. For the moment, however, it is enough to appreciate the difficulty of Schmidt's position in weighing alternative responses to the GDR's actions. He and other members of his cabinet were not at all averse to expressing their outrage at East Berlin's actions, which, they contended (to quote the government spokesman at the time, Klaus Bölling), "violated the goal of constantly raising the level of contacts between the peoples of both parts of Europe."[10] Still, it was by no means clear what Bonn could do to force East Germany's leaders to reconsider their decision. One possible recourse, which received considerable attention behind the scenes, was to push for a drastic reduction of the "swing" credit, since the inter-German trade agreement was up for renegotiation in 1981. However, unlike in 1974 when, as we have seen, the credit had been an effective lever against the GDR, the FRG had the disadvantage in 1980 of almost a decade's worth of carefully negotiated agreements with East Berlin. All these agreements could have been jeopardized, as the Schmidt government recognized, if it responded too forcefully to the East German move.[11]

The other recourse was, of course, to maintain some form of continued contacts with East Berlin with the aim of convincing the East German regime, through appeals to its self-interest, to reconsider its antagonistic stand. Yet here too Schmidt was confronted by his conservative opponents

[9]*Neues Deutschland* (hereafter *ND*), October 14, 1980.

[10]*Bulletin*, October 17, 1980, Bonn, Presse und Informationsamt.

[11]As one West German participant relates, "We thought of every way of applying pressure [on East Berlin]. But there was nothing for us to do; irrational responses wouldn't have accomplished anything. The GDR simply [was not] blackmailable." Author's interview, Bonn, February 4, 1988.

who were fully prepared to criticize him for ever having taken seriously the idea of meaningful dialogue with Honecker. After the raising of the currency exchange requirements, some fundamentalist elements within the Union ranks even called upon the chancellor to cancel the "swing" talks outright and to suspend all financial transactions with the GDR not tied to already negotiated contracts.[12] Under these circumstances, Schmidt could hardly be blamed for carefully weighing the potential risks and benefits of another meeting with his East German counterpart.

An East German Opportunity?

As the leader of a Marxist-Leninist state, Honecker had much less reason than the West German chancellor to worry about such domestic constraints. Nevertheless, precisely because the appearance of being taken seriously by his adversary was so important for the purposes of internal legitimation, the SED chief's interests in upgrading ties with his rival were bound to vary with the opportunites he found to pursue his objectives.

There can be little doubt that the primary stimulus behind the General Secretary's hopes of meeting with Schmidt lay in the events culminating in the INF decision of late 1979. At this early time, however, Honecker's aims were apparently quite modest. Those who were around the East German leader suggest that he was not for a moment inclined to question the Soviet Union's SS-20 deployments, regarding the new missiles as fully within the letter of the SALT agreements with the United States. He and most other members of the SED elite were even able to rationalize the Soviet invasion of Afghanistan on the grounds that it had been precipitated by provocative American actions in the Third World.[13]

Accordingly, up to December 1979 Honecker seems to have believed, like his Soviet colleagues, that by putting pressure on Schmidt and the SPD, they could conceivably prevent the West German government from going along with any decision to modernize NATO's nuclear forces. In October 1979 the East German government played host to a meeting with Brezhnev in East Berlin, in which Brezhnev made a much-publicized offer to reduce the number of his country's intermediate-range missiles provided that the West abandoned all consideration of its own INF deployments. In unmistakable terms, Honecker let Schmidt know his own views on the subject in a letter on October 12, in which he emphasized that any NATO decision to station the INF forces on German soil would "necessarily have

[12]*Neue Zürcher Zeitung*, October 15, 1980. For a representative statement, see the remarks by the CDU's spokesman for inter-German and Berlin affairs, Peter Lorenz, in *Deutschland-Union-Dienst*, October 26, 1980.

[13]Author's interview, Herbert Häber, East Berlin, June 1, 1989.

negative consequences for relations between the GDR and the FRG."[14] Finally, it can have been no coincidence that on November 28, just days before the SPD congress in Berlin, he again warned the chancellor about the danger of miscalculation.[15]

Some scholars may interpret the East German leader's actions as the predictable behavior of a Soviet bloc ally eager to carry out the dictates of his patrons in Moscow. But in fact, we do not have to appeal to Soviet wishes at all to account for the General Secretary's threats. By this time Moscow had already informed East Berlin that if the NATO deployments were to go ahead, the GDR would have to bear the brunt of an equivalent number of Soviet counterdeployments on its own soil. Hence, it is understandable that the entire East German leadership would have wanted to prevent the escalating East-West conflict from extending to its own territory.

For these same individuals, however, the turning point for the GDR's strategy seems to have come when Schmidt was able to convince his party to go along with the NATO dual-track decision.[16] From this point onward, officials in East Berlin reasoned, the only hope of defusing the tense situation was to encourage the chancellor himself to emphasize that aspect of Western policy which put primacy on searching for a negotiated solution to the crisis. In this sense, it said something for East German intentions as 1980 began that, in marked contrast to the harsher language from Moscow about Bonn's role in the INF question, Honecker and many of his colleagues in the SED leadership chose to underscore their regret at the extent to which the "so hopeful" developments between the Germanys had been threatened by international tensions.[17] At the Leipzig trade fair in March, East German representatives went to great lengths to broadcast their interest in maintaining favorable trade ties with the Federal Republic, and Günter Mittag repeated the message during an official visit to Bonn the following April. In this vein, too, it was predictable that Honecker was

[14]Honecker mentioned this letter in the politburo report before the Eleventh Central Committee Plenum, *ND*, December 14, 1979. An excellent analysis of the period is by Thomas Banchoff, "Die Rolle des NATO-Doppelbeschlusses in der sowjetischen Deutschlandpolitik, 1978–1984," unpublished Magisterarbeit, University of Bonn, 1988.

[15]The source is again Honecker's speech before the Eleventh Central Committee Plenum, *ND*, December 14, 1979.

[16]A central participant in the SED's internal discussions at the time described the period as follows: "My opinion is that in the course of the 1970s, we underestimated the SS-20s. We didn't reckon with INF. Perhaps the Soviets did not think that the SPD would follow through on INF. There was a kind of euphoric feeling about the SPD. They were sure that the party congress would not support the decision. Hence they wept when they saw they were wrong. The gravity of the problem was simply underestimated. To think that we could have saved ourselves these ten years!" Author's interview with Herbert Häber, June 1, 1989, East Berlin.

[17]*ND*, January 26–27, 1980.

eager to make the most of his exchange of views with Schmidt at Tito's May 1980 funeral, which he later described in upbeat terms as "underscoring the responsibility of both German states for peace."[18]

Finally, this background helps us to see why, from the GDR's perspective, the subsequent train of events surrounding the Polish crisis in the late summer and early fall of 1980 was very much an aberration for the East German leadership. There is every reason to think that Honecker still hoped to receive Schmidt in August and only very slowly began to back away from his pleas for dialogue as he and his colleagues grew aware of the gravity of the events in Poland, which included the rise of the Solidarity trade-union movement and the fully unexpected collapse of the Polish United Workers' Party. Years later, some of Schmidt's closest advisors could still wonder whether the raising of the minimum currency exchange rates in October was driven solely by the SED's fears that "the Polish fever"[19] might spread over the borders of the Oder and Neisse into the GDR. Some speculated that the Honecker regime also took advantage of a good opportunity to increase the amount of foreign exchange (*Devisen*) coming into East Germany, which was steadily becoming a concern for the government because of a rising level of international indebtedness.[20] There can be no question, however, that the storm of Western protest over the Soviet bloc's handling of the events in Poland elicited all of the SED's long-felt indignation at the West's "interference" in the "internal affairs" of other countries.[21]

This may be the best way to comprehend Honecker's surprise decision to respond to the political uncertainties on his country's Eastern border by endorsing a return to his government's maximal demands on the German question. The policymakers in the SED did not need to be told that Bonn would refuse to give ground on the citizenship issue or the exchange of

[18]*ND*, May 22, 1980.

[19]*ND*, September 4, 1980. As a contrast to the turmoil in Poland, the GDR's leaders were at pains to depict their country in terms that emphasized the virtues of stability, or in Honecker's words, "the spirit of hard work, the creativity, and [high] consciousness of our people," *ND*, October 8, 1980. For Honecker's assessment of the situation in Poland, complete with comparisons to the Prague Spring, see his remarks at a December 5, 1980, meeting of WTO leaders in Moscow (IV 2/1/363), CPA, Berlin.

[20]Author's interviews, Bonn, February 4, 1988. Although, if Leonid Brezhnev had anything to say about it, the GDR's action was more fundamental. In an August 3, 1981, meeting with Honecker on the Crimea, he expressed his government's full support for the East German steps: "They make it at least partly possible to reduce the flow of West Germans into the GDR." "These are all," he added, "visible elements of the necessary delimitation of the socialist GDR from the capitalist FRG. In the future, the West Germans must also grasp that without a solution to the basic issues which interest the GDR, a true normalization of relations with you is impossible." Unpublished transcript (IV 2/1/372), CPA, Berlin.

[21]See the reprints of Soviet articles by the pseudonymous observer, Petrov, in *ND*, September 22, 1980, and *ND*, September 29, 1980.

ambassadors. But at a time of escalating tensions between the super-powers, the party leadership probably reasoned that it did not make much difference anyway how conciliatory it was with the FRG. The inter-German relationship was bound to be strained as long as the threat of Soviet inter-vention in Poland hung over central Europe. In the meantime, it did not hurt the GDR to remind the FRG that, as the Basic Treaty itself affirmed, there were two separate and independent German states in Europe, each of which enjoyed the sovereign right to make decisions for itself.[22]

Additionally, one can also detect from this point onward another shift in Honecker's thinking about the inter-German relationship. Far from main-taining a merely defensive stance on the merits of further contacts with the West German government, the General Secretary and the majority of his coleaders evidently became emboldened by the opportunities presented to them by the East-West crisis. First, one does not have to look far to see why the FRG's inability to retaliate effectively to the increase in the currency exchange rates encouraged East Berlin to think that it was not nearly so dependent on Bonn's goodwill as common wisdom allowed. In a February 1981 address, Honecker practically taunted his adversaries by pointedly resurrecting the Ulbrichtian language of the 1950s to suggest that even the question of Germany's future condition remained unresolved: "Watch out!" he admonished. "One day, socialism will knock at your door, and when the day comes when the workers of the Federal Republic undertake the socialist transformation of the FRG, then the question of the unification of both German states will be seen in an entirely new light."[23]

Actually, there was nothing to suggest that the East German leadership was reconsidering its stand on the subject of German unity; quite to the contrary, most wanted to put the issue behind them forever. But the SED regime seemed intent upon demonstrating to the whole world, as it showed by initiating a number of diplomatic undertakings with various West Euro-pean states, such as France, Great Britain, Italy, Belgium, and the Scandina-vian countries, and other modern industrial powers, such as Japan, that the GDR could get by on its own, if need be, without assistance from the FRG.

There was also a second reason for the Honecker government's more pronounced sense of confidence at this time, which was related to the internal political situation in the Federal Republic as the debate about the implementation of the INF decision heated up. Just days before Honecker

[22]See Hermann Axen's defense of the new currency exchange rates in *ND*, November 8/9, 1980, and Herbert Krolikowski's statement in Madrid, *ND*, November 15/16, 1980. Cer-tainly, the Soviets encouraged them to think along these lines. As Brezhnev advised Honecker on August 3, 1981, about the possibility of a meeting with Schmidt: "It is important that you maintain a sense of suspense about this meeting. When you show West German politicians that you are capable of greater toughness, then they will begin to understand that they can't belittle our interests with impunity." Unpublished transcript (IV 2/1/372), CPA, Berlin.

[23]*ND*, February 16, 1981.

raised the stakes in the inter-German relationship in mid-October 1980, Helmut Schmidt had won a resounding victory over the Union candidate, Strauß, in the elections to the Bundestag. Nonetheless, in almost every respect, Schmidt's triumph was a pyrrhic victory. Many Social Democrats who now entered the West German parliament for the first time were representative of the party's left wing and were particularly harsh critics of the chancellor's support for the NATO build-up. Then, too, in part because of the challenge facing the SPD as a result of the rise of a new environmentalist party known as the Greens, Schmidt also found his entire governing philosophy under fire. Increasingly, party elders like Brandt and Wehner argued that the SPD had to reassess its domestic and international priorities if it hoped to retain the support of a rising generation of West German voters.[24] With the emergence in 1981 of a massive peace movement in the FRG, for the most part directed against NATO policy, such arguments met with growing favor within the party's ruling circles.

Thus, it was reasonable that the SED should have seen its opportunity in this politically fluid situation to promote discord among SPD members about INF. According to Honecker, ties between the two German states could be aided considerably—and hurt equally seriously—depending on the stand Schmidt took on the FRG's role in the missile question.[25] Yet, even more important for the GDR's specific purposes, there was also an additional dividend in the crisis atmosphere of the time. Beginning with a controversial interview that Günter Gaus granted to the Hamburg weekly, *Die Zeit*, in February 1981, just before his replacement as Bonn's representative to the GDR by Klaus Bölling, a number of prominent, primarily Social Democratic West German politicians were urging the government to rethink the purpose and practice of its German policy. Gaus probably went farthest of all in public by openly calling on Bonn to abandon the "concept of the nation." In his view, the traditional definition of German objectives only increased the likelihood that the GDR and the FRG would continue to engage in "shadowboxing" over old themes, whereas the times demanded greater cooperation between the blocs.[26] Still others in the party leadership, including Bahr, who met with Honecker in East Berlin in September, and Peter Glotz, the SPD's chief executive officer, appealed for a more elastic understanding of the inter-German relationship that proceeded from an

[24]See, for example, Willy Brandt, "Den eignen Weg neu finden," *Neue Gesellschaft* 28 (May 1981), pp. 396–404; or for a representative view from the younger generation, see Hermann Scheer, "Der verengte Sicherheitsbegriff," *Neue Gesellschaft* 28 (May, 1981), pp. 413–416.

[25]Consider Honecker's remarks at the SED's Tenth Congress in April 1981, in *Reden und Aufsätze* (hereafter *RA*), vol. 8 (Berlin: Dietz, 1983), p. 27.

[26]In particular, Gaus recommended that his government seek to move beyond considering the GDR as only a "police state" and come to accept ("internally recognize") its existence as an unavoidable reality; *Die Zeit*, January 30, 1981.

acceptance of the reality of the nation's division to embrace broader forms of dialogue in the interest of both states. Above all, these were to have included regular discussions on central European security.[27]

Evidently, there were some figures within the SED politburo who were unsure whether the GDR's needs, or even those of its allies in the Soviet government, would be best served by seeking to exploit these sentiments.[28] Yet from Honecker's perspective—and by this point, his views counted most in setting state priorities—the fact that at least some of his adversaries were willing to consider a more flexible definition of German concerns was quite encouraging. It showed that significant elements in the FRG were coming closer to treating his state as an "[equal] subject under international law" and "moving away from the presumption to speak 'for all Germans.' "[29]

This is not to say that one must regard the SED chief's professions of interest in discussions about European security as merely expedient. There is every reason to think that by 1981 he too was impressed with the dangers of the arms race between the superpowers.[30] West German officials attribute the General Secretary's more differentiated position in part to the greater level of information he was able to obtain, not only on NATO policy but also on Soviet objectives, from contacts such as the informal consultations between the two German foreign ministries; in July 1981 these talks were taken up on the ambassadorial level.[31] In addition, for the first time in

[27]Hendrik Bussiek, "Lieber getrennt leben als vereint sterben . . . ," *Vorwärts* 38 (September 1981), p. 3.

[28]For a blatant example, see the December 16, 1980, notes from politburo member Werner Krolikowski about Honecker, claiming that the GDR leader was carrying on "an irresponsible, two-sided zigzag policy" toward the FRG, first by making his "correct demands" at Gera and then by moving away from them. Cited in Peter Przybylski, ed., *Tatort Politbüro* (Berlin: Rowohlt, 1991), pp. 340–344. Also see Krolikowski's notes from a November 13, 1980, meeting between Willi Stoph and the minister of state security, Erich Mielke, both of whom echoed his reservations about Honecker, while at the same time admitting there was little they could do to pressure their leader to change course (Mielke: "Everyone is afraid of EH"), ibid., pp. 345–348. Presumably both sets of notes were passed on to Moscow.

[29]*RA*, vol. 8, p. 27.

[30]For example, Egon Bahr found Honecker to be a changed man after he learned more about the Soviet role in the arms buildup. "When I talked to Honecker in 1980 for the first time, he was in total agreement with Moscow. Yet, when I met with him again in 1981, he indicated that he didn't want to see any developments that would lead to the introduction of new Soviet missiles." Author's interview, Bonn, January 21, 1988. In addition, Honecker was not hesitant at all in warning Bahr that Schmidt's support for INF could hurt the SPD: "You've got to understand," the General Secretary lectured, "we are for the SPD coalition." "We are, too," Bahr replied. Unpublished transcript (IV 2/1/372), September 4, 1981, East Berlin, CPA, Berlin.

[31]Author's interviews, Foreign Office, Bonn, February 16 and March 10, 1988. At a meeting on July 3, 1981, the GDR was represented by Ambassador Ernst Krabatsch, the director of the Policy Planning Department in the Ministry of Foreign Affairs, and the FRG by Friedrich Ruth, the Foreign Office arms-control authority.

decades, an East German leader also faced the unique situation of having to contend with a faint expression of domestic opinion on security issues, as the massive antinuclear demonstrations in the FRG gave birth to a nascent GDR peace movement. This loose following was comprised largely of young people and church representatives who called on their government to take substantive steps to live up to its rhetoric about wanting peace and arms limits in Europe.

Under these circumstances, it is easy to see why, by 1981, Honecker should have been tempted to use the occasion of a meeting with Schmidt to lay the foundations for achieving two of his regime's principal objectives. He could demonstrate that the GDR was sincerely interested in assuming a position of responsibility in continental efforts to defuse tensions between the superpowers and, at least as pressing, he could also show that the two German states were finally prepared to deal with each other as the equals which, in Honecker's eyes, they already were. With regard to the latter pursuit, of course, the big unknown was how far Helmut Schmidt could be pushed, assuming that he was now ready to take the GDR seriously.

The Meeting at Werbellin

When the two German leaders finally managed to meet at Honecker's official hunting lodge on the Werbellinsee from December 11 to 13, 1981, the inter-German relationship unquestionably reached a turning point. Yet this was perhaps less because of the concrete agreements that emerged from the meeting than because the exchange of views in the GDR took place at all. Once one had gotten beyond the "sensational character" of the German-German encounter (to use the words of one senior East German participant), it was finally conceivable for Schmidt and Honecker to begin talking about normal ties between the two states.[32]

From the very first, "normality" had very different meanings for each of the German leaders. For Schmidt, who left Bonn with the critical eyes of the West German opposition bearing down upon him—Strauß apparently opposed the trip outright[33]—the main point of the meeting was to convince Honecker that some form of stable relations should be maintained *no matter what* happened between the superpowers. Although formal talks between the United States and the Soviet Union had begun a few months earlier in Geneva about limiting or eliminating altogether intermediate-

---

[32]Author's interviews, Herbert Häber, East Berlin, April 28, 1988.

[33]According to one of the West German planners of the trip, the CSU leader sent Schmidt a legal opinion from Dieter Blumenwitz (the lawyer who defended Bavaria's case against the Basic Treaty before the Constitutional Court in 1973), contending that the chancellor could not go to the GDR since the Wall was a violation of international law. Author's interviews, Bonn, February 4, 1988.

range missile systems in Europe, the new, avowedly anti-Communist Reagan administration in Washington and the few signs of real conciliation that were coming from Moscow suggested that there could be no guarantee that the German states would be spared the burden of a rapidly escalating arms race. Hence, Schmidt was all the more concerned to prevent a recurrence of the kind of disturbance to the daily conduct of business between his country and East Germany that had been touched off by the raising of the minimum border exchange requirements a year earlier.

In return for a modicum of what he termed "calculability" (*Berechenbarkeit*, a favorite concept of the chancellor), Schmidt made it clear that he was willing, in effect, to go halfway to meet the GDR's standard demands of his government. He was not about to cover up the fact, he told Honecker, that his administration and that of the SED still had basic differences on the national question, but by the same token, there was no point in Bonn any longer calling into question the GDR's "independence" and "sovereignty." In his estimation, the main consideration was that the two German states did "everything in [their] power, however limited, to hold on to their accomplishments, to preserve them and to strengthen them."[34] Somewhat more specifically, however, Schmidt also demonstrated through his handling of the exchange-rate controversy that he fully grasped the implications of his government's limited room for maneuver. Rather than introducing any ultimata, he suggested only that Bonn saw a strong "political-psychological" connection between the GDR's receptivity to greater citizen contacts and its own ability to foster a healthy economic relationship with the East German regime.[35] As a particularly pointed inducement to good behavior, he then presented Honecker with the outlines of a general treaty of economic cooperation that was to help the GDR solve some of its investment bottlenecks by establishing a common German credit institute, in which West German funds would necessarily play the greater role.[36]

For his part, Honecker preferred to keep the conversation on a loftier

[34]For Schmidt's remarks of December 11, see *Deutschland Archiv*, February 1982, p. 206. Or as one of the chancellor's deputies reflected, "this was our way of showing the GDR that we'd given up the *Alleinvertretungsanspruch*." Author's interviews, Bonn, January 11, 1988.

[35]The FRG government did not want to go so far as to establish a strict linkage (*Junktim*) between the exchange-rate issue and the two states' future economic relations because, as one of the decision-makers involved in the negotiations emphasized, "we considered intra-German trade to be a value in itself which one couldn't allow to be cavalierly placed in jeopardy." Author's interview, Hans-Jürgen Wischnewski, Bonn, January 11, 1988. But this does not mean the West Germans were hesitant to express their feelings in off-the-record discussions. For example, in his September 4, 1981, meeting with Honecker and Axen, Bahr emphasized that if the GDR expected to see progress in arms-control negotiations, there had to be equivalent progress on the exchange rates. Unpublished transcript (IV 2/1/372), CPA, Berlin.

[36]Author's interview, Hans-Jürgen Wischnewski, January 11, 1988. For a hint of this arrangement, cf. Bölling, *Die fernen Nachbarn*, p. 136.

level by emphasizing the special responsibility of his state and the FRG, in view of their troubled national past, to see to it "that war should never again emerge from German soil." In particular, he pleaded with Schmidt to reconsider his support for the NATO missiles. ("Why do you allow yourself to be a proponent of the American course? There's no sensible reason why you need these weapons.")[37] Yet one did not have to read much between the lines of the East German leader's arguments to appreciate that he was equally concerned to use this issue to assure that every step in the direction of greater inter-German contacts was also a guarantee that Bonn could never return to its old extraterritorial claims on the GDR.

To this end, the mere fact of the German summit was already a gain for Honecker, since the presence of the Federal chancellor alone in the GDR cannot but have helped to demonstrate, both to the East German population and to the onlooking world, that the one state that was historically inclined to question the legitimacy of the German Democratic Republic was steadily coming closer to accepting it as an equal. It remains an abiding paradox about the inter-German relationship, however, that had this been the only benefit of the discussions with Schmidt, Honecker's interest in exploring broader avenues of cooperation with Bonn might have been much more muted than it became by the mid-1980s. After all, the West German leader's visit to the GDR would soon lose its sense of immediacy, and there was no guarantee (aside from the chancellor's extension of an invitation to Honecker to visit the FRG at some unspecified future point) that he would reciprocate by making relations with East Berlin into a priority in the years to come. Yet two distinct events on the last day of Schmidt's visit seem to have assured the GDR party chief that greater promise lay in the inter-German future.

The first event, apparently unexpected by either German leader, was the announcement in the early hours of December 13 that martial law had been imposed in Poland.[38] There can be no question that, at the time, the declaration put Schmidt in the highly uncomfortable position of appearing to be on friendly terms with a regime, the SED, that had been among the most vocal critics of the Polish spring. For a few minutes, he and his

[37]Cited in Bölling, *Die fernen Nachbarn*, p. 141. Honecker tried to take advantage of Schmidt's troubles within the SPD by telling the chancellor that his political life would be easier if he abandoned INF: "You have made a big mistake," the General Secretary reportedly declared. "You've tied your political future to the missile decision." Author's interview, Herbert Häber, East Berlin, June 1, 1989.

[38]West German conservatives later argued that Honecker must have known that the Polish military and the Soviet Union were going to make this move on the last day of Schmidt's visit. However, I have been unable to find anyone involved in the visit, East or West German, who felt that Honecker had specific forewarning. According to West German participants, Schmidt believed that the GDR's leader was as surprised as he about the timing of the action. Author's interviews, East Berlin and Bonn.

advisors even considered cutting short the visit to the GDR in protest. That he did not opt for an early departure, however, essentially because such a gesture would have been sure to sour relations with East Berlin all the more, helped to establish a crucial principle from the SED's perspective: German interests would not necessarily be held hostage to events transpiring elsewhere in the socialist world.[39]

The second and even more telling event was the extent to which Honecker was able to control the domestic reaction to Schmidt's single encounter with the East German populace, which took place later in the day during a stopover in the Mecklenburg town of Güstrow. This time, unlike in 1970 when thousands of citizens had been able to cheer Willy Brandt upon his arrival in Erfurt, the West German leader was greeted by a carefully orchestrated demonstration of the SED state at its dictatorial best. Scores of policemen lined the city streets, and only a select handful of Güstrowers were allowed to come close to the chancellor. Given the heavy symbolic value Schmidt had placed on this part of his visit, it is no wonder that he was enraged by the deliberate manipulation of his presence. "It was a lousy deal," one of his advisors reflected, "*eine ganz große Scheiße!*"[40] Yet, at the same time, Honecker was also able to establish a principle of his own: acknowledging the GDR's sovereignty meant accepting its right to attend to its own internal affairs, which in turn also meant acknowledging its right to act as a Leninist state.

In these respects, it is hard to avoid concluding that East Berlin emerged as the net beneficiary of the meeting at Werbellinsee. Over the following months in 1982, the Communist regime arguably had to give up the least to sustain the momentum in the Germanys' relations. To be sure, Schmidt received the private assurances of his host that the GDR was also interested in maintaining a spirit of give-and-take in the two states' negotiations, and Bonn was subsequently able to make certain limited gains in the area of "human improvements." The duration of single-day visits by West Berliners to East Berlin was extended somewhat, and the East German regime promised to ease the requirements for those of its citizens seeking to visit the FRG in cases of "urgent family necessity." Despite Bonn's best efforts, however, the GDR still managed to emerge the victor on the issues of consequence in the inter-German relationship. The Honecker government refused to budge at all on the matter of the compulsory exchange requirements, keeping their levels at the previously high rates, and after some delay, the West Germans were finally induced to agree in June to a new multiyear extension of the "swing."

In short, had Honecker's rising interest in closer relations with his adver-

---

[39]Author's interview, East Berlin, May 25, 1988.
[40]Author's interview, Bonn, February 4, 1988.

saries been a sufficient basis for German-German cooperation, the preeminent obstacle to a flowering of the two states' relations would have been overcome by the spring of 1982. Indeed, Schmidt himself went a long way toward generating even greater goodwill in East Berlin at the time when he openly opposed an American plan to impose trade sanctions on the Eastern bloc in retaliation for the Polish crackdown. Nevertheless, as in the past, that which was possible between the Germanys was equally contingent upon the existence of the appropriate domestic climate within the FRG. Here, Honecker's successes appear to have come, almost ironically, at the cost of Schmidt's misfortune.

As a result of his decision to see his visit to the GDR through to the end, for example, the chancellor was immediately subject upon his return to Bonn to vilification by his conservative opponents. The Social Democratic leader had supposedly not been "bold" enough in condemning the imposition of martial law in Poland; either he should have left East Germany outright, his critics argued, or he should have at least made the issue a centerpiece of his discussions with Honecker.[41] Similar criticisms were again raised several months later when the governing coalition failed to get the GDR to back down on the exchange-rate issue, even after the renegotiation of the "swing."[42]

Against this background, the SED leadership could hardly complain of having been misled when Schmidt proved incapable of living up to his assurances of arranging a general economic treaty in 1982. By this juncture, the domestic constellation of forces necessary for hammering out such an agreement was just not to be found in the FRG. But from the perspective of the GDR's rulers, this disappointment was only symptomatic of an even greater danger looming on the West German horizon, which showed that liberalism and liberal institutions could not only be made to work for them but could also turn against them. As Schmidt's control over the SPD abated with every day the INF controversy remained unresolved and the polarization within his party grew, and as the chancellor's coalition partners in the FDP began to have justifiable worries about their ally's ability to maintain his governing majority,[43] policymakers in East Berlin had reason to be concerned, for the first time since the failed vote of no-confidence against Brandt in 1972, that the Christian Democrats might

[41]For example, see Strauß's criticism of Schmidt's "instinctless" reaction to the events in Poland, cited in *Frankfurter Allgemeine Zeitung*, December 14, 1981, or Eduard Lintner's critical remarks in *Deutschland-Union-Dienst*, March 16, 1982.

[42]For example, see the speeches by Peter Lorenz and Eduard Lintner in *Verhandlungen des deutschen Bundestages, Stenographischer Bericht*, 9th elec. period, 99th sess., May 12, 1982, pp. 5962–5963, 5965–5966.

[43]On the FDP's calculations at the time, see Johannes Merck, "Klar zur Wende? Die FDP vor dem Koalitionswechsel in Bonn, 1980–1982," *Politische Vierteljahresschrift* 28, no. 4 (December 1987), pp. 385–402.

soon return to power in the FRG. Paradoxically, by seeking to obtain maximal advantages from the SPD, the GDR may have helped to weaken the Social Democrats' base of support. East Berlin faced the very real possibility that its own gains were at risk.

The "Wende"

After the Schmidt-Honecker meeting, the formation of a new governing coalition between the CDU/CSU and the FDP under the leadership of Helmut Kohl on October 1, 1982, as well as the coalition's later confirmation in power in the national elections of March 1983, did indeed prove to be a *Wende*, or "turning point," in the history of GDR-FRG relations. But it was not the one that pessimistic observers of the two states' ties had anticipated. Rather, by finally including the opponents of the *Ostpolitik* in the normalization of German-German relations, the new West German government set in motion forces that locked Bonn more tightly than ever before into a manner of dealing with the GDR that confirmed the other state's independence.

Privately, East German officials had recognized for some time on the basis of back-channel discussions that the stereotypical image of the West German opposition as dominated by fire-breathing "revanchists" and "militarists" was inappropriate.[44] There were too many prominent officials within the CDU and even some within the CSU who, for a number of reasons, were already prepared to move their parties to accept more routine ties with the GDR. For some, like the mayor of West Berlin at the time, Richard von Weizsäcker, and the chief of Kohl's chancellery, Philipp Jenninger, this was merely a question of choosing the lesser of two evils, a qualified recognition of the existence of another German state in place of an insistence on the FRG's long-term national goals, in the hope that concrete benefits could be realized for ordinary people living in East Germany.[45] For others, and particularly for Kohl himself and CDU General Secretary Heiner Geißler, the shift had even deeper, political dimensions. It was a matter of bringing the Union parties back to the electoral mainstream by

[44]Says one, "The CDU always told us: 'We'll emphasize normal pragmatic relations with the GDR [when we come to power].' . . . Some, like [Werner] Marx, [Olaf von] Wrangel, [Gerhard] Reddemann, and [Manfred] Abelein, publicly stressed other things, but in private discussions they said 'normality.' " Author's interview, Klaus Zechmeister, East Berlin, June 8, 1988.

[45]"For me," one prominent CDU member of the Bundestag relates, "the question was, how can I personally improve the conditions for the people over there. There were many, many stories [involving peoples' lives there], which were in part quite moving [*dramatisch*]. I couldn't be responsible for making things worse. I wanted to make the Wall more permeable." Author's interviews, Bonn, January 20, 1988.

subscribing to a policy that was already approved by the vast majority of the West German population and for which public support seemed to grow as the fundamentals of the inter-German relationship were threatened by surrounding international tensions.[46]

Nevertheless, East German tacticians could also appreciate from past experience with the liberal democratic politics of the FRG that the existence of support alone for a change of course was no guarantee that any West German party would be willing to fight the internal battles required for serious innovation on the handling of the German question.[47] That the new governing coalition in fact proved to be at least as accommodating toward the GDR as Schmidt's SPD may be attributed to three more or less interrelated factors, all at best only indirectly tied to the substance of the national issue. The first had to do with the unusual circumstances in which the new chancellor, Kohl, found himself in 1982 and 1983. Unlike in earlier years, when the CDU leader had been constantly pressed to adjust his policies to accord with the less compromising stands espoused by Strauß and the CSU, Kohl's successful rise to power gave him the advantage of being able to say that the latter's inflexibility had only brought the Union parties a disastrous defeat at the polls in 1980. Thus, he proposed to base his government's policies on a "coalition of the middle" that would reach out to the broadest segments of the West German electorate possible, not unlike the way that Adenauer and the CDU's founders had originally crafted their party to be a true "catch-all" organization.

For Bonn's policy toward East Germany, this stand meant that Kohl was eager to show that his government would simply pursue a more "honest" and more "realistic" approach to the GDR by keeping those issues at the forefront of the public consciousness over which the FRG would never see eye to eye with East Berlin—the Wall, the barbed wire, and the "order to shoot" would-be escapees (*Schießbefehl*) at the East German border. Yet, while he insisted that his government would do its best to convince the GDR leadership to abandon its offenses against "the German fatherland," Kohl also emphasized that his administration, much as the SPD before it, in-

---

[46]Author's interview, CDU Bundesgeschäftsstelle, Bonn, March 8, 1988. For example, in May 1981 the Allensbach polling institute asked CDU/CSU voters, "Should the Federal government continue its détente policy toward the East in the future, or do you believe that there is no point in continuing the détente policy?" Fifty-five percent of the respondents favored continuing the old policy, while only 25 percent said the policy was pointless; 20 percent were undecided. In the same poll, 79 percent of SPD supporters and 84 percent of FDP supporters wanted to continue the policy. See E. Noelle-Neumann and E. Piel, eds., *Allensbacher Jahrbuch der Demoskopie, 1978–1983* (Munich: K. G. Saur, 1983), p. 637.

[47]In 1988, the deputy director of the East German foreign ministry department for FRG affairs observed that although his government's contacts with individuals like Biedenkopf and Kiep confirmed that there were sensible politicians in the CDU/CSU, the problem was that these figures had been in the opposition before, and possibly represented only minority opinion within their party. Author's interviews, Hans Schindler, East Berlin, May 12, 1988.

tended to use the four-power accord on Berlin and the Basic Treaty as its principal bases for negotiating with East Germany: "The GDR, ladies and gentlemen, can rest assured that we will remain true to already assumed obligations, while we expect only that the GDR likewise observes the letter and spirit of these treaties."[48]

Had Kohl in 1982–1983 needed any additional help in justifying his stand, he also had the advantage of a second circumstantial factor. His new coalition partners, the Free Democrats, literally required his regime to go along with the *Ostpolitik* they had developed with the SPD over the preceding decade.[49] As it was, at this early date in the coalition's history, the FDP's leader, Foreign Minister Genscher, was not nearly as provocative for Union fundamentalists as many of his colleagues. Genscher had been one of the key proponents of the INF decision; he had been an outspoken advocate of United States-FRG ties and a critic of Soviet "expansionism"; and at times, he was even known to harken back to the nationalistic inclinations at his party's roots.[50] Still, animosities between the FDP and the CSU ran deep, and on several occasions in early 1983, when the German-German relationship was burdened by new controversies—for example, the death of a West German citizen on the GDR's border—the governing coalition practically split into warring factions. Nonetheless, the FDP's hand was strengthened with the CDU/CSU's victory in the March 1983 elections. Although Kohl achieved only just short of an absolute majority in the parliamentary vote, he was conveniently able to silence his critics in the CSU with the admonition that the coalition could not survive without the support of the Free Democrats.[51]

This situation probably accounted for what was, arguably, the most important of all of the domestic changes in the FRG for the future of the inter-German relationship. By the spring of 1983, by virtue of Kohl's decision to embrace the rudiments of Social Democratic policy toward the GDR and the FDP's strengthened hand in foreign-policymaking, all of the world

---

[48] *Verhandlungen des deutschen Bundestages, Stenographischer Bericht*, 9th elec. period, 121st sess., October 13, 1982, pp. 7227–7228. Also see Clemens, *Reluctant Realists*, p. 257.

[49] This was the impression conveyed to me in every interview I conducted with members of the FDP Bundestag *Fraktion* in 1987 and 1988. One could easily detect the FDP's determination to preserve the *Ostpolitik* in its representatives' speeches around the time of the *Wende*. Consider Wolfgang Mischnik's statement on the very day of Kohl's appointment as chancellor, October 1, 1982: "We have been able to accomplish a great deal in the area of foreign policy and [the national] policy which wouldn't have been accomplished ten or fifteen years ago. We will preserve [these achievements] because we will also support this policy in the future. There is no other path than this one." *Verhandlungen des deutschen Bundestages, Stenographischer Bericht*, 9th elec. period, 118th sess., October 1, 1982, p. 7183.

[50] Olga Sandler, "Shades of Center: Hans-Dietrich Genscher and West German Policy towards the Soviet Union," unpublished manuscript, 1989, pp. 48–49.

[51] William Paterson, "The Christian Union Parties," in H. G. Peter Wallach and George Romoser, eds., *West German Politics in the Mid-Eighties* (New York: Praeger, 1985), p. 77.

could see (East Berlin included) that Franz Josef Strauß was threatened with the uncomfortable prospect of finding himself and his party relegated to a position of lesser political significance. Hence, it was no coincidence that in May 1983, shortly after the Federal elections, the Bavarian minister-president was approached by Honecker's personal representative, Alexander Schalck-Golodkowski, with the novel proposal that he, Strauß, aid the East German government in securing a substantial bank credit. In return, the SED was willing to make a number of key concessions on questions involving inter-German contacts.

In part, the GDR's motivations were clearly bound up with the health of its economy. By this juncture, although the truth was not widely known outside the SED's uppermost ruling circle, the regime's effort to maintain East Germany's reputation as the economic pacesetter of the socialist world was coming dangerously close to breaking down. In particular, thanks to Honecker's insistence upon maintaining high levels of consumer spending without cutting state subsidies, East Berlin had accumulated as much as $13 billion in foreign debts and desperately needed a quick infusion of foreign currency to meet the interest payments alone on these obligations. Thus, it made sense to go to one of the chief representatives of West German capitalism in seeking to make explicit a trade-off that had long been at the heart of the inter-German relationship.

But in addition, Honecker and his colleagues cannot have failed to appreciate how much their even broader interests might be served if they were to succeed in finally coopting Strauß, one of the *Ostpolitik*'s oldest critics, into the process of normalizing relations.[52] With the implementation of NATO's INF decision immediately before them—a decision the new coalition in Bonn was almost certain to ratify in November failing a U.S.-Soviet arms-control agreement—and with the equal certainty that the GDR's Soviet allies would then respond by deploying a new generation of missiles on East German soil, it made good sense for the SED to seek to eliminate all possible impediments to preserving a semblance of inter-German continuity.

In this respect, when Strauß chose to help the GDR resolve its liquidity problems by arranging a federally guaranteed bank loan of nearly DM 1

[52]Not only did East German officials intentionally seek to exploit Strauß's weaknesses in order to enlist him in the cause of better inter-German relations, but officials in the West German chancellery later insisted that they, too, had deliberately encouraged the Bavarian minister-president to get involved in the credit negotiations to co-opt him into supporting the Kohl government's policies as well. "It wasn't that important," one high-level participant told me, "that [Strauß] then claimed that it was all his idea, though it wasn't." Author's interviews, Bonn, January 20, 1988. This position is supported in Philipp Jenninger, "Kontinuität, was sonst? Deutsch-deutsche Beziehungen nach dem Regierungswechsel 1982 bis 1984," unpublished manuscript, 1991, pp. 41–43. For Strauß's views about his role, see *Die Erinnerungen* (Munich: Siedler, 1989), pp. 470–479.

billion in the summer of 1983, the nature of the bargaining relationship between East Berlin and Bonn was fundamentally transformed, and a host of opportunities were opened between the two states. This change took place for the not very complicated reason that Strauß, unlike Schmidt before him, did not have to worry about having the Bavarian head of the CSU questioning his every move. Given his hard-line credentials, Strauß could practically operate with political impunity.

In direct response to the minister-president's appeals, for example, the East German government intervened to ease the passage of Westerners entering the GDR at border control points and drastically reduced the number of vehicles searched by police officials on the transit routes to and from Berlin. Even more telling, however, in view of Schmidt's past frustrations, was the SED's decision in September 1983 finally to lift its compulsory exchange requirement for children under the age of fourteen. With this sign of flexibility, along with a simultaneous move to eliminate one of the bloodiest aspects of the GDR's border fortifications, the so-called self-shooting weapons (*Selbstschussanlagen*), the party regime almost seemed prepared to put its chief bargaining chip with Bonn—that is, control over access to its territory and population—up for negotiation.

What Honecker and his coleaders expected in return for such largesse was nothing less than a radical upward valuation of their country's place in Bonn's scale of priorities. The East German leader seemed to receive his wish in part with successive official visits to the GDR, by Strauß himself in late July, Richard von Weizsäcker in his capacity as mayor of West Berlin in September, and the FRG's finance minister, Gerhard Stoltenberg, in early November 1983. By themselves, such gestures of recognition for the GDR's sovereignty had to have been gratifying. Making each of these exchanges even more significant, however, was the way they increased the prospects of better ties between the two states. By fueling the fires of party competition in the FRG, a fact the SED was only too happy to exploit, they literally drove the Social Democrats into accelerating the pace of inter-German accommodation.

Under routine circumstances, it would have been understandable had the former architects of the *Ostpolitik* reacted with some mixed feelings and even rancor at the relative ease with which the CDU/CSU shed its old posture. No one wanted the German-German relationship to suffer with the change of government. But the unpleasant memory lingered that these were, in many cases, the same people who had once opposed ratification of the Basic Treaty and continually frustrated all subsequent attempts to normalize ties with East Berlin. Still, these were also far from normal times for the Social Democrats. With Schmidt's fall from the chancellorship and the loss of a galvanizing center within the party and with the appearance of any number of new challenges to the SPD's hopes of ever again regaining control of the government—not the least of which was the Greens' ability to garner 5.6 percent of the national vote in the March 1983 elections, in large part at the SPD's expense—the party was deprived of many of the internal constraints that might otherwise have forced its leaders to adhere to a more moderate line on the German question.

At first, only the Social Democrats' uncertainty at having to act as an opposition party at all was reflected in its leaders' statements on relations with East Berlin. For example, the SPD's candidate for chancellor in the March elections, Hans-Jochen Vogel, went to great lengths, after meeting with East German officials and talking with Honecker himself, to criticize the Union parties for ostensibly failing to maintain continuity with the German policy of Schmidt's time. Other party notables, such as Wehner, went even further, suggesting that the new government had no choice but to compromise with the GDR on the old sticking points in inter-German negotiations—such as the handling of East Germany's separate citizenship—if it hoped to make any progress in the area of "humanitarian improvements."[53] However, in the heated context of the INF debate, which was capped off with the SPD's formal rejection of the NATO missiles only four days before deployment actually began in the FRG on November 23, 1983, the Social Democratic left wing began to press for a radically different kind of dialogue with East Berlin than Bonn had conducted in the past.

Best known among these innovations was probably the idea of "common security," a nebulous concept that nevertheless seemed to offer the party a certain amount of talking ground with the SED. Its advocates underscored the dangers of a new Cold War and the opportunity before the German states to pressure their allies into seeking alternatives to the destabilizing consequences of nuclear deterrence. A year earlier, Egon Bahr had participated in a United Nation's commission led by Sweden's ex-premier, Olof Palme, which in May 1982 had proposed the creation of special nuclear-weapons-free zones on either side of the German border.[54] Above and beyond appreciating the security benefits of such arrangements, however, the Social Democratic leadership was also slowly brought around to the idea, in part thanks to the SED's subtle encouragement, that such discussions might provide a useful vehicle for the SPD to regain its leading role in the handling of the national question.

In championing such views, Bahr and his supporters drew on a little-noted article in the Basic Treaty that specified that the two German states could "contribute to security and cooperation in Europe," to undergird their claims that they were not advocating anything that had not been

---

[53]*Neue Zürcher Zeitung*, December 13, 1982; *Frankfurter Allgemeine Zeitung*, March 2, 1983.

[54]For Bahr's views, see his statement in *Der Spiegel*, May 31, 1982, pp. 34, 36.

previously envisioned in the days of Brandt's *Ostpolitik*.[55] Nevertheless, it is striking how quickly the SPD moved to raise the level of dialogue between the Germanys. In April 1983 the party's governing board took the controversial step of sending an official representative (although not Willy Brandt, as the SED had hoped) to an international conference of Communist and Socialist parties in East Berlin on the legacy of Karl Marx and its relevance to current world tensions. Then, in August 1983, Bahr met with Honecker and Hermann Axen to set up the first of what were to be regular working groups with the SED on ways the two parties could help to reduce the level of confrontation between the blocs. Finally, by the end of the year, the SPD and the SED had agreed to sponsor a series of discussions between a specially constituted Social Democratic commission and the East German Academy for Social Sciences on the subject of common social and political values. This undertaking was especially poignant in view of the deep ideological divisions that had separated the two parties ever since the SPD-East's forced merger with the KPD in 1946.[56]

A German "Coalition of Reason"

With the thaw in East Berlin's relations with the CDU/CSU and the prospect that the opposition Social Democrats were prepared to go beyond the limits of even their old conceptions of the inter-German relationship, it is easy to understand why the GDR's leaders would have been enthused at the possibility of making the dynamics of West German party politics work to their advantage. Even if the Union forces never matched the innovations of their rivals in the SPD, there was always the chance that all of the major West German parties together would nevertheless be brought around to a minimal acceptance of the GDR's sovereignty and equality.

These optimistic circumstances are in fact the best way of accounting for the sheer intensity with which Honecker personally fought to keep some form of inter-German dialogue alive in the late fall of 1983 and 1984, following the first deployments of Pershing II and cruise missiles in the FRG and other NATO member-states and the counterdeployments of Soviet

[55]Bahr later claimed authorship of this article, Article 5. With the exception of Bahr himself, however, all of the East German and West German officials with whom I have spoken who were involved in the negotiations on the Basic Treaty contend that the article was proposed by the GDR. East Berlin's motives seem to have had less to do with a foresightful appreciation of the future value of arms-control discussions than with its hopes of accentuating its independent image. Author's interviews, Foreign Office, Bonn, January 19, 1988 and Ministry of Foreign Affairs, East Berlin, May 31, 1988.

[56]For an early suggestion of what was to come, see the discussion organized by Peter Glotz in Bonn with the Academy's rector, Otto Reinhold, and *Einheit* editor Manfred Banaschak, "Karl Marx und die Sozialdemokratie," *Neue Gesellschaft*, March 1983, pp. 200–215.

SS-22s in the GDR. For the European missile crisis served to bring to the surface a nascent conflict between the East German leadership and its allies in Moscow about the very issue of contact between the Germanys. Were such ties to be regarded merely as instruments for serving the overarching needs of the Soviet bloc? Or, as the GDR's leaders were increasingly inclined to believe, could they not also be justifiably viewed as ends in themselves, worth pursuing regardless of external eventualities?

East German participants in the conflict with Moscow admit that well before the INF negotiations with the United States broke down in November 1983, the Soviet Union had shown signs of marked ambivalence about how far the German-German dialogue might be taken, particularly regarding its economic aspects. Even at the beginning of the decade, for example, their colleagues in Moscow had expressed concern that the level of the GDR's Western debt was growing too quickly. Some feared that Bonn might later use this condition as a lever against East Berlin.[57]

But the differences with the Soviet leadership were also due to a larger paradox built into the two allies' relationship. On the one hand, the SED could say that it was simply carrying out the Soviet Union's command in maintaining regular lines of communication with the West German parties, since the Kremlin itself had encouraged all of the fraternal regimes in East Europe to use their influence in the West to dilute support for NATO's armaments policy.[58] On the other hand, however, one could also not deny that Moscow had benefited directly over the years from the GDR's self-restraint in its dealings with Bonn. The memory of the Second World War was still alive in the minds of many in the Soviet leadership, as were the apprehensions, however seemingly irrational at the time, of a reawakening of German national feeling in the heart of Europe. Hence, it was almost predictable that when the SED undertook such independent initiatives as inviting the West German Social Democrats to participate in the Karl-Marx Conference of 1983, their Soviet counterparts were annoyed by what they viewed as an unwarranted expansion of the legitimate boundaries of German-German business.[59]

[57]For such concerns, see the unpublished transcript of Leonid Brezhnev's August 3, 1981, meeting with Honecker (IV 2/1/372), CPA, Berlin.

[58]East German participants note that support for such a policy of differentiation toward the West was particularly strong during the short reign of Brezhnev's successor, Yuri Andropov; but this sensitivity was lost during the equally short rule of Andropov's successor, Konstantin Chernenko. Author's interview, East Berlin, May 25, 1988. For signs of the former figure's comparative flexibility, see his first address as party leader in *Pravda*, November 22, 1982.

[59]For example, the East German planners of the conference had hoped that such potentially sympathetic Soviet personalities as Vadim Zagladin, the First-Deputy Director of the CPSU's International Department, would attend the conference but were disappointed when Moscow sent the hard-line Leningrad party boss, Gregori Romanov, who let it be known that

Consequently, East Berlin's insistence upon sheltering its ties with Bonn after the fateful developments of November 1983 can only have been seen as an affront to the USSR, for the SED's calls for moderation cut directly into the Soviet Union's definition of security. Up to this point, it must be noted, Honecker still seemed to be playing the role of the loyal follower of Soviet commands, since he linked his country's interests in better relations with the FRG to the latter's demonstrations of good faith on the crucial questions of peace, disarmament, and above all, INF. As a result, one did not have to read much between the lines of a letter the General Secretary dispatched to Kohl in early October 1983, in which he appealed to the latter, "in the name of the German people," to hold up deployment of the NATO missiles to avert an imminent "ice age" between the Germanys.[60] Were Bonn to implement the INF decision, or so the message seemed to read, there could be no inter-German détente.

The Soviets must have been taken aback, therefore, when Honecker assumed quite a different pose at the SED Central Committee's Seventh Plenum on November 25, only three days after the West German parliament had voted to support the deployment of the INF missiles. Although the East German leader emphasized that the United States and "especially the FRG" bore the chief responsibility for the tensions that were sure to engulf the blocs in the coming years, he also made it clear, in contrast to Soviet calls for retaliation, that his regime saw no point in jettisoning everything that it had accomplished over the preceding decade. Quite to the contrary, Honecker insisted, while the Western military buildup inflicted immeasurable harm, its occurrence made contacts all the more important to "limit the damage" that had already been done to the East-West relationship. "As genuine advocates of peace," he stressed, "we are always guided by the popular wisdom that ten times more negotiations are in any case better than firing one shot."[61]

From the very first, East German officials who were involved in the effort to maintain a semblance of normality in relations with the FRG sought to convince their colleagues in Moscow that there was really no contradiction at all between the Soviet Union's desire for tough countermeasures to restore the East-West military balance and their own interests in dia-

---

he disapproved of the whole undertaking. It was hard for many Soviet observers to understand why the East Germans would be discussing ideological questions with the Social Democrats. But when the SPD's representative hardly even mentioned Marx, preferring instead to stress international security concerns, these skeptics were dumbfounded. A high-placed Soviet official inquired of one of the conference's organizers: "What can this mean?" Author's interview with Joachim Böhm, East Berlin, June 28, 1988. Also see OHP (Böhm, December 5, 1990).

[60]*ND*, October 10, 1983.

[61]*RA*, vol. 10 (Berlin: Dietz, 1986), pp. 16–18.

logue.[62] Yet, as Honecker personally became more and more involved in such contacts, conspicuously receiving numerous Western visitors in late 1983 and 1984—Claude Cheysson, Pierre Trudeau, and Richard Burt—and even using the Moscow funeral of Brezhnev's short-lived successor, Yuri Andropov, to exchange a few words with Helmut Kohl, it was probably unavoidable that friction arose with the Kremlin over the idea that the GDR was competent to make such foreign-policy decisions on its own.

At first, for want of any other public forum, the Soviet–East German dispute was carried out in a curious exchange between two other East European states, Czechoslovakia and Hungary, which took the place of the USSR and the GDR in spelling out their differences. Through Czechoslovakia, the Soviets made known that their understanding of socialist solidarity meant absolute conformity in all views and the strict avoidance of any efforts to "gain unilateral 'advantages' from the capitalist world," an unmistakable reference to East Berlin's economic arrangements with the FRG. In defense of the East German position, however, the Hungarian party leadership argued that "individual initiatives" were allowable within the socialist bloc precisely because they would increase the prospects for peace.[63]

However, the real conflict was still to come over the particular steps that Honecker had in mind for sustaining his country's ties with Bonn. Beginning in the spring of 1984, at a time notably when the Soviet press was waging a campaign against ostensibly renewed manifestations of "revanchism" and "militarism" in the FRG, the East German regime announced that the General Secretary was eager to contribute to an easing of tensions between the blocs by making his first visit to the Federal Republic. Already, there had been signs that some sort of upgrading of the inter-German relationship was in the offing in gestures East Berlin and Bonn made to each other on the issue of free movement over their borders. In February the GDR had surprised West German observers with the unexpected decision to allow over twenty thousand of its most disenchanted citizens to emigrate to the West.[64] In return, the West German government

[62]This was by no means easy, because the Soviets and even some of their East European allies were bent upon punishing the West for going ahead with INF. For a time, Moscow considered withdrawing its ambassadors to the NATO states that had supported the move, while the Czechoslovak politburo passed a resolution that banned all contacts with offending parties. Author's interviews, Michael Geiger, East Berlin, June 6, 1988, and Herbert Häber, East Berlin, June 1, 1989.

[63]For these articles, see the useful collection by Ronald D. Asmus, "East Berlin and Moscow: The Documentation of a Dispute," *RFE Occasional Papers* (Munich), no. 1 (1985), pp. 25–30. On the evolution of the dispute, see Fred Oldenburg, "Werden Moskaus Schatten länger?" *Deutschland Archiv*, August 1984, pp. 834–842.

[64]This decision also backfired on the SED, and on many would-be emigrés. Because so many people—at least 100,000 at this time—had filled out applications to emigrate, the SED

had paid back the gesture a few months later by sealing off the inner offices of its mission in East Berlin during a period when other would-be East German emigrés had sought to use the building and several other embassies in the GDR to obtain political asylum.[65] Yet, by the summer of 1984, as the final preparations were being made for Honecker's trip, tentatively arranged for early September, the full extent of the German quid pro quo became manifest. The Kohl administration agreed to guarantee yet another sizable bank loan to the GDR, this time for DM 950 million, and East Berlin reciprocated with a number of significant measures (for example, a reduction in the compulsory minimum-exchange requirements for retirees) increasing West German access to its territory and its population.

For our purposes, it is less important to emphasize the harsh Soviet response to these developments—a series of articles in *Pravda* and other party newspapers obliquely accused the East Germans of having succumbed to the economic lure of the West and even took Honecker personally to task for, what one article termed, "pharisaical" notions such as "damage limitation"[66]—than simply to call attention to the SED's persistence in seeking to arrange Honecker's visit to the FRG. These efforts alone demonstrated how far the East German party had come in its valuation of the inter-German relationship. It was the General Secretary himself, however, who was most conspicuously at pains to show his Soviet colleagues why his government was determined "to continue its dialogue with the responsible politicians in Bonn and to work with those forces who were willing to take stock of reality and allow themselves to be moved by reason and good will." To counter the Kremlin's doubts, Honecker insisted that there were still realistic forces in the FRG who would not dare to turn their backs on the majority of the West German population who "opposed the new U.S. missiles and [favored] peaceful relations with the socialist world."[67] At the same time, accordingly, his representatives labored be-

---

could not allow some to leave without alienating thousands of others whose applications were denied. To further complicate the situation, because some East Germans had filled out such applications in the hope of then being provided with inducements (in the form of better apartments and higher salaries) to stay, they experienced a unique agony when their requests were accepted and they were forced to leave.

[65]The use of the FRG's Permanent Mission in East Berlin as a haven for would-be refugees was a problem that was as old as the mission itself. The first such incident was recorded in 1974, although East and West German authorities agreed not to publicize the problem, fearing that it would lead other East German citizens to copy the pattern.

[66]In Asmus, "East Berlin and Moscow," pp. 50–54.

[67]See Honecker's interview of August 17, 1984, in *RA*, vol. 10, p. 231. For a justification of why the East Germans felt that they could get away with a somewhat different position than the Soviet Union, see the book review by Harald Neubert, one of the SED's most influential international relations theorists, in *Horizont* 8 (1984). For Neubert's explanation, see OHP (Neubert, December 4, 1990).

hind the scenes to insure that the trip would also produce concrete results (for example, a settlement of the Elbe border dispute, the expansion of inter-German security talks), so that their leader would have the added advantage of being able to show Moscow the benefits that came from his more nuanced policy toward the West.[68]

Despite these efforts, however, on September 4, 1984, East Berlin precipitately announced that the visit would have to be postponed. In this case, a single telephone call from the Soviet leadership was enough to convince Honecker that this particular trip, at this particular time, was not worth the cost of a drawn-out battle with his Soviet patrons.[69] Of course, it is at least conceivable that the SED chief could have made the trip had he wanted; unlike Ulbricht in his challenge to the Kremlin more than a decade earlier, Honecker did have the advantage of a nearly unanimous politburo behind him.[70] Yet there could be little doubt that he would also have found himself largely isolated within the Soviet camp and later bereft of any chances of influencing his allies' behavior.

Nevertheless, for all of the controversy that attended the trip's postponement and the reminder that the GDR was still operating in the USSR's shadow, the prevailing political mood in East Berlin was illuminated by the fact that all of East Germany's leaders and Honecker in particular refused to consider themselves defeated in their exchange with Moscow. There was nothing in late 1984 to indicate that the SED had changed its stand on the merits of continuing contacts with the West. Quite the opposite, the regime's repeated emphasis that the visit had only been postponed and not canceled was evidence of the firmness of Honecker's intentions in the face of Soviet pressure—the trip would take place eventually. In a key October

[68]From the beginning, this was a difficult task since it was unclear that everyone in the FRG would welcome Honecker. Politburo member Herbert Häber made the case for the visit by outlining for the East German leader why all of the West German parties had reason to support the trip. Yet, by the end of the summer, following much foot-dragging by Kohl about what cities Honecker could visit and which diplomatic protocol would be used to receive him, it became apparent that the CDU/CSU had not overcome all of its misgivings. In a well-publicized remark in August, Alfred Dregger, the chairman of the Union's parliamentary *Fraktion*, observed that the FRG could survive without the visit. The problem with such utterances was not merely that they aggravated the SED but also that they made it that much harder for the party to justify the trip to the Soviet Union. "Mensch!" Honecker is said to have declared. "Don't they understand that they're playing right into the hands of the Soviets?" Author's discussion with Herbert Häber, East Berlin, March 21, 1990.

[69]Author's taped interview, Herbert Häber, East Berlin, March 19, 1990.

[70]Alfred Neumann, a deputy chairman of the Council of Ministers, appears to have been the only politburo member to oppose the trip outright, while Hermann Axen had initial reservations but eventually overcame them. The point is that, had the Soviets wanted to replace Honecker, they would not have been able to assure that his successor would think differently about the GDR's *Westpolitik*. Author's taped interview with Herbert Häber, East Berlin, March 19, 1990.

meeting between the GDR's leaders and Soviet foreign minister Andrei Gromyko, notable in part because the latter figure was one of the sharpest critics of East German policy, the SED even seems to have exacted a minor concession from its allies by convincing them to affirm their readiness in a joint communiqué "to conduct a serious and sincere dialogue with all forces who [were] genuinely interested in a healthy international situation."[71]

The greatest SED victory may have gone to Honecker himself. By virtue of his key role in defending the East German stand before the Soviet Union, the General Secretary seems to have gained something akin to folk-hero status within his country, or at least within his party. Over the course of the next year, as the SED chief was able with increasing credibility to present the GDR as one of the main reasons for hope that "the world situation would make a turn for the better," advocating such attractive notions as "a worldwide coalition of reason and realism in the interest of mankind's survival," he could not have helped but contribute to his regime's long-standing goal of securing a permanent niche for itself within the European fold.[72] Not only did other states suddenly start to regard the GDR with greater seriousness and sympathy—in the years to come, Honecker would receive personal invitations to visit practically every West European member of NATO, including Italy, Greece, and the Netherlands— but those who were around the General Secretary flattered themselves into thinking that their leader's popularity was growing among the East German population as well.

A New Era between the Germanys

It is essential to take note of the timing of the improvement of ties between East Berlin and Bonn. Because so much was to transpire in East-West relations in the mid- to late-1980s, one might easily gain the false impression that what happened between the Germanys was only a reflection of the dramatic developments that took place outside their borders. Above all, these were epitomized by the rise of the reform-minded Communist leader, Mikhail Gorbachev, in the Soviet Union in March 1985. Undeniably, Gor-

[71]*Foreign Affairs Bulletin*, October 19, 1984, p. 233. Indeed, Gromyko appears to have been a key Soviet opponent to the Honecker trip. On this period, see my interviews with Karl Seidel and Hans Schindler, former directors of the Ministry of Foreign Affairs department responsible for relations with the FRG, OHP (Seidel, July 8, 1991, and Schindler, October 3, 1991). On other Soviet critics, see the interview with the GDR's ambassador to Moscow, Egon Winkelmann, in *Junge Welt*, August 12, 1991.

[72]See his report to the Central Committee's Ninth Plenum of November 22, 1984, in *RA*, vol. 10, pp. 366–367.

bachev's appearance and the improvement of the Soviet-U.S. relationship in general following the reopening of INF negotiations in Geneva during the same month provided a uniquely favorable setting for the kinds of contacts envisioned by the two German regimes. Yet, quite independently of the behavior of their superpower patrons, policymakers in the GDR and the FRG were *already* prepared to enter into a qualitatively new stage in their relations.

In fits and starts in the mid-1980s, Honecker's government had grown inclined to make the sorts of demonstrations of goodwill toward Bonn that were necessary to sell an accommodating *Deutschlandpolitik* to many of the remaining FRG skeptics who doubted the efficacy of closer ties with the GDR.[73] For example, in July 1985 the East German regime implemented the first of a number of controls on tens of thousands of would-be asylum seekers from south- and southeast Asia who were using East Berlin's Schönefeld airport to gain access to West Berlin, explicitly requiring transit visas from Tamils who were seeking easy passage into the West.[74] By October 1986 this requirement was extended to all other nationalities as well. In November 1985 Honecker gave his consent to the negotiation of formal city partnerships between the GDR and the FRG, ties that various West German cities had sought to no avail since the early 1970s. This act led to the first such agreement, between Saarlouis and Eisenhüttenstadt in April 1986, and many more agreements in subsequent years. Finally, at the end of 1985, the East German regime made the concessions that were necessary to conclude an inter-German treaty on cultural cooperation, which had been envisioned in the *Grundvertrag* thirteen years earlier.[75]

It was in the area of human contacts, however, that East Berlin displayed the most important signs of readiness to compromise with the West. Up to this time, the biggest gains in the German-German negotiations on the subject had been confined to West German access to the GDR, that is, to questions of who could visit whom and under what circumstances, as well

---

[73]It is appropriate to speak of "fits and starts" because there were several incidents over this period that might have cast doubt on the GDR's readiness to cooperate with the West. For example, in May 1986, the SED regime caused an outcry from Berlin's Western occupiers when it sought to require all foreign diplomats in East Berlin to show their passports (and not simply identification cards) when passing into West Berlin. However, Western protests and behind-the-scenes pressure from Moscow quickly led to the repeal of this measure.

[74]Evidently, this step was the consequence of behind-the-scenes contacts between Franz Josef Strauß and Alexander Schalck-Golodkowski. See the article by Clemens Bollinger, "Strauß und Schalck—'Vertrauen gegen Vertrauen,' " *Die Welt*, September 19, 1991, based on the two personalities' communications.

[75]While West German authorities insisted that this agreement was yet another confirmation of West Berlin's "special" bond to the Federal Republic because the GDR gave in on the city's inclusion in the agreement, East German negotiators contended that the West Berlin–FRG tie was only for informational purposes.

as the entire issue of the cost of each visit—the consequence of the *Mindestumtausch*—for average citizens from the FRG and West Berlin. Bonn had proven willing to pay for every improvement with massive subsidies to the GDR, estimated to have run into hundreds of millions of Marks annually.[76] Yet, where the West German government had not been able to make comparable progress was on the more touchy question of whether East Germans could come in like numbers to the FRG. Ironically, for precisely the reasons the SED regime had proved to be such a difficult negotiating partner in the past—the confinement of most key decisions to a handful of policymakers and the ability of the East German elite to seal itself off from the pressures of its own citizenry—some two-and-one-half decades after the construction of the Berlin Wall the party was still information-poor. It continued to lack a reliable means of judging how its citizens would act if they were suddenly to be allowed to travel freely to the West.

As it was, the regime's decision to allow some twenty thousand East Germans to emigrate to the FRG in the early months of 1984 (for a total of forty thousand over the entire year) had not been greeted with unanimous enthusiasm within the upper reaches of the party, even among those who hoped for a change in policy. Some individuals within Honecker's circle of advisors felt that by simply ridding the country of its most disgruntled citizens, the SED had only put off the tougher matter of testing how far the GDR had come in stabilizing its relationship with its population.[77] Thus, one of the main approaches West German negotiators utilized in the following years in their efforts to convince East Berlin to liberalize its position on travel to the West was to emphasize that the FRG had nothing to gain by "depopulating" the GDR. Quite the opposite, Bonn's representatives contended. If East Germany's citizens were finally allowed to travel freely, they would no longer desire to leave the country permanently, and the SED's remaining uncertainties about its internal legitimacy would be resolved.[78]

Of course, when only retired citizens were allowed to travel with any regularity, the truth of this proposition could not be tested. Moreover, with the hindsight of knowing about the mass exodus that occurred only a few few years later when East Germany's borders to the West were completely opened, the reader may have difficulty imagining how Honecker could have found the confidence to begin the risky loosening of controls on the

---

[76]According to an internal U.S. Embassy (Bonn) study just after Honecker's trip to the FRG in September 1987, the FRG's provision of so-called welcome money to East Germans visiting the West amounted to about DM 90 million annually. But this was only one of Bonn's many expenditures. According to my own sources, payments for the ransoming of prisoners alone from the GDR came to around DM 200 million annually in the late 1980s. Author's sources, U.S. embassy, Bonn, and Federal chancellery, Bonn.

[77]Author's interview, East Berlin, June 7, 1988.

[78]Author's interview, Federal chancellery, Bonn, February 12, 1988.

number of citizens who were able to visit the FRG. Yet there is no denying that the SED regime changed its course in 1986, in essence signifying its agreement to the FRG's experiment. In that year alone, if one can take East German statistics seriously,[79] as many as 573,000 GDR citizens *under* retirement age were suddenly able to take advantage of a relaxed definition of the concept of "urgent family matters" to renew acquaintances and familial ties in West Germany; this total marked an increase of more than 400,000 visits over 1985.[80] In 1987 the number rose even further, as the regime allowed over 1.2 million individuals below retirement age to make trips to the FRG. If one adds to this sum the number of retirees who were regularly traveling to the West anyway, variously estimated at upward of 2 million individuals (and over 3.5 million total visits),[81] it is conceivable that between one-fifth and one-quarter of the total East German population found itself in the Federal Republic at one time or another in 1987.

The mystery behind the Honecker regime's newly acquired willingness to give ground on the question of freedom of movement becomes much easier to understand, however, if we recognize that East Berlin was also taking into account simultaneous developments within the FRG. At the same time that West German authorities were congratulating themselves for having convinced the SED about the potential payoffs of compromise—Honecker had noticeably softened his "Gera demands," and he and other party officials were increasingly inclined to insist only that Bonn "respect" East German citizenship[82]—the GDR leader could identify equally impressive grounds for assuming that the FRG's contending parties had entered a new era in the way they dealt with the national issue.

Among the GDR's possible partners in dialogue in West Germany, the SPD was unquestionably the most inviting candidate, since the rigors of opposition, in conjunction with its past role in the *Ostpolitik*, made its

---

[79]The reader may be surprised that anyone would take GDR statistics seriously. The problem is that West German authorities were never able to collect reliable figures on both the number of individuals visiting the FRG (particularly West Berlin) and on the age groups they represented. Thus, Bonn was curiously dependent on the GDR's help in calculating such visits. For example, the FRG's initial figure for visits by individuals under the retirement age in 1986 was 244,000; however, officials in the Federal chancellery informally calculated that as many as double the number of visits had taken place. The news service, ADN, later put the number at 573,000, although this figure may have included some individuals whom the FRG would have classified as retirees. Author's sources, Federal chancellery, Bonn.

[80]The West German estimate for 1985 was 66,000 visits under the retirement age, although as the preceding footnote suggests the actual figure may have been twice as high.

[81]The distinction between the total number of individuals and total visits has to be made in the case of retired citizens, who had much less trouble than other citizens in making return visits to the FRG and West Berlin.

[82]Peter Jochen Winters, "Nicht Eiszeit, aber Pause," *Deutschland Archiv*, March 1985, pp. 225–228.

leaders almost instinctively inclined to accommodate the GDR. By the middle of the decade, a variety of prominent personalities within the party leadership, including Brandt, Bahr, and even Schmidt's former defense minister, Hans Apel, had already gone on record regarding the need to move beyond presumably pointless debates about the "openness" of the national question.[83] Furthermore, a growing majority of middle-of-the-road Social Democrats seemed to agree. In late 1984, the party's parliamentary *Fraktion* called for both the abolition of the human-rights monitoring station in Salzgitter and a quick settlement of the Elbe dispute, and also recommended the immediate establishment of official ties between the Bundestag and the East German Volkskammer.[84] Other prominent Social Democrats, such as the outspoken minister-president of the Saarland, Oskar Lafontaine, and the leaders of some of the SPD's more left-leaning regional party organizations, urged the party to recognize a separate GDR citizenship and criticized the Kohl government for continuing to hand out passports to East Germans traveling to the FRG.[85] At least two well-known members of the SPD, Klaus Bölling, who retired as Bonn's official representative to the GDR in May 1982, and Jürgen Schmude, a former justice minister, dared to express the unthinkable by wondering aloud whether the FRG's interests would not be better served by rewriting the Basic Law's provisions about "the completion of the unity" of the German nation.[86]

Of even greater consequence for the GDR, because the accompanying achievements were more tangible, was the SED's ability to follow through on the discussions it had begun with the SPD on security questions and ideological matters. Both parties were careful to emphasize that they were only talking with each other and not conducting official negotiations, which was in any case not within the SPD's competence as an opposition party. Nevertheless, all of their agreements testified to how far the Social

[83]On the debate over Apel's remarks, see *Frankfurter Allgemeine Zeitung*, August 16, 1984. For even more explicit criticisms of the "life lies (*Lebenslüge*)" of past West German policy, as well as the source of the quotation that opens this chapter, see Willy Brandt, "Die Chancen der Geschichte suchen," in *Reden über das eigene Land: Deutschland*, vol. 2 (Munich: C. Bertelsmann, 1984), pp. 63–64.

[84]"Sozialdemokratische Thesen zur Deutschlandpolitik," *Politik* 17 (November 1984), Informationsdienst der SPD.

[85]*Frankfurter Allgemeine Zeitung*, November 16, 1985.

[86]The SPD never went so far as to endorse this last proposal publicly, although my impression at the time—in part, based upon interviews with Bölling and Schmude—was that the party leadership was less opposed to the substance of the proposal than to its timing, which allowed the CDU/CSU to criticize the Social Democrats for violating the sacred trust of "unity." Also see "Die offene deutsche Frage," *Der Spiegel*, April 18, 1985, pp. 52–53; and Jürgen Schmude, "Deutsch-deutsches Verhältnis," *Informationen der sozialdemokratischen Bundestagsfraktion* May 17, 1985. For the different currents within the SPD, see Wilfried von Bredow and Rudolf Brocke, *Das deutschlandpolitische Konzept der SPD* (Erlangen: Deutsche Gesellschaft für zeitgeschichtliche Fragen, 1987).

Democrats had come (or were willing to go) in their inclination to treat the GDR as a fully sovereign partner. In June 1985 the two parties' security groups, led by Bahr and Axen, issued a joint proposal for the creation of a chemical-weapon-free zone in central Europe, which, had it been implemented, would have prohibited the stationing, production, and transport of such weapons in the FRG, the GDR, and neighboring Czechoslovakia. This effort was followed by a similar proposal in November 1986 that envisioned a 300-mile wide nuclear-weapon-free corridor between the German states. Finally, in late August 1987, the SPD's Basic Values Commission and the SED Academy for Social Sciences released a joint paper, "Conflicting Ideologies and Common Security," which endorsed a new level of discourse between the blocs (a "culture of political argumentation," as the document called it). According to this paper, the Germanys would demonstrate how the two world systems could recognize each other's right to exist and mutual "capacity for peace and reform" even while they continued to compete on an ideological level. Apparently, Honecker was so intent upon seeing the agreement realized that he personally intervened to support the initiative, despite the misgivings of some of his closest colleagues on the politburo and evidently without the previous approval of the Kremlin.[87]

In comparison, no one in the GDR can have realistically expected that the governing parties in Bonn, the CDU/CSU and the FDP, would have been prepared to go so far in stretching the limits of acceptable dialogue with East Berlin. But from the SED's perspective, even with this necessary qualification, they may still have gone far enough to meet the party's minimal expectations of the relationship. Since the *Wende* of 1982/83, the FDP by itself had proven to be very comfortable playing the role of the "balancer" between the West German extremes, regularly criticizing the SPD for moving too quickly to accommodate the East German leadership but at the same time also finding fault with the remaining hard-liners in the Union ranks who refused to recognize the realities of dealing with the GDR.[88] Although Free Democratic spokespersons continued to lay some weight on

[87] "Der Streit der Ideologien und die gemeinsame Sicherheit," *Politik* 3, (August 1987), Informationsdienst der SPD. One of the authors of the joint paper pointed out at the time that such discussions would not have been conceivable between governments: "Governments can't talk about ideological issues, they can only issue communiqués!" Author's interview, Rolf Reissig, East Berlin, May 4, 1988. Yet, although the SED hardly represented a voice distinct from the East German government, the point does hold true for the SPD and is one of the reasons the party was so attractive to East Berlin. On these contacts, see Ann Phillips, *Seeds of Change in the German Democratic Republic: The SED-SPD Dialogue* (Washington, D.C.: AICGS, Research Report no. 1, December 1989). Also see OHP (Erich Hahn, February 28, 1991).

[88] Author's interviews, FDP Bundestag *Fraktion*, Bonn, October 1, 1987, and December 10, 1987.

the "openness" of the German question, the onlooking SED regime cannot have failed to appreciate such nuances as the disappearance of the word "reunification" from the party's official vocabulary or the Liberals' explicit disavowal of any policies that might lead to a "destabilization" of the situation in Central Europe.[89] Particularly under Genscher's influence, whose decade-long association with the Foreign Ministry assured his presence as an independent force within the Kohl government, the FDP's national policy became almost exclusively identified with efforts to reduce East-West tensions—including confidence-building measures, Helsinki, and arms control—which Genscher himself increasingly described as the foundations of a "European peace order."[90]

Most important of all from the GDR's standpoint were the changes in the CDU/CSU's official definition of its national priorities. True, in the period leading up to the parliamentary elections of 1987, the Union forces were always prepared to make political capital out of what they regarded as the excesses in the SPD's dealings with East Berlin. Their leaders readily contended that their opponents had endangered the FRG's security and its relations with the United States by conducting a "shadow foreign policy" (Nebenaußenpolitik), warning the West German electorate that a vote for the SPD could only result in an extremist Social Democratic coalition with the Greens.[91] Yet, by the same token, the Christian Democrats were not at all averse to using the SPD's contacts with the SED to further inter-German ties when it suited their interests. In the process, this strategy helped to improve their image as capable foreign-policymakers in the West German public mind.[92]

---

[89]For example, *Frankfurter Allgemeine Zeitung*, April 27, 1984, and the FDP's *Information Bulletin* January 29, 1986.

[90]Although the Free Democrats regularly criticized the SPD for its security talks with the SED, the FDP-dominated Foreign Office accelerated its own arms-control "consultations" with the GDR Ministry of Foreign Affairs. Five formal sessions were held between May 1985 and December 1987, the last with Deputy Foreign Minister Kurt Nier. These meetings were supplemented by regular discussions between Genscher and Foreign Minister Oskar Fischer at the United Nations. Author's interviews, Foreign Office, Bonn, February 16, 1988. On Genscher's national views, see "Taking Gorbachev at His Word," speech at the World Economic Forum, Davos, Switzerland, February 1, 1987, *Statements and Speeches* 10, no. 3 (February 6, 1987), New York, German Information Center; and "Fostering Detente and Disarmament," *Statements and Speeches* 10, no. 13 (August 12, 1987). On the evolution of Genscher's thinking, see Sandler, "Shades of Center," pp. 64–80.

[91]On the so-called *Nebenaußenpolitik*, see Volker Rühe, "Nebenaußenpolitik der SPD schadet deutschen Interessen," *Die Entscheidung* October 1985, pp. 20–21.

[92]Even in the mid-1980s, the SPD continued to enjoy a much better reputation for its foreign-policy competence than the CDU/CSU. In a 1985 survey by Infratest, 47 percent of those queried regarded the SPD as most likely to contribute to better relations with East Berlin while only 19 percent spoke in defense of the Union forces. Deutsche Presse-Agentur press release, August 5, 1985.

10. Erich Honecker (First Secretary, later General Secretary, of the Socialist Unity Party, GDR, May 3, 1971–October 18, 1989) and Helmut Schmidt (chancellor, FRG, May 16, 1974–October 1, 1982) met for the first time at the Helsinki Conference on European Security and Cooperation, July 30–August 1, 1975. (Courtesy GIC)

11. Bavarian minister-president Franz Josef Strauß, originally an outspoken critic of the *Ostpolitik*, was later a practitioner of the policy. Behind him, Helmut Schmidt. (Courtesy GIC)

12-13. Egon Bahr and Willy Brandt, top, and Günter Gaus (FRG permanent representative to the GDR, 1974–1981) were early advocates of improved inter-German ties. (Courtesy GIC)

14. Erich Honecker, fifth from left, bottom row, reviewing a military parade on the thirtieth anniversary of the GDR's founding, October 7, 1979. Fourth from left, Soviet General Secretary Leonid Brezhnev. (Courtesy GIC)

15. Helmut Schmidt and Erich Honecker, during the Werbellinsee meeting, September 11–13, 1981. (Courtesy GIC)

16. Socialist Unity Party politburo member, Hermann Axen, and Egon Bahr, at a meeting of the joint SED-SPD working group on arms control, May 30, 1986. (Courtesy GIC)

17. Helmut Kohl (chancellor, FRG, October 1, 1982–), left, and Erich Honecker, on the occasion of the East German leader's official visit to Bonn, September 7, 1987. (Courtesy GIC)

18. Helmut Kohl, under light umbrella, at official opening of the Brandenburg Gate, December 22, 1989. At the microphone, GDR prime minister Hans Modrow. Next to Modrow, on the right, West Berlin governing mayor Walter Momper; FDP chairman Otto Graf Lambsdorff; and FRG foreign minister Hans-Dietrich Genscher.

Thus, when Hermann Axen visited Bonn in the early spring of 1985 as part of the SPD-SED talks on chemical weapons, he was quietly but officially received in the Federal chancellery by Kohl's special minister, Wolfgang Schäuble. During a similar visit by Volkskammer president Horst Sindermann a year later, in February 1986, the SPD's guest conducted side discussions with nearly the entire leadership of the CDU and CSU, bringing the first indications that the GDR was about to liberalize its policy on private travel to the West, as well as a great deal of public anticipation that Honecker might soon make his own trip to Bonn.

The governing parties could insist that by taking up such contacts they were merely pursuing every conceivable avenue to enmesh the GDR in the broadest web of commitments to the inter-German relationship. But for the East German regime, it was equally significant that the Union forces thereby slowly became bound to the success of this undertaking. If East Berlin's openness to ever greater contacts between the German populations was contingent upon its leaders' confidence in the internal stability of the GDR, then the CDU/CSU cannot have helped but acquire a stake in what transpired within East Germany in the process.

True to the model that Strauß had already established with the bank credits, it was by no means surprising that one of the levers to which Kohl and his advisors turned in seeking to convince the SED to relax the controls on its citizenry was economic. For example, only half a year before the Honecker regime implemented its new travel policy, the Federal government responded to the GDR's growing desire to reduce its foreign debt and its recurrent failure to devote sufficient resources to capital investment projects, by agreeing to raise the annual level of the "swing" credit to DM 850 million (its level before the minimum-exchange-rate controversy of 1980). It also consented to guarantee the delivery of certain finished industrial products, machines and high-technology goods, which were integral to the modernization of the East German economy.[93]

Even more telling, albeit on a considerably more subtle level, was the Union parties', and especially the CDU's, inclination to give in where giving counted most for the SED, on the handling of the national question. If the greatest source of insecurity for the East German leadership lay in the ever-present reminders to its population that there was another German state with a standard of living and a style of life far different from that to be found under socialism, the greatest gesture that the conservative parties could make to the GDR was in the way they addressed the entire subject of the national future. Few members of the CDU/CSU would have been willing to abandon references in the Basic Law to the task of "completing the unity" of the German nation. Yet even this specification was sufficiently

---

[93]Ilse Spittmann, "Weichenstellung," *Deutschland Archiv*, August 1985, pp. 786–788.

vague to allow the majority of leading figures within the Union ranks—President von Weizsäcker; West Berlin's governing mayor, Eberhard Diepgen; Kohl advisors Schäuble, Jenninger, and Rühe; and the chancellor himself—considerable room for leeway in defining their terms. Hence, as with the FDP, most references to concrete goals like "reunification" and the reestablishment of the old "national state" simply vanished from the Christian Democrats' speeches, only to be replaced with less provocative references to the need to "reduce the burdens of division" and to make the Germanys' borders "more permeable." Most suggestive, the Union parties seem deliberately to have fought off the temptation to say anything about how they envisioned their long-term relationship with the GDR, arguing only that the nation's unity would be restored on that distant day when the division of Europe itself was overcome.[94]

In this respect, there may have been a liberating quality to the less antagonistic relationship with East Germany. The more Kohl and his colleagues could feel that they had put their tensions with East Berlin behind them, the easier it also became to portray the FRG to its West European neighbors as a state just like theirs, eager to play its part in bringing the continent together again. By the mid-1980s, in fact, the chancellor himself was defining his priorities, much like Adenauer before him, increasingly in European terms, allying himself closely with President François Mitterrand of France and actively promoting the cause of West European economic and political unification. Thus it was with some self-assurance that Kohl could repeatedly assure his listeners that there was no contradiction between his country's national interests and its European identity: "European policy and German policy are like two sides of a coin for us. It is part of our national mission, the raison d'être [Staatsräson] of the Federal Republic from the very beginning, to be a motor for the unification of Europe."[95]

---

[94]Of many examples, see Richard von Weizsäcker, Von Deutschland aus (Munich: dtv, 1987), p. 53; Wolfgang Schäuble, "Deutschlandpolitik im fünften Jahrzehnt der Teilung," in Tutzinger Materialien 23 (1985), pp. 1–26; Helmut Kohl's State-of-the-Nation address of March 14, 1986, in Bulletin, March 15, 1986; Eberhard Diepgen, "Perspektiven statt Illusionen," Deutschland Archiv, March 1986, pp. 268–278; and Volker Rühe's remarks in "Wie geht es weiter in den deutsch-deutschen Beziehungen?" unpublished conference report, Friedrich-Ebert-Stiftung, June 3, 1987, pp. 7–11. One major exception to this rule was the widespread publicity attending an internal discussion paper by a CDU Bundestag deputy, Bernhard Friedmann, in 1987 that sought to reawaken thinking on the theme of reunification by proposing a special deal with the USSR. But even Kohl dismissed Friedmann's reflections as nonsensical. See "Thesenpapier: Die Wiedervereinigung der Deutschen als Sicherheitskonzept," May 16, 1987, unpublished letter in author's possession.

[95]From a representative speech, on March 15, 1984, reprinted in Europa Archiv 20 (1984), p. D591. A major analytical treatment of the relationship between European policy and German national policy is Eberhard Schulz, Die deutsche Nation in Europa (Bonn: Europa Union, 1982), esp. chap. 5.

A Working Visit to Bonn

Against this background, who could doubt, when Erich Honecker made his long-anticipated visit to West Germany from September 7–11, 1987, that the Germanys had arrived at the workable compromise which had eluded them for years? Simultaneously, each government could think that the East German leader's presence in the FRG was a demonstration of the success of its respective stand on the national question. West Germany could hope that the progress that had been made since Schmidt's visit to the Werbellinsee in 1981 would be enough to keep alive inter-German commonalities and contacts for years to come. East Germany, in contrast, could assume that every gesture of respect for the SED General Secretary was a confirmation of the permanence of the national divide. There was no way of knowing for sure which of the two states had actually come closest to achieving its objective—the denouement of the Wall's collapse was still a couple of years from providing the answer to this question—but for the first time, it was at least arguable that the evidence lay with the GDR.

Predictably, Bonn was careful to define Honecker's trip as only a "working visit" and not a "state visit," which would have entitled him to a slightly higher level of protocol. His discussions with Kohl, von Weizsäcker, Strauß, and other notables were at best businesslike and formal; Honecker was, after all, as one participant could insist, "still the builder of the Berlin Wall."[96] Throughout the SED chief's stay, West Germany's leaders also emphasized the two German governments' "different views" on the national question. The "consciousness of the unity of the nation is as awake as ever," Kohl contended, "and the will to preserve it is unbroken."[97]

Yet no one could deny the changes in the tenor of FRG policy. When Honecker had first hoped to visit West Germany in 1984, there had been some doubt about whether he would be received by the Federal president. In addition, the meeting that was planned for him with Kohl was to have taken place outside of the capital. Three short years later, however, thanks in large part to the dynamics of party politics in the West, the major reservations about the General Secretary's presence in Bonn had apparently been worked out. Not only were many of his former critics now agreeable to being seen with him publicly, but virtually no subject, including the controversial matter of security questions, was taboo during the visit.[98] Most important of all was the incalculable symbolic value of Hon-

[96]Author's interview, Burkhard Dobiey, Bonn, October 8, 1987. Yet this did not keep individual politicians from exploiting the visit to serve their political purposes. For a humorous characterization of Strauß's efforts to keep the "free state" of Bavaria from being upstaged by Bonn, see OHP (Schindler, October 3, 1991).

[97]See Kohl's welcoming remarks of September 7, 1987, in *Bulletin* September 10, 1987.

[98]For example, in 1984 Kohl had insisted that one subject he would not discuss with the East German leader was security affairs, whereas in 1987 this issue (and particularly the

ecker's presence in the FRG. The images of Honecker being taken seriously by his adversaries that were beamed back to the GDR population via
East and West German television, from a casual conversation with von
Weizsäcker at the Villa Hammerschmidt to a formal dinner with Kohl at
the Bad Godesberg Redoute, were simultaneously images of a confirmed
order of German priorities for the 1990s. The bulk of the two states' efforts
would be concentrated (to quote Kohl again) on the "do-able" (*das Mach-
bare*), and not on issues that were "at the moment unresolvable."[99]

Given the governing coalition's emphasis on relieving the travails of
those who suffered most under the burden of national division, some
members of the CDU/CSU had reason to feel encouraged when on one of the
final days of Honecker's visit, in the town of his birth, Neunkirchen in the
Saarland, the General Secretary admitted that the conditions on the inter-
German border were "still not quite what they should be." What these
politicians may have missed, however, was the significance of his following
remark. The day would come, Honecker prophesied, in which such
"borders no longer separate us but unite us." By this remark the East
German leader undoubtedly meant that all German citizens would only
truly come together again when the FRG had fully and irrevocably recognized that the GDR was a state like any other.[100]

---

contribution that the FRG could make to the INF negotiations between the superpowers)
played a central role in Honecker's confidential talks with both Kohl and the CDU/CSU
parliamentary leader, Alfred Dregger. Author's interviews, CDU/CSU Bundestag *Fraktion*,
Bonn, March 3, 1988.

[99] See Kohl's remarks on September 7, 1987, in *Bulletin* September 10, 1987.

[100] Author's interviews, CDU/CSU Bundestag *Fraktion* Bonn, September 25, 1987. For
Honecker's remarks of September 10, 1987, see *RA*, vol. 12 (Berlin: Dietz, 1988), pp. 539–
540.

VI

The Fall of East Germany

Both states [agree] to preserve and to build upon
everything which they have achieved by
respecting each other's independence and
autonomy in its internal and external affairs. A
readiness to show understanding and realism
shall be the guiding rules in both states' efforts to
cooperate constructively in the pursuit of
practical goals.
(Joint communiqué between the GDR and the
FRG, September 8, 1987)

[I]f everything had gone as I wanted, the GDR
would still exist.
(Erich Honecker, October 10, 1991)

IN LATE 1987, Erich Honecker appeared to be at the height of his career after his journey to the FRG, having successfully overcome the decades of West German opposition to treating the GDR as an independent state that had been so much a part of Bonn's national policy since Adenauer's days. Although one would have had no trouble finding politicians in West Germany who still felt some discomfort at the sight of the two German flags flying in tandem before the Federal chancellery or at the image of the FRG's president and the General Secretary chatting amicably on the grounds of the Villa Hammerschmidt, the maintenance of good relations with East Berlin had nevertheless become an integral part of West German foreign policy.

Not far below the surface of party rhetoric, however, there were signs that all was not well in the German Democratic Republic. The primary uncertainty had to do with the fact that the new Soviet General Secretary, Mikhail Gorbachev, was proving to be just as interested in the cause of socialist domestic reform as, from East Berlin's standpoint, in the quite welcome amelioration of tensions between the superpowers. Yet, when the Honecker government showed that it was not willing to subscribe to many of the Soviet leader's more daring economic and political initiatives, it found itself confronted by some of the GDR's best-known intellectuals, artists, and church representatives. First hesitatingly and then ever more demonstrably, they demanded that their government prove its fealty to the homeland of the October Revolution by following Gorbachev's example. Then, too, despite the liberalized procedures for travel to the FRG, the number of East Germans filing applications for permanent emigration to the West was rising at an alarming rate. Even within the SED, visitors could detect an internal migration of a sort as individual party members lost the faith they had once seemed to have in their leadership's ability to adapt to changing conditions. Many found no other recourse than to retreat into their private lives.

Nevertheless, the intriguing feature of the relationship between East Berlin and Bonn at the end of the 1980s was how little room it allowed for such dissonance. This suggested just how much the GDR and the FRG had adapted to the accommodating norms and mores of inter-German cooperation. In East Germany, as we shall see, the awkward reality was that the situation grew worse just as the relationship appeared to be getting better. The closer the Honecker government came to achieving the national goals the General Secretary had pursued since rising to power in 1971 and the greater his personal involvement in the process grew, the more incapable the SED regime seemed of reacting with subtlety and creativity to what it perceived to be unacceptable challenges to its sovereignty. Yet, in the FRG too, the more that West German authorities grew accustomed to the existence of a second German state and accepted the need to emphasize their respect for their adversaries' equality and independence, the harder it was for them to take the East German regime to task when the SED failed to live up to their hopes for internal reform.

This accommodation to the status quo was of no small effect. It meant that when hundreds of thousands of East German citizens destroyed the tranquility of the inter-German relationship in the summer and fall of 1989 by seeking to escape from their country to the West or, if they wished to remain, by calling for fundamental political changes from within, West German politicians did not know how to react. They were conspicuously lacking in the means, and even the vocabulary, for dealing with those who sought to challenge the old East German elite. It would take months before the great majority of policymakers in the FRG were able to return to the all-German themes that they and their predecessors had slowly abandoned one or more decades earlier. Even in this case, however, to speak as though one favored the re-creation of a unitary German state was by no means the same as being fully prepared to accept the consequences of the unexpected event.

The Illusion of Success

In order to understand the thinking of the SED's leaders in the period leading up to their sudden fall from power, it is crucial to appreciate that, in one key respect, the party could not have been more self-satisfied in the late 1980s. Because East Berlin's relations with West Germany were not merely relations with any other country but also integrally related to the GDR's identity as a sovereign state, the dramatic increase in inter-German contacts during the decade added to the East German elite's confidence. After all, if the one country in the world that had a continuing stake in questioning the existence of two separate German states was, for all practical purposes, finally coming to terms with the division of the nation, it was reasonable to conclude that the international community would never again treat the GDR as anything but an accepted fact.[1]

Honecker's diplomatic schedule in the months after his trip to the Federal Republic seemed to testify to the depth of his regime's accomplishments. The General Secretary was received with full diplomatic honors by the king and queen of Belgium in Brussels in mid-October 1987, by the French prime minister in Paris in January 1988, and by the Spanish royal family and prime minister in Madrid in early October 1988. At the same time, SED officials did not hide their eagerness to lay the groundwork for similar visits by their chief to the two principal NATO allies and former German occupation authorities, Great Britain and the United States.[2] Furthermore, all of Honecker's trips were accompanied by equally energetic efforts to bring leading politicians from the nonsocialist West to East Berlin for personal meetings with the East German leader. The Greek prime minister visited in January 1988, the Austrian chancellor in June, and the Danish prime minister in September.

In addition, as Soviet-U.S. relations warmed and tensions between the blocs decreased, Honecker's government also showed a provocative inclination to cast itself in a special role at the side of the Soviet Union in promoting world peace. When, for example, in early December 1987 Moscow and Washington were finally able to reach an INF agreement under which both superpowers eliminated their entire stocks of inter-

---

[1]Consider, for example, the following Central Committee report about Volkskammer president Horst Sindermann's visit to the FRG in early 1986: "Wide coverage of H. Sindermann in the FRG. Everyone is scrambling to get to Horst. [North Rhine-Westphalia minister-president Johannes] Rau is home in bed with the flu, but still requests that H. S. make a house visit! . . . Even [CDU/CSU *Fraktion* leader] Dregger and his 'steel helmets' [i.e., hard-liners] are horny for Horst. Without us, policy just can't be made there any more." The words are Heinz Geggel's, one of the Central Committee's propaganda chiefs, in Ulrich Bürger, *Das sagen wir natürlich so nicht!* (Berlin: Dietz, 1990), p. 146.

[2]Author's interview, Manfred Uschner, East Berlin, June 3, 1988.

mediate-range nuclear missiles, the SED acted as though the two states, and its chief ally above all, were merely coming to recognize the wisdom of arms-control measures that had long been apparent to East Germany's leaders. No one could doubt, as the SED politburo report to the Central Committee's Fifth Plenum of December 16 advised, that the INF treaty had been brought about to a great extent thanks to the "courageous, initiative-filled, and dynamic foreign policy" of the new Gorbachev leadership. It was, however, also true that Moscow had not acted alone. "Thanks to a commonly worked-out approach," the party report emphasized, "and to a constant process of coordination and collaboration, our Soviet comrades could be confident of the support of all of the states of our alliance during the negotiations. It is recognized internationally that the constructive position of our country helped to make possible the conclusion of the treaty on intermediate-range weapons."[3] Honecker could only agree. "As is well known," he stressed, "the GDR has in no small way contributed to the now agreed-upon elimination of the devil's ordnance [Teufelszeug]."[4]

In view of the acrimonious level to which East Berlin's relations with the Kremlin had descended in the fall of 1984, when Honecker had first sought to visit the FRG, it was easy to understand why East German policymakers should have been inclined to engage in a modicum of self-congratulation at the apparent success of their calls for dialogue with the West. It may also have been predictable that Honecker himself would be eager to benefit personally from the attention his government's foreign policy successes had brought to the GDR. Was it not he, one could ask, who had shown the greatest courage in standing up to the hard-liners in Moscow at a time of "speechlessness" between the blocs? And was it not also he who deserved the greatest credit for earning his country the respect and esteem of the world community?[5]

Nonetheless, these displays of self-satisfaction also seem to have played a

[3] Cited in Ilse Spittmann, "Irritationen zur Jahreswende," Deutschland Archiv, January 1988, p. 1. The East Germans had also sent similar messages to Moscow in earlier years. For example, in late December 1986, after Gorbachev's ascent to power but before his February 1987 decision not to link any preconditions to INF negotiations with the United States, Honecker used an address before his country's military academy to put the GDR at the forefront of those campaigning for peace: "In times of speechlessness," he stressed, "we never broke off the dialogue." Neues Deutschland (hereafter ND), September 25, 1986.

[4] ND, December 17, 1987. Also, see Eberhard Schulz, "Das 'Neue politische Denken' und die Deutschen," Deutschland Archiv, September 1988, pp. 963–979.

[5] Consider the assessment of Horst Sindermann, a full member of the SED politburo and president of the Volkskammer: "Who was kissed-up to [poussiert] more often by the world community than Honecker? There was no Western politician who wouldn't gladly have met with Honecker. Foreign statesmen and numerous parliamentary leaders would never have come had I not been able to promise that they could speak with Honecker. . . . He used this for his own personal purposes." Cited in Peter Kirschey, Wandlitz Waldsiedlung—die geschlossene Gesellschaft (Berlin: Dietz, 1990), pp. 31–32.

key role in compounding the East German leadership's inability to contend with the very specific challenges that were to haunt the GDR in the late 1980s. These included Mikhail Gorbachev's well-known calls for *glasnost* ("openness") and *perestroika* ("restructuring") under socialism and, the equally troublesome, if initially more subtle, internal dilemmas that were to emerge as a result of East Germany's opening to the Federal Republic. Just as the Honecker regime seemed to come close to attaining its most prominent objectives from the West, even the most loyal members of the SED could admit confidentially that their party's leader and those around him had become infected with an almost unfathomable sense of complacency about their achievements. This attitude blinded them to the need to reassess any aspect of their policies.[6]

Had the GDR not enjoyed any international successes during the 1980s, a man like Honecker was not likely to have been an ideological soulmate of an individual like Gorbachev in any case. The two Communist leaders came from distinctly different generations and backgrounds, the one directly tied to the struggle against Nazism and the other, in contrast, to the failures of two decades of Brezhnevism. Despite an initial show of East German enthusiasm in 1985 for the new Soviet General Secretary's more egalitarian style with other states, Honecker's and Gorbachev's conceptions of their governments' priorities were bound to diverge. Hence, as early as April 1986, when the Soviet leader first traveled to East Berlin to speak before the SED's Eleventh Congress and used the forum casually to broach the idea that the GDR might also benefit from a "restructuring" of its economy, Honecker responded to his guest's intimations with a mixture of disbelief and incomprehension: "The young man has been making policy for only a year, and already he wants to take on more than he can chew!"[7]

Over the following year, however, the Soviet leader continued to push through measures in his own country that represented even greater deviations from the East Germans' conservative understanding of socialist discipline. These included the introduction of looser controls over the party press, the promotion of agricultural reforms and economic cooperatives, and radical experiments in democratic participation. Quite frequently, all that Honecker's government could do to stay in line with its patron and ally was to emphasize the one domain on which there was still manifest agreement with Moscow—foreign policy and (to quote the SED chief himself) the merits of the "persistent efforts on the part of the Soviet party and state leadership to secure the peace."[8]

---

[6]Author's impressions, 1988 and 1989, East Berlin.

[7]Cited in Günter Schabowski, *Das Politbüro* (Reinbek bei Hamburg: Rowohlt, 1990), p. 34.

[8]See Honecker's September 2, 1987, address in Moscow, in *RA*, vol. 12, p. 647.

The logic of such an argument might have seemed forced. Yet, for many East German officials, this polite denial of the Soviet reform initiatives was only a matter of drawing on the SED's long-felt sense that the GDR had already made its own distinctive contribution to socialism. Why, a majority of party members asked at the time, should a state like theirs, which had first begun to experiment with economic reforms in the 1960s and had then registered some of the most impressive growth rates in the bloc, now run the risk of large-scale reforms? Or, why should its government undertake experiments in even more sensitive areas (for example, with its media and information policy or with the election of its public officials), when the daily conditions under which it operated, given East Germany's location on the boundary between capitalism and socialism, were so very different from those faced by the Soviet Union?[9]

If Gorbachev and his supporters were swayed by this reasoning, they did not show it. In 1988 they moved on to take up themes that touched on some of the most troublesome questions of the GDR's existence—the responsibility of the German Communists for Hitler's rise to power, the East German workers' uprising of 1953, and even a subject as sensitive as the Berlin Wall.[10] When the Soviets insistently pressed the East German leadership to go along with their initiatives, the SED regime reacted almost as though it had acquired a new enemy. Honecker and the small circle of his advisors who were responsible for the government's information policy responded to these assaults in a manner that would have been unthinkable a decade and a half earlier. To the surprise of even some members of the politburo—most of whom were quite characteristically kept in the dark about party policy—issues of prominent Soviet publications such as *New Times* and *Sputnik*, which addressed themes that were not to the General Secretary's taste, were simply banned in the GDR. Gorbachev's own speeches were increasingly printed only in partial form and often only in tandem with other articles attacking his reforms. For the first time ever, the East German media began to make scarcely veiled references to the darker side of everyday socialism in the USSR, including rising alcoholism, homelessness, and food shortages.[11]

---

[9]This was the tenor of many interviews I conducted at institutions such as the Central Committee's Academy of Social Sciences and the Institute for Marxism-Leninism throughout the spring of 1988 in East Berlin.

[10]For some of the Soviet heresies, from the SED's perspective, see Ilse Spittmann, "SED setzt auf Zeitgewinn," *Deutschland Archiv*, July 1988, pp. 689–691; and Fred Oldenburg, "Sowjetische Deutschlandpolitik nach den Treffen von Moskau und Bonn 1988/89," *Berichte des Bundesinstituts für ost-wissenschaftliche und internationale Studien* 63 (1989).

[11]At times, one might have thought *Neues Deutschland* was covering the United States. On the banning of *Sputnik*, which provoked instant controversy throughout the SED, one member of the party politburo, Erich Mückenberger, later observed: "We weren't even asked"; *ND*, January 10, 1990.

Finally, Honecker and his closest colleagues introduced an idiom into their public references to the homeland of the October Revolution that might equally have suited their discourse with the FRG. In a particularly bitter report before the SED's Seventh Central Committee Plenum in December 1988, the East German General Secretary emphasized for the benefit of his Soviet counterparts that the GDR was a sovereign state that was entirely capable of making decisions for itself. It was all fine and good to speak about fraternal solidarity within the socialist bloc, but true cooperation was only possible on the basis of accepting each country's "equality, independence, and autonomy." This entailed recognizing, Honecker instructed, that there was no model that was universally applicable for all socialist states and that it was fully up to the GDR, as was the case with all of its East European neighbors, to decide "its responsibility before its own people."[12]

If Gorbachev's policies alone had been at the root of the SED's difficulties at this juncture, Honecker and the other members of the party elite who were nervous about what was happening in the USSR might have justifiably been able to ascribe their problems to the invidious influences of a new type of external threat. Nonetheless, quite independently of Gorbachev's influence, it is significant that the SED regime itself helped to provide fertile ground for the Soviet leader's initiatives with every new development in its *Westpolitik*. For in the process of opening the GDR to the Federal Republic, even on a selective basis, the Honecker government raised the East German population's expectations of social and political change far more quickly than it could ever have managed to fulfill. Furthermore, the regime may also have prepared the way for precisely the sorts of challenges to its authority that would culminate in the GDR's collapse in late 1989.

In part, these developments may be regarded as an unintended consequence of the SED's efforts to create the right kind of climate for its "peace policy," including its calls for dialogue with the FRG. For example, at just around the time that Honecker traveled to Bonn in the fall of 1987, the East German government made a number of notable symbolic gestures to its population—allowing a group of independent peace activists to take part in an official demonstration, the Olof Palme Peace March; televising debates between East and West German politicians; and perhaps most im-

---

[12]*ND*, December 2, 1988. For the first of many such declarations of independence from the Soviet reforms, see politburo member Kurt Hager's April 1987 interview with the West German weekly, *Der Stern*, in which he treated Gorbachev's innovations as a matter of significance only for the USSR itself: "Would you, by the way, feel obliged to redo the wallpaper in your apartment just because your neighbor has put up new wallpaper?" Reprinted in *ND*, April 10, 1987. For Hager's reflections on his remarks, see OHP (Hager, December 3, 1990, and July 11, 1991). Also see Johannes Kuppe, "Offensiv in die Defensive," *Deutschland Archiv*, January 1989, pp. 1–7.

important of all, giving wide publicity to the signing of the joint document with the SPD on the "culture of political argumentation." These steps had to have awakened hopes that inter-German détente would have immediate and substantive consequences for the quality of intellectual and spiritual life within the GDR.[13]

No doubt the SED regime was confident that it could still present itself as the final voice on what issues constituted legitimate subjects of discussion and which groups would be entitled to debate them. Thus, in early 1988 and then with ever-increasing intensity in the ensuing months, it showed its determination to maintain this authority by cracking down on a number of unauthorized protests and organizations, such as the participation of dissidents in a march honoring Rosa Luxemburg in January 1988 and the opening of a small environmentalist exhibit at the Zionskirche in East Berlin. The more the regime sought to reassert its control by using force, however, the more other groups seemed inclined to demand the right to express their views, ranging from proponents of nuclear disarmament to prominent East German literary and cultural personalities and from environmental activists to the hierarchy of the country's Lutheran churches. Gradually, it became clear that the party itself had sown the seeds for a political phenomenon that was completely new to the GDR. For the first time in the country's history, a widespread if diffuse network of informal groupings and interests had come into being, which were all in many ways no longer beholden to nor completely dependent upon state authority. Moreover, these groups were primed to take advantage of whatever signs of discontent they could find—economic, religious, and otherwise—among the East German population.[14]

At the time, it may not have mattered much to Honecker and his closest colleagues that many of these potential critics became embittered when the regime failed to respond positively to their demands for expanded oppor-

---

[13]Yet, for an indication that some East German dissidents felt the SPD did not push the common document far enough, see OHP (Markus Meckel, June 10, 1991). Also, see Walter Süß, "Perestroika oder Ausreise," *Deutschland Archiv*, March 1989, pp. 286–301. For an example of the very limited kind of leeway the SED was willing to allow its artists, see *Neue Deutsche Literatur* 36 (March 1988), which first published some of the controversial proceedings, by the standards of the time, of the Tenth Writer's Congress of November 24–26, 1987.

[14]Internal SED opinion polls in the 1980s confirmed that these quasi-independent groups had rising levels of popular discontent to build upon. For example, in surveys among worker apprentices in 1983, the Leipzig Institut für Jugendforschung found that 46 percent showed a "strong" identification with socialism, 45 percent "with qualifications," and only 9 percent had "little or no" identification. Yet, by May 1988, the "strong" category had fallen to 28 percent, those "with qualifications" had risen to 61 percent, and 11 percent were in the final group. By October 1988, only 18 percent were in the "strong" category, 54 percent were in the middle category, and 28 percent showed "little or no" identification with socialism. See Peter Förster and Günter Roski, *Die DDR zwischen Wende und Wahl* (Berlin: Links Druck, 1990), p. 39.

tunities for political participation, greater freedoms of religious worship, or for swifter steps to clean up the GDR's polluted environment. Yet the position of the SED's leaders was made considerably more complicated by growing disgruntlement within the party's own ranks as well, and even among the rank and file of the East German security organs. In particular, many of the party faithful were unhappy about the discrepancies they perceived between their government's more accommodating postures toward the outside world—the SED/SPD common document, for example, spoke explicitly of *both* Germanys' "capacity for reform"—and the upper leadership's seeming obliviousness to the many shortcomings and problems of daily life in the GDR. These were the maladies with which average party officials and policemen were most closely acquainted, and many held Honecker himself personally responsible for the country's misfortunes.[15]

Those who knew something about the actual state of health of the GDR economy, as opposed to its mythically pristine character at the head of the Soviet bloc, were unhappy with Honecker's insistence on pursuing an East German road to socialism ("socialism in the colors of the GDR," as he called it), which seemed to be little more than a pretext for avoiding responsibility for the country's economic problems and for failing to undertake drastically needed changes in strategy.[16] The regime could no longer afford the massive subsidies that were hidden behind many of the General Secretary's consumerist policies: its indebtedness to Western lending institutions was rising dangerously (indeed, at an even faster rate than in the 1970s), and necessary investments in plant modernization and research and development had long been postponed in the name of fleeting, short-term economic gains.[17]

[15]Because there were few if any public forums for expressing such discontent, few of the internal grievances within the SED ever saw the light of day. To the extent that criticisms of party policy or even veiled statements of support for Gorbachev's reforms were published at all, they appeared only in an arcane form that was comprehensible to the initiated or in the form of interviews with the Western press. Two prominent examples of the former were the writings of the East German social philosopher, Uwe-Jens Heuer, in such publications as the *Deutsche Zeitschrift für Philosophie*, or the supposedly metaphorical family biography, *Die Troika* (Berlin: Aufbau, 1989), by the ex-deputy minister of state security and purported Gorbachev enthusiast, Markus Wolf. An example of the latter was Jürgen Kuczynski (e.g., "Die Bürokratie muß vernichtet werden," *Konkret*, May 1987, pp. 23–25), who could get away with giving interviews to the Western media because of his personal ties with Honecker.

[16]Indeed, Honecker was not at a loss for excuses. In a meeting with Wojciech Jaruzelski on May 22, 1989, he observed to the Polish president that "even 'hot' supporters of *perestroika* and *glasnost* [would not] think about making any changes in their own policies"; unpublished transcript (IV 2/1/438), Central Party Archives (hereafter CPA), Berlin.

[17]Author's interview, Günter Schabowski, East Berlin, October 30, 1989. To cite one early example, on April 5, 1986, the Ministry for State Security called for drastic measures to repair and upgrade the GDR's power plants and its entire system for transmitting electrical energy, for fear that the country could no longer meet its needs for electricity in the 1990s. See the interview with Wolfgang Schwanitz, the director of the short-lived Office of National Security, in *ND*, November 23, 1989.

In the meantime, as Honecker's direct influence on even the most mundane aspects of official policymaking had grown to become almost unchallengeable, economic experts in the party had good reason to worry that the General Secretary was falling prey to the same excessive estimation of his country's world-historic position for which he had once criticized Walter Ulbricht. Best known among the schemes he advocated was a plan by economics authority Günter Mittag, in the second half of the 1980s, to transform the GDR into a world leader in the field of microtechnology by developing a one-megabyte computer chip. In the end, the new technology not only cost the East German economy a staggering one billion Marks but was also outmoded by the time it was brought into production.[18] Despite the repeated efforts of some of the government's most distinguished economic authorities to make the case for a more moderate course to Honecker personally, however, the SED leader became all the more distant and unreachable.[19]

More troublesome, the East German government faced a fundamentally different set of challenges than it had only a few years earlier. This situation was a result of the GDR's new relationship with the FRG and, in particular, Honecker's determination to continue the risky policy of allowing his country's citizens greater freedom to travel to the West. By the end of the decade, the right to visit the Federal Republic had become an unexpectedly divisive issue among the East German people because there was no way of applying it universally. As it was, some citizens simply lacked the familial ties and friendships in the FRG to facilitate such trips. More aggravating still, other groups within the population—key party officials, soldiers, and even members of the secret police—were not allowed to venture into "capitalist foreign territory" at all, by virtue of their supposed connection with the country's security interests. In no small part because of the material benefits these individuals lost as a result of their inability to visit the West, many of these citizens complained that the GDR was quickly becoming a two-class society in which, ironically, loyalty to the regime could guarantee a lower quality of life.[20]

Even this problem could not compare with the greater turmoil that was

[18]It was said, at the time, that the GDR was going to develop the world's biggest microchip.

[19]For example, the SED's chief of state planning, Gerhard Schürer, tried repeatedly in 1988 and 1989 to appeal directly to Honecker for a more cautious economic strategy but was never able to overcome the opposition of Mittag, the General Secretary's confidant on economic affairs; author's interview, Otto Reinhold, East Berlin, March 23, 1990. Also see Peter Siebenmorgen, "Vom Retter zum Sündenbock," Die Zeit, May 10, 1991. For Schürer's reflections, see my interview with him in OHP (Schürer, July 10, 1991).

[20]The problem snowballed when the regime tried to appease its dissatisfied loyalists by giving them special rights to Western consumer goods and cash bonuses, paid in West-Marks, at the end of the year. When word of these measures spread among the general public, new resentments arose among those who could travel but did not receive the benefits.

generated by the manifest failure of the travel policy itself. After two years of dramatic increases in the numbers of East Germans who were allowed to visit the West, it was becoming clear that the overall gamble with more open borders was not working out. Although both East and West German negotiators could note with pride that less than one-half of one percent of the millions of GDR citizens who went to the FRG annually actually chose to remain there, *neither* side was willing to admit publicly the more revealing datum about what happened when these individuals returned to their homes in the East. Too often, the first act of many East German citizens was to file applications for themselves and for their families for permanent emigration. As a consequence, by 1988 several hundred thousand East Germans, among them all of the categories of skilled workers who had fled from the GDR in the 1950s, were once again poised to throw the country into disorder by leaving it behind.[21] Evidently, after seeming to come so close to achieving its perennial objective of domestic stability, the SED had to recognize that its efforts to combine a greater degree of openness to the West with a reinvigorated sense of domestic pride in the GDR's achievements were being eroded from within.

A Path of Least Resistance

In the increasingly more optimistic atmosphere of the late 1980s, after so much progress had been made between the Germanys and following the even grander changes that were to be registered in the Soviet-American relationship, it would have been unusual had West German politicians not shown some sign of concern at the suddenly less-than-encouraging turn of events in the GDR. In fact, in the first few months of 1988, when East Berlin turned to punitive measures to quell discontent among its artistic community and churches and expelled some of its best-known critics to the West, among them the dissident songwriter Stefan Krawczyk, his wife, the theater-director Freya Klier, and one of the founders of the antiestablishment "church from below," Vera Wollenberger, a pall was thrown over the inter-German relationship. At least some of those politicians in Bonn who had idealistically sought to promote dialogue with the East German regime were shocked to find how little their counterparts had changed in their ability or willingness to tolerate disagreement.

[21]Author's interviews, Klaus Bölling, West Berlin, June 8, 1987, and Wolfgang Vogel, East Berlin, May 7, 1988, and March 20, 1990. For the Ministry of State Security's warnings to the SED about the problem, see the interview with Wolfgang Schwanitz in *ND*, November 23, 1989. One gains a glimpse into the genesis of such discontent in the interviews throughout L. Niethammer, A. von Plato, and D. Wierling, eds., *Die volkseigene Erfahrung* (Berlin: Rowohlt, 1991), esp. pp. 354–381.

The Social Democratic coauthors of the SPD/SED common document, Erhard Eppler and Thomas Meyer, lost no time in voicing their apprehensions that the whole point of the two parties' talks had been thrown into jeopardy; "dialogue with the outside world will not function in any lasting sense," Eppler asserted, "if dialogue with [internal forces] fails to take place or if it is disparaged."[22] The West German Greens as well, many of whom had been forbidden to enter the GDR because of their contacts with dissident groups, expressed their indignation that the only way in which the SED regime could see fit to deal with its problems was by ostracizing those who dared to disagree.[23] Oddly, in these critiques the Left may even have found some uneasy grounds for agreement with those on the West German Right who had been dubious all along about the lasting value of any sustained interactions with the East.

Nevertheless, the great majority of politicians in the Federal Republic still reacted to these developments with a noteworthy degree of caution and self-restraint, almost to the point of going out of their way to avoid provoking the Communist regime. For example, when some younger members of the Social Democratic Party called upon their party's leadership to expand its contacts with the East to include parallel channels of communication with the newly emerging social and political forces in the GDR,[24] their senior colleagues, all veterans of the early *Ostpolitik*, vetoed the idea, arguing that the SPD had no legitimate discussion partners outside of the SED elite.[25] Experience had shown that there was no easy path to reforming the GDR, prominent figures like Brandt and Bahr were quick to advise. Moreover, precisely because the East German regime faced risks that did not exist in the West, one had to appreciate that meaningful change in its behavior would not come about overnight.[26]

[22]Eppler's comments in an interview on January 27, 1988, unpublished press report, Archives of the German Bundestag. Another participant relates that many Social Democrats' disappointment was due to their high expectations of their interlocutors. "We had always had the impression that these GDR people were already thinking in terms of Gorbachev-type reforms," Thomas Meyer noted in early 1988. "[But] we now doubt this today." Author's interviews, Bonn, March 11, 1988.

[23]See, for example, Petra Kelly's remarks in *Stenographische Berichte des deutschen Bundestags*, 11th elec. period, 57th sess., February 3, 1988, p. 3953.

[24]For example, in an unpublished internal discussion paper of early 1988, "Zur Handlungsorientierung und den Schwerpunkten sozialdemokratischer Außenpolitik," SPD Bundestag member Hermann Scheer called for "communications with nonstate reform groups." Author's sources, Bonn.

[25]The only prominent exception to this rule was the East German Lutheran church. Yet even here, West German politicians took great care in the way they handled such contacts, since they did not want to impair the church's freedom of maneuver by making it appear too political. They also strictly avoided contacts with more independent religious groupings below the Lutheran hierarchy.

[26]Author's interview, SPD Bundestag *Fraktion*, Bonn, March 9, 1988. Also see Gunter Hofmann, "Ich bin doch auch nur ein Mensch," *Die Zeit*, February 12, 1988.

Even more telling, however, was the extent to which this understanding of the possibilities and limits of political change in East Germany was actually suffused through all of the major parties in Bonn.[27] Indeed, when two special sessions of the Bundestag were called in February 1988 to debate the developments in the East, one West German party could scarcely be distinguished from another in the assessments of what needed to be done to put matters aright between the Germanys. Everyone could agree that the SED's hard-fisted manner of dealing with its critics had been deplorable, that the exhibition of a greater degree of "tolerance and more generosity" was required of its government, and that good-neighborly relations between East Berlin and Bonn presupposed a strict adherence to the letter and spirit of the Basic Treaty. Yet what also stood out, in contrast to the bitter interparty debates of the 1970s, was the absence of any call by any of the West German parties for retribution or punitive action against the East German government. A prominent FDP parliamentarian, Uwe Ronneburger, summed up the collective attitude of the Bundestag best when he candidly observed: "I believe we all have occasion in the current situation to do exactly that which we have tried to impress upon the GDR leadership during the last weeks, namely to react calmly."[28]

Additionally, it is compelling to consider the extent to which the parliament's consensus on policy toward East Germany may also have left the FRG's leaders paradoxically dependent on the maintenance of social and political stability in the GDR. Even if the East German regime was suffering the most as increasing numbers of its citizens opted to leave for the West, Bonn still relied upon East Berlin's goodwill in keeping the doors to East-West contacts open. Just as the FRG had benefited from the Communist regime's decision to make the Berlin Wall more permeable in the first place, there was no question that the GDR's leaders were equally capable of reconstricting their population's access to the outside world should the risks of further contacts with West Germany have been perceived to outweigh their advantages. Thus it is hardly surprising that few politicians in the West were anxious to provoke the SED by reawakening old differences. As one participant exclaimed about East Berlin's more liberal travel policy

[27]Consider the observation of a leading official in the Foreign Office in the spring of 1988: "We don't have any choice but to work with this socialist government. Only its leaders can make real concessions. Anything else is inconceivable." Author's interview, March 10, 1988, Bonn.

[28]For his remarks, and also those of Eduard Lintner (CSU), Minister of Intra-German Affairs Dorothee Wilms (CDU), Hans Büchler (SPD), and Heinrich Lummer (CDU), see *Stenographische Berichte*, 11th elec. period, 57th sess., February 3, 1988, pp. 3952–3963. Even members of the Greens, who regularly attacked the establishment parties for ostensibly colluding with the SED to limit the influence of opposition groups, appear to have been constrained by their own demands that Bonn recognize the GDR's independence. This meant not interfering in its internal affairs. See the speech by Peter Sellin, in *Stenographische Berichte*, 11th elec. period, 59th sess., February 5, 1988, p. 4105.

in 1988: "These visits are worth a thousand speeches about German reunification!"[29]

For these reasons alone, as tensions rose even more between the Honecker government and its population in late 1988 and early 1989, West German negotiators found themselves frequently cast in the uncomfortable role of advocating East German interests. On several occasions, for example, when GDR citizens sought refuge in the FRG's permanent mission in East Berlin and in West German embassies in other East European capitals, hoping to acquire free passage to the West, it was left up to officials of the Federal Republic to convince such would-be refugees to return to their homes to obtain the right to leave their country through appropriate channels. On the broader question of travel itself, West German representatives also endeavored to convince Honecker and his colleagues that it was still in the FRG's interest as well to keep East Germany's citizens right where they were; again, it was not the policy of the Federal government to "depopulate" the GDR. If excessive numbers of East Germans were seeking to emigrate to the West, they contended, this was only a result of continuing uncertainties in the GDR about who could travel and under what circumstances. These could be resolved simply by allowing more individuals to go abroad on a regular basis and by introducing more formal and predictable procedures (what one participant, appealing to Gorbachev's terminology, called "transparency")[30] to handle the whole issue of freedom of movement.

In this single respect, in fact, the SED regime seems to have gone along with its adversaries' reasoning. Despite (or perhaps even because of) the worsening state of relations between rulers and ruled in the GDR, the Honecker government decided to open up the country even more than before. Thus, in 1988, the number of total trips by East Germans to the West was allowed to rise from its previous high of 5 million visits in 1987 to over 6.7 million; in the first half of 1989, these figures were even higher, up 9 percent to the FRG and over 20 percent to West Berlin. Furthermore, over 30,000 individuals were allowed to emigrate from the GDR in 1988 (a significant increase from only 11,500 during the previous year); and, in the first seven months of 1989 alone, this number rose even higher, to over 48,000.

No doubt with the aim of extracting significant economic remuneration from the West in return, East Berlin also began to take exactly the kinds of steps that hopeful Germans on both sides of the national divide might have interpreted as marking the beginning of the end of the Wall. On November

[29]Author's interviews, Bonn, January 20, 1988.
[30]Author's interview, Federal chancellery, Bonn, March 24, 1988. Also see Dorothee Wilms, "Zweimal vierzig Jahre," *Deutschland Archiv*, May 1989, pp. 497–500.

30, 1988, the regime introduced a new "statute on travel by citizens to foreign countries" that went a long way toward codifying the legal conditions under which average East Germans could apply to leave their country, either for short visits abroad or permanently, and toward specifying the kinds of procedures that public officials would be required to follow in turning down such requests. On January 15, 1989, at a follow-up meeting of the European Conference on Security and Cooperation in Vienna, the Honecker government went even further, affixing its imprimatur to an international document that affirmed "the freedom of every individual" to leave his country and to return to it on his own volition. Finally, in mid-June 1989, Honecker himself seemed to proclaim the end to the single most offensive practice along the Wall and the inter-German border, the *Schießbefehl*, or "command to shoot" anyone who attempted to flee the GDR, when he announced that East German border guards would henceforth use their weapons only in clear instances of self-defense.[31]

Under normal circumstances, if these had been the only significant developments to have emerged from the GDR, those involved in talks with the SED might have had grounds for guarded optimism that East Berlin was slowly beginning to make the difficult transition to a more trusting relationship with its citizenry. Yet this would have been to deny the other side of the government's policies in late 1988 and early 1989. Just below the surface, there were many indications that the internal situation in East Germany was becoming impossibly polarized. Representatives of the GDR's Lutheran churches and even the country's smaller Roman Catholic community had moved beyond the advocacy of such relatively straightforward issues as their parishioners' right to emigration to embrace much broader, even more provocative themes, like the need for a "comprehensive dialogue" between the government and its people and the evils of bureaucratism and centralism.[32] Then, too, for the first time ever, loosely organized citizens' groups actually monitored the conduct of an official election, the statewide municipal elections of May 7, 1989, and later went public with numerous allegations of irregularities and fraud in the electoral process. And, among the population as a whole, enthusiasm was growing for the positive examples of socialist reform that were just then beginning to emerge in Hungary and neighboring Poland.

Yet, rather than seek to appease those who were nervously anticipating similar changes in their own country, perhaps to be set in motion with the appearance of a new, younger group of officials in the SED politburo, the

---

[31] For his interview with the *Washington Post*, see *ND*, June 13, 1989.

[32] Gisela Helwig, "Plädoyer für Umgestaltung," *Deutschland Archiv*, June 1989, pp. 609–612. For a thorough account of the political transformation of the East German churches, see Robert F. Goeckel, *The Lutheran Church and the East German State* (Ithaca, N.Y.: Cornell University Press, 1990), esp. chaps. 8 and 9.

regime took a more explicitly unforgiving tone than ever. Party leaders accused their critics of playing directly into the hands of "counterrevolutionary forces" and called for an unequivocal definition of the "friends and foes" of socialism. More ominously, in June 1989 the Honecker government issued an unmistakable warning to all of its citizens when it unabashedly came to the defense of the government of the People's Republic of China, only weeks after the latter had suppressed the Chinese democracy movement in the bloody massacre at Tiananmen Square.[33]

The outside observer is struck, in comparison, by the relatively restrained public stands taken by many West German politicians on these developments. To be sure, there was a steady stream of prominent visitors from the FRG into East Berlin during the first six months of 1989, including Walther Leisler Kiep, Ernst Albrecht, and Lothar Späth of the CDU, Olaf Feldmann of the FDP, and Björn Engholm, Johannes Rau, and Hans-Jochen Vogel of the SPD, all of whom used the opportunities provided by their confidential talks with the East German leadership to express varying degrees of concern about the deteriorating internal situation in the GDR.[34] Yet, above and beyond the necessity of preserving their country's ability to conduct business with the SED regime, by the end of the 1980s very few of the leaders of the major West German parties were eager to contemplate an abrupt change in their relationship with East Berlin.

At least in part, this attitude may have resulted from the fact that the governing forces in Bonn had become comfortably accustomed to their newly acquired ability to present the FRG as a force for stability in European affairs, and not as a nagging threat to the status quo. For example, Hans-Dietrich Genscher and the FDP had enjoyed phenomenal success, both at the polls and, for that matter, in wresting foreign-policy authority away from the Federal chancellery, by selling the idea of Bonn's role in a "European peace order" (europäische Friedensunion) to the West German people. In Genscher's vision, both Germanys would work together "to

[33]See the defiant politburo report at the Central Committee's Eighth Plenum of June 22, 1989, in ND, June 24–25, 1989, as well as the continuous, positive press coverage of the events in China earlier in the month.

[34]Although West German politicians took care in many of these meetings to criticize a recent shooting at the Wall, the tone of their conversations with Honecker can hardly be described as hostile. For example, in his April 27 meeting with the SED chief, Ernst Albrecht coupled his insistence that the government of Lower Saxony would not give in on the definition of the Elbe River boundary with the assurance that he was nevertheless open to "practical solutions." For his part, Honecker seemed intent upon cultivating friendly ties with each visitor. For example, he assured the Social Democratic minister-president of North Rhine–Westphalia, Johannes Rau, that "the GDR [was] intent upon supporting the Rau government, even if this did not always please the Federal Chancellor." See the unpublished transcripts (IV 2/1/438) of the meetings with Engholm (January 31), Späth (February 23), Rau (March 12), Albrecht (April 27), and Vogel (May 25), CPA, Berlin.

make the division of [the continent] into an anachronism, step by step through cooperation."[35] Kohl, too, ever sensitive to the demands of the West German electorate, was quite pleased to continue depicting the CDU as the pillar of reasoned accommodation with the East.

In the spring of 1988, in fact, only the presence of a handful of hard-line critics within the ranks of the chancellor's party had kept the Christian Democratic leadership from adopting a platform that would have explicitly put the task of overcoming the division of Europe ahead of the goal of restoring German unity.[36] Over the following year, even after the reformers' proposal had been watered down through intraparty compromises and the CDU found itself challenged to reaffirm its conservative credentials by a small right-wing party known as the Republikaner, the CDU still could not get over the habit of wanting to portray West Germany as a European power like any other.

In this sense, it was understandable that CDU moderates, including the chancellor, carefully avoided provocative references to any theme that might have seemed to call prevailing European boundaries into question, preferring instead to describe their national goals in ways that were so innocuous as to have been palatable to any of the Federal Republic's continental neighbors.[37] As late as July 1989, for example, Kohl's chief foreign-policy advisor, Horst Teltschik, could speak about his government's working relationship with the GDR as though it represented the only conceivable way of acting on the national question: "We have recognized the existence of the GDR as a separate state, and in this sense we must also take into account its existence as a state in any future solution [to the German problem]. For us, the German question is not primarily a matter of seeking

[35]Hans-Dietrich Genscher, "Ein Plan für das ganze Europa," *Die Zeit*, October 28, 1988, p. 3.

[36]See "Unsere Verantwortung in der Welt: Christlich-demokratische Perspektiven zur Außen-, Sicherheits-, Europa- und Deutschlandpolitik," *CDU-Dokumentation* 6 (1968), sec. 4. The reformers who drafted the proposed policy statement, among them Horst Teltschik, Dorothee Wilms, Wolfgang Schäuble, and Wulf Schönbohm, regarded the document as a way of modernizing CDU national policy to make it more competitive with that of the SPD and FDP. "Our problem," one of the key authors explained, "[was] the old continuing assumption that the German question [had] to be on the agenda [*Tagesordnung*]." Author's interview, Federal chancellery, Bonn, March 17, 1988.

[37]Consider Kohl's State-of-the-Nation address in December 1988, which, although designed to appease his fundamentalist critics, can hardly have offended anyone: "So long as the contradiction between freedom and the absence of freedom [*Unfreiheit*] continues to hinder the overcoming of the division of Europe and, with it, of Germany," he declared, "it is our task to do whatever is possible and responsible to lessen the East-West conflict in Europe and to work toward overcoming it." *Bulletin*, December 2, 1988, p. 1502, Bonn, Presse und Informationsamt. On Kohl's objectives, as well as the continuing contradictions within the CDU, see Clay Clemens, *Reluctant Realists* (Durham, N.C.: Duke University Press, 1989), pp. 294–298.

a territorial solution. . . . Now the question is one of harmonizing German goals and desires with developments throughout Europe."[38]

At this point in 1989, quite unlike the situation during an earlier decade, no major political party in the FRG had either the inclination to welcome a severe deterioration of relations with East Berlin or the awareness that it had much to gain from such an eventuality. In this setting, the West German regime seemed to be left with two fairly straightforward options, both of which amounted to following paths of least resistance. The first, which the Kohl government appeared to pursue throughout the spring of 1989, was simply to continue those contacts with the GDR that still worked to both states' mutual advantage. Sister-city exchanges proceeded apace, new agreements were signed in the field of scientific and technical cooperation, and East Berlin and Bonn also began several joint projects in the area of environmental protection. Not to be outdone, the Social Democrats maintained their own search for an even higher level of inter-German dialogue in international security affairs. They regularly met with East German officials up to June 1989 to discuss a host of possible areas of collaboration, including the opening of formal contacts between the National People's Army and the Bundeswehr, proposals for dismantling European battlefield weapons, and such novel concepts as the need for an "ecological security partnership."[39]

In contrast, Bonn's second option, which became more and more attractive as the internal situation in the GDR worsened, was simply to avoid East Berlin altogether. In this regard, Kohl himself seems to have found that it was at times much easier to make his party's case for détente simply by going to the sources of positive innovation in the socialist world. Thus, in mid-June 1989, he welcomed Mikhail Gorbachev to a triumphant reception in Bonn, and over the ensuing summer months he and others in the CDU began to lay the foundations for what they hoped to be a closer relationship with the reformist governments of Hungary and Poland.[40] To the extent that a similar temptation existed within the ranks of the Social

[38]*General Anzeiger*, July 6, 1989.

[39]It must be said, however, that some Social Democrats—Erhard Eppler directly and Oskar Lafontaine and Horst Ehmke behind the scenes—criticized SED policy in their discussions in the GDR. On this theme and the general evolution of GDR-FRG affairs in the final months before the East German explosion, see Thomas Ammer, "Politische Kontakte Bundesrepublik-DDR im ersten Halbjahr 1989," *Deutschland Archiv*, September 1989, pp. 1019–1027.

[40]On the events leading up to this visit, see Michael Sodaro, *Moscow, Germany and the West, from Khrushchev to Gorbachev* (Ithaca, N.Y.: Cornell University Press, 1991), pp. 355–362. Kohl advisor Horst Teltschik was largely responsible for Bonn's decision in the late 1980s to diversify its contacts with the East, although efforts to improve relations with Poland in 1989 were still complicated by pressures from the Union right wing to accentuate the FRG's special relationship with that country's remaining German population.

Democratic opposition, it was signaled by a push by party moderates in July 1989 to move in the opposite direction. With the enunciation of a new platform, "European Security 2000," members of the SPD leadership who had watched the party's chances of regaining control of the government dwindle since 1982 tentatively began to shift away from the era of grandiose experiments in East-West security cooperation toward a reassertion of trans-Atlantic commonality and closer ties with the United States.[41]

Both of these trends might have led students of inter-German affairs to predict something of a downturn in Bonn's relations with East Berlin in the months to come. The East German government seemed to be irrationally bent upon turning itself into a less appealing discussion partner for the FRG, while policymakers in the Federal Republic were turning their attention to other concerns. Nonetheless, there was nothing that could have prepared politicians in either of the countries, let alone the onlooking world, for the kind of disorder that was to engulf the Germanys as a result of a single decision made outside of East Germany's borders that would, in effect, mark the death of the Berlin Wall.

A New Political Force

The beginning of the end of the GDR should be dated May 2, 1989, although this fact was by no means self-evident at the time. On that day, the Hungarian government, already well along the path of instituting its own domestic reforms, began to remove the barbed-wire fence and fortifications along its border with Austria as a demonstration of its desire to be more fully included in the European community. At once, the conditions were created that made the Wall in Berlin superfluous. At first, only a handful of East German citizens managed to elude Hungarian border patrols to reach the West. Nevertheless, over the ensuing summer months, as word traveled about the unanticipated opportunity to escape the GDR "via socialism," thousands more East Germans sought to take advantage of the new opening to the outside world. Hundreds of others streamed into West German embassies in Budapest, Prague, and Warsaw, and even into the FRG's Permanent Mission in East Berlin in the hopes of compelling the Bonn government to facilitate their emigration. Over thirty thousand individuals fled to the FRG by the end of September 1989, with no end in sight to the exodus.

From this point onward, East Germany's collapse may well have been

---

[41]The new platform was partly developed through consultations with prominent members of the U.S. Congress. For similar trends in Social Democratic domestic politics, see Peter Merkl, "The SPD after Brandt: Problems of Integration in a Changing Urban Society," *West European Politics* 11, no. 1 (January 1988), pp. 40–53.

inevitable. Without the artificial conditions that had for almost three decades allowed the SED leadership to impose its will freely upon its population, individual GDR citizens suddenly found themselves in the position, much like an earlier generation in the 1950s, where they could decide their state's fate simply by voting with their feet. As escalating numbers of skilled professionals, doctors, engineers, and craftsmen left the GDR for the West, the country's survival was literally determined by the choice these people made.[42]

Despite these dire circumstances, however, it is noteworthy how hard it was for the two German governments to come to terms with the issues exposed by the refugee exodus. To a great extent, both up to and following the opening of the Berlin Wall on November 9, East Berlin and Bonn each still seemed bound by the categories that had made their relationship manageable in the 1970s and 1980s. In the FRG, the unexpected circumstance of finding the GDR regime no longer fully in control of its borders meant that West Germany's leaders were temporarily at a loss to know how to adapt their policies to the existence of a new constituency, the East German people. In the case of the GDR, the consequences were even more severe. The Honecker regime's defiant refusal even to admit to the problems it faced may have actually accelerated the pace of the state's dissolution and, in the process, done a great deal to insure that the totally unanticipated pressures for German reunification were upon it before the end of the year.

Certainly, on an abstract level, one can conceive of an alternate scenario taking place in the GDR in the summer of 1989. Had those within the SED politburo who eventually were to topple Honecker on October 18 only managed to marshal their forces some two months earlier, the speed of the East German collapse might have been slowed and the conditions under which the country was absorbed into the Federal Republic significantly altered. By immediately taking a more open stand on the need for political reforms, by engaging in honest dialogue with their critics outside of the party, and by promulgating an even more liberal travel code—all steps that were later taken by the post-Honecker government of Egon Krenz—a revamped SED might have collected just enough domestic support, both from the East German populace and, perhaps more important, from its own ranks, to postpone at least that sense of utter hopelessness that descended upon the country beginning in the fall of 1989.

---

[42]Otto Reinhold, rector of the Academy for Social Sciences, captured the SED's dilemma by suggesting early in the crisis that the GDR did not have the luxury of falling back on an uncontested claim to national identity should its population lose faith in socialism: "[The GDR]," he noted, "is only conceivable as an anti-fascist and socialist alternative to the FRG. What justification would a capitalist GDR have next to a capitalist Federal Republic?" Cited from an unpublished transcript of his remarks, Radio GDR II, August 19, 1989.

Nevertheless, even to construct such an alternate scenario for the GDR is to miss the point about the constraining character of policymaking in the SED as it had existed long before Erich Honecker ever came to power. Precisely the exaggerated degree of centralism that made the GDR such an effective bargainer with the West in the past also made it nearly inconceivable that an effective challenge to the General Secretary's policies could have been mounted, until of course the party found itself in the worst sort of crisis. It made no difference that as early as the summer of 1989, there were a number of key figures within the SED politburo who favored a change of leadership, evidently including the Berlin party chief, Günter Schabowski; the head of state planning, Gerhard Schürer; several of the district (*Bezirk*) party bosses who were most sensitive to the daily frustrations of the East German populace; and, very tentatively, Krenz himself, long regarded as Honecker's most likely successor.[43] Still, what all of these individuals lacked was in actuality the most crucial skill of all, the ability to organize against their leader and, in the face of decades of training in the norms of "revolutionary discipline," to articulate an alternative conception of the GDR's priorities while Honecker still remained in office. "One would have sooner committed sodomy," Schabowski later observed, in a telling admission of the exasperation felt by many of his colleagues, "than to have allowed oneself to have been guilty of factionalism."[44]

As a result, however, as those with reservations about their party's course kept their feelings to themselves, the SED's reaction to the growing refugee exodus was, at least at first, strangely divorced from the reality of the situation it was facing. Most accounts of the period suggest that Honecker was obsessed with presenting an image of the GDR that was simply problem-free and unblemished. The country was preparing to celebrate the fortieth anniversary of East German socialism on October 7, and with Gorbachev expected to be in attendance, the SED chief clearly wanted to avoid giving his guest any opportunity to think that he had been right about the applicability of the Soviet reform model to the GDR.[45] Hence, in

[43] Author's interview, Otto Reinhold, March 23, 1990. Also, Peter Siebenmorgen, "Vom Retter zum Sündenbock," *Die Zeit*, May 10, 1991, p. 6.

[44] Günter Schabowski, *Das Politbüro*, p. 25. Or as another member of the SED's highest organ, Siegfried Lorenz, explained: "The argument about the unity and closed ranks (*Geschlossenheit*) of the party leadership kept Egon Krenz, me, and other comrades from acting much earlier on important decisions. From today's perspective, this was clearly a mistake (*falsches Verhalten*)," *ND*, December 1, 1989. However, Schabowski also notes that Honecker reinforced his coleaders' weaknesses by deliberately playing these individuals off against each other. See *Das Politbüro*, pp. 24–25.

[45] This is not to say that Honecker himself was unable to get a definitive picture of what was transpiring in the GDR. For a collection of secret police reports from the summer of 1989, see Armin Mitter and Stefan Wolle, eds., *Ich liebe euch doch alle!* (Berlin: Basis Druck, 1990). The important question was what Honecker and his colleagues *wanted* to see. For a strong

mid-August, as thousands of East German citizens were desperately seeking to escape their country, Honecker acted as though nothing were happening at all, telling a visiting delegation of microelectronics workers from
Erfurt that the GDR's march to victory was unstoppable: "Neither an ox
nor an ass will halt socialism on its appointed course."[46] When at this same
juncture, Krenz seems to have privately intimated to the General Secretary
that the SED might indeed have to consider some minor adjustments to its
policies, Honecker not only refused to listen to his deputy's advice but
promptly sent Krenz on vacation to insure that no one could challenge his
command of the politburo.[47] Then the East German government practically shut down when Honecker himself was suddenly taken out of action
by a gall bladder operation on August 21, not to return to his official
functions until the end of September. The absence of their leader seemed to
deprive even those in the party's highest echelons of any sense of how to act
in their country's best interests.

From this point onward, therefore, with almost no initiative coming
from the supposedly leading force of the GDR, the SED found itself steadily
driven onto the defensive. When the first loosely organized opposition
groups began to spring up in late August and early September, including
such citizens' movements as Neues Forum, Democratic Awakening, the
United Left, and even the rudiments of an East German Social Democratic
Party (called the SDP to distinguish it from its Western cousin), the party's
reaction was confused and uncertain. The faceless leadership charged with
representing Honecker during his absence went from initially ignoring its
new critics, hoping perhaps that such troubles could be resolved through
the "administrative" means (that is, the police) that had been used so often
in the past, to finally taking on its challengers directly, accusing them of
"defamatory" and "antistate activities" that played right into the hands of
those in the FRG who wanted to destabilize the GDR.[48] In language that
increasingly resembled the party's vocabulary at the height of the Cold
War, the West too was criticized for ostensibly promoting the flight of East
Germans for the basest economic and nationalistic purposes.[49] But significantly, there was no hint that the regime recognized even the possibility that

---

suggestion of the General Secretary's unwillingness to accept what was happening before his
eyes, see his later interview in the *Wochenpost* 47 (1990), p. 27: "These reports from the
Ministry of State Security . . . were just not that reliable. I myself didn't give these reports a
lot of credence, because you could find everything in them in the Western media."

[46]*ND*, August 15, 1989.

[47]Egon Krenz, *Wenn Mauern fallen* (Vienna: Paul Neff Verlag, 1990), pp. 28–29. On this
point at least, Krenz's sometimes questionable reinterpretation of this period is supported by
other sources. See, for example, the interview with Horst Sindermann in *ND*, December 27,
1989.

[48]For example, "Warum berichtet die *Junge Welt* nicht," *Junge Welt*, September 6, 1989.

[49]For example, *ND*, September 12, and *ND*, September 19, 1989.

it might have to consider changing its ways. Indeed, one of Honecker's first acts upon returning to work on September 25 was to use the official news service, ADN, to announce that his government would not allow itself to be moved by those who dared to leave the GDR. There should be "no tears shed," he dictated, at the loss of individuals who had "trampled on the moral values [of socialism]" and then of their own volition chosen to "exclude themselves from our society."[50]

This lack of any self-correcting mechanisms within the institutional apparatus of the SED was, of course, the same problem that the party had confronted in the fall of 1970 in the period leading up to Ulbricht's removal from office. Only when the most extreme conditions arose could one even begin to think of moving beyond the established conventions of the past and risking that most uncertain of all challenges to the policies of a reigning General Secretary. Whatever the SED might have done, however, by 1989 it was probably too late. Two events in particular confirmed that the Honecker era was definitively at an end.

On October 6–7, Gorbachev attended the GDR's fortieth anniversary celebrations. However, he not only failed to give a warm endorsement of his counterpart's policies at the time but also implicitly touched off the social revolution that was to undermine both Honecker and the entire East German socialist system. Gorbachev never criticized the SED directly. Yet, by pressing for the same kinds of values that were at the heart of his own reforms in the Soviet Union ("democratization, openness, socialist legality, and the free development of all peoples and their equal inclusion in [their country's] affairs"), he effectively told the GDR's citizens all they needed to know to take their bottled-up grievances into the streets: the USSR would no longer intervene, as it had on Ulbricht's behalf in June 1953 and perhaps later in 1957/58, to keep the Honecker regime in power.[51] The second signal came on October 9, when over seventy thousand East German citizens, in open defiance of the authorities, gathered in the center of Leipzig for what was to be only the first of months of mass demonstrations throughout the GDR calling for far-reaching political and economic reforms.[52]

We know that these events provided just the kind of impetus that Egon Krenz and other putative reformers at the very top of the SED needed to oust Honecker at the Ninth Plenum of the party's Central Committee on October 18. Still, in view of the even greater tumult that was to engulf the GDR

[50]In ND, October 2, 1989.

[51]See the General Secretary's speech in ND, October 9, 1989, and Sodaro, Moscow, pp. 377–378.

[52]On the transition up to the opening of the Berlin Wall, see Elizabeth Pond, "A Wall Destroyed: The Dynamics of German Unification in the GDR," International Security 15, no. 2 (Fall 1990), pp. 35–60. Also see DDR Journal zur Novemberrevolution (West Berlin: Tageszeitung, 1990).

by year's end, what stands out about Honecker's immediate successors is not only that the new party leadership was very late in coming, but also, perhaps more telling, that its capacity to conceive of fundamental political changes was much more constrained than its words seemed to convey. True, Krenz, Schabowski, and others in the revamped SED politburo did bring a manifestly more accommodating political style to their party's public persona, openly admitting to past mistakes and candidly expressing the hope that it was not too late to undertake "a sincere domestic dialogue" (Krenz) with all of the forces that sought to make life in their country better, including even those in the new opposition groups.[53] However, it was on the issues that counted most at this point to generate trust among the populace—the need for deep, structural reform within the party, the calling of truly democratic elections, and the legalization of other political parties—that the new General Secretary and his coleaders proved to be stubbornly wedded to the past. In a fashion characteristic of the SED throughout its history, many blamed the misfortune that had befallen them not on their own shortcomings but on the malicious intentions of outside agencies like the FRG.[54]

On the most crucial question of all, the right to travel, the Krenz government's hesitancy clearly sped up its own downfall. As thousands continued to flee the GDR by way of neighboring states and as literally hundreds of thousands of their compatriots mustered the courage to demonstrate at home for the freedom to leave the country *and* return, the SED's rulers evidently still believed that they could avoid addressing the issue of freedom of movement directly by concentrating instead on incremental domestic reforms.[55] Only on November 6, almost three weeks after Honecker's

[53]See Krenz's report to the Central Committee's Ninth Plenum on October 18 in *ND*, October 19, 1989. Also see Ilse Spittmann, "Eine Übergangsgesellschaft," *Deutschland Archiv*, November 1989, pp. 1201–1205.

[54]As late as October 30, when I spoke with Schabowski, the politburo spokesman seemed still to be firmly wedded to the past. To his credit, Schabowski was prepared to alter how he and his colleagues dealt with controversial issues, but he opposed any steps that might have compromised the party's leading role. Thus it was inconceivable that a state post as important as the premiership be headed by a non-Communist, that such groups as Neues Forum be legalized as competitive parties, or even that the politburo itself be bound by the kind of formal rules that might limit the hand of its General Secretary—one didn't want to restrict the crucial role of "personal qualities," Schabowski noted. Author's interview, Günter Schabowski, East Berlin, October 30, 1989. Others, however justified their caution by insisting they were simply trying to be realistic. "Now the question is," Markus Wolf told me, "how does one change socialism without losing it, without allowing forces to disturb this process [of reform] which don't want socialism?" Author's interview, East Berlin, October 31, 1989.

[55]As late as October 31, 1989, officials at the Ministry of Foreign Affairs were still considering solutions to the refugee crisis that implied the West's acceptance of a separate GDR citizenship. Author's interviews, Ministry of Foreign Affairs, East Berlin. For an optimistic account of the possibilities by a key participant, see OHP (Hans Schindler, October 3, 1991).

fall, did the Krenz government formally enunciate a new travel law. Still, although the revised code in principle seemed to allow the GDR's citizens the right to leave the country for up to thirty days annually, it was so full of qualifications and ambiguities that even the Volkskammer rejected it as inadequate. Finally, only after 750,000 demonstrators had returned to the streets in several cities to protest the government's hesitancy and the regime was faced with the prospect of widespread industrial strikes did Krenz and his colleagues decide to go all the way.

When Günter Schabowski made his almost matter-of-fact announcement before Western reporters on November 9, that all of the GDR's citizens could henceforth travel as they wished to the West, there could be no doubt that the regime was making one last desperate move to restabilize the country. It would allow its population to decide for itself, really for the first time since August 13, 1961, whether there should be a separate and socialist East German state.[56] What was much less clear by this late juncture, however, was whether a functioning government still existed in East Berlin that could have any say in the matter.

The West German Response

In the first few days after Schabowski's announcement, millions of East Germans flowed into West Berlin and over the inter-German border into the FRG seeking their first uncontrolled opportunity to visit the West. Although the SED regime hoped that its action would help to calm the internal situation in the GDR by demonstrating that one no longer had to emigrate to obtain the precious right to travel, nothing could have prepared East Germany's new leaders for what was still to come. The opening of the Wall not only failed to halt the outflow of refugees; thousands continued to leave the GDR every week, evidently hoping to take advantage of the chance for an instant improvement in their life-styles in the West. But even more unexpected, by mid-November, as domestic conditions grew steadily more tense and the SED proved incapable of meeting its citizens' ever-rising demands for reform, the first cries were heard in the street demonstrations of Leipzig and then numerous other municipalities for the one goal that unequivocally called East Germany's existence into question—national reunification.

To say that even the revamped leadership of the SED, Krenz and the reform communist Hans Modrow, who became the GDR's prime minister on November 13, had no way of responding credibly to such appeals is

---

[56]For various interpretations of the period, see Pond, "A Wall Destroyed," pp. 47–48; Schabowski, *Politbüro*, pp. 134–139; and Krenz, *Mauern*, pp. 176–182.

hardly controversial. After all, a party that had survived by propagating the notion that socialism and capitalism were as compatible as "fire and water" (to use one of Honecker's favorite expressions) would have enjoyed only a very dubious existence in a German national state that was dominated by the capitalist FRG. By the logic of the SED's own all or nothing reasoning, socialism would have to be abandoned. Nevertheless, it is noteworthy that the leaders of the Federal Republic were themselves not much better prepared for this development. Even if one were to have found a few mainstream West German politicians who had somehow managed to resist the temptation to downplay the goal of national unity during the heyday of inter-German détente—many, to the contrary, had written off reunification altogether—one fact was undeniable: Bonn's national policy simply did not provide for the possibility that the East German people might act on their own behalf.

This was the impression conveyed by the West German government's first halting attempts to handle the refugee crisis as it swelled out of control in the late summer of 1989. As they struggled with the problem represented by the growing numbers of refugees in their embassies, Kohl and his co-leaders emphasized that their main concern was "to help the people." Nonetheless, there was no mistaking Bonn's equally frantic efforts to preserve the rudiments of a working relationship with East Berlin. The SED may have been a difficult negotiating partner in the past, but the dictatorial party regime was at least readily identifiable and manageable in a way that the mass of potential East German emigrés never could be. Thus, the Federal chancellery's spokesman, Rudolf Seiters, set the tone for the West German government's approach to the crisis by going to great lengths to reassure the Honecker regime that the Federal Republic had nothing to gain by depopulating the GDR. Quite the opposite was true, in Seiters's official view. His country's leaders had always understood that their foreign missions could not be used to resolve the emigration problem and, he averred, they were as interested as ever in continuing along the path of "sensible cooperation" with the East.[57] In the same vein, Kohl made known his readiness to meet with Honecker personally at the earliest possible moment to discuss the crisis. In return for the latter's willingness to entertain the possibility of serious political and economic reforms, he even began to drop hints that his government would be forthcoming with major economic assistance.[58]

It was also at this juncture, however, that the ruling parties in Bonn first seem to have become aware that the refugee crisis did bring some unexpected *domestic* political opportunities in its wake. For reasons that were

[57]For representative remarks by Seiters, see *FBIS*, WEU-89-151, August 8, 1989, pp. 2–3.
[58]See, for example, Kohl's interview with the *Süddeutsche Zeitung*, August 23, 1989, and his interview with the *Bild Zeitung*, in *FBIS*, WEU-89-192, October 5, 1989, p. 3.

quite tangential to the FRG's foreign relations (for example, the continuing strong showing of the Republikaner in West German municipal elections and in the elections to the European parliament), Kohl's position at the helm of the CDU had come under steadily increasing fire in the summer of 1989. Accordingly, both he and the party's new General Secretary, Volker Rühe, were very willing to take advantage of the practical benefits to be gained by portraying the Christian Democrats as the one force capable of realizing the country's national goals. Normally without using the term "reunification"—the chancellor's discomfort with the concept was still manifest throughout the early fall of 1989[59]—Union parliamentarians began to go out of their way to cultivate an image for West German voters according to which the CDU and the CSU had never really given up on the goal of German unity.

In this case, the Union parties clearly benefited from the fact that they had never gone as far as the SPD in their reassessments of the national issue. Rühe, in particular, appears to have taken personal responsibility for exploiting the issue. He pointedly recalled to public attention just how close the Social Democrats' policy of "change through rapprochement" (Rühe now termed the approach, "change through chumming up" [*Wandel durch Anbiederung*]) had ostensibly brought the Federal Republic to abandoning the East German people. The SPD's long-standing talks with the SED were a "humiliation of all Social Democrats," he stressed, made all the more remarkable because the party had still not seen the error of its ways.[60]

In this context, it can have been little solace to the fathers of the Social Democratic *Ostpolitik* that merely by calling on the East German government to reform its policies, the CDU and, for that matter, its coalition partners in the FDP were demonstrating that they too had come to accept the appropriateness of Bahr's famous policy regarding the GDR's capacity for change, its *Reformfähigkeit*.[61] The SPD leadership was in fact thrown into a quandary by the East German crisis, to such an extent that some party members immediately took up the call for a downgrading of contacts with the Honecker regime. Norbert Gansel, a member of the Bundestag

[59]For example, in an interview with the *Bild Zeitung* on September 14, Kohl managed to say that he was "firmly convinced" about reunification without even mentioning the term. See *FBIS*, WEU-89-178, September 15, 1989, p. 3.

[60]*FBIS*, WEU-89-179, September 18, 1989, p. 4. Also see Gunter Hofmann, "Kanzlerstark, aber kopflos," *Die Zeit*, September 22, 1989, p. 4.

[61]Consider, for example, the encouraging language that CDU Labor minister Norbert Blüm used in a letter to Honecker on October 10, when he pressed the East German leader to endorse necessary reforms: "I would like you and your state to be remembered in a positive way by the people." Cited in *FBIS*, WEU-89-195, October 11, 1989, p. 5. Similarly, on the same date, the FDP's Genscher expressed the wish that Honecker would soon use his authority to push for "urgently needed reforms." Cited in ibid., p. 5. Also see Carl-Christian Kaiser, "Immer reden—aber mit wem?" *Die Zeit*, September 29, 1989, p. 4.

and the head of the SPD's governing council, issued a plea for a new policy of "change through distance" (*Wandel durch Abstand*), which would allow for dialogue only with those in the SED who were willing to push for serious reforms in their country.[62] All the same, even these critiques seem to have been based on the assumption that it was still not the prerogative of the SPD to question the legitimacy of the East German regime.

For that matter, in view of the ongoing refugee exodus, key figures within the Social Democratic leadership like Oskar Lafontaine continued to insist that their party's overriding orientation should be to "respect" the existence of a separate East German citizenship.[63] Still others, like Bahr and the mayor of West Berlin, Walter Momper, openly opposed any speculation about long-range German national goals, on the grounds that such talk was inflammatory and detrimental to the cause of East German reform.[64] Additionally, it was no doubt a consequence of such attitudes that it took the SPD until well into October 1989 even to extend an official welcome to the East German SDP. Even then, however, the party's desire to avoid doing anything that could have endangered its presumably long-term relationship with the SED was palpable: "It is not up to us," one Social Democratic spokesman cautioned, as if seeking to maintain proper distance from the East German opposition, "to guide these people and to act on their behalf."[65]

That the SPD was only expressing publicly the private sentiments of all of the other West German parties, however, became fully apparent in late October and early November, when Egon Krenz's government showed unmistakable signs of no longer being able to master the challenges before it. For even if some politicians were slowly beginning to acclimatize themselves to the previously unthinkable prospect that the two German peoples might realistically find themselves together again, few of the country's leaders were prepared for the speed with which this development was being thrust upon them. For one thing, the welcome that many West German citizens were ready to extend to the growing numbers of refugees from the GDR was already beginning to be exhausted. Not only were the tens of thousands of East German resettlers imposing severe strains on municipal

[62]See his interview with the Deutschlandfunk on September 24 in *FBIS*, WEU-89-185, September 26, 1989.

[63]*FBIS*, WEU-89-185, September 26, 1989, p. 7.

[64]See Bahr's interview with *Die Zeit*, September 1, 1989, p. 6, and Momper's interview with the same newspaper, October 6, 1989, p. 14. Even as late as October 30, the SPD's aversion to the concept of reunification was spelled out in a statement by the party presidium which expressed its respect for the "request made by all reform forces in the GDR not to begin the emotional rhetoric of reunification." See *FBIS*, WEU-89-211, November 2, 1989, p. 6.

[65]*FBIS*, WEU-89-195, October 11, 1989, p. 8. On August 27, the SPD chairman, Hans-Jochen Vogel, had said that "other things were more urgently required" than formal contacts with the SDP, likening such an act to putting the "[cart] before the horse." *FBIS*, WEU-89-165, August 28, 1989, p. 8.

social services throughout the Federal Republic, but these "other" Germans also represented an equally weighty, if less tangible, psychological burden on the sense of calm and orderliness that characterized middle-class life in West Germany.

Even more consequential, the possibility that the reunification of Germany might actually precede the realization of such lofty ideals as the economic and political unification of Europe was also disconcerting for reasons of foreign policy. It threatened to undermine all of the efforts that figures like Kohl and Genscher had made to convince their neighbors that they no longer had anything to fear from an active German role on the continent. When the FRG's foreign minister was questioned about the East German crisis by the French daily Le Figaro on November 2, only a few days before Günter Schabowski was to make his unexpected announcement about the Wall, Genscher seemed almost self-consciously to avoid dwelling upon the theme of national reunification, preferring instead to underscore less controversial issues such as the primacy of "European rapprochement" and the FRG's "immutable place in the [EEC]." In particular, he emphasized the right of those whom he called the "GDR Germans" to determine their own place on the continent by expressing "their views freely in their own state."[66]

It can have hardly been a surprise, therefore, that, when the Wall was finally opened on November 9, West German politicians of all shades reacted with the mixed feelings of joy and apprehension that came with their lack of preparation for the event. In an interview with Der Spiegel, Walter Momper was almost defiant about what the barrier's fall could not mean: "Berlin has longed for this for twenty-eight years," he declared. "But this is not the festival of reunification, it is a festival of seeing each other again."[67] For his part, Genscher was the model of sobriety and caution about the East German population's next move, as hundreds of thousands flowed dramatically into the West: "We do not want to replace one kind of patronage in the GDR with unwanted advice from us," he stressed, as if hoping that the situation would stabilize long enough for his ministry to sort out the best response.[68] It was Kohl, however, who best captured the ambivalence felt by his colleagues. He observed that henceforth he would do "everything in [his] power to make the responsible people in the GDR carry out reforms immediately," not to hurry along reunification, but instead to assure that "as many Germans as possible would stay in the GDR."[69]

---

[66]FBIS, WEU-89-214, November 7, 1989, p. 10.

[67]FBIS, WEU-89-217, November 13, 1989, p. 7.

[68]Ibid., p. 11.

[69]Ibid., p. 8. Or as his deputy, Rühe, advised the onlooking East German population the day the Wall opened, "Whoever has freedom at home, has no need to seek it by fleeing." International Herald Tribune, November 10, 1989.

Unity Despite the Germanys

Against this background, it is not hard to understand why, for at least the
first couple of weeks after the Wall's fall, a curious sort of unspoken consensus existed between the ruling parties in Bonn and what remained of a
viable government in East Berlin. Whatever was coming to East and West
Germany, both sides had very definite interests in slowing the process down
to accommodate the transition away from their recent, self-confident conceptions of what was most appropriate for the nation.

Undoubtedly, this motivation was uppermost in every speech that
Helmut Kohl delivered during this short period. He simultaneously offered
the GDR every form of assistance to weather its crisis *and* called upon the
East German people to "remain calm." Evidently, "calmness" meant stay-
ing behind in the GDR to keep the country and its economy from completely falling apart—Kohl noted, almost hopefully, that the pace of emigration *seemed* to have slowed after November 9—while at the same time
recognizing that, if reunification were indeed to come, it could not be
brought about in the FRG alone. For both international and domestic
reasons, neither East nor West Germany could afford the instability that
would arise with the wholesale collapse of the GDR.[70]

Similarly, although with an understandably greater degree of vehemence
and desperation, Hans Modrow used his inaugural address as prime minister to emphasize the reasons why a separate and socialist German state was
still feasible and warranted. All of the reforms that should have been in-
stituted years earlier in the GDR—the creation of a true "state of laws"
(*Rechtsstaat*), a reduction of unnecessary impediments to economic initiative, the introduction of a new educational system, and even greater attention to the environmental dangers facing the country—would now be set
into motion. Modrow also emphasized that East Germany would finally
open itself without reservations to the outside world, assuming a closer
relationship with the European Economic Community and accepting the
need for a qualitatively new kind of "cooperative coexistence" with the
FRG. This higher stage of inter-German cooperation would be based upon a
"community of treaties" (*Vertragsgemeinschaft*) going well beyond anything ever envisioned in the Basic Treaty. Yet the new East German prime
minister still insisted that it was in the interest of all of the GDR's neighbors,
Bonn above all, "not only to look upon the changes in our state with favor
but also to help them along, both politically and economically." "The
stability of the GDR," he added, "is a condition of stability in Central
Europe, indeed in the whole of Europe."[71]

[70]See Kohl's November 16 address to the Bundestag, *FBIS*, WEU-89-220, November 16,
1989, p. 10. These considerations are artfully captured in the diary of Kohl advisor, Horst
Teltschik, *329 Tage* (Berlin: Siedler, 1991), pp. 11–86.
[71]*ND*, November 18–19, 1989.

Only a few weeks earlier, such a declaration might have been greeted with a resounding show of support from the West. The glaring problem with both Modrow's appeal for assistance and even Kohl's calls for societal calm in the East was that they no longer had anything to do with the actual domestic situation in the country. At this late date, for the countless individual East Germans who had learned to expect considerably less from decades of SED leadership and were contemplating leaving their country for good, there was no longer any GDR there.

This fact accounts for what has to be one of the most ambiguous episodes in the months leading up to Germany's reunification. Despite East Berlin's and Bonn's hopes, over seventeen thousand East German citizens applied for and received permission to emigrate in only the first week and a half following the Wall's fall. As the population drain from the GDR continued apace, Kohl made one last effort to stabilize the situation by outlining a ten-point plan before the Bundestag on November 28 in which he, somewhat ambiguously, appealed for the creation of future "confederal structures" between the Germanys.[72] Although the speech itself was supposed to be a bold effort to chart the coming course of German unity, everything about the details of Kohl's plan testified to its architect's desire to slow the march to national unity by confining it within certain commonly acceptable parameters. Not only did the chancellor conspicuously avoid the strong term "confederation," but the fact that he repeatedly emphasized the FRG's broader transnational goals, European integration, the elaboration of the Helsinki process, and the need for further progress in the fields of arms control and disarmament showed that he, too, was at a loss to predict what the next development would be between the Germanys.[73]

Naturally, Kohl and his advisors cannot have failed to appreciate the domestic political advantages of taking the lead in providing a coherent framework for reunification. For precisely this reason, the ten-point plan itself was prepared under conditions of greatest secrecy, so that the West German leader would not run the risk of being scooped in his initiative by one of his competitors, especially the foreign minister. Nevertheless, for all of the plan's cautiousness, its announcement was explosive. More than any other gesture, ironically, it had the combined effect of putting the official seal of approval on all subsequent discussion of the sensitive subject of reunification and accelerating the collapse of the GDR. Coming from the most powerful figure in German politics, Kohl's imprimatur on the issue of national unity amounted to an unrefusable challenge to everyone else with

[72]"A Ten-Point Program for Overcoming the Division of Germany and Europe," *Statements and Speeches* 12, no. 25 (December 19, 1989), New York, German Information Center.

[73]Author's sources, Federal Chancellery, Bonn. For a perceptive analysis of Kohl's strategy, see Pond, "A Wall Destroyed," p. 57.

an interest in the question. Others would have to emulate, if not also improve upon, the chancellor's overture.

Quite predictably, in the immediate weeks thereafter, all of the other major West German parties struggled to articulate their own positions on the path to German unity, not only with a view to retaining the support of their voters in the FRG but also to curry favor among future generations of an as yet undefined East German electorate.[74] For their part, the Germanys' neighbors and allies hastened to express their own opinions about Kohl's initiative and, where they dared, to attempt to impose conditions upon the process. Nonetheless, the most important event had already taken place. In sharp contrast to the seemingly orderly character of the inter-German relationship only two years earlier on the occasion of Honecker's triumphant visit to Bonn, the mystique of two separate German states had been shattered by the collapse of the SED regime. The reunification of a single German nation was already underway.

[74]This was by no means an easy task, if the SPD's behavior was any indication. Although the Social Democrats supported Kohl's ten-point plan in principle, their conception of German unity was, for a time, even vaguer than his reference to "confederal structures." As Oskar Lafontaine, for example, noted: "It is clear that the conservative right wing of the Union has the old national state as its point of orientation. But this isn't appropriate anymore, and it certainly has nothing to do with the current wishes and feelings of the people of the GDR." *Süddeutsche Zeitung*, November 25–26, 1989.

VII

Germany without a Wall

The German question will remain open as long
as the Brandenburg Gate remains closed.
(Richard von Weizsäcker, June 8, 1985)

WHEN WEST GERMAN president von Weizsäcker made the above observation in a speech before a congress of his country's Lutheran Church in the mid-1980s, it is more than a little bit doubtful that he was thinking about ways of acting upon the distant goal of Germany's reunification. Already, most efforts to deal with the decades-old national question had been reduced for the most part to making the Berlin Wall, best symbolized by the fortifications at the Brandenburg Gate, more permeable. In this sense, for every visit that East or West German citizens were able to make to their counterparts in the other part of Germany, for every telephone call or letter exchanged, the Federal government should have come one step closer to resolving the German question. Still, implicit in von Weizsäcker's remark was also the suggestion that the Wall itself was at the heart of the dilemma of German identity. Accordingly, one just might have expected the removal of the barrier in its entirety to be the final step in settling the national problem for all time.

By early 1991, however, not much more than a year after the barricade surrounding the Brandenburg Gate was actually removed, most Germans, East and West, were asking themselves whether the Wall's absence was, by itself, sufficient to bring the nation together again.[1] Contrary to all previous predictions, the GDR was legally incorporated into the FRG on October 3, 1990, fulfilling the formal act of national reunification. Nonetheless, after all the years of enforced separation, the factors that still divided the two German populations loomed large. Very few western German politicians would have dared publicly to express their private misgivings about the desirability of the sudden end to the Communist system in the GDR. But this did not keep many from actively seeking to exploit those negative sentiments that had first arisen in response to the influx of eastern Germans

---

[1] For politicians' views on the depth of the problem, see the Bundestag debates over Helmut Kohl's government declaration of January 30, 1991, in *Das Parlament*, February 8/15, 1991, pp. 2–12.

to the FRG in late 1989 and that failed to die down in the wake of reunification. By 1991 many average western Germans were clearly frustrated at
having to finance the exorbitant costs of economic recovery in the East.
Taxes had been raised and government subsidies cut for social programs in
the West. There was also anxiety about the potential competition represented by eastern German labor. Even for those individuals who were not
directly touched by the burdens of reunification, many western Germans
felt a nagging sense of discomfort at having the customary tranquility of life
in their country upset by the reappearance of national obligations that had
long been dismissed as empty rhetoric.

In eastern Germany, signs of popular resentment were even more manifest. Almost no one in the East wanted to return to the days of the old
German Democratic Republic, particularly in the form the state had assumed under Honecker's not-so-enlightened tutelage. With the region beset by rising levels of unemployment, however, and much of its population
demoralized and relegated, in the perception of many, to a second-class
status by the economic and political might of the FRG, it was not uncom-
mon for former GDR citizens to feel that they had gone from one form of
helplessness before an all-powerful state to another.[2] They had voted for
reunification—in fact well before the first democratic elections to the country's Volkskammer on March 18, 1990—by letting their West German
cousins know that they wanted the quickest possible route to national
unity. Yet, from that point onward, many lamented that just about every
decision relating to the fate of their popular revolution had been trans-
ferred to Bonn.

Of course, no one imagined in 1990 and 1991 that the reunification of
the German nation would be easily accomplished. Nevertheless, the existence of such difficulties gave rise to an intriguing, if also disturbing, prospect. Was it not possible that the inter-German tensions of times past, far
from disappearing with the fall of the Wall, might instead be redefined in
the form of a new type of conflict between the eastern and western German
populations? The question that all German politicians were driven to ask
at the time, and which none could answer to satisfaction, was how quickly
they could convince the peoples on both sides of the old national divide
that their interests were best served by emphasizing what they shared in
common and not what still set them apart.

---

[2]For example, in an Emnid poll in March 1991, 85 percent of East Germans who were
surveyed felt that they would remain "second-class" citizens for some time; *Der Spiegel*,
March 18, 1991, p. 57. A particularly appropriate sense of their feelings at the time was
conveyed by the term *Bevormundung* ("patronization"), which was often used by East German dissidents and intellectuals during the fall of 1989 to criticize the Honecker and Krenz
governments' policies.

Inter-German Tensions of a New Type

From the beginning, the course of national reunification in 1990 was paradoxical. On the one hand, the year provided the setting for an outpouring of democratic self-expression throughout Germany. For the first time in more than half a century, Germans between the Elbe and the Oder were able to exercise the right to select their representatives in a series of unprecedented free elections—in the parliamentary election to the Volkskammer on March 18, in municipal and state elections on May 6 and October 14, and finally in the first all-German election of December 2. On the other hand, however, as the citizens of both parts of the nation confronted the trials before them, it was equally significant that each side could find plausible reasons for thinking that it had never really been able to choose the Germany it received.[3]

It was an ironic consequence of the inter-German successes of the 1980s that as the national question itself was defined increasingly as a humanitarian issue and not as a matter of immediate, existential concern for all Germans, more and more of the FRG's citizens had focused their attention on issues other than the GDR. Despite the progress between the Germanys, for example, Paris and London remained the preferred travel destinations for the great majority of West Germans, and not East Berlin or Dresden. Furthermore, unlike in the late 1960s and early 1970s, when the inter-German relationship had been a matter of intense controversy, few aspiring politicians could any longer imagine tying their political futures to an issue as nebulous as the *Deutschlandpolitik*. Although most West German citizens still gave affirmative replies when they were asked in public opinion surveys if they were in favor of Germany's eventual reunification, polling experts rarely even bothered to inquire whether they would also be willing to make personal sacrifices if this unlikely event were to come to pass. So much was the GDR a part of German reality, therefore, that almost no one in the FRG was prepared for the speed with which the issue of national unity was laid before them. Yet, in a country in which a dictatorial party had claimed the right to total power, it was true almost by definition that the SED's fall would lead to the complete and total collapse of the state it represented.

Clearly, this maxim held true for the fate of the East German pseudo-

---

[3]As Claus Offe has argued about the GDR in particular, the East Germans' pursuit of reunification "cannot be explained in terms of categories of 'will.'" See his "Prosperity, Nation, and Republic: Aspects of the Unique German Journey from Socialism to Capitalism," *German Politics and Society* 22 (Spring 1991), pp. 18–32, and also Klaus von Beyme, "The Legitimation of German Unification between National and Democratic Principles," ibid., pp. 1–17.

parliament, the Volkskammer, which made a feeble plea for democratic legitimation on December 1, 1989, by changing the GDR constitution to omit the SED's "leading role." As an organ that had functioned for nearly forty years as little more than a rubber stamp for the decisions of the party politburo, the parliament never stood a chance of becoming anything more than a short-lived, transitional vehicle for the passage to German unity. It was in fact viewed in this light by most who ran for its offices in the spring of 1990. Early on, a number of the so-called bloc parties within the Volks-kammer, the non-Communist but totally powerless equivalents to the SED, sought to carve out independent profiles by distancing themselves from their former allies. These included an East German variant of the Christian Democratic Union, the Liberal Democratic Party of Germany, the National Democratic Party, and various other holdovers from the GDR's campaigns for leadership on the national question during the 1950s. Nonetheless, although some of these parties' representatives had been among the first to raise cautious challenges to the Honecker regime in October and November 1989, the public memory of their years of subservience before the SED was too great for any of them to have a chance of survival, except as appendages of West German sister-parties if they had such ties.

Even more suggestive of the GDR's fragility, however, was that even the disparate citizens' groups that had provided the intellectual and spiritual rationale for the revolution of 1989 were unable to present themselves as credible spokesmen for the population of East Germany. In part, the failure of such popular movements as Neues Forum and Democracy Now to retain the support of those who had initially followed them into the streets de-rived from their manifest organizational shortcomings. Not surprisingly, their leaders had almost no practical experience with politics, the move-ments themselves were based upon little more than decentralized mass followings, and they all faced the overwhelming challenge of having to craft coherent and appealing visions for the East German future at a time when the ongoing flight of refugees from the GDR threatened to destroy the region's economy.

Aside from these weaknesses, the majority of those who had risen from the loose ranks of the East German opposition in the 1980s proved to be revealingly incapable of moving out of the shadow of the SED dictatorship, almost as though the years of subservience before the party regime had tied their own identities inextricably to the old order.[4] Many were simply opposed to transforming their movements into formal political parties; even as late as February 1990 one of the cofounders of Neues Forum could

---

[4]This bond with the GDR past was reflected in the ambivalent reaction of many prominent dissidents to the Wall's fall. As Sebastian Pflugbeil, a leader of Neues Forum, told reporters about the barrier's opening: "This is what we wanted for 28 years, but we did not want it like this and we did not want it right now"; New York Times, November 13, 1989.

still describe his organization's primary function as that of providing "therapy," not of winning votes.[5] Then, too, far from welcoming the escalating calls for national reunification around them, most of the opposition critics remained wedded to the notion that their overriding political purpose, as in an earlier era, was to "develop a socialist alternative to the Federal Republic."[6]

For these reasons alone, it is fair to say that the burden of the GDR's absorption into the Federal Republic practically fell onto the shoulders of West Germany's policymakers, as political power drained out of the few remaining centers of authority that still existed in the East. For a short time, the East German premier, Hans Modrow, enjoyed modest support among the population, thanks to his reputation for having taken principled stands against the Honecker government when he was SED First Secretary in the Dresden *Bezirk*.[7] Nevertheless, the prime minister's popularity proved to be fleeting as a result of his, perhaps understandable, inability to keep pace with his population's escalating demands for social and economic change.[8]

For an equally short period, there was also a glimmer of hope to be found in the formation in mid-December 1989 of a quasi-parliamentary body known as the Round Table, which allowed various parties from the Volkskammer and opposition representatives to exercise the self-appointed task of scrutinizing government policy. Yet this organ, too, failed to make the natural passage to legitimacy. The Round Table's few successes—exposing past crimes and corruption in the SED, for example, or campaigning against such measures as Modrow's attempt in early 1990 to reconstitute the former Ministry for State Security—merely served to deprive the East German state of any remaining grounds for existence.

In these uncertain conditions, the exodus of the GDR's population for the West, far from decreasing in 1990, actually rose to over sixty thousand in

---

[5] To quote Jens Reich, as cited in Daniel Hamilton, *After the Revolution: The New Political Landscape in East Germany*, German Issues, no. 7 (Washington, D.C.: American Institute for Contemporary German Studies, 1990), p. 35.

[6] The quotation is from an appeal by a number of prominent intellectuals and church officials of November 26, 1989, including Günter Krusche, Ulrike Poppe, Konrad Weiß, and Pflugbeil, in *DDR Journal zur Novemberrevolution* (West Berlin: Tageszeitung, 1990), p. 154. Such attitudes, which I encountered in interviews with members of Neues Forum in fall 1989, remained prevalent among East German intellectuals well into 1990. Also, see Detlef Pollack, "Außenseiter oder Repräsentanten?" *Deutschland Archiv*, August 1990, pp. 1216–1223; and, Hamilton, *After the Revolution*, pp. 32–40.

[7] It was widely assumed in the GDR in the late 1980s that Modrow was one of the Honecker regime's greatest critics from within the SED elite. For this reason, his long-awaited promotion to the politburo never came to pass. Nonetheless, when some members of the leadership, including Günter Mittag, tried to have Modrow replaced in the spring of 1989, Honecker himself intervened to prevent the demotion. See OHP (Schürer, July 10, 1991).

[8] On this, see Elizabeth Pond, "A Wall Destroyed: The Dynamics of German Unification in the GDR," *International Security* 15, no. 2 (Fall 1990), p. 61.

January alone. As average East Germans surveyed the chaotic situation into which their country had descended, many came to the not unreasonable conclusion, given the circumstances, that their chances of surviving the reconstruction of the German nation were better served by starting over in the FRG. Predictably, their departure then compounded the crisis of confidence in the GDR. At a later date, representatives of the West German government would argue that it was precisely this situation that gave them no other choice than to speed up the pace of the GDR's incorporation. Kohl officially signaled the decision on February 7, 1990, by calling for the unification of the two German monetary systems and the introduction of the Deutsche Mark to East Germany. Nevertheless, while the chancellor may have been intent upon putting the weight of responsibility for his administration's actions onto the East, it was here that critically inclined citizens of the GDR could find all the reasons they needed, although far different from the complaints being raised in the FRG, to feel that they, too, were not getting the Germany that they wanted. While the Communist state collapsed, the political system of the FRG literally moved into East Germany to fill the void.

Had 1990 not been an election year in the Federal Republic, the leaders of the largest political parties in the West probably would not have been eager to get involved in the GDR elections. Presumably, it would have been easier to wait to assess the potential benefits and pitfalls of reunification before commiting themselves prematurely to one or another vision of the German future. Yet, because both the governing coalition and the Social Democratic opposition faced the possibility of having to compete in an all-German vote less than a year later—the Basic Law required that Federal elections be conducted in late 1990 or early 1991—few politicians in Bonn could afford to be indifferent to every development in the East. Viewed optimistically, this was an opportunity to shape the voting habits of the emerging East German electorate. Just as consequential, however, no one was willing to incur the likely penalties of failing to do so.

The first signs of what might be called inter-German cooperation of a new type were already evident in mid-January 1990, as several West German parties first sought to take advantage of their existing or possible counterparts in the East by utilizing them as vehicles for reaching out to new voters. After a few months of initial hesitation in which it waited for the GDR's fate to become clearer, the leadership of the SPD-West finally got around to forming a committee to provide technical assistance to the East German Social Democratic Party, which obligingly changed its name to the SPD. Likewise, the Bavarian CSU actively began to court a varied group of conservative parties in the southern regions of the GDR, Thuringia and Saxony. The decisive point came, however, on January 28. In a desperate effort to halt the flight of the country's citizens and avert a total collapse of the East German economy, the Modrow government and the Round Table announced that the Volkskammer elections, previously planned for May 6, would be moved up to March 18. From this date onward, Kohl's CDU hastily put together its own electoral alliance ("Alliance for Germany") with the CDU-East and two other parties, the German Social Union and the citizens' movement Democratic Awakening, and the FDP bound together a like coalition of East German Liberal parties. The GDR's fate was perforce caught up in the logic of party competition in the FRG.

East German names were outwardly associated with the election campaigns leading up to the Volkskammer vote—Ibrahim Böhme for the SPD, for example, and Lothar de Maizière for the CDU, both individuals who had risen to political prominence in the revolutionary fall of 1989 and who would each later see their political careers destroyed following revelations of their past association with the GDR's secret police. Yet, as preparations were undertaken for the first democratic elections on East German soil, few participants doubted that the names which counted most for the country's voters were those of the better-known West German personalities who stood behind such figures. These included Willy Brandt and the SPD's likely chancellor candidate in the Federal elections, Oskar Lafontaine; Hans-Dietrich Genscher for the FDP; and, most important because of his visibility as chancellor, Helmut Kohl. The unintended consequence of the appearance of these West German notables at campaign rallies throughout the GDR in February and March 1990, however, was that it simultaneously raised questions about who was really sovereign in East Germany. While the majority of the members of the Round Table tried and failed to pass a resolution barring Western involvement in the election, this West German presence practically assured that complaints would later be lodged that the Volkskammer elections had been "hijacked" by the FRG.[9]

As intellectuals from both states lamented subsequently, the idea that there might be a distinct act of East German self-determination before the GDR disappeared had already become a lost cause. To the extent that the country's citizens were able to say anything about their destiny, this voice was merely defined by the political tactics of West Germany's parties and the overwhelming economic strength of the Federal Republic. Admittedly, many of these complaints were exaggerated. But there was a certain amount of truth to them as well. For, just about every positive signal the East German population received from the West seemed to be combined with a qualification of Bonn's commitments that reflected the underlying interests of the FRG.[10]

[9]See, for example, Klaus Hartung, "Abwahl der DDR," in DDR Journal Nr. 2: Die Wende der Wende (West Berlin: Tageszeitung, 1990), p. 156.

[10]For Willy Brandt's candid reflections on this theme, see Gunter Hofmann, "Die Republik wird am Ende nicht mehr die alte sein," Die Zeit, September 21, 1990, p. 5.

For reasons that had as much to do with his own electoral calculations in the Saarland as the needs of the GDR, for example, Oskar Lafontaine brought a message of patience and sobriety to the people of East Germany, telling them that it was in their interest to remain at home and slow the transition to national unity. Nonetheless, while many of Lafontaine's listeners may have agreed with this wisdom, the Social Democratic leader undermined his credibility by seeking at the same time to win votes in the FRG through appeals to his own compatriot's anxieties about the speed and costs of reunification.[11] Naturally, Kohl brought almost the opposite message to the East. In contrast to Lafontaine, he contended that the region's interests could only be served by the immediate adoption of West German political and economic institutions. Yet, although the chancellor spoke optimistically of an era of abundance and prosperity for all who went along with his plan to transform the GDR, his assurances also came with the implicit, bittersweet proviso that every decision of consequence would be made in Bonn.

For some time, observers assumed that Kohl's promises of "thriving landscapes" (blühende Landschaften) to come would run into immediate conflict with the stark reality of economic and social conditions in the GDR, where only a massive program of government assistance was likely to facilitate the region's transition to capitalism and democracy. Because the Social Democrats, notwithstanding Lafontaine's mixed signals, still seemed best equipped to lead such an effort and because the party had also enjoyed considerable support within the country's southern, working-class towns in the period before World War II, it was commonly held that the SPD would win the Volkskammer election.

That the East German electorate voted as it did on March 18, 1990, however, giving the conservative Alliance for Germany a decisive victory over the Social Democrats (48 percent of the vote versus the SPD's 21.8 percent) seems considerably less startling in retrospect than it did at the time. Many East Germans simply cast their vote for what appeared to be the fastest and least painful route to national unity. Few wanted to risk the possibility of any further delays in the dismantling of the GDR's socialist economy. Moreover, many were attracted by the fact that Kohl was not only readily inclined but, as chancellor, best positioned of all the FRG's politicians to force through such difficult steps as currency union and the lifting of the remaining four-power constraints on German sovereignty.[12] In fact, so great was the electorate's antipathy to any political current

[11]For some of the mixed signals that Lafontaine was sending the East Germans, see his December 1989 interview in Der Spiegel, December 25, 1989, pp. 66–67. Also see Brandt's reflections in Hofmann, "Die Republik," p. 5.

[12]Max Kaase and Wolfgang Gibowski, "Deutschland im Übergang: Parteien und Wähler vor der Bundeswahl 1990," Aus Politik und Zeitgeschichte, September 14, 1990, p. 25.

associated with the prospect of an independent GDR that the very citizens' movements that had launched the popular revolution in 1989 were themselves nearly closed out of the election, receiving less than 5 percent of the vote. For its part, the CDU did not miss the opportunity to reinforce this sentiment by deliberately equating the SED and the Social Democrats in the East German voter's mind ("Never again socialism!" one campaign slogan ran). Conveniently ignoring the record of their own relations with the GDR, the Union forces even hinted that their rivals had compromised the national cause by dealing so closely with Honecker and the old SED elite.

Yet, who was to say that either of the two West German parties' policies really had anything to do with the unexpected events of 1989? It may have given the Christian Democrats some solace to think that their refusal to give in on basic principles (such as the existence of a single German citizenship) had helped to keep alive East German hopes for eventual reunification. By the same token, however, their counterparts in the SPD could retort that it was their practical efforts to improve the quality of contacts with the GDR (such as the 1987 common document with the SED) that had given the country's citizens the courage to rise up against their government. Nonetheless, even if on these grounds the CDU and the SPD were prepared to defend themselves before the court of history, the more important fact may have been the extent to which the Volkskammer vote would remain with the Federal Republic long after the ballots were counted. Up to the FRG's national elections, which were finally held in December 1990, the vote's outcome meant that not one of the major German parties was poised to speak on behalf of the East German population per se.[13] The two state treaties that led to economic reunification on July 1 and then to political union on October 3 were almost wholly formulated in Bonn. Similarly, the negotiations surrounding the restoration of German sovereignty over Berlin and allowing for the removal of Soviet troops from eastern Germany by 1994 were also dominated by the Federal government.[14] Finally, barely more than one-third of those representatives who were elected to the East German parliament in March were able to enter the Bundestag in the shadowy period between October 3 and December 2, when the first all-German assembly was constituted. Even then, those who did make

[13]One could argue that the West German Greens were an exception to this rule. Yet they were ambivalent about the entire theme of reunification and, unlike their East German counterparts, they also failed to receive the 5 percent of the West German vote in December 1990 that is necessary to remain in the Bundestag.

[14]Just who had the real leverage over the path to German unity was demonstrated at the February 1990 "Open Skies" Conference of NATO ministers when, under West German pressure, what had previously been called the "four plus two talks" on reunification ("four" referring to the former German occupation powers) was renamed "two plus four." "Two," as GDR representatives quickly realized, really meant "one," the Federal Republic.

the journey to Bonn were only allowed to play the role of nonvoting observers.[15]

Although some East German intellectuals were quick to object at this point that their revolution had been absorbed by another government and another system, they were for the time being overtaken by events. The overwhelming victory of Kohl's ruling coalition over the SPD on December 2, 1990, showed that a majority of former GDR citizens were eager to complete the transition to liberal democracy as quickly as possible. Together, the CDU/CSU and the FDP won 54.7 percent of the total vote in the East, and Germans on both sides of the old national divide were temporarily united in a single act of democratic self-expression. But this was merely the first stage of national reunification.

A Liberal Democratic Germany

When the social and economic difficulties of German unity became fully apparent to the citizens of both parts of the new nation in early 1991, it would have been unusual if many individuals had not fallen prey to the easy temptation of blaming their travails on their counterparts. Objectively speaking, many of these complaints may have been unfounded. Yet eastern and western Germans alike could easily find all the justification they needed from a selective reading of the recent past to make the leap to a simple conclusion: for all that had been won, their side had been unfairly victimized by the costs of reunification.

Was it not high time, many former GDR citizens asked, that their western German cousins were made to pay the price for their national identity? For decades, the FRG had enjoyed all of the benefits of Western alignment and capitalist well-being, while they had been forced to pay for the Second World War by suffering under Soviet domination and Communist dictatorship. Given the record of West Germany's relations with the GDR in the 1980s, there was even some question of whether Bonn had forgotten its obligation to work for the liberation of its eastern countrymen and become overly concerned with appeasing the Honecker regime. Thus, from the East German perspective, anything less than complete equality with the West was a betrayal of the national cause. Naturally, average western Germans saw the situation quite differently. In fact, in a mirror image of their counterparts' complaints, many inquired why the eastern Germans were not being made to bear even greater sacrifices in the passage to capitalism.

[15]On these issues, see Marc Fisher, "When *Ost* Meets West, *Ost* Gets an Elbow in der Face," *Washington Post* (National Weekly Edition), September 10–16, 1990, p. 25; Carl-Christian Kaiser, "Die 'Ossis' in Bonn," *Die Zeit*, November 16, 1990, p. 5; and Peter Bender, "Die geeinte Nation—zutiefst geteilt," *Die Zeit*, February 22, 1991, p. 3.

Had not the population of the old FRG already proven its democratic credentials decades before, they argued, and therefore earned the right to an undiminished claim to its benefits?

In these respects alone, it was as if a recipe for conflict had been built into the inter-German relationship. With the passing of the euphoric feelings that had accompanied the Wall's opening and the first unhampered contacts between the two German peoples, each side expected the other to give first before the remaining barriers between them ("new walls," as they were increasingly called) would be overcome and the way paved toward true national unity.[16] By itself, this was a powerful statement of the dilemmas inherent in the unification process. However, the existence of these tensions also had the additional advantage of shedding light upon the larger issue of what Western democracy, as it had for so long been exemplified only in the FRG, would mean for the transformation of the new German state, particularly for those who hoped for both a quick and a complete integration of the two parts of the nation.

Eastern Germans clearly could take heart in one aspect of the unambiguous outcome of their revolution. Unlike the experience with four decades of Leninism, which in the final analysis had left the Honecker regime blind and for the most part indifferent to the everyday shortcomings of socialism, the liberal democratic order that replaced the GDR at least held out the promise that eastern German interests would eventually be incorporated into official government policy.[17] In this sense, the region's population enjoyed an incalculable advantage over the socialist states of East Europe, such as Hungary, Poland, and Czechoslovakia, which were simultaneously undergoing their own democratic transformations. Because none of the GDR's former allies shared its good fortune in inheriting an elaborated system of democratic ground rules to guide them through the difficult transition to a new political age, their governments all found themselves in an unenviable position in the early 1990s. They had to build such institutions from the ground up *at the same time* that they wrestled

---

[16]As Berlin's Christian Democratic mayor, Eberhard Diepgen, contended in the spring of 1991, it was still necessary to dismantle "the wall in our heads." Cited in John Tagliabue, "What Divides Berlin Now?" *New York Times Magazine*, April 7, 1991, p. 56. Also, see Peter Schneider, *The German Comedy* (New York: Farrar, Straus, and Giroux, 1991). The tense relationship between the German populations was not due to cultural differences alone. It might also be likened to a game of "chicken," in which both parties' determination not to be the first to give ultimately leads to their mutual harm. See Kenneth Oye, "Explaining Cooperation under Anarchy," *World Politics* 38, no. 1 (October 1975), p. 8.

[17]On why liberal-democratic institutions are optimal, but not necessarily ideal, for resolving conflicts, see Robert Dahl, *After the Revolution?* (New Haven, Conn.: Yale University Press, 1990), pp. 36–37; Samuel Huntington, *Political Order in Changing Societies* (New Haven, Conn.: Yale University Press, 1968), pp. 397–432; and Giuseppe Di Palma, *To Craft Democracies* (Berkeley: University of California Press, 1990), pp. 90–91.

with the economic and social cleavages that had been generated over four decades of Communist rule.

Eastern Germany scarcely had to face this dilemma. In the event that the Federal government's desire to promote economic rationality and higher rates of productivity got the better of its leaders, the Basic Law imposed a formal obligation on the decision-makers in Bonn to insure "equal conditions of life" throughout Germany. This norm gave the citizens of the old GDR a powerful argument to which they could appeal when seeking to mitigate the harsher effects of the transition to capitalism. Additionally, eastern Germans could be encouraged by the fact that five new *Länder* were formed in the place of the GDR (six, if one counted the full city of Berlin as a new voting power). This assured them a significant presence in the upper house of the German parliament, the Bundesrat, and with it, eventually, an important voice in the allocation of Federal finances. Finally, they also had the more abstract comfort of knowing that few politicians in either part of the nation could comfortably afford to ignore the potential impact of sixteen million new voters upon the elections of the German future.[18]

The problem, however, with this almost instantaneous adoption of democratic institutions in the GDR was that politics was also sure to get in the way of the equally important task of achieving inter-German harmony. As we have seen in the case of the old FRG's uncertain adaptation to its changing international environment between the 1960s and 1980s, liberal democracy may have eventually provided the basis for a sound domestic consensus on the handling of the German question. But this understanding among West Germany's key political parties was only reached after sufficient time had passed for all of them to recognize that there was more to be gained by collaborating than by seeking fleeting political advantages over their competitors. In the new Germany as well, there was just as little to keep the major parties from putting short-term objectives, like the pursuit of political office, ahead of the more consequential, long-term challenge of national integration.

In the final months before the Federal elections of December 1990, Helmut Kohl could not have helped but recognize that the real costs of reunification were going to be much higher than they had seemed at the time of the Volkskammer vote; in fact, this was a softly spoken, secondary theme in many of his speeches. Nevertheless, although the chancellor might have chosen to lay greater weight on the sacrifices that all Germans would have to bear to smooth the way for East Germany's integration into the Federal Republic, the temptation of gaining electoral capital over his opponents seems to have overcome him. The main thrust of his reelection

---

[18]For these points, see Beyme, "Legitimation," p. 8.

campaign remained on the optimistic side of reunification—for both parts
of Germany—that was sure to rebound to the advantage of his party. While
he continued to tell his listeners in the East that prosperity would soon
come their way, in the same breath he also assured his West German
supporters that there would be "no new taxes to finance unity."[19] As the
subsequent problems of reunification were to show, however, neither proposition could have been further from reality.

Lest one think, however, that virtue was only to be found in the ranks of
the West German opposition, the chancellor's challengers in the SPD were
themselves no more inclined to rise above the play of partisan politics.
Thus, rather than focusing on the positive steps that his party might have
taken to encourage Germans on both sides of the Elbe to work together to
rebuild the nation, the SPD's candidate, Lafontaine, devoted most of his
campaign to seeking to discredit the CDU and Helmut Kohl personally.
Beyond arguing that the governing coalition had made a fatal error by
accelerating the pace of reunification, as if administration policy had been
the sole reason for the speed with which the GDR had collapsed, he also
accused the chancellor of deliberately lying about his government's intention to forgo new taxes.[20] This essentially negative strategy meant that the
Social Democrats practically took themselves out of the position of offering
the East German population an alternative vision of their own for the
German future.

After the election campaigns were concluded, those individuals in the
former GDR who were hardest hit by the economic and social impact of
their region's incorporation into the FRG may have found some grounds for
hope in a marked shift in political rhetoric from Bonn. In early 1991 the
Kohl government and the Social Democratic opposition finally began to
put politics behind them, or at least on a secondary level, and paid greater
attention to the task of, in the chancellor's understated terminology,
"bringing Germany together."[21] Notably, by February and March 1991,
Kohl had altered his earlier optimistic tone to emphasize the more difficult
side of reunification. Backing away from his preelection assurances, he
agreed to a number of controversial tax increases to cushion the impact of
unemployment in the East, and, at the same time, he nearly doubled the
amount of public funds to be invested in the region's economy.[22] In like

[19]See Simon Head, "The East German Disaster," *New York Review of Books*, January 17,
1991, pp. 41–44.

[20]Peter Jansen, "Oskar Lafontaine sorgt für Stimmung," *Das Parlament*, November 23,
1990, p. 3.

[21]See his government declaration of January 30, 1991, in *Das Parlament*, February 8/15,
1991, p. 2.

[22]See Kohl's first hint that taxes would be raised and his justification for the move, which
put the blame largely on the FRG's contributions to the U.N.-sponsored Gulf War of 1991
against Iraq, in *Das Parlament*, ibid., p. 2. If the outcome of the April election in Kohl's own

fashion, the leadership of the SPD reciprocated by toning down some of its more acerbic attacks on government policy.[23]

Yet, if the eastern German population was at all reassured by these shifts, it may have been only with the implicit understanding that those politicians who now claimed to speak for its interests really had no other recourse than to make such gestures. Throughout the first half of 1991, tens of thousands of the region's most highly skilled laborers continued to seek better opportunities for themselves and their families in the West as a result of the full-scale collapse of eastern German industry, the closing of old smokestack industries, and the loss of former markets in the East. By year's end, over 200,000 individuals had left the former territory of the GDR for good. In comparison, the number of western Germans moving in the opposite direction remained depressingly small. In March a new dimension was added to the dynamics of the inter-German relationship when, for a time, hundreds of thousands of eastern German workers took to the streets of Leipzig, Dresden, and other municipalities to protest the Federal government's policies.[24] Perhaps most disconcerting of all was the assassination in early April of Detlev Karsten Rohwedder, the director of the primary Federal agency, the Treuhandanstalt, charged with privatizing eastern German industry. Although the act was carried out by western German terrorists, the symbolism of the event was enough to disabuse many Germans of the notion that any sort of easy accommodation would be found between the two parts of the nation.

These developments were by no means an indictment of German liberal democracy. But they were an indication that one could not count upon institutions alone to heal the wounds of forty years of national separation. True to this spirit, in the spring of 1991 a number of prominent German politicians, among them Kurt Biedenkopf and Manfred Stolpe, the minister-presidents of the new states of Saxony and Brandenburg, and Klaus von Dohnanyi, the ex-mayor of Hamburg, publicly urged their contemporaries to look beyond the exigencies of democratic competition. In their view, it was necessary to find higher, symbolic means of convincing the two German peoples that they were part of the same common enterprise.[25]

Land, the Rhineland-Palatinate, was any indication, many Western Germans must not have accepted the chancellor's explanation for the tax hike. The CDU-dominated government was thrown out of office for the first time in forty-four years.

[23] Werner A. Perger, "Bühne frei für den Großen Konsens," *Die Zeit*, April 19, 1991, p. 3.

[24] Cf., *The German Tribune*, March 31, 1991, p. 3. In a revealing defense of the Kohl government's policy, the chancellery's spokesman, Dieter Vogel, tried to convince his listeners that the demonstrators in Leipzig were not really protesting against the Federal government but against forty years of socialist mistakes. Ibid., p. 3.

[25] See the interview with Biedenkopf and Stolpe, in *Die Zeit*, March 1, 1991, pp. 3–5, and also Klaus von Dohnanyi, "Brücken auf dem Weg zur Einheit," *Die Zeit*, April 12, 1991, p. 3.

In the former GDR, the need for such "political craftsmanship" may have become self-evident, since the problems associated with Germany's transformation presented the potential danger that average eastern German citizens would be made permanently cynical about the benefits of liberal politics.[26] One only had to consider the extent to which eastern Germans were included—or, in many instances, not included—in significant positions in the Bundestag that was elected in December 1990. Only three ministers out of a total of nineteen in Kohl's cabinet of 1991 came from the former GDR, all of whom were appointed to relatively minor posts. In the SPD, only a single eastern German was selected for one of the party *Frakt-ion's* nine vice-chairmanships.[27] Making the situation more disheartening from the Eastern vantage point, the region's seeming good fortune in experiencing both federal and state elections in 1990 came with what was at the time an almost unnoticed cost—it would be four years before the citizens of the old GDR would once again have the opportunity to express themselves politically in major elections.

In this light, it was no accident that when the Bundestag began its deliberations in 1991 about whether Bonn or Berlin should become the political heart of the new German nation, many parliamentarians were instinctively disposed to support the long-isolated city of Berlin. Formally, the second state treaty on reunification had already declared Berlin to be the German capital. Still, it was unclear whether the city would be merely the site for a few official functions, such as the residence of the Federal president, or instead replace Bonn as the true seat of German government. For those who were looking for a gesture that would underscore the FRG's commitment to the psychological unity of the nation—an austere collection of individuals including Brandt, Genscher, and the new interior minister, Wolfgang Schäuble—the choice of Berlin seemed to be ideal. Not only was the city Germany's prewar capital and the subject of the most prominent conflicts over the national question at the height of the Cold War, but as the former capital of the GDR as well its selection represented the perfect act of conciliation to the East German people.[28]

[26]For the provocative notion of "crafting democracies," see Di Palma, *To Craft De-mocracies,* pp. 76–77. On the challenge of convincing individuals that their interests will ultimately be met under the conditions of "institutionalized uncertainty" typical of liberal democratic politics, see Adam Przeworski, "Some Problems in the Study of the Transition to Democracy," in G. O'Donnell, P. Schmitter, and L. Whitehead, eds., *Transitions from Au-thoritarian Rule* (Baltimore: Johns Hopkins University Press, 1986), pp. 56–59.

[27]For a sense of the bitterness felt by some East German Social Democrats at not being fully included in the SPD, consider the remarks of SDP cofounder Markus Meckel, in OHP (Meckel, June 10, 1991). In the fall of 1989, Meckel emphasizes, the SPD-West would have "completely fallen on its nose" had there been no SDP: "It would have been an absolute disaster for the SPD. For where [else] should they have looked for partners in the East? To the SED?"

[28]For other possible gestures that were suggested in the spring of 1991, see Hans-Peter Schneider, "Die parlamentarische Demokratie stärken," *Das Parlament,* February 22, 1991, p. 7; and Rosemarie Will, "Auch gesellschaftliche Verhältnisse regeln," ibid.

If only the German nation could have been patched together solely by appeasing the disgruntled citizens of the GDR, the challenge before German politicians in the early 1990s would have been reasonably straightforward. Nonetheless, one could get a glimpse of the immensity of the task before them by noting that when the Bundestag finally chose Berlin on June 20, 1991, to be the Federal Republic's seat of government after eleven hours of intense debate, the vote for the city (338 for Berlin versus 320 for Bonn) was surprisingly close. In supporting Bonn, many parliamentarians, from Bundestag president Rita Süßmuth to minister of labor Norbert Blüm and North Rhine-Westphalia president Johannes Rau, refused to abandon a symbol which, in their view, had been at the heart of the FRG's political identity since Adenauer's time. For these politicians, Bonn's geographical location alone in the Rhineland identified the country with the Atlantic alliance and the ideals of Western democracy.[29] The fact that many of these individuals then reacted bitterly to losing the vote bespoke an even greater truth about the German future: it might be just as hard, if not harder, to convince the citizens of the old FRG to make sacrifices for the cause of national unity as any of their counterparts in the East. As long as many western Germans viewed the fall of the GDR as little more than a victory of their system over its longtime rival, it was not self-evident why they should give up their own images of a successful past, like Bonn itself, to accommodate their still distant countrymen.

The New Germany and the New Europe

How capably will the German politicians of the coming years cope with the twofold challenge before them—convincing the citizens of the former GDR of their inclusion in the institutions and ideals of the new Germany while at the same time persuading the citizens of the old FRG that they have not been unfairly victimized by the material and psychological burdens of reunification? Undoubtedly, much will depend on how long it takes to rebuild the economies of the five new *Länder* and, correspondingly, how great the costs of this undertaking are for the whole German economy. Similarly, the new Germany's options will also be shaped by the likes and dislikes of the successor generation of younger politicians, now only faintly visible on the political horizon, which rises to replace personalities such as Kohl and Genscher, Brandt and Bahr, after decades in which these individuals have been at the forefront of decision-making.

---

[29]On this subject, compare the speeches of June 20, 1991, by Norbert Blüm, Friedbert Pflüger, and Peter Glotz with those by Wolfgang Thierse, Wolfgang Schäuble, and Willy Brandt, in *Das Parlament*, June 28, 1991, pp. 1–7.

For all that is unforeseeable about the German future, however, it is easy to appreciate why the Federal Republic's neighbors and allies were quietly posing exactly these questions as the 1990s began.[30] Despite the intuitive wisdom contained in Richard von Weizsäcker's 1985 intimation that the vitality of the German question was directly related to the Wall's existence and the absence of movement through the Brandenburg Gate, the opening of the barrier and the unification of the GDR and the FRG seem merely to have given rise to new types of uncertainties, in effect, new questions about the age-old problem of German identity.

Such concerns might have been merely academic issues for the FRG's neighbors were it not for the fact that, as long as the GDR was around, the West German state had been far more than an average participant in European affairs. Since Brandt and Schmidt's time in particular, when the question of rational reunification had begun to lose much of its official primacy, the Federal Republic had become involved in just about every transnational undertaking on the continent, from the promotion of the Helsinki process on security and cooperation to the maintenance of stable monetary and trade relations and, especially in the later part of the 1980s, the economic and political unification of the European Community. In itself, Bonn's active role in such endeavors was an indication of how much the dependence of many European states on the FRG had grown since the later years of Adenauer's reign when West German priorities and continental interests had seemed distinctly at odds with each other. Accordingly, when the GDR suddenly ceased to exist and Germany was reunified in the early 1990s, all of these powers had reason to be concerned about the potential international impact of every event that transpired within the Federal Republic.

Given the financial and political strains that were involved in rebuilding eastern Germany and reconciling the eastern and western German populations, it is not surprising that some Europeans feared that the FRG would be tempted to turn inward and to retreat from its formerly activist role. Making matters worse, the possibility of such a shift in the Federal Republic's orientation arrived at a time when the whole continent was threatened by a series of previously unthinkable dangers. These included the crumbling of the Soviet empire and its replacement by the palpably fragile Commonwealth of Independent States, the prospect of massive waves of immigrants coming from the East to seek economic and political security in the

---

[30]For example, for a Polish view, see Janusz Tycner, "Der Planet vor der Haustür," *Die Zeit*, July 26, 1991, p. 15; for a Czech view, see "Strenger als der Vater sein," ibid.; for British reflections, see "Should Germany Cheer?" *The Economist*, September 14, 1991, pp. 15–16. For American reflections, see Andrei Markovits and Simon Reich, "Should Europe Fear the Germans?" *German Politics and Society* 23 (Summer 1991), pp. 1–20; and for a French view, see Anne-Marie LeGloannec, "Mißtrauen kann man schwer abbauen," *Der Tagesspiegel*, October 3, 1991, p. 4.

West, and the outbreak of new nationalist conflicts in countries such as Yugoslavia and the old Soviet republics. As politicians in Bonn quarreled about how best to settle their internal differences and as diverse manifestations of antiforeign sentiment and even of right-wing radicalism began to make their presence felt in the FRG, many worried that Europe as a whole would suffer from a loss of leadership at its heart. Who, if not the Germans, would provide the aid required to reconstruct the economies of Eastern Europe after decades of Communist mismanagement? Furthermore, at a time of increasing indications of U.S. retrenchment, who if not the Germans would provide the extra resources that were needed to usher the Western security system into the twenty-first century?[31]

In stark contrast, however, many other Europeans and even some Americans were concerned that Germany's reunification might actually go too well, and in the process, the new Federal Republic could be transformed into something far different and far more unpredictable than the old West German state writ large. In particular, these individuals worried that with the inclusion of former GDR citizens in the making of their country's foreign policy, new and very different attitudes about the FRG's role in NATO, its relations with the Soviet Union (or what was left of it), and its international obligations would find their way into the calculus of German priorities. Who was to say that an activist FRG would necessarily continue to abide by the interests of its longtime allies? For that matter, who could know what foreign-policy orientation would result from the melding of eastern and western German positions?[32]

It would have been a strange occurrence indeed if, after forty years of separate development, the two German populations had come together without exercising some meaningful influence upon the political character of their government. As the Kohl administration began to apply itself to the concrete tasks of completing the "internal unification" of the nation in the spring and summer of 1991, however, the country's European neighbors could at least have taken heart at one aspect of German policy that had evidently not changed since the second half of the 1980s. All of the Federal Republic's chief foreign-policymaking authorities, including the chancellor and his foreign minister, were still prepared to go out of their way to emphasize German acceptance of the continental status quo. For that mat-

---

[31]Hence, during the Gulf War against Iraq, both European and American officials worried openly that the distraction of reunification was keeping the German government from contributing its fair share to the allied costs of the engagement.

[32]For somewhat contrasting studies of the impact of the incorporation of East German citizens into West German foreign-policymaking, see Hans-Joachim Veen, "The Germans' Allegiance to the West—Recent Trends," *Occasional Paper Series*, no. 14-91 (Washington, D.C.: Konrad-Adenauer-Stiftung, 1991), pp. 5–22, and Ronald Asmus, *German Unification and Its Ramifications* (Santa Monica, Calif.: RAND Corporation, R-4021-A, 1991), pp. 66–80.

ter, Bonn showed itself to be ready, following the loosening of the Soviet hold over Eastern Europe, to act as the primary advocate for the integration of many of the formerly socialist states into the broad European fold. On March 15 the Bundestag ratified a treaty of good-neighborly relations, partnership, and cooperation with the Soviet Union, which not only outlined a number of areas in which Germany would contribute to the USSR's economic and technological development, but also explicitly promised to bring the Soviet state, as it then existed, "back to Europe." Then, on June 17, the FRG signed a long-awaited treaty of friendship and cooperation with the democratic government of Poland, underscoring its acceptance of the Oder-Neisse border and pledging to support Poland's admission to the European Community and to work to create a new security order on the continent to replace the Warsaw Pact. This accord was ratified by the Bundestag on October 17, 1991.[33]

Of course, no one would have dared to underestimate the scale of the challenges still before the FRG as its leaders struggled to balance the internal tasks of reunification with the increasingly complex external demands of a continent that was no longer neatly divided into opposing blocs. Yet, how great the contrast was from those times in the 1950s and 1960s when the old governments of the GDR and the FRG had been conspicuously out of step with the conciliatory impulses of many of their neighbors. At many points, in the eyes of leaders such as Ulbricht and Adenauer, attention to the national conflict had seemingly taken precedence over all of the other trials around them. But since then, the Germans' sense of their horizons had widened. Naturally, the reunification of Germany itself had a lot to do with the Federal Republic's ability finally to overcome any remaining uncertainties about its readiness to live with the prevailing territorial order on the continent. Helmut Kohl emphasized this attitude in an impassioned address before the Bundestag in 1991, in which he stressed that after two hundred years, the efforts of generations of German politicians to find a balance of their country's "political constitution, its internal order, and its place in Europe" had finally "had a happy end."[34]

---

[33]On the general theme of German reconciliation with postwar Europe, see Richard Ullman, *Securing Europe* (Princeton, N.J.: Princeton University Press, 1991), pp. 31–36. However, on the continuing danger that domestic politics might impair such agreements, see Clay Clemens's discussion of Union infighting over the treaty with Poland, in "Helmut Kohl's CDU and German Unification," *German Politics and Society* 22 (Spring 1991), p. 39. Some Europeans worried that the German government came close to violating the principle of reconciliation when in mid-December 1991 it practically compelled the other members of the European Community to recognize the breakaway Yugoslav states of Croatia and Slovenia. Still, German policymakers rationalized that this step was the only realistic way of keeping the intra-Yugoslavia conflict in check as that state disintegrated following the collapse of communism. Cf. *New York Times*, December 16, 1991.

[34]See Kohl's Bundestag address of January 30, 1991, in *Das Parlament*, February 8/15, 1991.

Nonetheless, if one is to do justice to the historical record, it will be essential for future students of German affairs to recall that attitudes like Kohl's were much more than merely the happy outcome of the drive to national unity. A great part of the story behind the Federal Republic's accommodation to existing realities in Europe must be viewed as the unexpected consequence of years of persistent efforts in an earlier age to normalize relations between two distant states, the GDR and the FRG. As a result of these struggles, by the 1980s most German politicians, in the East and in the West, assumed that they had no other choice than to make their peace with the burden of national division. What remained to be seen in the 1990s, however, was how successful the liberal democratic order of the newly reunified German nation would be in insuring that no other tendencies would intrude to challenge this accommodation.

APPENDIXES

Appendix A _____

Interview Locations, 1985–1990

Bonn

All-German Institute
Federal Chancellery
Federation of Expellees
Foreign Office
    Emissary for Questions of Disarmament and Arms-Control
    Legal Department
    Office of Coordinator for German-American Cooperation
    Office of Coordinator for German-French Cooperation
    Office of the Foreign Minister
    Office of Parliamentary Affairs
    Planning Staff
    Political Department
Friedrich Ebert Stiftung
German Bundestag
    Office of the President
    Parliamentary Parties:
        Christian Democratic Union
        Christian Social Union
        Free Democratic Party
        The Greens
        Social Democratic Party of Germany
    Parliamentary Committees:
        Committee on Foreign Relations
        Committee on Intra-German Relations
Konrad Adenauer Stiftung
Ministry of Intra-German Relations
Office of Berlin Affairs
Office of the Federal President

Embassy of the Republic of France
Embassy of Great Britain
Embassy of the Union of Soviet Socialist Republics
Embassy of the United States of America
Permanent Representation of the German Democratic Republic

West Berlin

Central Institute for Social Science Research-6
Mission of the United States of America
West Berlin Senate

East Berlin

Academy of Sciences
    GDR History
    General History
    Institute of State and Law
    Institute of Philosophy
Academy of Social Sciences of the Central Committee of the SED
Central Committee of the Socialist Unity Party
    Einheit
    International Department
    Politburo
    USA Department
    West Department
College of Economics, "Bruno Leuschner"
Federation of Evangelical Churches of the GDR
Free German Youth
Institute of International Relations
Institute of Marxism-Leninism
Institute for International Politics and Economics
League of People's Friendship
Ministry of Foreign Affairs
    FRG Department
    Foreign Minister's Office
    Legal Department
    Policy Planning Department
    USA Department
    West Berlin Department
Ministry of State Security
Neues Forum
Volkskammer of the GDR
    Committee on Legal Affairs
    Committee on Foreign Affairs
Embassy of the Union of Soviet Socialist Republics
Embassy of the United States of America to the GDR
Permanent Representation of the Federal Republic of Germany

Appendix B ————————————

GDR Oral History Project Interviews

A. James McAdams, Principal Investigator

With the assistance of Thomas Banchoff, Heinrich Bortfeldt, Daniel Hamilton, Matthew Siena, and John Torpey
  (*Archives of the Hoover Institution, Stanford University*)

Böhm, Joachim: December 5, 1990
Brie, Michael: December 23, 1991
Ebeling, Fred: January 28, 1992
Eberlein, Werner: February 2, 1992
Elmer, Konrad: December 5, 1991
Eppelmann, Rainer: December 12, 1991
Fischer, Peter: December 23, 1991
Gysi, Klaus: January 3, 1990 and December 28, 1991
Häber, Herbert: March 19, 1990
Hager, Kurt: December 3, 1990 and July 11, 1991
Hahn, Erich: February 28, 1991
Harich, Wolfgang: December 12, 1990
Herger, Wolfgang: January 30, 1992
Heuer, Uwe-Jens: November 14, 1991
Hilsberg, Stephan: June 14, 1991
Just, Gustav: February 1, 1992
Keller, Dietmar: November 25, 1991
Loetsch, Manfred: January 28, 1992
De Maizière, Lothar: November 12, 1991
Mebel, Moritz: February 27, 1991
Meckel, Markus: June 10, 1991
Montag, Claus: July 9, 1991
Neubert, Harald: December 4, 1990
Ortleb, Rainer: December 19, 1991
Plagemann, Karl-Ernst: November 17, 1990
Reich, Christiane and Jens: December 28, 1989 and December 23, 1991
Reinhold, Otto: January 29, 1991
Runge, Irene: December 19, 1991
Schindler, Hans: October 3, 1991

Schirdewan, Karl: July 9, 1991
Schürer, Gerhard: July 10, 1991
Seidel, Karl: July 8, 1991
Templin, Wolfgang: February 3, 1992
Ullmann, Wolfgang: November 12, 1991
Uschner, Manfred: October 4, 1991
Wroblewsky, Vincent von: December 17, 1991

Select Bibliography

Adenauer, Konrad. *Erinnerungen.* 4 vols. Stuttgart: Deutsche Verlags-Anstalt, 1967.

Adomeit, Hannes. "Gorbachev and German Reunification." *Problems of Communism* 39, no. 4 (July–August 1990), pp. 1–23.

Ammer, Thomas. "Politische Kontakte Bundesrepublik-DDR im ersten Halbjahr 1989." *Deutschland Archiv,* September 1989, pp. 1019–1027.

Ardagh, John. *Germany and the Germans.* New York: Harper and Row, 1987.

Aron, Raymond. *Democracy and Totalitarianism.* New York: Praeger, 1968.

Artner, Stephen J. *A Change of Course: The West German Social Democrats and NATO.* Westport: Greenwood, 1985.

Ash, Timothy Garton. "Mitteleuropa." *Daedalus* 119, no. 1 (Winter 1990), pp. 1–21.

Asmus, Ronald D. "The Documentation of a Dispute." *RFE Occasional Papers* 1. Munich: Radio Free Europe, 1985.

Asmus, Ronald D. *German Unification and Its Ramifications.* Santa Monica, Calif.: RAND Corporation, R-4021-A, 1991.

Bahr, Egon. *Zum europäischen Frieden.* Berlin: Siedler, 1988.

Banchoff, Thomas. "Die Rolle des Nato-Doppelbeschlusses in der sowjetischen Deutschlandpolitik, 1978–1984." Unpublished Magisterarbeit, University of Bonn, 1988.

Bandulet, Bruno. *Adenauer zwischen Ost und West.* Munich: Weltforum, 1970.

Baring, Arnulf. *Außenpolitik in Adenauers Kanzlerdemokratie.* Munich: R. Oldenbourg, 1969.

Baring, Arnulf. *Machtwechsel: Die Ära Brandt-Scheel.* Stuttgart: Deutsche Verlags-Anstalt, 1983.

Baring, Arnulf. *Uprising in East Germany, June 17, 1953.* Ithaca, N.Y.: Cornell University Press, 1972.

Bark, Dennis, and Gress, David. *A History of West Germany.* Oxford: Basil Blackwill, 1989.

Barzel, Rainer. *Auf dem Drahtseil.* Munich: Droemer Knauer, 1978.

Baylis, Thomas A. "Explaining the GDR's Economic Strategy." *International Organization* 40 (Spring 1986), pp. 381–420.

Behrendt, Wolfgang. "Die innerparteilichen Auseinandersetzungen um die Ostpolitik in der SPD, 1960 bis 1969." Unpublished Diplomarbeit, Free University, West Berlin, 1972.

Bender, Peter. *Neue Ostpolitik.* Munich: dtv, 1986.

Beschloss, Michael. *The Crisis Years: Kennedy and Khrushchev, 1960–1963.* New York: HarperCollins, 1991.

Besson, Waldemar. *Die Außenpolitik der Bundesrepublik.* Munich: R. Piper, 1970.

Bethkenhagen, J.; Kupper, S.; and Lambrecht, H. "Die Aussenwirtschaftsbezieh-

ungen der DDR vor dem Hintergrund vom kalten Krieg und Entspannung."
Beiträge zur Konfliktforschung 4 (1980), pp. 39–72.

Beyme, Klaus von. "The Legitimation of German Unification betweeen National
and Democratic Principles." *German Politics and Society* 22 (Spring 1991),
pp. 1–17.

Birnbaum, Karl E. *East and West Germany: A Modus Vivendi.* Westmead, England: Saxon House, 1973.

Bloemer, Klaus. "Außenpolitische Vorstellungen und Verhaltensweisen des F. J.
Strauß." *Liberal*, July–August 1980, pp. 609–24.

Bölling, Klaus. *Die fernen Nachbarn.* Hamburg: Goldmann, 1985.

Brandt, Heinz. *The Search for a Third Way.* Garden City, N.Y.: Doubleday, 1970.

Brandt, Willy. "Die Chancen der Geschichte suchen." In *Reden über das eigene
Land: Deutschland*, vol. 2, pp. 57–70. Munich: C. Bertelsmann, 1984.

Brandt, Willy. "Den eignen Weg neu finden." *Neue Gesellschaft* 28 (May 1981),
pp. 396–404.

Brandt, Willy. *People and Politics.* London: William Collins, 1978.

Braunthal, Gerard. "The Policy Function of the German Social Democratic Party."
Comparative Politics 9 (January 1977), pp. 127–145.

Braunthal, Gerard. *The West German Social Democrats, 1969–1982.* Boulder,
Colo.: Westview, 1983.

Bredow, Wilfried von, and Brocke, Rudolf. *Das deutschlandpolitische Konzept der
SPD.* Erlangen: Deutsche Gesellschaft für zeitgeschichtliche Fragen, 1987.

Bruns, Wilhelm. *Deutsch-deutsche Beziehungen.* Opladen: Leske, 1982.

Brzezinski, Zbigniew, and Huntington, Samuel. *Political Power: USA/USSR.* New
York: Viking, 1966.

Buchstab, Günter, ed. *Adenauer: Es mußte alles neu gemacht werden.* Stuttgart:
Clett-Cotta, 1986.

Bundesministerium für innerdeutsche Beziehungen. *Zahlenspiegel*, February 1979.

Bürger, Ulrich. *Das sagen wir natürlich so nicht!* Berlin: Dietz, 1990.

Bussiek, Hendrik. "Lieber getrennt leben als vereint sterben . . ." *Vorwärts* 38
(September 1981), p. 3.

Carr, Jonathan. *Helmut Schmidt: Helmsman of Germany.* London: Weidenfeld
and Nicolson, 1985.

Catudal, Honoré M. *Kennedy and the Berlin Wall Crisis.* Berlin: Berlin Verlag,
1980.

Childs, David. "The Ostpolitik and Domestic Politics in East Germany." In *The
Ostpolitik and Political Change in Germany*, ed. Robert Tilford, pp. 59–76.
Westmead, England: Saxon House, 1975.

Cioc, Mark. *Pax Atomica.* New York: Columbia University Press, 1988.

Clemens, Clay. "Helmut Kohl's CDU and German Unification." *German Politics
and Society* 22 (Spring 1991), pp. 33–44.

Clemens, Clay. *Reluctant Realists.* Durham, N.C.: Duke University Press, 1989.

Conradt, David. *The German Polity.* 4th ed. New York: Longman, 1989.

Craig, Gordon. *From Bismarck to Adenauer: Aspects of German Statecraft.* New
York: Harper and Row, 1958.

Cramer, Detmar. "Zwischen Kollision und Kooperation." *Deutschland Archiv*,
February 1974, pp. 113–118.

Croan, Melvin. "Entwicklung der politischen Beziehungen zur Sowjetunion seit 1955." In *Drei Jahrzehnte Aussenpolitik der DDR*, ed. Hans-Adolf Jacobsen et al., pp. 347–379. Munich: R. Oldenbourg, 1979.

Dahl, Robert. *After the Revolution?* New Haven, Conn.: Yale University Press, 1990.

DDR Journal zur Novemberrevolution. West Berlin: Tageszeitung, 1990.

DDR Journal Nr. 2: Die Wende der Wende. West Berlin: Tageszeitung, 1990.

Dean, Robert W. *West German Trade with the East: The Political Dimension*. New York: Praeger, 1974.

dePorte, Anton W. *Europe between the Superpowers: The Enduring Balance*. New Haven, Conn.: Yale University Press, 1979.

Deuerlin, Ernst. *DDR 1945–1970: Geschichte und Bestandsaufnahme*. Munich: dtv, 1972.

Deutsch, Karl, and Edinger, Lewis. *Germany Rejoins the Powers*. Stanford, Calif.: Stanford University Press, 1959.

Diepgen, Eberhard. "Perspektiven statt Illusionen." *Deutschland Archiv*, March 1986, pp. 268–278.

DiPalma, Giuseppe. *To Craft Democracies*. Berkeley: University of California Press, 1990.

Doering-Manteuffel, Anselm. *Die Bundesrepublik in der Ära Adenauer*. Darmstadt: Wissenschaftliche Buchgesellschaft, 1983.

Dokumente zur Deutschlandpolitik. 5 Series. Frankfurt am Main: Alfred Metzner, 1939–1968.

Drummond, Gordon D. *The German Social Democrats in Opposition*. Norman: University of Oklahoma Press, 1982.

Edinger, Lewis J. *Kurt Schumacher*. Stanford, Calif.: Stanford University Press, 1965.

Eltermann, Ludolf; Jung, Helmut; and Kaltefleiter, Werner. "Drei Fragen zur Bundestagswahl 1972." *Aus Politik und Zeitgeschichte*, November 17, 1973, pp. 1–22.

End, Heinrich. *Zweimal deutsche Aussenpolitik*. Cologne: Verlag Wissenschaft und Politik, 1973.

Fischoff, Baruch, "For Those Condemned to Study the Past: Heuristics and Biases in Hindsight." In *Judgment under Uncertainty*, ed. D. Kahneman, P. Slovic, and A. Tversky, pp. 335–354. Cambridge, U.K.: Cambridge University Press, 1982.

Förster, Peter, and Roski, Günter. *Die DDR zwischen Wende und Wahl*. Berlin: Links Druck, 1990.

Frey, Eric. *Division and Detente: The Germanies and Their Alliances*. New York: Praeger, 1987.

Fricke, Karl Wilhelm. *Opposition und Widerstand in der DDR*. Cologne: Verlag Wissenschaft und Politik, 1984.

Gaddis, John Lewis. *Strategies of Containment*. Oxford: Oxford University Press, 1982.

Gaus, Günter. "Die Elbe—ein deutscher Strom, nicht Deutschlands Grenze." *Die Zeit* January 30, 1981, pp. 3–4.

Gaus, Günter. *Wo Deutschland liegt—Eine Ortsbestimmung*. Hamburg: Hoffmann und Campe, 1983.

Geißler, Heiner. *Zugluft—Politik in stürmischer Zeit*. Munich: C. Bertelsmann, 1990.

Genscher, Hans-Dietrich. "Fostering Detente and Disarmament." *Statements and Speeches*, August 12, 1987.

Genscher, Hans-Dietrich. "Taking Gorbachev at His Word." Speech at the World Economic Forum, Davos, Switzerland, February 1, 1987. *Statements and Speeches*, February 6, 1987.

Gerstenmeier, Eugen. *Streit und Friede hat seine Zeit*. Frankfurt: Propyläen, 1981.

Glaeßner, Gert-Joachim. *Die andere deutsche Republik*. Opladen: Westdeutscher Verlag, 1989.

Glotz, P.; Reinhold, O.; and Banaschak, M. "Karl Marx und die Sozial-demokratie." *Neue Gesellschaft*, March 1983, pp. 200–215.

Goeckel, Robert F. *The Lutheran Church and the East German State*. Ithaca, N.Y.: Cornell University Press, 1990.

Gould, Stephen Jay. *Wonderful Life: The Burgess Shale and the Nature of History*. New York: W. W. Norton, 1989.

Grabbe, Hans-Jürgen. "Konrad Adenauer, John Foster Dulles, and West German-American Relations." In *John Foster Dulles and the Diplomacy of the Cold War*, ed. R. H. Immerman, pp. 109–132. Princeton, N.J.: Princeton University Press, 1990.

Grewe, Wilhelm. *Rückblenden: 1976–1951*. Frankfurt: Propyläen, 1979.

Griffith, William. *The Ostpolitik of the Federal Republic of Germany*. Cambridge, Mass.: MIT Press, 1978.

Häber, Herbert. "Das Wesen der Demokratie und Freiheit: Der Kampf um demokratische Verhältnisse in Deutschland." Unpublished lecture, Central Committee of the SED, July 8, 1966, Archives of the Akademie für Gesellschafts-wissenschaften, East Berlin.

Hacke, Christian. "Parlamentarische Opposition und Entspannungspolitik—Die Position der CDU/CSU zur KSZE." In *Verwaltete Außenpolitik*, ed. H. Haften-dorn, W.-D. Karl, J. Krause, and L. Wilker, pp. 263–278. Cologne: Verlag Wissenschaft und Politik, 1978.

Hacke, Christian. "Von Adenauer zu Kohl: Zur Ost- und Deutschlandpolitik der Bundesrepublik, 1949–1985," *Aus Politik und Zeitgeschichte*, December 31, 1985, pp. 3–22.

Hacker, Jens. *Deutsche unter sich*. Stuttgart-Degerloch: Seewald, 1977.

Haftendorn, Helga. *Sicherheit und Entspannung*. Baden-Baden: Nomos, 1983.

Hamilton, Daniel. *After the Revolution: The New Political Landscape in East Germany*. German Issues, 7. Washington, D.C.: American Institute for Contemporary German Studies, 1990.

Hanrieder, Wolfram. *Germany, America, Europe*. New Haven, Conn.: Yale University Press, 1989.

Head, Simon. "The East German Disaster." *New York Review of Books*, January 17, 1991, pp 41–44.

Heep, Barbara. *Helmut Schmidt und Amerika*. Bonn: Bouvier, 1990.

Heidenheimer, Arnold. *Adenauer and the CDU*. The Hague: Martinus Nijhoff, 1960.

Helwig, Gisela. "Plädoyer für Umgestaltung." *Deutschland Archiv*, June 1989, pp. 609–612.

Hildebrand, Klaus. *Geschichte der Bundesrepublik Deutschland: Von Erhard zur Grossen Koalition, 1963–1969*. Stuttgart: Deutsche Verlags-Anstalt, 1984.

Hofmann, Jürgen. *Ein neues Deutschland soll es sein*. Berlin: Dietz, 1989.

Hofmann, Gunter. "Kanzlerstark, aber kopflos." *Die Zeit*, September 22, 1989, p. 4.

Hofmann, Gunter. "Die Republik wird am Ende nicht mehr die alte sein." *Die Zeit*, September 21, 1990, p. 5.

Honecker, Erich. *Reden und Aufsätze*. 12 vols. Berlin: Dietz, 1975–1988.

Huntington, Samuel. *Political Order in Changing Societies*. New Haven, Conn.: Yale University Press, 1968.

Jacobsen, Hanns-Dieter. "Strategie und Schwerpunkte der Aussenwirtschaftsbeziehungen." In *Drei Jahrzehnte Aussenpolitik der DDR*, ed. H.-A. Jacobsen, Gert Leptin, Ulrich Scheuner, and Eberhard Schulz, pp. 298–308. Munich: R. Oldenbourg, 1980.

Jäger, Wolfgang, and Link, Werner. *Geschichte der Bundesrepublik Deutschland: Republik im Wandel*. Stuttgart: Deutsche Verlags-Anstalt, 1987.

Jänicke, Martin. *Der dritte Weg*. Cologne: Neuer Deutscher Verlag, 1964.

Jansen, Peter. "Oskar Lafontaine sorgt für Stimmung." *Das Parlament* November 23, 1990, p. 3.

Jenninger, Philipp. "Kontinuität, was sonst? Deutsch-deutsche Beziehungen nach dem Regierungswechsel 1982 bis 1984." Unpublished manuscript, 1991.

Joffe, Joseph. "The View from Bonn." In *Eroding Empire: Western Relations with Eastern Europe*, ed. Lincoln Gordon, pp. 129–187. Washington, D.C.: Brookings Institution, 1987.

Kaack, Heino. *Zur Geschichte und Programmatik der FDP*. Meisenheim am Glan: Verlag Anton Hein, 1976.

Kaase, Max. "Die Bundestagswahl 1972, Probleme und Analysen." *Politische Vierteljahresschrift* 14 (1973), pp. 145–190.

Kaase, Max, and Gibowski, Wolfgang. "Deutschland im Übergang: Parteien und Wähler vor der Bundeswahl 1990." *Aus Politik und Zeitgeschichte*, September 14, 1990, pp. 14–26.

Kaiser, Carl-Christian. "Gespaltene Opposition." *Die Zeit*, July 11, 1975, p. 4.

Kaiser, Carl-Christian. "Immer reden—aber mit wem?" *Die Zeit*, September 29, 1989, p. 4.

Kaiser, Karl. *German Foreign Policy in Transition*. London: Oxford University Press, 1968.

Kaltefleiter, Werner. *Vorspiel zum Wechsel: Eine Analyse der Bundestagswahl 1976*. Berlin: Duncker und Humblot, 1977.

"Karl Schirdewan: Fraktionsmacherei oder gegen Ulbrichts Diktat?" *Beiträge zur Geschichte der Arbeiterbewegung* 32, no. 4 (1990), pp. 498–512.

Katzenstein, Peter J. *Policy and Politics in West Germany*. Philadelphia: Temple University Press, 1987.

Keithly, David. *Breakthrough in the Ostpolitik*. Boulder, Colo.: Westview, 1986.

Kennan, George. *Russia and the West under Lenin and Stalin*. Boston: Little, Brown, 1961.

Kiep, Walther Leisler. "Zur Entspannungspolitik—Bilanz und Ausblick." *Sonde* 1 (1975), pp. 72–78.

Kirschey, Peter. *Wandlitz Waldsiedlung—die Geschlossene Gesellschaft.* Berlin: Dietz, 1990.

Kleßmann, Christoph. *Zwei Staaten, eine Nation.* Göttingen: Vanderhoeck und Ruprecht, 1988.

Koch, Klaus-Uwe. "Das Problem der Nation in der Strategie und Taktik der SED in der zweiten Hälfte der sechziger Jahre." Unpublished dissertation, Akademie für Gesellschaftswissenschaften, East Berlin, July 1985.

Kohl, Helmut. "State of the Nation Address of March 14, 1986." *Bulletin* March 15, 1986. Bonn: Presse und Informationsamt.

Kohl, Helmut. "A Ten-point Program for Overcoming the Division of Germany and Europe." *Statements and Speeches*, December 19, 1989. New York: German Information Center.

Krenz, Egon. *Wenn Mauern fallen.* Vienna: Paul Neff, 1990.

Krisch, Henry. *The German Democratic Republic: The Search for Identity.* Boulder, Colo.: Westview, 1985.

Krone, Heinrich, "Aufzeichnungen zur Deutschland- und Ostpolitik, 1954–1969." In *Adenauer Studien III*, ed. R. Morsey and K. Repgen, pp. 134–201. Mainz: Matthias-Grünewald Verlag, 1971.

Kuczynski, Jürgen. "Die Bürokratie muß vernichtet werden." *Konkret*, May 1987, pp. 23–25.

Kuppe, Johannes. "Offensiv in die Defensive." *Deutschland Archiv*, January 1989, pp. 1–7.

Kupper, Siegfried. "Politische Aspekte des innerdeutschen Handels." In *Handelspartner DDR—Innerdeutsche Wirtschaftsbeziehungen*, ed. C.-D. Ehlermann et. al. Baden-Baden: Nomos, 1975.

Langguth, Gerd, ed. *Offensive Demokratie.* Stuttgart: Seewald, 1972.

LeGloannec, Anne-Marie. *Die deutsch-deutsche Nation.* Munich: printful, 1991.

Lehmbruch, Gerhard. "Die improvisierte Vereinigung: Die dritte deutsche Republik." *Leviathan* 4 (1990), pp. 463–486.

Leonhard, Wolfgang. *Child of the Revolution.* Chicago: Henry Regnery, 1967.

Lippmann, Heinz. *Honecker and the New Politics of Europe.* New York: Macmillan, 1972.

Livingston, Robert Gerald. "East Germany between Moscow and Bonn." *Foreign Affairs*, January 1972, pp. 297–309.

Löwenthal, Richard. "Vom kalten Krieg zur Ostpolitik." In *Die zweite Republik*, ed. R. Löwenthal and H.-P. Schwarz, pp. 626–644. Stuttgart: Seewald, 1974.

Ludz, Peter C. *Die DDR zwischen Ost und West.* Munich: C. H. Beck, 1977.

McAdams, A. James. *East Germany and Détente.* Cambridge, U.K.: Cambridge University Press, 1985.

McCauley, Martin. *The German Democratic Republic since 1945.* New York: St. Martin's, 1983.

Mahncke, Dieter. "Abschluss der Neuordnung der Beziehungen zwischen der Bundesrepublik Deutschland und Osteuropa." In *Die Internationale Politik 1973/1974*, pp. 193–215. Munich: R. Oldenbourg, 1980.

Mahnke, Hans Heinrich, ed. *Dokumente zur Berlin-Frage, 1967–1986*. Munich: R. Oldenbourg, 1987.

March, James, and Olsen, Johan. "The New Institutionalism: Organizational Factors in Political Life." *American Political Science Review* 78 (September 1984), pp. 734–779.

Martin, Ernst. *Zwischenbilanz: Deutschlandpolitik der 80er Jahren*. Stuttgart: Bonn Aktuell, 1986.

Meissner, Boris, ed. *Die deutsche Ostpolitik: 1961–1970*. Cologne: Verlag Wissenschaft und Politik, 1970.

Merck, Johannes. "Klar zur Wende? Die FDP vor dem Koalitionswechsel in Bonn, 1980–1982." *Politische Vierteljahresschrift* 28 (December 1987), pp. 385–402.

Merkl, Peter. "The SPD after Brandt: Problems of Integration in a Changing Urban Society." *West European Politics* 11 (January 1988), pp. 40–53.

Meyer, Gerd. *Die DDR-Machtelite in der Ära Honecker*. Tübingen: Francke, 1991.

Mitter, Armin, and Wolle, Stefan, eds. *Ich liebe euch doch alle!* Berlin: Basis Druck, 1990.

Moersch, Karl. *Kurs-Revision: Deutsche Politik nach Adenauer*. Hof: Societäts-Verlag, 1978.

Moreton, Edwina. *East Germany and the Warsaw Alliance*. Boulder, Colo.: Westview, 1978.

Moreton, Edwina, ed. *Germany between East and West*. Cambridge, U.K.: Cambridge University Press, 1987.

Nakath, Detlef. "Zur Geschichte der Handelsbeziehungen zwischen der DDR und der BRD in den Jahren 1961 bis 1975." Unpublished dissertation, Department of History, Humboldt University, East Berlin, May 1988.

Naumann, Gerhard, and Trumpler, Eckhard. *Der Flop mit der DDR-Nation*. Berlin: Dietz, 1991.

Naumann, Gerhard, and Trumpler, Eckhard. *Von Ulbricht zu Honecker*. Berlin: Dietzg, 1990.

Nawrocki, Joachim. *Relations between the Two States in Germany*. Bonn: Verlag Bonn Aktuell, 1985.

Nickel, Erich. *Die BRD: Ein historischer Überblick*. Berlin: VEB Deutscher Verlag der Wissenschaft, 1988.

Niclauß, Karlheinz. *Kontroverse Deutschlandpolitik*. Frankfurt: Alfred Metzner Verlag, 1977.

Niethammer, Lutz; von Plato, Alexander; and Wierling, Dorothee. *Die Volkseigene Erfahrung*. Berlin: Rowohlt, 1991.

Noelle-Neumann, Elisabeth, ed. *Allensbacher Jahrbuch der Demoskopie: 1977*. Vienna: Molden, 1977.

Noelle-Neumann, E., and Neumann, E. P. *Jahrbuch der öffentlichen Meinung, 1968 bis 1973*. Allensbach: Verlag für Demoskopie, 1974.

Noelle-Neumann, E., and Piel, E., eds. *Allensbacher Jahrbuch der Demoskopie, 1978–1983*. Munich: K. G. Saur, 1983.

Offe, Claus. "Prosperity, Nation, and Republic: Aspects of the Unique German Journey from Socialism to Capitalism." *German Politics and Society* 22 (Spring 1991), pp. 18–32.

Oldenburg, Fred. "Sowjetische Deutschlandpolitik nach den Treffen von Moskau und Bonn 1988/1989." *Berichte des Bundesinstituts für ost-wissenschaftliche und internationale Studien* 63 (1989), pp. 834–842.

Oldenburg, Fred. "Werden Moskaus Schatten länger?" *Deutschland Archiv*, August 1984, pp. 834–842.

Osten, Walter. *Die Außenpolitik der DDR*. Opladen: Leske, 1969.

Oye, Kenneth. "Explaining Cooperation under Anarchy." *World Politics* 38 (October 1985), pp. 1–24.

Paterson, William. "The Christian Union Parties." In *West German Politics in the Mid-Eighties*, ed. H. G. Peter Wallach and George Romoser, pp. 60–80. New York: Praeger, 1985.

Pfeiler, Wolfgang. *Deutschlandpolitische Optionen der Sowjetunion*. Melle: Verlag Ernst Knoth, 1987.

Phillips, Ann. *Seeds of Change in the German Democratic Republic: The SED-SPD Dialogue*. Washington, D.C.: American Institute for Contemporary German Studies, Research Report 1, December 1989.

Planck, Charles R. *The Changing Status of German Reunification in Western Diplomacy*. Baltimore: Johns Hopkins University Press, 1967.

Pollack, Detlef. "Außenseiter oder Repräsentanten?" *Deutschland Archiv*, August 1990, pp. 1216–1223.

Pond, Elizabeth. "A Wall Destroyed: The Dynamics of German Unification in the GDR." *International Security* 15 (Fall 1990), pp. 35–61.

Prauß, Herbert. "CDU/CSU Außenpolitik—nichts dazugelernt." *Neue Gesellschaft* 25 (May 1978), pp. 402–406.

Pridham, Geoffrey. "The CDU Opposition in West Germany, 1969–1972." *Parliamentary Affairs* 26 (Spring 1973), pp. 201–217.

Pridham, Geoffrey. *Christian Democracy in West Germany*. London: Croom Helm, 1977.

Protokoll der Verhandlungen des III. Parteitages der SED. Berlin: Dietz, 1951.

Przeworski, Adam. "Some Problems in the Study of the Transition to Democracy." In *Transitions from Authoritarian Rule*, ed. G. O'Donnell, P. Schmitter, and L. Whitehead, pp. 56–59. Baltimore: Johns Hopkins University, 1986.

Przybylski, Peter, ed. *Tatort Politbüro: Die Akte Honecker*. Berlin: Rowohlt, 1991.

Public Papers of the Presidents: John F. Kennedy, 1961. Washington, D.C.: Government Printing Office, 1962.

Pulzer, Peter G. J. "The German Party System in the Sixties." *Political Studies* 19 (1971), pp. 1–17.

Reinhold, Jochen. "Die Beziehungen zur DDR in der Regierungspolitik der SPD von 1973 bis 1982." Unpublished dissertation, Akademie für Gesellschaftswissenschaften, East Berlin, July 1983.

Reinhold, Otto. Transcript of radio remarks. Radio GDR II, August 19, 1989.

Richert, Ernst. *Die Sowjetzone in der Phase der Koexistenz*. Hannover: Niedersächsischen Landeszentrale, 1961.

Roth, Reinhold. *Aussenpolitische Innovation und politische Herrschaftssicherung*. Meisenheim am Glan: Verlag Anton Hain, 1976.

Rühe, Volker. "Nebenaußenpolitik der SPD schadet deutschen Interessen." *Die Entscheidung*, October 1985, pp. 20–21.

Rühe, Volker. "Wie geht es weiter in den deutsch-deutschen Beziehungen?" Unpublished conference report of the Friedrich-Ebert-Stiftung, June 3, 1987, pp. 7–11.

Sandler, Olga. "Shades of Center: Hans-Dietrich Genscher and Western German Policy towards the Soviet Union." Unpublished manuscript, April 14, 1989.

Säuberlich, Dietmar. "Das Problem der Nation in der Strategie und Taktik der SED." *Forschungen zur Geschichte der deutschen Arbeiterbewegung*, ser. A, no. 48, pp. 61–80. Berlin: Akademie für Gesellschaftswissenschaften, 1985.

Schabowski, Günter. *Das Politbüro*. Reinbek bei Hamburg: Rowohlt, 1990.

Schäuble, Wolfgang. "Deutschlandpolitik im fünften Jahrzehnt der Teilung." In *Tutzinger Materialien* 23 (1985), pp. 1–26.

Scheer, Hermann. "Der verengte Sicherheitsbegriff." *Neue Gesellschaft* 28 (May 1981), pp. 413–416.

Shevardnadze, Eduard. *The Future Belongs to Freedom*. New York: The Free Press, 1991.

Schlesinger, Arthur M., Jr. *A Thousand Days*. Greenwich, Conn.: Fawcett, 1965.

Schmid, Günther. *Entscheidung in Bonn: Die Entstehung der Ost- und Deutschlandpolitik, 1969/1970*. Cologne: Verlag Wissenschaft und Politik, 1979.

Schmid, Günther. *Politik des Ausverkaufs*. Munich: tuduv, 1975.

Schmidt, Helmut. "The 1977 Alastair Buchan Memorial Lecture." *Survival* 20 (January–February 1978), pp. 2–10.

Schmidt, Helmut. *Die Deutschen und ihre Nachbarn*. Berlin: Siedler, 1990.

Schmidt, Helmut. *Menschen und Mächte*. Berlin: Siedler, 1987.

Schmidthammer, Jens. *Rechtsanwalt Wolfgang Vogel*. Hamburg: Hoffmann und Campe, 1987.

Schmude, Jürgen. "Deutsch-deutsches Verhältnis." *Informationen der sozialdemokratischen Bundestagsfraktion*, May 17, 1985.

Schneider, Hans-Peter. "Die parlamentarische Demokratie stärken." *Das Parlament*, February 22, 1991, p. 7.

Schneider, Peter. *The German Comedy*. New York: Farrar, Straus, and Giroux, 1991.

Schönbohm, Wulf. *Die CDU wird moderne Volkspartei*. Stuttgart: Ernst Klett, 1985.

Schulz, Eberhard. *Die deutsche Nation in Europa*. Bonn: Europa Union, 1982.

Schulz, Eberhard, and Danylow, Peter. "Bewegung in der deutschen Frage?" *Arbeitspapiere zur Internationalen Politik* 33 (April 1985). Bonn: Deutsche Gesellschaft für Auswärtige Politik.

Schulz, Hans-Dieter. "Die Entspannung kann weitergehen." *Deutschland Archiv*, November 1980, pp. 1121–1123.

Schwarz, Hans-Peter. *Adenauer: Der Staatsmann, 1952–1967*. Stuttgart: Deutsche Verlags-Anstalt, 1991.

Schwarz, Hans-Peter. "Das aussenpolitische Konzept Konrad Adenauers." In *Adenauer Studien*, vol. 1, ed. R. Morsey and K. Repgen, pp. 71–108. Mainz: Matthias Grünewald, 1971.

Schwarz, Hans-Peter. *Geschichte der Bundesrepublik Deutschland: Die Ära Adenauer, 1949–1957*. Stuttgart: Deutsche Verlags-Anstalt, 1981.

Schwarz, Hans-Peter. *Geschichte der Bundesrepublik Deutschland: Die Ära Adenauer, 1949–1957*. Stuttgart: Deutsche Verlags-Anstalt, 1981.

Schwarz, Hans-Peter, ed. *Konrad Adenauer, Reden: 1917–1967*. Stuttgart: Deutsche Verlags-Anstalt, 1975.

Schweigler, Gebhard. "German Questions or the Shrinking of Germany." In *The Two German States and European Security*, ed. F. Stephen Larrabee, pp. 73–105. New York: St. Martin's Press, 1989.

Schweigler, Gebhard. "Normalität in Deutschland." *Europa Archiv* 6 (1989), pp. 173–182.

Siebenmorgen, Peter. "Vom Retter zum Sündenbock." *Die Zeit*, May 10, 1991, p. 6.

Slusser, Robert. *The Berlin Crisis of 1961*. Baltimore: Johns Hopkins University Press, 1963.

Smith, Gordon; Paterson, William; and Merkl, Peter, eds. *Developments in West German Politics*. London: Macmillan, 1989.

Smith, Jean Edward. "The Berlin Wall in Retrospect." *Dalhousie Review* 47 (Summer 1967), pp. 174–184.

Smith, Jean Edward. *The Defense of Berlin*. Baltimore: Johns Hopkins University Press, 1963.

Sodaro, Michael. *Moscow, Germany, and the West: From Khrushchev to Gorbachev*. Ithaca, N.Y.: Cornell University Press, 1991.

Sodaro, Michael. "Ulbricht's Grand Design: Economics, Ideology, and the GDR's Response to Detente." *World Affairs* 142 (Winter 1990), pp. 147–168.

Sorensen, Theodore C. *Kennedy*. New York: Harper and Row, 1965.

"Sozialdemokratische Thesen zur Deutschlandpolitik." *Politik* 17 (November 1984). Informationsdienst der SPD.

Spittmann, Ilse. "Eine Übergangsgesellschaft." *Deutschland Archiv*, November 1989, pp. 1201–1205.

Spittmann, Ilse. "Irritationen zur Jahreswende." *Deutschland Archiv*, January 1988, p. 1.

Spittmann, Ilse. "SED setzt auf Zeitgewinn." *Deutschland Archiv*, July 1988, pp. 689–691.

Spittmann, Ilse. "Weichenstellung." *Deutschland Archiv*, August 1985, pp. 786–788.

Staritz, Dietrich. "Die SED, Stalin, und der 'Aufbau des Sozialismus' in der DDR." *Deutschland Archiv*, July 1991, pp. 686–700.

Steininger, Rolf. *Eine vertane Chance: Die Stalin Note vom 10. März 1952*. Bonn: Dietz, 1985.

Steininger, Rolf, ed. *Deutsche Geschichte: 1945–1961*. 2 vols. Frankfurt: Fischer, 1987.

Steinmo, Sven; Thelen, Kathleen; and Longstreth, Frank, eds. *Structuring Politics: Historical Institutionalism in Comparative Analysis*. New York: Cambridge University Press, 1992.

Stent, Angela. *From Embargo to Ostpolitik*. Cambridge, U.K.: Cambridge University Press, 1981.

Stern, Carola. *Ulbricht*. Cologne: Kiepenheuer und Witsch, 1964.

Strauß, Franz Josef. *Bundestagsreden.* Bonn: Verlag AZ Studio, 1968.

"Der Streit der Ideologien und die gemeinsame Sicherheit." *Politik* 3, August 1987, Informationsdienst der SPD.

Stultz-Herrnstadt, Nadja. *Das Herrnstadt Dokument.* Reinbek bei Hamburg: Rowohlt, 1990.

Stützle, Walther. *Kennedy und Adenauer in der Berlin Krise, 1961–1962.* Bonn–Bad Godesberg: Verlag Neue Gesellschaft, 1973.

Süß, Walter. "Perestroika oder Ausreise." *Deutschland Archiv,* March 1989, pp. 286–301.

Tagliabue, John. "What Divides Berlin Now?" *New York Times Magazine,* April 7, 1991, pp. 30, 56–60.

Teltschik, Horst. *329 Tage: Innenansichten der Einigung.* Berlin: Siedler, 1991.

Teltschik, Horst. "Plädoyer für eine konstruktive Ost- und Deutschlandpolitik." In *Offensive Demokratie,* ed. Gerd Langguth, pp. 162–187. Stuttgart: Seewald, 1972.

"Tenth Writers' Congress of November 24–26, 1987." Proceedings. *Neue Deutsche Literatur* 36 (March 1989).

Texte zur Deutschlandpolitik. 3 Series. Bonn: Deutscher Bundes-Verlag, 1966–1989.

Trachtenberg, Marc. *History and Strategy.* Princeton, N.J.: Princeton University Press, 1988.

Turner, Henry A. *The Two Germanies since 1945.* New Haven: Yale University Press, 1987.

Ulam, Adam. *Expansion and Coexistence.* New York: Praeger, 1968.

Ulbricht, Walter. *Zur Geschichte der deutschen Arbeiterbewegung.* Berlin: Dietz, 1966.

Ullman, Richard. *Securing Europe.* Princeton, N.J.: Princeton University Press, 1991.

"Unsere Verantwortung in der Welt: Christlich-demokratische Perspektiven zur Außen-, Sicherheits-, Europa- und Deutschlandpolitik." *CDU-Dokumentation* 6 (1968).

Uschner, Manfred. *Die Ostpolitik der SPD.* Berlin: Dietz, 1991.

Veen, Hans-Joachim. "The Germans' Allegiance to the West—Recent Trends." *Occasional Paper Series* 14–91. Washington, D.C.: Konrad-Adenauer-Stiftung, 1991.

Verträge, Abkommen und Vereinbarungen. Bonn: Presse und Informationsamt der Bundesregierung, 1973.

Vogel, Barbara. "Die Politik zur Herstellung verträglicher Beziehungen zwischen der DDR und der BRD in der ersten Hälfte der siebziger Jahre." Unpublished dissertation, Akademie für Gesellschaftswissenschaften, East Berlin, July 1987.

"Warum berichtet die *Junge Welt* nicht . . ." *Junge Welt,* September 6, 1989.

Weber, Hermann. *Kleine Geschichte der DDR.* Cologne: Verlag Wissenschaft und Politik, 1980.

Weber, Hermann, ed. *DDR: Dokumente zur Geschichte.* Munich: dtv, 1986.

Weidenfeld, Werner, ed. *Politische Kultur und deutsche Frage.* Cologne: Verlag Wissenschaft und Politik, 1989.

Weizsäcker, Richard von. *Von Deutschland aus*. Munich: dtv, 1987.

Wettig, Gerhard. "Dilemmas der SED-Abgrenzungspolitik." *Berichte des Bundesinstituts für ost-wissenschaftliche und internationale Studien* 22 (1975).

Wettig, Gerhard. *Die Sowjetunion, die DDR und die Deutschland-Frage*. Stuttgart: Verlag Bonn Aktuell, 1977.

Will, Rosemary. "Auch gesellschaftliche Verhältnisse regeln." *Das Parlament* February 22, 1991, p. 7.

Willis, F. Roy. *France, Germany, and the New Europe*. Greenwich, Conn.: Fawcett, 1965.

Wilms, Dorothee. "Zweimal vierzig Jahren." *Deutschland Archiv*, May 1989, pp. 497–500.

Windsor, Philip. *Germany and the Management of Detente*. London: Chatto and Windus, 1971.

Winters, Peter Jochen. "Nicht Eiszeit, aber Pause." *Deutschland Archiv*, March 1985, pp. 225–228.

Wolf, Markus. *Die Troika*. Berlin: Aufbau, 1989.

Wollweber, Ernst. "Aus Erinnerungen. Ein Porträt Walter Ulbrichts." *Beiträge zur Geschichte der Arbeiterbewegung* 32, no. 3 (1990), pp. 350–378.

Zehn Jahre Deutschlandpolitik. Bonn: Bundesministerium für innerdeutsche Beziehungen, 1980.

Zieger, Gottfried. *Die Haltung von SED und DDR zur Einheit Deutschlands, 1949–1987*. Cologne: Verlag Wissenschaft und Politik, 1988.

Zimmermann, Hartmut. "The GDR in the 1970s." *Problems of Communism* 27, no. 2 (March-April 1978), pp. 1–40.

Zolling, Hermann, and Bahnsen, Uwe. *Kalter Winter im August*. Oldenburg: Gerhard Stalling, 1967.

Zündorf, Benno. *Die Ostverträge*. Munich: C. H. Beck, 1979.

Abelein, Manfred, 127, 152n
Abgrenzung. See delimitation
Adenauer, Konrad: and the CDU, 32–33,
46–47, 68; and France, 60; and FRG re-
lations with Western allies, 19, 58–60,
66, 223; on the policy of strength, 17,
19–20; political style, 32, 66; response
to the Berlin Wall, 53; and the USSR,
34–35; views on the national question,
19–20, 31, 225
ADN (*Allgemeine Deutsche Nachrichten*),
167n
Adzhubei, A. I., 62n
Afghanistan, Soviet invasion of, 135, 137,
141
Albania, 120
Albertz, Heinrich, 66
Albrecht, Ernst, 129, 190
Alleinvertretungsanspruch ("claim to sole
representation"), 7
Alliance for Germany, 213–14
Andropov, Yuri, 159
Apel, Hans, 178
Arab-Israeli War of 1967, 103
Aron, Raymond, 22
Augstein, Rudolf, 64
Austria, 177
Axen, Hermann, 12n, 71, 72n, 76, 91,
121n, 130n; on inter-German security,
158, 169, 171

Bad Godesberg, meeting at, 47
Bahr, Egon: on the division of Germany, 7,
51, 102, 168; on inter-German relations,
66–67, 96, 106, 111n, 186, 201; security views, 137, 146n, 157–58, 169
Barzel, Rainer, 81, 95n; as CDU/CSU
Fraktion leader, 81; and the battle over
the Eastern treaties, 84–85
Basic Law (*Grundgesetz*), 7, 168, 171, 212,
218
Basic Treaty (*Grundvertrag*), 8, 14, 56, 83,
86–88, 93–95, 114, 116, 133, 140; ambiguities of, 9, 96–100, 102–11, 128,

131, 144; implementation of in 1980s,
154, 158n, 165, 187
Belgium, 144, 177
Berlin, as capital of Germany, 221–22;
conflicts over, 22, 63; East German
claims to, 22, 29, 49n; Soviet policy on,
24; Western occupation rights, 18, 22–
23; West German claims to, 108–10
Berlin accord (Quadripartite Accord), 80,
84, 92–93, 108
Berlin Wall: as bargaining advantage, 7,
139; construction of, 49–55; impact of,
5, 7, 16; opening of, 3–5, 14, 193, 217;
responses to, 14, 56–57, 61, 71, 153,
187; sphinxlike character of, 8, 166
Biedenkopf, Kurt, 119, 131, 153n, 220
Biermann, Wolf, 130
Blüm, Norbert, 201n, 222
Böhme, Ibrahim, 213
Bölling, Klaus, 140, 145, 168
Bonn, as capital of FRG, 221–22
Brandenburg Gate, 207, 223
Brandt, Willy, 94, 110; as challenger to Ad-
enauer, 53–54; fall from power, 113,
116; as foreign minister, 69; handling of
national question, 56–57, 66, 83–85,
99–100, 168n; as proponent of an ex-
panded *Ostpolitik*, 132, 137, 168; re-
sponse to Berlin Wall's construction, 53;
role in the SPD, 33–34, 79–81, 87, 94,
99, 118
Brentano, Heinrich von, 66
Brezhnev, Leonid, 76, 89–90, 112n, 136,
141–42, 143n, 144n
Bulganin, Nikolai, 28
Bulgaria, 65, 75
Bundesrat, 218
Bundestag, 13, 67, 168, 187
Bundeswehr, 22, 192
Burt, Richard, 161

Carter, Jimmy, 136–37
Castro, Fidel, 62
CDU. *See* Christian Democratic Union

CDU/CSU parliamentary party (*Fraktion*), 33, 72, 81, 84, 119
Ceausescu, Nicolae, 116
"change through rapprochement," 67, 117
Chernobyl, 103n
Cheysson, Claude, 161
China, People's Republic of, 50, 190
Christian Democratic Union (CDU): early contacts with GDR, 127, 141; lack of preparedness for reunification, 200–201; as a modern *Volkspartei*, 32, 119; and the national debate, 65, 80, 119–20, 154, 171, 191–92; and party politics, 65–66, 81n, 82–85, 170; relations with GDR in late 1980s, 171–72, 191–92; response to reunification, 213. *See also* Konrad Adenauer; Helmut Kohl; *Wende*
Christian Social Union (CSU): and the national debate, 81, 84; relation to the CDU, 33, 119, 152–53; response to reunification, 212. *See also* Franz Josef Strauß
citizenship, East German views on, 98, 100–101, 147, 167; West German views on, 7, 69, 98–99, 127, 168, 202
Cold War, 157, 196, 221
COMECON (Council for Mutual Economic Assistance), 24, 104
Cominform (Communist Information Bureau), 24
Common Document, SED-SPD, 169, 182–83, 286, 215
Common Market. *See* European Economic Community
Commonwealth of Independent States, 223
Communist Party of Germany (KPD), 31, 37, 158
Communist Party of the Soviet Union (CPSU), 17
confederation plan, 28–29, 41, 76, 77; in contrast to "confederal structures," 205
Conference on Security and Cooperation in Europe ("Helsinki conference"), 116, 119–20, 124n, 129–30, 170, 189, 223; background to, 76
Constitutional Court, 99
Council of Europe, 31
CPSU. *See* Communist Party of the Soviet Union
CSU. *See* Christian Social Union

"culture of political argumentation" (*Kultur des politischen Streits*), 169, 182
Czechoslovakia, 3, 57, 69–70, 75, 79, 97, 161, 169

damage limitation, 160, 162
De Gaulle, Charles, 52, 60
Dehler, Thomas, 32
delimitation (*Abgrenzung*), 91; Soviet origins of concept, 91n
Democracy Now, 210
Democratic Awakening, 196, 213
Denmark, 177
détente, 6, 60, 84, 138, 160
Diepgen, Eberhard, 172, 217n
Dohnanyi, Klaus von, 220
Dregger, Alfred, 174n
Dulles, John Foster, 20, 22–23, 44

Eastern Europe, Soviet relations with, 6, 20; West German policy toward, 69, 116
economic relations, between the Germanys, 9, 26, 100, 105, 140n, 148, 171; special credits, 155–56. *See also* swing credit
Eden, Anthony, 21
Egypt, 103
Ehmke, Horst, 137, 192
Elbe River dispute, 128–29, 140, 163, 190n
Engels, Friedrich, 26
Engholm, Bjorn, 190
England. *See* Great Britain
Environmental Protection Office, 108–10
Eppler, Erhard, 186, 192n
Erfurt, meeting at, 83, 88–89, 150
Erhard, Ludwig, 65–66
Erler, Fritz, 33, 68
European Defense Community, 31
European Economic Community, 105, 114, 204, 223, 225
European peace order, 170, 190
European Security 2000, 193

FDP. *See* Free Democratic Party
Federal Republic of Germany (FRG): as a European power, 14, 191, 203, 209, 222–26; official policy on the GDR, 7, 31; relations with the Soviet Union, 19–21, 34–35; relations with Western occupiers, 18–23. *See also* Konrad Ade-

nauer; Willy Brandt; Christian Democratic Union; reunification; Social Democratic Party

Federation of Expellees (*Bund der Vertriebenen*), 20, 70, 81

Feldmann, Olaf, 190

France, 4, 17, 44, 60, 104

free city, Berlin as a, 18, 30, 49n, 52

Free Democratic Party (FDP): coalition with SPD, 79–80; domestic political position of, 70, 75, 169; views on the national question, 32, 67, 154, 170

FRG. *See* Federal Republic of Germany

Friedmann, Bernhard, 172n

Gansel, Norbert, 201–2

Gaus, Günter, 109n, 123–24; on inter-German relations, 126–27, 132, 145

GDR. *See* German Democratic Republic

Geheimnisträger ("secret-carrier"), 102

Geißler, Heiner, 131, 152

Genscher, Hans-Dietrich: domestic political calculations of, 190; and East-West relations, 154, 170, 190–91; views on the national question, 108–10, 203, 221

Gera demands, 140, 167

German Democratic Republic (GDR): debates over socialism, 37–43, 89, 91–92; founding of, 36; relations with the Soviet Union, 6, 24–27, 90–92, 179–80; relations with the West, 35, 103–4; fall of, 193–206. *See also* Erich Honecker; reunification; Walter Ulbricht

German Social Union, 213

Gerstenmaier, Eugen, 46n, 47, 70n

Gierek, Edward, 116

glasnost ("openness"), 179, 183n

Globke, Hans, 46

Glotz, Peter, 145

Gomulka, Wladyslaw, 42n

Gorbachev, Mikhail, 164–65, 175–76, 178n, 183n, 186n, 188, 192; differences with Honecker, 179–81, 183; and the fall of the GDR, 195–97

Grand Coalition, 68–70, 75–76, 78

Great Britain, 4, 17, 44, 104, 144, 177

Greece, 164, 177

Greens, the, 145, 157, 170, 186, 187n, 215n

Grewe, Wilhelm, 35n, 58–59

Gromyko, Andrei, 58, 164

Grotewohl, Otto, 25–26, 37

Grundvertrag. See Basic Treaty

Guillaume, Günter, 116

Gulf War of 1991, 219n, 224n

Güstrow, 150

Haack, Dieter, 132

Häber, Herbert, 127, 163n

Hager, Kurt, 42n, 49n, 71, 72n, 91, 181n

Hallstein, Walter, 35n

Hallstein Doctrine, 35, 46, 65, 69, 75

Heinemann, Gustav, 88

Heisenberg, Werner, 64

Helsinki conference. *See* Conference on Security and Cooperation in Europe

Herrnstadt, Rudolf, 38n, 39–41

Herter Plan, 45

Heuer, Uwe-Jens, 183

Honecker, Erich: domestic policies, 7, 122, 130–31, 183; and the FRG, 74, 95, 144–47, 175; interest in foreign policy, 122–25, 129–30, 144, 149, 177–78, 181; policymaking role, 11n, 121; political style, 92–93, 179, 195–97; and the Soviet Union, 25n, 142, 159–64; views on the national question, 89, 144; visit to Bonn, 173–74

Hungary, 65, 75, 161, 189, 192, 217; opening of western border, 3, 14, 193

Intermediate-range Nuclear Forces controversy (INF), 134–37, 141, 142n, 144–45, 149, 155, 157–60; reopening of negotiations, 165, 177–78

Italy, 144, 164

Japan, 104, 144

Jaruzelski, Wojciech, 183n

Jaspers, Karl, 64

Jenninger, Philipp, 152, 172

JUSOS. *See* Young Socialists

Kadar, Janos, 116

Kaiser, Jakob, 31, 34n

Kanzlerdemokratie ("chancellor democracy"), 32, 66

Kassel, meeting at, 83, 88–89

Kennan, George, 22

Kennedy, John F.: and the Berlin question
    50, 58–60; meeting with Khrushchev,
    50–51
Khrushchev, Nikita: and the Cuban missile
    crisis, 62–63; demands during the Berlin
    conflicts, 17–18, 45, 61; exchange of let-
    ters with Kennedy, 61; internal position,
    50; relationship with Walter Ulbricht,
    30, 61–63
Kiep, Walther Leisler, 127, 153n, 190
Kiesinger, Kurt-Georg, 65; as chancellor,
    68–69, 77, 80, 81n
Klier, Freya, 185
Kohl, Helmut: and national reunification,
    203–6, 214, 218–19, 224; political
    calculations of, 119, 152–53; relations
    with the GDR, 127, 131–32, 173–74,
    191–93; views on the national question,
    131, 152–53
Kohl, Michael, 86, 106–7, 132n
Korean War, 20
Kosygin, Alexei, 76
KPD. See Communist Party of Germany
Krawczyk, Stefan, 185
Krenz, Egon, 194–99, 202, 208n
Krone, Heinrich, 23, 59n, 70n
Kuczynski, Jürgen, 183n

Lafontaine, Oskar, 168, 192n, 202, 206n,
    213–14
Lamberz, Werner, 76
liberal democracy: in the FRG, 12–13, 94,
    125; in reunified Germany, 216–22
Liberal Democratic Party of Germany
    (LDPD), 32, 210
Ligachev, Yegor, 4n
London Declaration, 18
Lorenz, Siegfried, 195n
Lutheran church, 64, 182, 189

Macmillan, Harold, 52
Main Economic Task, 44, 48, 122
Maizière, Lothar de, 213
Mann, Golo, 64
Marx, Karl, 26; conference on, 158–59,
    160n
Marxism-Leninism, in the GDR, 10–12,
    195, 198, 209–11, 217
Matern, Hermann, 37n
Meckel, Markus, 221n
Mende, Erich, 67

Menschengemeinschaft ("human com-
    munity"), 78, 89, 92n
Mettke, Jörg, 131
Meyer, Thomas, 186
Mikoyan, Anastas, 45
Mindestumtausch (minimum exchange re-
    quirement), 110–12, 139–43, 148, 166
Ministry for State Security, 183n, 185n,
    196n, 211
Mittag, Günter, 91n, 142, 184
Mitterrand, François, 172
Modrow, Hans, 199, 204–5, 211, 213
Momper, Walter, 202–3
Moscow Treaty, 82, 84–85, 88, 97
Mückenberger, Erich, 180n
Müller, Vincenz, 28n

National Democratic Party, 210
National Front, 101
National People's Army (NVA), 192
NATO. See North Atlantic Treaty
    Organization
Netherlands, the, 164
Neues Deutschland, 39
Neues Forum, 196, 198n, 210
Neumann, Alfred, 92n
New Economic System, 72
New Times, 180
Nier, Kurt, 109n, 170n
Nixon, Richard, 80
Norden, Albert, 101
North Atlantic Treaty Organization
    (NATO): and German reunification, 19–
    20; policies of, 19, 22, 32, 135–36;
    West Germany's entry into, 20, 27, 36.
    See also Intermediate-range Nuclear
    Forces controversy

Oder-Neisse boundary, 20, 64, 70, 82, 225
Ostpolitik, 29, 61, 64–65, 69, 75, 79, 82,
    85, 87, 110, 118, 152, 156, 167, 186;
    second phase of, 115, 125

Palme, Olof, 157; peace march named af-
    ter, 181
Paris Agreements, 18
Pawelczyk, Alfons, 137
peace policy, 181
peace treaty, 18, 50, 61–62
perestroika ("restructuring"), 179, 183n
permanent missions, 71, 95, 98, 106–7

Pervukhin, M. G., 49n
Pfleiderer, Karl Georg, 32
Pflugbeil, Sebastian, 210n
Pieck, Wilhelm, 25–26, 48
Poland, 35, 65, 79, 82, 189, 192, 217, 225; crisis of, 1980–1981, 135, 139, 143; imposition of martial law, 149–51. See also Oder-Neisse boundary
policy of movement, 65
policy of strength, 17, 20–21, 33–34, 53, 65
Ponomarev, Boris, 89

Rau, Johannes, 190, 222
Reagan administration, 148
Reddemann, Gerhard, 127, 152n
refugee exodus: before 1961, 5, 48, 52; post-1989, 176, 193
Reich, Jens, 211n
Reinhold, Otto, 194n
Republikaner, 191, 201
reunification: early proposals for, 22, 27, 45; European response to, 222–25; FRG policy on, 7, 9, 26; GDR policy on, 25–26, 40, 48, 93, 101; German preparedness for, 3–4, 200–9; "internal," 225; as a mixed blessing, 213–22; unlikelihood of, 4, 5n, 15–16
Rohwedder, Detlev Karsten, 220
Roman Catholic Church, 189
Romania, 65, 69, 75
Ronneburger, Uwe, 187
Round Table, 211, 213
Rubin, Hans-Wolfgang, 70
Rühe, Volker, 172, 201, 203n
Rusk, Dean, 58

SALT. See Strategic Arms Limitation Treaty
Salzgitter, monitoring station at, 140, 168
Schabowski, Günter, 4, 122n, 183n, 195, 198–99, 203
Schäffer, Fritz, 28n
Schalck-Golodkowski, Alexander, 125, 155, 165n
Schäuble, Wolfgang, 171–72, 191n, 221
Scheel, Walter, 70, 81
Scheer, Hermann, 186n
Schießbefehl ("command to shoot"), 153, 189
Schirdewan, Karl, 37n, 42–43
Schmid, Carlo, 33

Schmidt, Helmut, 80, 84, 112n; and the INF crisis, 135–37, 142; on inter-German relations, 113–21, 151–52; political calculations, 113–14, 117, 120, 136–68. See also Werbellinsee meeting
Schmude, Jürgen, 168
Schollwer, Wolfgang, 67, 70, 102
Schönbohm, Wulf, 119n, 191n
Schröder, Gerhard, 65–66
Schumacher, Kurt, 31–33
Schürer, Gerhard, 105n, 184n, 195
Schütz, Klaus, 66
Schwanitz, Wolfgang, 183n, 185n
SDP (Social Democratic Party, East Germany), 196, 202, 221n
SED. See Socialist Unity Party of Germany
Seiters, Rudolf, 200
Shevardnadze, Eduard, 4n
Sindermann, Horst, 171
sister-city exchanges, 134, 192
Smirnov, Andrei, 35
Social Democratic Party of Germany (SPD): electoral strategy of, 33–34, 47, 68, 136–37, 156–57; and German reunification, 31, 212, 219; lack of preparedness for reunification, 201–2; national policy of, 31–33, 67, 70–71, 74, 168; relations with the GDR, 168, 186, 192; relations with the United States, 53, 137, 193
Socialist Unity Party of Germany (SED): early debates within, 37–43, 91–92; founding, 31; national policy, 71–72, 91, 100–1; reasons for collapse, 182–84, 176, 194–95; structure of policy-making, 10–12
Soviet Union (USSR): and the Eastern treaties, 79–82; and a European security conference, 76; and German reunification, 24–28, 31; policy toward Berlin, 17–18, 24; relations with the GDR, 24, 27; relations with the United States, 6. See also German Democratic Republic
Spain, 177
Späth, Lothar, 190
SPD. See Social Democratic Party of Germany
SPD-East, 221n
Sputnik, 180
Stalin, Josef, 24, 26, 27n, 39
State Council (Staatsrat), 48, 107, 124

State Secretariat for All-German Affairs, 73, 77
Stobbe, Dietrich, 139n
Stolpe, Manfred, 220
Stoltenberg, Gerhard, 156
Stoph, Willi, 69, 83, 88, 91, 146n
Strategic Arms Limitation Talks (SALT), 115, 135, 141
Strauß, Franz Josef: as chancellor-candidate, 136, 138, 145; early contacts with the GDR, 127; political calculations of, 173; role in the inter-German credits, 155–56, 171; views on the *Ostpolitik*, 66, 82, 118, 147; views on reunification, 82n
Sudan, 103
Suslov, Mikhail, 89
Süßmuth, Rita, 222
Sweden, 157
swing credit, 105, 111–12, 140, 150, 171
Syria, 103

Teltschik, Horst, 191, 192n
Tiananmen Square, 190
Tito, Josip Broz, 138
Treuhandanstalt (trust agency), 220
transit treaties, 86, 93, 116
travel, between the Germanys, 102–3, 110–11, 167, 188–89, 199; FRG encouragement of, 8–9, 67, 166, 187; GDR views on, 100–1; unintended consequences of, 9, 100, 161, 162n, 185
Trudeau, Pierre, 116

Ulbricht, Walter: and the Berlin Wall, 49–50, 54–55; demands on Berlin, 29–30, 41, 48, 53, 90; differences with colleagues, 36–44; domestic policies of, 7, 38, 41, 43–44, 48–49, 91–92; fall of, 92–93; leading role in SED, 44, 87; and the national question, 6, 17, 225; relations with the FRG, 74–79; relations with the Soviet Union, 30, 62–63, 89–90
UNESCO, 104
United Nations, 22, 93, 104, 157

United States, 104; evolving Berlin policy, 21–23, 44–45, 51–52, 80; relations with the FRG, 19–23; relations with the Soviet Union, 57–63. *See also* Berlin accord; John Foster Dulles; John F. Kennedy
USSR. *See* Soviet Union

Verner, Paul, 92n
Vienna Convention on Diplomatic Relations, 106–7
Vogel, Hans-Jochen, 190, 125, 202n
Volkskammer, 101, 168, 171, 208–10, 213–15, 218
Volkspartei ("people's party"), 32, 119

Warsaw Treaty, 82, 84–85, 97
Warsaw Treaty Organization (WTO), 21, 25
Wehner, Herbert, 53, 68, 71, 74, 80, 132, 137, 145
Weimar Republic, 32
Weizsäcker, Carl Friedrich von, 64
Weizsäcker, Richard von, 99, 152, 156, 172–74, 223
Wende ("turning point"), 152, 154n, 169
Werbellinsee, meeting at, 147–51, 173
Wilms, Dorothee, 191n
Wischnewski, Hans-Jurgen, 132
Wolf, Hanna, 92n
Wolf, Markus, 183n, 198n
Wollenberger, Vera, 185
Wollweber, Ernst, 42
World Health Organization, 104
World Postal Union, 104
World War II, 4, 56, 159, 216
Wrangel, Olaf von, 127, 152n

Young Socialists (JUSOS), 136
Yugoslavia, 35, 69

Zaisser, Wilhelm, 39–41
Zentralinstitut für Jugendforschung, 182n
Zhivkov, Todor, 116
Ziller, Gerhard, 42
Zionskirche, 182